D1642617

Mike Dash is the author of four pre
Tulipomania and *Batavia's Graveyard*. A
in London. He is presently completing
American policeman ever to be executed for murder, to be published by Granta. www.mikedash.com

'Enthralling . . . Mike Dash has written what is easily the best and most judicious book on this bizarre episode. He surpasses every previous account, both in the thoroughness of his research and in the clarity and cogency of his narrative. Even better, Mr Dash writes superbly. I read his book practically at one sitting, and have been having stealthy, silken nightmares ever since' *New York Sun*

'A gripping read' *Daily Mail*

'Dash peppers his fascinating story with anecdotes and pictures that bring it alive . . . his account reads like a thriller' *South China Morning Post*

'Fascinating and immensely readable' *Times Literary Supplement*

'Extraordinary . . . Mike Dash is an amazing storyteller. Apart from the beauty and eloquence of his prose, the book is painstakingly researched' *Deccan Herald*

'Admirable . . . captures the poignancy and excitement of the macabre' *Independent*

'Storming narrative grounded in historical and political detail . . . the thrillerish pace is kept up throughout' *Geographical*

'Glorious . . . Dash has produced a history that is stylistically riveting, thorough in detail and rich in analysis' *Outlook India*

'A strange, sometimes bizarre and often gruesome tale . . . This is a fine book, well sourced, engagingly written, level-headed and clear-eyed' *Sunday Herald* (Glasgow)

THUG

The True Story of India's Murderous Cult

MIKE DASH

Granta Books
London

Granta Publications, 2/3 Hanover Yard,
Noel Road, London N1 8BE

First published in Great Britain by Granta Books 2005
This edition published by Granta Books 2006

Copyright © 2005 by Mike Dash

Mike Dash has asserted his moral right under the
Copyright, Designs and Patents Act, 1988, to be
identified as the author of this work.

All rights reserved. No reproduction, copy or
transmissions of this publication may be made without
written permission. No paragraph of this publication
may be reproduced, copied or transmitted save with
written permission or in accordance with the provisions
of the Copyright Act 1956 (as amended). Any person
who does any unauthorized act in relation to this
publication may be liable to criminal prosecution and
civil claims for damages.

A CIP catalogue record for this book
is available from the British Library.

1 3 5 7 9 10 8 6 4 2

ISBN-13: 978-1-86207-846-8
ISBN-10: 1-86207-846-7

Typeset by M Rules

Printed and bound in Great Britain by
Mackays of Chatham plc

For my parents, who made so much possible

CONTENTS

AUTHOR'S NOTE

This book tells the story of the Thugs of India, from the earliest days described in their own oral histories to the final months of the last surviving members of their gangs. It is based on three years of research among the voluminous records of the East India Company, which still fill literally miles of shelf space in archives in London, Delhi and Bhopal, and incorporates material exhumed from thousands of pages of centuries-old manuscripts – trial transcripts and official correspondence, private letters and legal memoranda – not to mention dozens of volumes of memoirs, travelogue and academic history. I have done my best to ensure that it takes account of the most up-to-date research on the subject.

At this point most readers will probably want to turn to the opening pages of the book itself. But a few words of further comment may be of interest to those with knowledge of the historiography of India.

The pursuit, arrest and conviction of the Thugs caused a huge sensation in the Subcontinent of the 1830s. Their crimes were so monstrous, and the number of their victims so enormous, that they quickly assumed the stature of bogeymen. Several historical accounts of their depredations, based to a large extent on official papers, were published – albeit in relatively obscure journals or in books produced only in small editions. Many of the authors had been involved themselves in the campaign to eradicate 'Thuggee', and their works contained, as might be expected, a certain amount of exaggeration and glorification of the parts that the writers had played in the whole affair. The homogeneity of the Thug gangs and of their methods was exaggerated, making the gangs seem more formidable than they had been. The prisoners' motives were also distorted, and in particular far greater stress was placed on their religion, and their devotion to Kali, the Hindu 'goddess of destruction', than had been the case when the Thugs themselves were brought to trial.

These early accounts influenced the way in which Thuggee was perceived, both in India and elsewhere. They were expanded on in a hugely successful contemporary novel entitled *Confessions of a Thug* (1839)*, written by Meadows Taylor, a British officer based in Hyderabad. Taylor turned his own experiences of the anti-Thug campaign into what was widely acclaimed as the greatest 'chiller' of its day, and his protagonist (a murderer named Ameer Ali, whose 'confession' was based on the deposition of a real Thug) was more ruthless, more successful and more free from the pangs of conscience than even the killers whose confessions had peppered the first historical accounts. Ali's 'guiltless confessions of multiple murder' were – a reviewer in the *Literary Gazette* declared – 'enough to freeze the blood in our veins'; the young Queen Victoria herself was so impatient to read the final chapters that she could not wait for the pages to be bound, asking that the running sheets to be sent directly to her as they came off the press.

A few years later, the French writer Eugene Sue inserted another murderous Thug – this one a cultivated, clever man, lethal as a panther, who haunted the salons of Paris rather than the forest paths of India – into the pages of his novel *The Wandering Jew*. This book, too, was astonishingly successful, and by the second half of the nineteenth century the popular image of the Thugs themselves had become more or less fixed. They were perceived as a fearsome cult of religiously inspired killers, for whom the act of murder was akin to human sacrifice. The robbery of their victims – which captured Thugs had always acknowledged as their motive for murder – was relegated to the status of a secondary objective, and it was generally accepted that the Thugs formed a hereditary fraternity, devoted to killing solely by strangulation and thus without shedding blood. At about the same time the number of killings assigned to the gangs became exaggerated, a consequence of the misinterpretation of some unpublished manuscripts and of some generous assumptions concerning the antiquity of Thuggee. By the time James Sleeman published his book *Thug, Or A Million Murders* in 1920, it was commonly accepted that the Thugs had murdered somewhere between 40,000 and 50,000 victims a year over the course of perhaps

---

*The book was written in the course of a voyage home from India and the completed manuscript was fortunate to survive its passage through quarantine in Malta, where, Taylor recalled, 'the three volumes were first scored through with knives, then smoked with sulphur till the ink turned pale, and finally delivered to [the author's cousin] by means of long tongs, through a narrow slit in the grating'.

seven centuries. Thuggee was now described as 'a hideous religion of murder'.

Books and theses based on these early accounts continued to be published for several decades. (One of the last, by the German historian Gustav Pfirmann, set out a detailed account of the apparent religious beliefs of the gangs.) But, beginning in the 1950s, historians began to reassess the portrayal of the Thugs: Hiralal Gupta, Stewart Gordon, Christopher Bayly and Radhika Singha have all published critiques that portray the murderers as more or less ordinary criminals. For Gupta, the Thugs were a product of British dominion in India – mostly soldiers thrown out of work by the imposition of the *Pax Britannica* on the Subcontinent. For Gordon, they were marauders hired by minor rajahs and other landholders to generate the revenues required for state building. Bayly and Singha saw them as bandits of no fixed modus operandi, who had been given the label 'Thug' by their British captors.

These studies have been followed by those of a new generation of literary critics such as Parama Roy who – ignoring the mass of manuscript material contained in the East India Company archives, and arbitrarily designating a variety of published texts as a coherent 'Thug Archive' – assume that the 'Thugs' picked up by the British authorities in India were actually no more than a miscellany of ordinary bandits, thieves, rebels against British rule and innocent men. Thuggee, in the view of this group of revisionists, never existed at all.

The latter view has proved very influential. It is certainly 'politically correct', for it turns on their heads all the colonial histories of Thuggee – filled as they are with tales of corrupt, demonic Hindu devotees thwarted by altruistic British officers – and offers in their place a potent criticism of imperialism itself.

The revisionists do make valuable points. It is true, as they suggest, that the thousands of men put on trial as Thugs after 1829 were scarcely the products of 'organized crime' in the modern sense. They possessed no central organization; there was no 'Chief Thug' and no complex Thug hierarchy; nor were punishments meted out to traitorous stranglers or their immediate families. Captured Thugs admitted to killing in a variety of ways. And it seems certain that their crimes were not committed in the name of any religion. All this does not mean, as the revisionists suggest, that Thuggee cannot be succinctly defined and that it is therefore impossible to distinguish the Thugs themselves from other sorts of highwaymen and bandits. Yet their rejection of the reality of Thuggee rests on precisely this assumption.

Criticisms advanced by Parama Roy and her colleagues betray their lack of familiarity with the primary sources. To suggest that Thuggee was a construct because not all the Thugs' victims were strangled, because some Thugs shed blood, because not every member of the Thug gangs was descended from a long line of murderers, or because few if any of their crimes were religiously inspired is to ignore the fact that the men captured and tried by the British did indeed possess a unique modus operandi. The distinguishing feature of the Thugs was that they invariably murdered their victims before robbing them. This remarkable habit has no parallel, so far as I am aware, anywhere else in the world, and yet it crops up time and time again in hundreds of depositions and other accounts compiled by dozens of Company officers, travellers and others over a period of well over half a century. In the earliest cases, at least, it is clear that the writers of individual accounts were unaware that very similar reports were being made from elsewhere in India.

This is not all. By the 1830s a huge mass of evidence for the reality of Thuggee had been compiled, not only by British prosecutors, but by the authorities in various independent Indian states who tried and punished Thugs from time to time. It is certainly true that the most important statements against the alleged murderers came from 'approvers' – informers who had saved their own lives by turning King's Evidence. But the officers of the East India Company went to considerable lengths to keep their informants isolated, and to check the testimony they obtained from each new source against that already obtained from other approvers. In addition, a considerable quantity of evidence was collected from the families of Thug victims. Finally, and perhaps most importantly of all, the bodies of nearly a thousand men, women and children killed by various Thug gangs were exhumed from the places where they had been buried – spots successfully identified by approvers who had taken part in the murders themselves. The Thug trials conducted in India between 1829 and 1848 may have been deficient by modern standards, not least in the entire absence of counsel for the defence. But they were not unusual by the standards of the time. Thousands of men have been convicted of murder, in India, in Europe and America, on far less evidence than that assembled against many Thugs.

I am not alone in my conviction that Thuggee was very real. Stewart Gordon accepts the existence of 'a small core of families, members of which had been murderers for several generations'; Radhika Singha notes that 'the existence of band lore, a common slang, and a shared knowledge of major attacks does suggest long terms of association, as does the ability to coordinate action in large gangs'. Within the last year or two, moreover, a new generation of historians has returned to the manuscript sources and begun to take issue with the arguments advanced by the revisionists. Acceptance of the Thugs as worthwhile objects of study is thus growing once again. Given the controversial nature of the subject, however, I feel it is important to make my own position on the matter clear.

A note on currency

The prevailing rate of exchange in India in 1830 was two Madras rupees to the pound sterling, and one pound in 1830 was worth the equivalent of £30 today. Thus one rupee in the Thugs' time would be worth around £15 now, and a *lakh* of rupees (Rs 100,000) had a value equal to £1,500,000 in 2004.

There were 16 annas to the rupee, four pice to the anna, and thus 64 pice (each worth about 23 modern pence) in a rupee. A Thug willing to kill for eight annas – which some were – received a little over £7 for committing murder.

India was vast enough to support more than a hundred different currencies and coins. Among those most commonly met with by the Thugs were pagodas (gold coins from the Deccan, each worth 4 rupees) and mohurs (each worth 16 rupees).

A note on place names

The approved spelling of Indian place names has altered considerably since the heyday of the Thugs. The current trend is to abandon, or at least modify, British colonial names. Calcutta has become Kolkata, Madras is now Chennai, the Jumna river the Yamuna, and Bombay has changed its name to Mumbai; but the changes have been spotty, and in search of consistency – and also, I confess, because I find the old place names evocative – I have stuck with early nineteenth century Anglo-Indian usage as it appears in the manuscript sources and the gazetteers of the time. For this reason, readers will find themselves in Jubbulpore rather than Jabalpur, crossing the Nerbudda river instead of the Narmada, and traversing not Rajasthan but Rajpootana.

Mike Dash
London, May 2004

GLOSSARY OF INDIAN WORDS

adalat	court of justice
barkandaze *(burkindaz)*	watchman or guard, armed with a sword and shield or matchlock
bebee (bibi)	woman; often applied to the Indian lovers and mistresses of East India Company men
Brahmin	member of the highest Hindu caste
cakari	military service
chokie (chauki)	customs post or guardhouse
chaukidar	village watchman
chuprassee	messenger, courier – usually a government servant
cutcherry	'private office', or courtroom, often in a magistrate's home, where new cases were brought before the Company authorities and decisions were taken as to which should be referred to trial
dacoit	member of an organized gang of robbers
dafadar	sergeant; the head of a party of police
darogah	head of a police *thanah*, and the most senior police officer likely to be encountered by an Indian villager
datura	poison made from the seeds of the thorn apple, used by Thugs and other robbers to stupefy their victims
dhoti	cotton loincloth or wrap for the lower body
ghat	either a mountain pass or a river landing stage – frequently, in the latter case, one with a customs post
godna	needle used to make tattoos; also tattooing itself
jagir	a grant for the maintenance of troops; the term also described the lands generating revenues for this purpose
jemadar	native officer, equivalent to an army lieutenant; leader of a Thug gang
khunjur	low-caste herdsmen from one of India's 'wandering tribes'

lakh, lac	one hundred thousand
lathial	armed retainer, usually employed by a zamindar to collect rents and enforce his decisions
mofussil	the countryside, the provinces – as used by the inhabitants of Calcutta, Madras or Bombay, a somewhat derogatory expression
moonshee	teacher of Indian languages; the term was also applied to the secretaries or confidential agents of East India Company residents and other senior officers
nujeeb	mounted militiaman
nullah	gully or watercourse, frequently dry outside the monsoon season
pargana	district, comprising anything up to 200 villages, that was the main component of both the Mughal and Company revenue collection systems
pundit	learned Brahmin, specifically a student of Sanskrit
rumal	scarf or kerchief; the Thugs' strangling cloth
sepoy, sipahi, sepahee	Indian soldier
seth	banker
shikari	big game hunter
sirdar	headman; also the headquarters of district administration
subadar	native officer, equivalent to an army captain; senior Thug leader
tank	small reservoir or man-made pond, providing drinking water for men and animals and used for washing and sometimes irrigation
thanah	regional police station or militia post; an area of jurisdiction under both the Mughals and the Company
zamindar	under the Mughals, a local notable with powers to collect taxes and recruit militias, and the duty to improve the lands placed in his charge; under Company rule he became a landholder with obligations to pay rents due on his property
zillah	district – one of the major building blocks of the Indian revenue administration

GAZETTEER

Place names are shown as they were in 1830

PLACE	GRID REFERENCE	PLACE	GRID REFERENCE	PLACE	GRID REFERENCE
Agra	G9	Ellichpore	I9	Midnapore	I15
Allahabad	B3, G11	Etawah	G9, K17	Mirzapore	H12
Allygurh	F9	Furruckabad	G10	Moradabad	F9
Alumpore	G9	Futtehpore	G11	Murnae	M17
Arcot	D3	Ganges	B5, H15	Mynpooree	G9
Aurangabad	J7	Ghazeepore	G13	Mysore	D2
Banda	G10	Gohud	G9	Nagpore	C3, I10
Bangalore	D3	Gorruckpore	G12	Nasik	J6
Baroda	C2, I6	Gujerat	C1	Nepal	B4
Barrackpore	I15	Gwalior	B2, G9	Nerbudda river	C2
Benares	B4, H12	Hattah	H10	Nursingpore	H10
Berar	I9	Himalayas	A3	Oomroutee	I9
Bhilsa	H9	Himmutpore	M19	Orissa	C4
Bhopal	C3, H9	Hindustan	B2	Oudh	G10
Bhurtpore	H11	Hoshangabad	H9	Patna	B4, G13
Bihar	B4, I4	Hyderabad	C3	Poona	C2, J7
Bindachul	H11	Indore	C2, I8	Punjab	A2
Bindawa	M17	Indus river	B1	Rampoora	K17
Bombay	C2, J6	Jhalna	J7	Rewah	H11
Borhanpore	I8	Jhalone	G9, O19	Roy Barelly	G11
Bundelcund	C3, H10	Jhansee	G9	Saugor	C3, H9
Calcutta	C5, I15	Jubbulpore	H10	Sehore	H8
Candeish	I6	Juggernaut	C4, J14	Seonee	I10
Cape Cormorin	E3	Jugmunpore	N19	Sewagunge	H11
Cawnpore	G10	Jumna river	F9, L18	Shekoabad	G9
Chambel river	G8, K6	Jypore	B2	Sinde river	H9, M16
Chittoor	D3	Kamptee	I10	Sindouse	M18
Chourella	M18	Kotah	H8	Sleemanabad	H10
Chupara	I10	Lahore	A2	Surat	I6
Coharry river	L6	Lower Provinces	C4	Sursae	M18
Coimbatoor	E2	Lucknadown	I10	Tapti river	C2
Coimbatoor	E2	Lucknadown	I10	Tapti river	C2
Coimbatoor	E2				
Coimbatoor	E2				
Coimbatoor	E2				
Dacca	B5	Lucknow	B3, G11	Tehngoor	M17
Deccan	D2	Madras	D3	Tehree	H9
Delhi	B2, F8	Malwa	H7	Western Provinces	B3
Doab	G9	Meerut	F9		

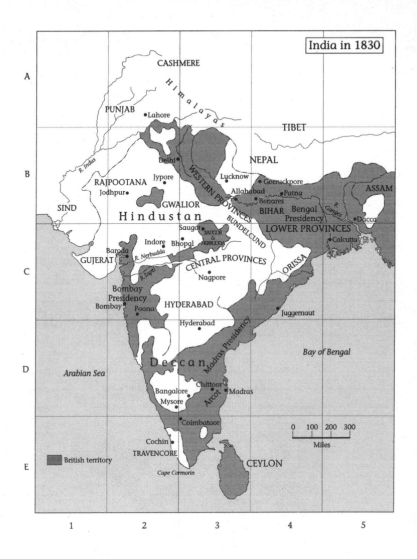

India in 1830

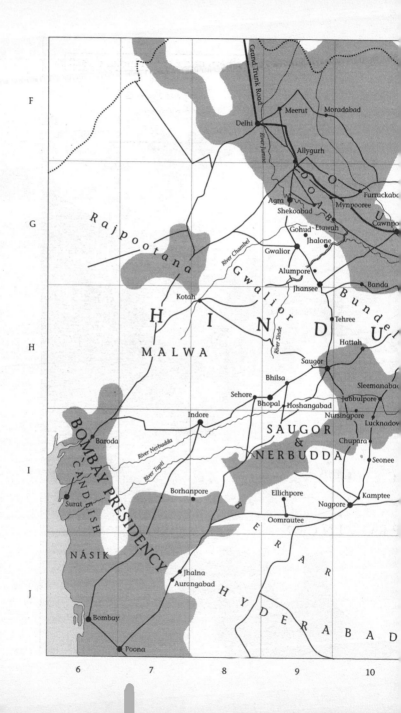

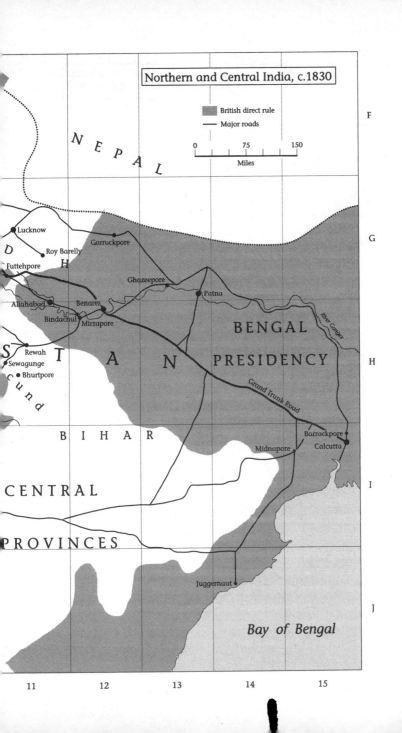

Northern and Central India, c.1830

British direct rule
Major roads

0   75   150
Miles

NEPAL

Lucknow
Roy Barelly
D   Gorruckpore
H
Futtehpore
         Ghazeepore
Allahabad   Benares   Patna
Bindachul
         Mirzapore   BENGAL

Rewah
Sewagunge   PRESIDENCY
Bhurtpore
und
                    Grand Trunk Road

B I H A R
                    Barrackpore
                    Midnapore   Calcutta

CENTRAL

PROVINCES

                    Juggernaut

                    Bay of Bengal

F

G

H

I

J

11   12   13   14   15

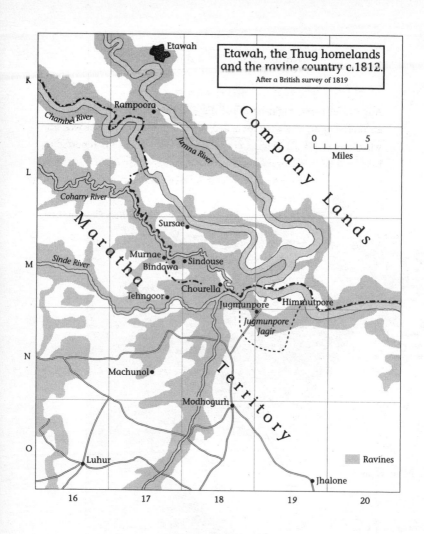

Etawah

Etawah, the Thug homelands
and the ravine country c.1812.
After a British survey of 1819

Company Lands

Rampoora

Chambel River

Jumna River

0   5
Miles

L

Coharry River

Maratha

Sursae

Sinde River

Murnae
Bindawa

Sindouse

Chourella

Tehngoor

Jugmunpore

Himmutpore

Jugmunpore
Jagir

Machunol

Territory

Modhogurh

Ravines

Luhur

Jhalone

16   17   18   19   20

Any skilful party might have had three or four *affairs* a night without anyone being any the wiser for it. People knew not what Thuggee was, nor what kind of people Thugs were. Travellers were frequently reported to have been murdered by robbers, but people thought the robbers must be in the jungles; and never dreamed that they were murdered by the men they saw every day about them.

From the interrogation of Hurree Singh by William Sleeman, 1835

The Road to Lucknadown

'bote hona – to fall into the snares of Thugs'

The sentries on the old fort saw it first: a dark cloud something like a dust devil, spinning madly on the last ridge south of the village of Chupara. It was visible from nearly a mile away, spiralling up over the crest of the hill and bulging outwards like a rising loaf of bread. The cloud billowed and surged, swallowing the road up as it came, and it was only as it descended to the valley floor that the guards were able to make out the cause of the disturbance.

The dust was thrown up by a group of travellers, picking their slow way along the unmade track that ran towards the fort. They were led by a middle-aged Muslim man, bearded and turbaned and riding a horse. Next came a young girl and a woman carrying a newborn baby, both mounted on ponies led by grooms. Five more servants brought up the rear, grouped around a bullock pulling a cartload of possessions.

It was an early evening in February 1823 – late in the cold season by Indian reckoning, more than three months after the end of the monsoon and only a few weeks before the onset of the next hot weather. Chupara was at its most pleasant at this time of year. The monsoon humidity had ebbed; the sun was tolerable, even in the heat of the day; and the rains had turned the country green, ripening crops in the fields, filling streams and replenishing the little man-made reservoirs, called tanks, that dotted the whole country. It was the best time to be on the roads. Next month it would be hotter, and the temperature would continue to rise until the land was brown and burned, nothing moved under the noonday sun, and those who had to travel did so only after dark.

The little party had been on the move all day, and by the time the travellers passed under the walls of Chupara's fort the sun had almost set. They halted nearby, close to the river that ran through the village, and before long a small tent had been pitched and the servants were busy preparing the evening meal. The grooms led their horses down to the riverbank, where they washed away the grime of the day's travel; the woman disappeared into the tent with her children; and the bearded man – her husband – settled himself down on a length of carpet that had been unrolled on the grass close by.

The man's name was Bunda Ali, and he was a *moonshee* – a teacher of languages – from the little town of Jhalna, 380 miles to the south-west. He had worked there, off and on, for about five years, while his children grew around him. Now, though, his eldest child was 10, and old enough to take the husband the moonshee had found for her in Hindustan. The family was going north to celebrate the wedding.

It was an arduous journey. They had already been on the road a month, and still had more than a hundred miles to go before they reached their destination. But this was only to be expected, for most roads in the central provinces were little more than tracks and even the highway from Jhalna to the holy city of Benares – an important route that was crowded with pilgrims for much of the year – was unpaved and rutted by bullock carts.

The Jhalna road wound first east, then north, for 700 miles. Along the way it passed through the territory of the Rajah of Nagpore. Much of the Nagpore countryside was nothing more than barren waste, unfit for human habitation, and even when the road emerged into richer country north of the city, there were still places where it narrowed to become a mere path threading its way through thick jungle that closed in on every side. This was one of the most dangerous parts of the whole journey. The jungle concealed a variety of animals – wolves, jackals, snakes, boar, and a large number of tigers – that on occasion attacked passers-by. It also offered protection to gangs of *dacoits*, robbers who preyed on the local peasantry and sometimes killed those who resisted them. Travellers who escaped these threats unmolested might still be robbed in the night, by thieves from local

villages who crept through camps and into tents so silently that they were
very hard to catch.*

Bunda Ali knew something of the risks he faced, but he had never been
given to exaggerating danger. In Jhalna – where he had worked as moonshee
for a regiment of cavalry, drilling native languages into each fresh draft of
British officers – he had sometimes been called on to interrogate men picked
up near the cantonment on suspicion of assault or robbery. He would put
questions to the prisoners in their own language and translate their replies for
his superiors, and he sometimes found the allegations levelled against his
countrymen implausible. On one occasion, early in 1819, a group of 18 well-
dressed men had been brought before him accused of strangling a bullock
driver. Bunda Ali had questioned them carefully, noting that they had walked
to Jhalna all the way from northern India, a matter of 300 miles, apparently
in search of work. He had taken down the men's statements, checking them
carefully, and – finding no discrepancies – recommended their release.
'Moonshee Bunda Ali,' one of the prisoners recalled, 'urged the improbabil-
ity of so large a body of robbers coming so far to murder one poor bullock
driver. This argument had weight, [and] we were let go.'

The moonshee, then, was not inclined to overstate the dangers of the
road. But his salary, 360 rupees a year, was lavish at a time when many Indians
lived on wages of 5 rupees a month or less, and since he was so obviously
wealthy – few Indians travelled with a retinue – even he preferred to be cautious. His party would, he knew, make a fine target for dacoits; hidden among
the baggage was more than 200 rupees' worth of jewels and cash, five years'
savings, hoarded to pay for his daughter's wedding and provide her dowry.

The safest thing would be to join a larger party. Men walking the Jhalna
road often banded together for mutual protection; bandits rarely attacked
large groups, and new companions could help to pass the long days of drudg-
ery. So Bunda Ali was pleased to be approached, as dusk drew in, by two men
who wandered over from another campsite some way off. They belonged to

---

*'There were most expert thieves in former days,' the British diarist Harriet Tytler recalled in the middle
of the century. 'They were closely shaved and oiled all over, so that if caught they could slip out of your
grasp like eels.' These men were capable of stealing a woman's clothes from her body without being
detected, which they did by creeping into the tent at night and tickling their sleeping victim's ear with a
feather so that she moved from side to side while they loosened her nightdress. On one occasion, when
Tytler was on the road with a Mrs Beckett, her companion 'awoke feeling very cold, and found to her
horror that she had no covering over her; not even her night garments were left'.

a substantial party, about a hundred strong, and when they discovered that the moonshee was making for the Nerbudda river they announced that they were going the same way, and invited the whole family to join them. The river was still three days' march off, and they would be glad of the company of an educated man along the way.

Any concerns that Ali had were swiftly swept away. His new acquaintances belonged to a group so large it would be safe from all attack. They were polite, indeed deferential, and seemed likely to be interesting companions. And they were evidently trustworthy. The first, a man named Dhunnee Khan, proved to be a policeman who had come to Chupara on government business. The other, Essuree, was an officer of the magistrate's court at Etawah, in Hindustan. Both men wore badges of office to emphasize their official standing.

The two parties broke camp early the next morning and left the village in company. They were heading for the little town of Lucknadown, about 20 miles further up the road. It was a full day's journey – a walk of 12 or 15 miles would have been more usual. But the road from Chupara was good, and the terrain unchallenging. The track ran almost directly north, deviating only a little so as to run around the rolling hills and ridges of the Lucknadown plateau rather than across them. The soil here was black and stony and unsuited to agriculture, but the jungles to the south had given way to a forest fringe and there were only two rivers to be forded along the way. Bunda Ali rode between Essuree and Dhunnee Khan, and found the men to be fine company. By the time the group reached Lucknadown, late in the afternoon, he would have been glad to ride with them all the way to Hindustan.

They made camp in a shaded bamboo grove on the outskirts of the village and a quarter of a mile from a small stream. A short while later, a detachment of soldiers came up from the south and pitched their tents only a hundred yards away. They were an advance party of Native Infantry, led by British officers and sent ahead to prepare for a convoy of magazine stores that would reach Lucknadown next day. The two camps were so close that the men in one could easily have called to those in the other, and there was nothing between them but a few bamboos and a pair of horses that Essuree had tethered there. The sound of voices drifting over from the army camp added to Bunda Ali's sense of security, and by eight o'clock, when the sun began to set, he was thoroughly content.

The moonshee had settled himself outside his tent as usual when he was joined by several of his new companions. Two of them had brought a sitar, and they began to wail a jangling tune. Another pair of Dhunnee's men, Bhawanee Jemadar and Sheikh Bazeed, came up, Bhawanee sitting down to Ali's right and Sheikh Bazeed to his left, by the tent. Others followed, until more than two dozen members of the police party had gathered to listen to the music. A second group of men wandered down towards the stream, where the grooms were standing with their horses, and the slight figure of Essuree could just be made out among the bamboo shadows at the edge of the grove, standing alone in the gathering darkness. It was late in the evening now, and the soldiers' camp receded slowly from view as the night drew in. The moonshee's world had contracted to the little circle of family and friends gathered around his campfire. He could feel the flames' warmth on his face.

It was shortly after nine o'clock that Bunda Ali began to sense something was wrong. Dhunnee Khan's men could not be bandits, he was sure; dacoits were invariably direct in their attacks. But they were crowding in a little close, and he became uncomfortably aware that his own servants were nowhere near him. He reached down for the sword he had laid at his feet, but it was gone – two of his companions had picked it up and were loudly admiring its workmanship. Seriously alarmed now, Ali stumbled to his feet, shouting for his men, and as he did, a voice called out *'Tumbakoo lao'* – 'Bring tobacco' – and there was a huge commotion over by the bamboos. Essuree had loosed the horses, and the night air was suddenly full of noise and chaos. In the next instant the moonshee felt Bhawanee Jemadar behind him, and something soft and twisted slipped over his head. He tried to turn, but another of Dhunnee's men seized his hands and held them tight, while a third kicked his legs from under him and brought him crashing to the ground. A length of cloth tightened around Ali's neck and bit into his throat as Bhawanee crouched over him, one knee pressed into his back. The *jemadar's* hands were crossed behind the moonshee's head, and now he jerked them hard apart, brutally throttling his victim. Bunda Ali's body twitched convulsively, once, twice, and then fell still.

Down by the stream, the moonshee's grooms glanced up to find themselves surrounded. One went down quickly under the combined assault of three more men, but his friend, reacting swiftly, ducked under his horse's belly and made for the water, screaming murder in a voice that could scarcely be heard above the din made by the escaping horses. Two more of Dhunnee's men went after him, catching the man on the riverbank and strangling him there. The same scene was played out five more times around the camp as Ali's other servants were cut down with the same detached efficiency.

The commotion brought the moonshee's wife to the flap of her tent, carrying her baby. When she saw what was happening, she made a despairing attempt to run, but Sheikh Bazeed was waiting for her and he threw his own cloth noose around her neck and pulled it tight. A second pair of hands reached out for the baby, and two more figures pushed past into the tent as the mother gasped and died. These men found Bunda Ali's other daughter, the ten-year-old bride-to-be, lying on her makeshift bed, and together they squeezed the life from her as she tried to rise. Eight men, a woman and a child had died in less time than it took to say a prayer. And the soldiers a hundred yards away, whose presence had given the moonshee comfort, had been so distracted by stampeding horses that they had noticed nothing untoward.

Quietly, in the darkness, Dhunnee's men crouched over the bodies of the fallen men, searching them for valuables. Essuree himself hunted through the moonshee's clothing, removing a few coins and a valuable watch. Then he and his comrades took the corpses, broke their joints, and used knives to slice through the sinews in their legs and arms. The mutilated remains were dragged through the long grass to two deep pits by the river, which had been dug there earlier that day. The killers forced the bodies into the makeshift graves, twisting limbs and crushing them together until they were tightly packed. As they did so, they made long, jagged incisions in the belly of each corpse so that, as it decomposed, gas would not build up inside them, bloating the cadavers and displacing earth until the grave pits were revealed.

A man named Gubbil Khan stood holding Bunda Ali's baby, scooped up from her dead mother's arms. 'She is mine,' one member of the party heard him say. 'I will take her, bring her up and marry her to my son.' But his comrades would not allow this. 'A child from parents of such exalted rank would be recognized and lead to our discovery,' one argued. So Gubbil threw the child, alive, into the grave pit, and the black earth of the bamboo grove was shovelled over her and carefully pressed down until there was no sign of any disturbed soil. Later that night the assassins packed up Bunda Ali's tent and the rest of his possessions. When they left the grove an hour before dawn, there was no sign that the dead man and his family had ever been there.

CHAPTER 1

'Murdered in Circumstances Which Defied Detection'

'*bajeed* – safe, free from danger'

Thomas Perry's scalp itched. He could feel it prickle almost unendurably as beads of sweat rose, in rapid succession, to the surface of his skin and rolled slowly down his neck, inside the stiff, high collar that he wore, and on along the line of his spine until they pooled unpleasantly in the small of his back. His shirt clung damply to his body in half a dozen places, and more rivulets of perspiration carved zigzag trails in the thin patina of wind-blown dust that coated his forehead, just as it covered every inch of his crowded court-room in the ancient town of Etawah, 250 miles north-west of Lucknadown.

It was a hot day during the hot weather of 1811, in a station noted for its intolerable climate:* the sort of conditions that made even magistrates such as Perry, acutely conscious of their dignity, long to mop their faces dry with handkerchiefs. But the room was crowded with Indian officials and servants – clerks, witnesses, the local moonshee, his arms filled with papers and depositions, the court clerk toting his seal of office – and most Britons felt

---

*At this time the great plain of the Doab, which stretched east from Etawah's city walls, was renowned for its baking winds – said to be the worst to be encountered anywhere in India – which, during the hot weather, blew from dawn till dusk, and sometimes through the night as well, carrying with them choking clouds of dust and practically roasting the inhabitants. 'Every article of furniture,' one visitor to Etawah reported, 'is burning to the touch; the hardest of wood, if not well covered with blankets, will split with a report like a pistol.' The nights, the same writer added, 'are terrible, every apartment may be compared to a hot oven', while the transition to the monsoon was via a 'furious tornado', with winds so loud that they drowned out the sound of thunder, and rains so thick that even lightning failed to penetrate the murk.

compelled, in such circumstances, to make a show of self-restraint. So Perry groaned inwardly and returned his attention to the matter in hand: the interrogation of an Etawahan farmer who had made an unpleasant discovery close to the High Road leading into town.

The farmer, Perry heard, had gone to a well to draw water for his animals. But the bucket, lying at the bottom of the well shaft, some 10 or 15 feet below him, had refused to rise. No matter how hard the farmer tugged upon the rope, it had remained resolutely stuck. At length, he had clambered down into the water, reaching into the muddy shallows to feel for the obstruction. His fingers had closed around something large and soft; an object had broken the surface; and as it did so, the stench of rotting flesh had struck his nostrils. Had some animal fallen into the well and drowned there? Heaving again at the heavy burden, the man had at last succeeded in hauling the obstruction into his bucket. It was slippery and yielding, and even in the gloomy dankness of the well it was all too obvious that it was no animal. It was the bloated body of a middle-aged man: broken, naked, and quite dead.

The farmer's deposition completed, Perry dismissed the witness and laid down his pen. The discovery of corpses in the local wells was scarcely a novelty; innumerable farm animals, and even a handful of unlucky travellers, stumbled into such shafts each year and drowned. But there was no room to doubt that this was a case of murder. If the corpse's nakedness suggested it, the terrible wounds the body bore confirmed it. Telltale blotches around the throat hinted at death by strangulation. Worse, having suffered the indignity of being stripped of its clothes, the dead man's body had been savagely mutilated. His unknown killers had carved jagged gashes across his belly, exposing the stomach and the folds of the intestines, and then gouged out both his eyes.

Dully, Perry reviewed the evidence scattered about him. There was little enough of it. The dead man's name was quite unknown; there were no identifying marks upon the body, no possessions that might be traced back to their owner. Since no local people had been reported missing, he had almost certainly been a stranger to Etawah, probably a traveller without friends or relatives in the district to raise the alarm when he failed to return home. Nor was there anything about the torn remains to suggest the dead man's profession. He might have been a soldier going home on leave or a merchant travelling to a distant market, but there was not a single witness to help trace the victim's progress or point out his next of kin. 'The inhuman precaution,' Perry scribbled in his letter-book, 'of the Perpetrators of this crime by destroying all living testimony to the fact precluded the possibility of any complaints being preferred to the Magistrates or the local Police Office.'

The identity of the murderers themselves was equally mysterious. Their motive, apparently, was robbery; no valuables had been found on the body or in the well, and the dead man's missing clothes had no doubt been taken by his killers. That apart, however, there were practically no clues. The dead man's assassins had taken every care to leave no trace of their presence. Perry could not even find witnesses who recalled the appearance of a group of strangers in the district, or remembered anything that might point to the assassins' current whereabouts. Both the killers and their victim seemed to have come from nowhere and, the deed done, the murderers had swiftly disappeared.

The one thing that Perry knew for certain was that this had been no isolated crime. East India Company officers in the Etawah district had long been plagued by the discovery of unidentifiable corpses along the district's dusty roads. No fewer than 28 had been found in 1808, and another 39 the next year – so many that, bizarrely, the number of murders committed around the town dwarfed the total of common-or-garden robberies, assaults and petty crimes reported during the same period. Half a dozen of the bodies had been found roughly concealed beside the roads themselves. The rest – 60 or more corpses – had been hauled, like this most recent discovery, from 'wells adjacent to the High Road'. Not a single victim had been identified; nor had any of the murderers been caught. Every one of the dead men, Perry was compelled to admit, had been 'murdered in circumstances which defied detection'. And there was no reason to believe that this latest mystery would prove any easier to solve.

Etawah had long possessed a reputation as a lawless place. It stood at one of the historic crossroads of India, just to the east of the parched lands of Rajpootana and to the north of the holy river Jumna. There the high road from the great cities of Delhi and Agra met routes that led into the central provinces of India. Etawah was a natural gateway to the Doab* – which, despite its inclement climate, was one of the richest and most fertile provinces in the Subcontinent – and to the wealthy Kingdom of Oudh, 50 miles to the east. But by 1810 the city's great days were long past. Etawah had reached the peak of its prosperity in the time of the Delhi Sultanate, a state that had ruled much of northern India from the twelfth century to the sixteenth. After 1550 it had become a stronghold of the Great Mughals, Muslim emperors belonging to the last and most magnificent of the dynasties of India. But as successive Mughal rulers pushed the borders of their empire east and south, until eventually they controlled nine-tenths of the Subcontinent, Etawah lost much of its *raison d'être*. A merchant passing through in 1608 found its citadel and walls lying in ruins. By the beginning of the eighteenth century, the city had declined into a place of little importance: a mere market town renowned for oils and sweetmeats, grains and cloths, standing secure at the very heart of one of the richest, most powerful and celebrated empires that the world had ever seen. There was no longer any need for elaborate fortifications when the Mughal Emperors ruled over more than 200 million subjects, enjoyed an annual income estimated at 230 million rupees, and commanded what was probably the largest army on earth.

In the years of the Mughals' pomp, so far as one can tell, Etawah's history was little different to that of any other modest Indian town. But even the immense and wealthy Mughal Empire could not grow indefinitely, and although the last of its great rulers, Aurangzeb, extended the boundaries of the state as far south as Mysore, his four decades of ceaseless campaigning drained the imperial treasury almost dry. When the old man died, aged nearly 90, in 1707, he left his country weaker, in important respects, than it had ever been before.

The Empire had grown too large and too diverse. Its ruler's Muslim religion was alien to two-thirds of his subjects; its heavily equipped armies moved at a snail's pace; its finances were in a state of disrepair. Most important of all, so much power was reserved to the monarch himself that only a man of the greatest ability and energy could govern successfully. Over six generations and 180 years, the Mughals had produced half a dozen such rulers. But Aurangzeb's successors were mere ciphers. With his death, the Empire entered into steep decline.

---

*The lands between the rivers Ganges and Jumna. The word means 'two rivers'.

The eighteenth century thus proved to be a turbulent time for India. In only a few short decades, Aurangzeb's creation disintegrated, to be replaced by a land of warring independent princedoms much like the one that had existed before the Mughals first appeared in Hindustan. As early as 1720, many of the imperial checkpoints on the Grand Trunk Road that ran all the way from the Afghan border to Bengal were lying empty, abandoned by officers who had received no pay and been deserted by their men. By 1750, the Empire's richest provinces had broken away altogether, their governors setting themselves up as rulers on their own account and paying little more than lip service to a feeble young Emperor whose writ now barely ran outside the walls of his capital. The Marathas – warlike Hindus from central India whom even Aurangzeb had never completely subdued – were busy carving out lands of their own east of Bombay. Dozens of petty rajahs and small city states scrabbled over what remained of the old Emperor's inheritance.

Etawah suffered as much as any other part of India in the confusion of these times. The city changed hands on no fewer than 10 occasions in the course of the century, passing from Mughal control into the possession of a dynasty of Afghan adventurers, and thence to the Marathas, before finally falling under the sway of the King of Oudh in 1773. The last quarter of the century witnessed a small recovery under the benign and able rule of a vizier named Mian Almas Ali Khan, who – having no children of his own – devoted his considerable wealth to building projects designed to help the people of the district. But for all these ministrations, Etawah remained a poor and ruined place, bypassed by the construction of the Grand Trunk Road, which ran some 20 miles to the north of the city. A handful of its inhabitants might be comparatively wealthy, and there was a small class of merchants and farmers who owed their livelihood to the philanthropy of Ali Khan, but the remainder of the population was far from rich. Almost every Etawahan family suffered amid the tumult of the late eighteenth century.

It is hardly surprising, in these circumstances, that the number of burglaries, murders and other acts of violence committed in the district rose sharply during the final years of the old century. But those who deplored this inexorable rise in crime invariably assumed the problem was a local one, and that the robbers, murderers and thieves who ranged themselves along the roads were isolated bands of limited sophistication. The Mughals had believed this, as had the King of Oudh. And when in 1803 Etawah fell under British sway, the new rulers of the city thought so too.

The British were no strangers to India. Several European states – first Portugal, then Britain, the Netherlands and France – had long maintained a presence on the fringes of the Subcontinent. The first Englishmen had appeared along the coast during the sixteenth century, coming as traders to purchase spice and other eastern luxuries and even seeking grants of land on which to build their warehouses and forts. In time the merchants of the English East India Company established themselves at Madras, Bombay* and Calcutta. But for more than a hundred years, no European wielded any influence over local affairs. For all their wealth and grand ambitions, the few hundred Britons scattered across India were, as one of their own number admitted, no more than 'fleas on the back of the imperial elephant'.

All this changed with Aurangzeb's death. The decay of the Mughal Empire was bad for business, and as parts of the interior descended into civil war and chaos, the trading companies dotted around India became concerned for their profits. At the same time, rapid advances in Western military tactics and technology began to offer even small detachments of European soldiers decisive advantages over local troops. Improved muskets, better doctrine and, in particular, rapid-firing artillery meant that a well-led force of a few thousand men could defeat an army 20 times as large and, by the 1750s, when the final disintegration of the Mughal state began, both the English and the French East India companies had transformed themselves into minor powers along the coast. Their actual possessions were still minimal: a few strips of land around their ports and a handful of isolated trading posts in the interior. But both companies were shipping regiments of their own soldiers out from

*Bombay became British in 1661, when it passed to Charles II as part of the dowry of his Portuguese bride, Catherine of Braganza. Finding the cost of maintaining the place entirely prohibitive, the Merry Monarch leased it to the East India Company in 1668. 'The actual transfer,' one historian records, 'was by letters patent which, presumably for reasons of bureaucratic convenience, described Bombay as being "in the Manor of East Greenwich in the County of Kent".'

Europe, and both recruited *sepoys* (native infantry) whom they equipped and trained to fight alongside their own troops.

The first British conquests in India dated from 1756, when, in one lightning campaign – the 'Famous Two Hundred Days', it became known – Robert Clive and a mixed force of British troops and sepoys routed a large Indian army and took possession of Bengal. The Company ruled the province through a puppet *nawab*, who depended almost entirely on British arms to quash intrigue and oppose the horde of rival states emerging from the ruins of the Mughal Empire. Clive and his successors were happy to oblige him, maintaining a large standing army that was – at least in theory – at the new ruler's command. But British help came at a considerable cost. In order to fund the upkeep of his European regiments, the new nawab was forced to transfer ever larger portions of his dominions to the Company's control. The rising British Empire in India was thus based not so much on conquest as on gifts of land* and trading rights made, reluctantly, by native rulers in return for military service.

This simple formula served the East India Company well for many years. By the 1790s Bengal had passed entirely under its control. Several incursions from the inland provinces of Bihar and Oudh were beaten off, with the consequence that the Company began acquiring lands and interests deep in the interior. It was firmly established in the city of Benares and had been gifted territory along the north bank of the Ganges in wealthy and populous Oudh. By the time the process had run its course, the Company's influence stretched across almost the whole of Hindustan. Its most distant outposts lay within 200 miles of Delhi. And the profits it was extracting from its lands and its new privileges far outweighed existing revenues from trade.

The transformation of the English East India Company from a merchant venturer into what amounted to an imperial power took a long time and was far from easy. The Company of 1756 had excelled at trading, shipping and generating enormous dividends for its investors, and was developing a fair degree of competence in military affairs. But it utterly lacked the infrastructure required to run any country, much less one as huge as India. In not much more than half a century, it was forced to develop an entirely new administrative system, one peopled with governors

*Or, to be exact, the right to raise revenues from designated tracts of land – which in eighteenth-century India amounted to much the same thing.

and political officers, 'Collectors' to assess and gather revenues, magistrates and police to keep the peace, and hundreds of clerks to labour over a vast mountain of paperwork. This it was plainly ill equipped to do, and it was only with the passage of the India Act of 1784, which placed the directors of the East India Company under the supervision of a government-appointed Board of Control and made it in effect an arm of the British state, that affairs in Bengal were fully regulated.

As late as 1790 there was no great wish, either in parliament or in the Company's headquarters at East India House, to see British rule stretch across the whole of India. Indeed the costs of conquering and holding down the whole of the Subcontinent were so obviously colossal that streams of orders enjoining caution and strict economy flowed from London to Calcutta. The most valuable British territories, notably Bengal, were to be surrounded by pacified client states that would guarantee their security, but that was all. There were to be no further wars of conquest in the interior.

Unfortunately for the Company's directors, two substantial obstacles now arose to prevent this moderate policy from being carried through. The first, for which they themselves were responsible, was the appointment of the bellicose Richard Wellesley* as Governor General of British India. Wellesley, a brilliant and ambitious nobleman, was sent out to Calcutta in 1798 with strict orders to keep the peace. But – much to the Company's dismay – he soon showed himself to be a determined empire-builder so anxious to destroy the surviving native states that he 'had barely touched Indian soil before he was preparing for battle'. In his path stood the second great barrier to peace in the Subcontinent: the Maratha warlords of the central provinces, whose aggressive posturings now provided Wellesley with the excuse he needed to plunge the Company into another Indian campaign.

The principal Maratha leaders were Sindhia of Gwalior – who had already conquered Delhi and subdued so many enemies that his lands now butted up against the British territories in Oudh – and the Holkar of Indore, whose own

---

*He was the elder brother of Arthur Wellesley, later the Duke of Wellington, whose own military skills were largely honed campaigning in central India.

domain stretched as far as the borders of Bengal. Sindhia and Holkar were bitter rivals, and at least as likely to go to war against each other as they were to attack the Company's possessions. But both possessed formidable armies, and Wellesley quickly became convinced that the threat they posed was very real.

The secret of the Marathas' military success lay in their willingness to wage war in the Western style. Both Sindhia and Holkar had made it their business to recruit European mercenaries – the men they hired were mostly French, but they included a few British officers as well – to purchase the latest guns and cannon and to train their sepoys to fight like the Company's own infantry. Their new regiments were highly effective and conquered much of central and northern India; even the British regarded them as dangerous. But they were so expensive that it proved to be quite beyond the capacity of either ruler to support them.

Some older Maratha states had developed sophisticated administrations and ruled with fairness and even leniency over some of the richest lands in India. But Sindhia and Holkar could only maintain their armies by using them to extort taxes from their own subjects and ordering a never-ending cycle of attacks on other rulers. Starting with their nearest neighbours in the last years of the eighteenth century, the Marathas proceeded to devastate much of central India with such thoroughness that the land took decades to recover. By 1802, most of the territory east of Delhi had been ravaged by Sindhia's men, while Holkar's armies had left 'not a stick standing within 150 miles of Poona; the forage and grain were consumed, the houses pulled down for fuel, and the inhabitants with their cattle compelled to fly from the destruction that threatened them'. The Marathas' next target was Bihar, on the borders of Bengal. Inevitably, Sindhia's raiders soon exceeded their orders and crossed into British territory, too.

The consequences were catastrophic. Wellesley seized the longed-for opportunity to make war. Company armies from Bengal and Bombay drove into the interior and the Marathas' well-trained regiments were destroyed in a series of hard-fought battles. By 1804, both Sindhia and Holkar had been compelled to accept alliances with the British and the unwelcome presence of 'Residents' – political officers whose purpose was to keep Indian rulers in line – in their capitals. Only the displeasure of the Company's directors, shocked by the horrific cost of Wellesley's campaign, saved their lands from outright annexation.

For the people of the central provinces, the wars were even more disastrous. Great swathes of territory had been looted and burned, often more
than once. Crops had been seized and forts, workshops and looms destroyed.
Mile after mile of countryside had been depopulated. And – with Wellesley
recalled to London in disgrace – most of the lands overrun by the Company's
armies were now abandoned so hastily that they fell into what amounted to
a state of anarchy. The British did retain the Doab, and they guarded their
flank by taking possession of Delhi, Agra and Etawah. But the thousands of
square miles to the south were left effectively ungoverned, prey to famine,
newly unemployed sepoys, rapacious local rajahs and bankrupt landholders
forced to earn a living by their swords.

It was in these circumstances that Thomas Perry arrived in Etawah in the
year 1811. Perry was a Londoner, an experienced Company magistrate who
had first come to India more than a decade before his posting to the Doab.
He had a good deal more experience of the interior of India than was
common at the time, spoke the local languages well, and knew something of
the difficulties of governing difficult and fractious territories. But the task
confronting him was nonetheless a daunting one. For one thing, Perry
reached Etawah to find that the town's first British Collector, WO Salmon,
had left the place in 'a very disorganized and impoverished state'. Salmon
had been forced by the Company's incessant demands for revenue to auction
off large swathes of the land around the city, and fear of seeing their established rights snatched away by wealthier rivals had led many desperate
landholders to offer 'a much larger sum that the estates could have yielded
without all sorts of oppression'. Before long several Etawahan notables had
failed to make good their guarantees and been dispossessed; others had
resorted to extorting the required excess from their increasingly distressed
tenants. A short while later Salmon's successor, a Mr Batson, had further
increased rents in several districts, so that 'revenues had been run up to a
ruinous extent'.

The consequences were predictable. Several more important men
were ruined, and others driven into poverty. Company rule in Etawah became
increasingly unpopular, and there was a good deal of unrest. 'During the
short period that I have been in charge of this office,' Perry was forced to

report to his superiors, 'almost daily reports have reached me of the commission of offences of the most heinous and aggravated nature.'

This might not have mattered so much in Bengal, where the bulk of the Company's army was based, but Perry was almost wholly isolated. The nearest large military station was at Roy Barelly, several hundred miles away, and communication with Calcutta took weeks and sometimes months. The few assistants posted to the city with him were young and lacked experience of service in the *mofussil*, as the interior of India was known. Yet the magistrate was expected not only to impose the Company's regulations upon the half-million people of the district and suppress the rising tide of banditry and violence sweeping up from the Maratha lands, but also to control the unrest festering within the town itself.

It was for these reasons that Perry was concerned by the discovery of so many unknown corpses in his jurisdiction. Keeping the peace in Etawah was a hard enough job in normal circumstances. The last thing he needed was dead bodies in the wells.

CHAPTER 2

'An Independent Race of Men'

'kullooee – to steal'

The city that Perry was having so much difficulty governing was a strange and unique place. It lurked around a sharp bend in the Jumna, squatting along the edge of a line of cliffs that tumbled down towards the muddy, sacred waters far below, and it was quartered by precipitous ravines. Although a few narrow, fragile-looking bridges had been thrown this way and that across the chasms, linking the more important public buildings on their pinnacles of higher ground, most of the inhabitants dwelled down among the ravines themselves, where clusters of their low, brick, whitewashed houses clung like limpets to every niche and ledge. By the beginning of the nineteenth century, the place had acquired a faded look. Its buildings were ramshackle and ageing. Even along the cliff tops, where many of its richer merchants lived, the flights of wooden steps that led down to bathing plat-forms at the river's edge were ragged and decaying, and the skeletons of numerous abandoned temples offered mute testimony to the failing fortunes of a once-great city.

To the east, it is true, the land was civilized and cultivated. The monsoon greened the Doab so rapidly that it was said that any interested observer with two hours to spare in the vicinity could literally watch grass grow, and a profusion of orchards and melon groves stretched away from Etawah's mud-brick walls, speckling the edges of the road that ran towards the city of Allahabad. But the land to the west, on the far bank of the Jumna, was bleak as anywhere in India: a sparsely inhabited wilderness of bare rock, cliffs and crevices with 'only here and there a patch of culturable ground'.

Here were the notorious Chambel ravines, an all but impenetrable maze of steep-sided channels and gorges carved out over millennia by the monsoon rains. The ravine country stretched away south of Etawah for miles, butting up against the Maratha lands and running along both sides of the Chambel river. Two other, lesser streams, the Sindh and the Coharry, also threaded their way through the district. For much of the Chambel's journey through the district, the Company's border with Maharajah Sindhia's territories ran down the middle of the river. But south of Etawah itself, the boundary shifted further south, to the banks of the Coharry.

It was here that Perry's efforts to pacify and regulate his district were most bitterly resented. The lands south of the Jumna were, the magistrate informed his superiors soon after his arrival in the city, among the most difficult and dangerous in India. The district had been inhabited for the best part of a thousand years by a people known as the Parihars – 'always a desperate and lawless community' – and they had never submitted willingly to Oudh or to the Maratha armies. The inhabitants paid rents and taxes for their lands only sporadically, concealing much of their wealth. The whole district, in short, was peopled by what Perry came to recognize as 'a bold, spirited and independent race of men . . . accustomed to submit to no authority but that of the sword', in which 'the greater part of the inhabitants are extremely averse and in fact openly hostile to the forms and principles of our Government'. Secure in their remote fastnesses, tucked away in fortified villages concealed amidst the gorges, the men of the ravine country proved almost impossible to bring to heel. As late as 1812, a few pockets of nominally British territory still seethed with men of 'very turbulent and criminal habits' and remained 'hardly conquered'.

The ravine country was poor and unproductive land, and few of the inhabitants were farmers with fields to till or animals to herd. Some had always made their living as sepoys, selling their services as mercenaries to the Marathas or the King of Oudh. These men had done well for much of the eighteenth century, fighting and plundering their way across Hindustan as sepoys in one or other of the armies carving up the Mughal Empire. But ever since the Company had first appeared along the River Jumna, it had become harder and harder for the soldiers of the ravines to find employment. Most of the rulers who employed them had been defeated by the British armies and disarmed by British diplomacy. The Company itself recruited its sepoys predominantly from Oudh, regarding the soldiers of the ravine district as too ill-disciplined and venal to make good troops.

By the first years of the new century, then, many of the soldiers of the Chambel valley found themselves destitute and desperate for work. A good number of them turned naturally to the other occupation for which the men of their district were known. For generations, hundreds, perhaps thousands of the most determined bandits and robbers of India had made their homes in the Chambel ravines, where they were difficult to find and felt safe from pursuit. Now, their ranks swollen by unemployed soldiers, these men did what they had always done: they left their homes and went out on the roads to steal.

India had long been plagued by highwaymen and thieves.

The very earliest texts referred to it. The Vedas – that vast collection of Sanskrit hymns compiled around 1000 BC – included several tales of the god Rudra that portray him as both a robber and lord of highwaymen, and the Chinese pilgrim Hsuan Tsang, whose description of the 15 years he spent criss-crossing Hindustan in search of Buddhist manuscripts is one of the earliest accounts we have of India, narrowly escaped a violent death at the hands of river pirates in the seventh century AD. Little seems to have changed in the millennium that followed, for bandits continued to loom large in the histories of the Subcontinent. A handful were do-gooders, robbing the rich to feed the poor or resisting invaders and alien rule, but most were little more than ambitious mercenaries, out to enrich themselves and often willing to sell their services to the highest bidder. The most notorious were men so powerful that their hordes of followers numbered in the thousands. Leaders of this sort could and did loot entire towns, and their exploits, real and imagined, became the subject of folk tales and ballads that are still told and sung today.

Not even the greatest of the Mughal Emperors could guarantee safe passage through the interior of India. Travel on the busiest of roads was so notoriously risky that William Hawkins, a British merchant making his way inland from the port of Surat in the year 1609, was forced to hire a troop of 50 soldiers to protect his caravan, since 'the country is so full of outlaws and thieves that a man cannot stir out of doors without great forces'. These same precautions were not enough to save his colleague Nicholas Withington a few years later; on his journey to Agra, Withington was not only set upon by a large gang of highwaymen but attacked by his own guards, who held up the merchants they were supposed to be protecting, took the Englishman prisoner, and robbed and hanged three Indian traders riding with the party. Native caravans, too, were seldom safe in the interior. In one infamous incident, which occurred around the year 1700, a substantial Mughal convoy protected by a numerous armed guard was cut to pieces only 60 miles from Delhi. Not a single member of the party escaped with his life.

By the middle of the eighteenth century, brigandage was already so common throughout the Subcontinent that thousands of men earned their living entirely from robbery, and roving gangs were a common feature of life in the mofussil. Most of these bandits were dacoits,* members of large and well-disciplined gangs of burglars and thieves who operated, more or less openly, in many towns and villages. Some were highway robbers, stealing from merchants and other travellers on the roads. Others again were both.

There is no doubt that the dacoits were more greatly feared than any other group. Although in no sense part of any grand confederacy, most dacoit gangs used similar techniques to terrorize their victims. They generally worked by night. A gang, numbering anywhere from 50 to 300 men, would assemble at a predetermined place, armed with spears, swords, guns and torches. Its target might be a specific house – perhaps the fortified home of a rich merchant or banker – or an entire village. Most were taken by a frontal assault, launched without warning and carried through with considerable daring. It was rare for such gangs to pay more than lip service to careful planning, or devote any effort to subtlety or concealment. They relied, instead, on sheer numbers and their own fearsome reputations to cow their enemies.

Dacoits moved 'with incredible rapidity', one contemporary observed. They 'would sweep down on some distant town or village, plunder some house previously selected for the purpose, and before any pursuit could be organized they were far advanced on their homeward journey'. Larger gangs sometimes attacked well-defended targets – in 1818 one group, 80 strong, assaulted a fort outside the city of Lucknow and stole treasure valued at

*The word derives from the Hindi *daka parna*, meaning to plunder, and perhaps ultimately from *dakna*, to shout.

6,500 rupees from under the noses of its escort of 30 regular soldiers. When they had plundered what they could, the members of a dacoit band would disperse and reassemble at some prearranged meeting spot to divide their loot. It was almost impossible, in such circumstances, to pursue them effectively. In the words of one official who tried, they were like 'a ball of quicksilver, which, if pressed by the finger, divides into many globules, all certain to come together again and cohere as firmly as before'.

Such bandit gangs were unsparingly violent, even though they did not plan to kill their victims and there are accounts of dacoits loading their muskets with shot rather than ball so as to maim, not murder. They ruthlessly disposed of those who dared to resist them, and never flinched at brutally interrogating prisoners in their search for hidden valuables. Blazing torches were the preferred implements of torture, but some gangs would open deep cuts with a spear or knife and rub mustard seeds or chillis into the exposed wound. Another favourite technique was to force a cotton bag filled with hot ash over some victim's head until he had inhaled the burning cinders. In some gangs the application of torture was known colloquially as *tuhsul kurro*, a phrase that means 'to make the revenue collection'.

In Mughal times, dacoit gangs had sometimes hidden out, like outlaws, 'in colonies in the midst of wild jungles difficult of access'. Others had been formed from 'tribals' and 'foresters' – indigenous peoples who inhabited the remoter hills and more impenetrable jungles of India, kept themselves largely to themselves, supported their families by hunting, and emerged occasionally from their hiding places to raid the people of the plains. But amid the chaos of the eighteenth century, most were composed of ordinary peasants, who lived and worked among the people that they robbed. Almost all operated with the approval of the local rajah or one of the many village landholders – known as *zamindars* in northern India and as *polygars* in the south – whose revenues had been badly dented by the wars. The zamindars offered the dacoits a secure base and protection against arrest, commonly employing them as village watchmen, guarding fields, or as *lathials* ('clubmen'): enforcers who worked as revenue collectors and formed what amounted to a village militia. In return, the bandits' protectors claimed a large share of their loot, often well in excess of a quarter – so much, indeed, that one robber complained that were it not for this informal tax, 'we would undoubtedly, in a couple or three years, become men of fortune and there would be no more necessity for our stealing any more'.

The attractions of dacoity were obvious. Impoverished peasants and labourers could earn far more, more easily, by theft than they could on ravaged and depopulated farms. They were most unlikely to be punished; even in the relatively well-policed districts of lower Bengal only a minuscule proportion – it was thought less than six per cent – were ever caught and tried. The profession of dacoity, with its attendant risks, was even seen as a prestigious one, akin to soldiering in the minds of the robbers' less daring neighbours. Since dacoits contributed a good deal to the local economy, bringing home quantities of loot and cash that could never be generated within their village themselves, they were often well respected in their own communities and in many cases robber bands doubled as a sort of local defence force, raiding rival towns and settlements, protecting their own homes from other gangs, and even collecting rents and taxes for their zamindars. As one policeman wearily explained:

> A crime committed by an individual of a village is perfectly disregarded by the rest unless it be against the community. If a man perpetrates a highway robbery in sight of his village he is as well received as before, and if he gives away part of the plunder, he is a patron.

For all these reasons, dacoity had long been common in India, even at the height of the Mughal Empire. But it became considerably more widespread during and after the Maratha wars, and particularly with the advent of a British rule, which so often entailed sharp increases in demands for rent. Figures from the Company's possessions in Bengal suggest that violent crimes rose rapidly after 1793, the number of people tried for what were then termed 'heinous offences' increasing by nearly a third between 1794 and 1801. It seems entirely likely that robbery and violence were even more prevalent in the Doab and among the central provinces of India, where the authorities were weaker, the police almost non-existent, the lot of the peasantry considerably worse and the bandits of the Chambal ravines lurked.

Dacoits rarely worked out in the countryside itself, preferring to launch their raids on homes in towns and villages and to depend on surprise and superior numbers to achieve their aims. In the course of Perry's first year in Etawah, for instance, a gang of dacoits ransacked an Etawahan banker's house, stealing 2,000 rupees and leaving 13 servants injured and another dead; an armed band seized a large quantity of jewels; then, shortly before Christmas, a third gang burst into an important local temple and looted it of all its treasure, carrying off some 60,000 rupees' worth of cash and goods. But even in the first years of the nineteenth century, when British rule was well-established throughout much of the Subcontinent, rural districts could be just as hazardous as the largest cities – and here again the men of the Chambel played their part. Thomas Perry's attention might have been focused principally on dacoity in Etawah. But the magistrate would have been still more concerned had he known that other groups of thieves and robbers from his jurisdiction were active many miles from his headquarters. These men made their living on India's dangerous roads.

Before the advent of the Great Mughals, even the most important Indian highways were not much more than unpaved tracks, dusty and pitted and liable to turn into impassable quagmires during the rainy season. Travel through the mofussil was almost always slow and frequently uncomfortable. But the sheer size of the Empire made it important to ensure swift communication and the free movement of armies. By 1700 the busiest roads had been roughly surfaced with gravel, gathered from riverbeds, and stones collected from the fields to make them more resistant to the rains and to the grinding wear and tear inflicted by the wheels of bullock carts.

Several new routes were also opened up through the interior. Most were in the Mughal heartlands in the north and west of the Subcontinent; few led far into the south, and only a handful stretched as far east as Bengal. But the longest of them – the celebrated Grand Trunk Road, which ran from Dacca up to Delhi and then on to the Afghan border – was 3,000 miles from end to end and thickly lined with trees to offer shade and shelter. All the most vital imperial arteries were provided with mosques and wells for the convenience of travellers; 30-foot pillars known as *kos minars* were thrown up to act as milestones, and comfortable inns and caravanserais were built every few miles so that messengers could change horses and wealthy travellers engage fresh relays of bearers. The Great Mughals were conscious of the importance of this work. For years, repairs to bridges and inns along the Empire's major highways were paid for by the Emperor himself, out of his private purse.

By the early eighteenth century travel through the heartlands of the Empire had thus become comparatively easy. The imperial postal service, manned by the fabled messengers known as *hucarras*,* was capable of 50 miles a day across unbroken country, while well-off Indians in palanquins – the elaborate litters widely regarded as the most comfortable form of transport then available – moved at twice that speed on major roads by changing bearers frequently. The cost of crossing the interior by palanquin was, however, so staggering – as much as a rupee a mile, excluding tips – that almost no one could afford it, and the vast majority of ordinary travellers made their way through India on foot, or (if they were moderately well off) on the backs of the little ponies known as *tattoos* that were a common sight in every province.

Away from the handful of major roads, though, little changed during the Mughal period. Much of the terrain was arduous, and almost nothing was done to improve the web of minor tracks and paths that criss-crossed the mofussil. In poorer districts there was often 'not a vestige of a road to be found, and nothing but impoverished villages to be encountered' for mile after mile. Dried-up riverbeds were used as roads during the dry season, and such paths as did exist were dusty and uneven, being broken up by 'cracks crossing and recrossing one another, some so large that the soil in between was in isolated, loose, irregular squares, and the cracks difficult to jump over'. All were badly scarred by the wheels of innumerable carts. Thomas Bacon, a British officer making his way inland from Calcutta in 1831, complained bitterly of the impossibility of following 'in the ruts of what the natives call a road. When the traffic has been limited to one narrow line, be the soil sandy or swampy, the ruts are sure to be knee-deep.'

There were no milestones or signposts to guide men forced to travel on these lesser roads, and it was often difficult to persuade bearers or palanquin boys to venture away from the established routes. Other forms of transport were more or less unheard of. 'Such conveniences as stage coaches, public wagons, and boats' – London's *Foreign Quarterly Review* observed – simply 'did not exist',

---

*These low-caste confidential messengers began their training at the age of six with regular 'walking practice'. A year later, chosen boys started to run three miles at a stretch, moving at 'a handsome trot', and gradually increased this distance so that by the age of nine they could cross 10 miles of rough country without rest. Training continued for a further nine years until, at the age of 18, a freshly qualified *hucarra* would be issued with a water bottle, bread pan and other equipment and set to work. By then he would be capable of running anything up to 100 miles a day, and would be expected to possess a detailed knowledge of the sacred Vedic texts, astronomy, music, five Indian languages and six varieties of script – not to mention being a master of disguise.

and it was impossible to find 'any conveyances which a person might hire from stage to stage'. Even as late as 1840, those proceeding on foot or horseback through the central and southern provinces of India, or across the western deserts or the badlands of Hindustan, found it a most unpleasant business.

The physical discomforts of life on the road were so ever-present and inevitable that few Indians bothered to mention them. But it was rare for travellers on the minor roads to spend the night in any of the villages they passed. The few inns dotted through the mofussil were shabby and dirty and, during the cold season at least, the climate favoured those who wished to camp outdoors in some bosky grove. Men who knew the roads – the most experienced wayfarers were merchants, pilgrims and soldiers going to and from their homes on leave – carried everything they needed with them: 'a blanket or a quilt for a bed, a pot of brass or copper to boil pulse in or make a curry, a smaller one to drink out of'. Round plates of sheet iron raised on stones or clods of earth were used as stoves, little fires of sticks or dried cow dung being kindled underneath. Those who could afford to cooked rough *chapattis* and ate them with a little dried fish, spiced rice, or vegetable curry prepared with ingredients bought locally or carried with them. The staple diet of the impoverished traveller was, however, considerably less appetizing, consisting as it did of the intoxicating betel nut, chewed to sustain those on the road, and lumps of coarse and dampened flour known as *suttoo*, rolled into the shape of sausages and eaten raw.

It was left to foreign visitors, more accustomed to the roads of Europe, to grumble at the heat and choking dust, the insects, poor food, contaminated water, lack of privacy and sheer tedium that combined to take their toll on even hardy spirits making their way through India. 'The traveller,' Bacon complained, 'often has to find his way over trackless plains, or through crops and jungul, without any better guide than the sun', and the highly cultured Fanny Eden – who set out on an unhurried tour 'up the country' during the 1830s – was so appalled by the conditions she encountered that she copied down one of the reports compiled by scouts sent to survey the road ahead:

This is tomorrow's [itinerary]: '1st mile – ruff and dusty (he evidently thinks ruff a more emphatic mode of spelling), 2nd, 3rd and 4th mile rugged and sandy, 5th mile a brute no water, very bad passage – better go on the left of it; 6th, 7th and 8th miles, very rugged and heavy, 9th, 10th and 11th miles, better but ruff and dusty – encamping ground dusty and not good.

Fanny's sister Emily, who had joined the progress in order to escape the hor-rors of summer in an Indian city, was just as much dismayed by the experience. 'I shall,' she sighed in her own journal, 'always respect marching, for making me like Calcutta.'

Thomas Perry's main concerns were with the roads around Etawah itself.

In the first years of the nineteenth century, highway robbers of all sorts found it easy enough to prey on men and women travelling through India. Even armed parties were vulnerable to attack. Once away from the main roads, there were few police and no patrols to offer protection, and many isolated spots were well suited to ambush. Robbers fleeing the scene of an attack could lose themselves amid the spider's web of minor tracks and paths that threaded through the mofussil, and it was only rarely that the alarm could be raised in time to mount an effective pursuit.

Etawah, under British rule, was as poorly policed as it had been decades earlier. Within weeks of his arrival in the city, Perry was ordered to cut the costs of his patrols by 32,000 rupees, a severe reduction that forced the mag-istrate to reduce the number of policemen he employed and to revise the salaries of those who remained. In consequence, all the outlying areas in his district were left poorly protected, and the loyalty of the men serving in Etawah itself was greatly tested. By the first months of 1809, Perry's police found themselves badly outnumbered by the groups of armed retainers assembled by the district's more powerful zamindars, and more or less pow-erless to prevent local landholders from flouting the Company's authority. 'Daily experience,' the magistrate vainly protested to his superiors, 'teaches them that they have nothing to fear from any force that the [police] can bring against them, and ignorant as they profess to appear of our System of Government, they have acuteness enough to discern that military aid cannot be resorted to except in cases of the most pressing necessity.' So it was scarcely surprising, all things considered, that the bodies of murdered men continued to appear in ditches and wells along the main routes leading into the city from both the east and west.

There were no suspects, for the sheer ruthlessness of the murders sug-gested they were not the work of dacoits or any ordinary criminals. And there were no precedents for how best to proceed, for homicide, even in those violent times, was not especially common in India. Such cases as did occur were almost always the products of land disputes or domestic violence and were, as such, rarely difficult to solve. Cold-blooded murder – visited, apparently, by one or two gangs on a succession of strangers – was more or less unknown.

The magistrate responded as best he could. He set up a checkpoint, manned by a dozen policemen, on the main road between Mynpooree and Agra, where a good proportion of the bodies had been discovered. He offered a large reward – 1,000 rupees, the equivalent of well over 10 years' earnings for most peasants in the Doab – in exchange for information leading to the murderers themselves. Then he settled back to wait.

For the better part of 18 months, nothing happened – nothing, that is, but the discovery of yet more mutilated bodies in the Etawahan wells. The new checkpoint proved utterly ineffective, no arrests were made, and no informants came forward with worthwhile information. Perry may even have begun to doubt that he would ever solve the mystery that tormented him. Then, in the first weeks of the new hot season, news came from nearby Shekoabad that 'private information of a very important nature' had at last been received from a police informant. Eight men had been arrested on suspicion of murder and questioned by local police officials. Each, in turn, had been asked his name and occupation. One, 20 years old, had talked.

'My name,' the boy confessed, 'is Gholam Hossyn. And I am a Thug.'

CHAPTER 3

'Awful Secrets'

'kyboola – a novice Thug'

The word 'thug'* is an ancient one. It first appears in India's sacred Sanskrit tongue – in which *sthaga* means to cover or conceal – and crops up in a variety of guises in several other languages, including Hindi and Hindustani, Gujerati and Marathi. Its literal meaning is almost always 'robber' or 'cheat', but as early as the twelfth century the word was being used as a synonym for 'rogue', 'imposter' and 'deceiver' too, and over the next several hundred years it was employed to describe a wide variety of swindlers. A pair of counterfeiters were condemned as 'thugs' in the first years of the seventeenth century, while in the western province of Gujerat, 'alchemists deservedly came to be classed with them'. Virtually all the 'thugs' encountered in Indian history and literature before the year 1800 turn out to have been members of this class of knaves and thieves.

When Gholam Hossyn identified himself as a thug, however, he had in mind a very different meaning. His Thugs were not so much tricksters and rogues as robbers and murderers: men whose methods were quite distinct from those of dacoits, thieves and other common criminals and formed, indeed, a modus operandi of such startling and original brutality that it had had no exact parallels elsewhere in the world. The defining characteristics of

---

*Properly spelled *thag* and pronounced 't'ug'.

these Thugs were that they wandered the roads of India, seeking likely victims among the travellers whom they met along the way; that they wormed their way into the confidence of these potential victims, stealing only from those whom they had befriended; and that they invariably killed their victims before they robbed them. It is not hard to see how a word used for centuries to describe minor swindlers came to be applied to these far more dangerous criminals; Hossyn's Thugs were 'cheats' and 'deceivers' in that they inveigled their way into the company of travellers, 'imposters' because they never openly declared themselves in the manner of dacoits, and 'robbers' and 'rogues' since they made their living from violence and theft. But they were also ruthless and cold-blooded killers, a meaning that was not reflected in the definition of the word until it found its way into the English language as a direct consequence of the Company's encounter with the murderers of Hindustan.

The young Thug did not volunteer his information willingly. Although he was taken to Etawah almost immediately, his interrogation continued for several days, Perry probing for information, his prisoner deflecting his questions or varying the answers that he gave, gradually admitting to more and more as the stunned magistrate pressed him on each point time and again. On the first occasion that the shackled prisoner was dragged into the courtroom, Gholam Hossyn confessed to nothing more than 'standing two fields off' while his companions had robbed and killed a pair of travellers. On the second, he admitted taking an active part in those same killings. Under further examination, though, the number of his victims rose, to four at first and then 14, until by the end of the third day of relentless questioning, the young Thug had confessed to his involvement in nearly 60 killings. By the time Perry had taken Hossyn through his evidence for a fourth time, the total of his victims stood at 95, all murdered in a mere eight years of robbery. It was a confession so horrific as to be without precedent.

'These examinations,' the magistrate concluded,

are undoubtedly the most extraordinary which ever came before a Court of Justice; they contain the avowal of crimes which could never be presumed to have had existence in one place under the protection of the British administration. They afford also an abundant proof of the shocking depravity and merciless unfeeling disposition of a great portion of the Inhabitants of these provinces. They are in fact so extraordinary that the whole might be considered fabulous, were we not aware that it is no unusual circumstance to discover six or eight murdered bodies, and sometimes a greater number, in pits and wells.

The thing that puzzled Perry most of all at first was the sheer mystery that surrounded the Thugs. 'It is certainly a matter of astonishment that we should have held the administration of justice for so many years, without any information of this detestable association,' he wrote. But as he continued his interrogations, gradually assembling the details of the Thug gangs' methods and techniques, Perry came to understand the reasons for this silence. His prisoners were no ordinary murderers. They were, in fact, the strangest and most remarkable criminals of the day.

Day by day, and gradually, Perry pieced together the story of the Thugs. Some of the evidence he took from Hossyn, some from men arrested with him, who likewise yielded under close questioning. All of it he set down in court records, preserving it for ever.

Thugs worked the lands on both sides of the Jumna, from Lucknow to Jypore. There were, Perry's informants thought, about 1,500 of them living north of the river, and more to the south, ranging as far east as Benares – far more, certainly, than the magistrate had ever imagined existed. They lived under the protection of the zamindars of their home villages and worked in small groups, leaving their homes 'whenever they have nothing left to live on'. The more experienced members of the gangs killed by 'strangling with any part of their clothes'. Less expert Thugs sometimes poisoned their victims with *datura* – the finely ground seeds of the thorn apple, a deadly relative of belladonna, 'which deprives the object of his senses, when they plunder him'.

Several of Hossyn's fellow Thugs, arrested along with the boy, eventually confessed to committing numerous murders over lengthy criminal careers. One, a 60-year-old man named Dullal, had strangled 15 or 16 victims and taken a considerable quantity of loot: 'Much have I plundered and expended, beyond all account.' A second Thug claimed to have witnessed 50 murders in only three years. A third had killed 45 men in eight years, strangling all of his victims with his bare hands.

These men's gang had been led by a man named Ujba, who lived a few miles outside Etawah and supplemented his income as an armourer with the proceeds of Thug expeditions into the Doab. Gholam Hossyn had joined this group after spending a short period as an agricultural labourer, perhaps because he found the prospect of life on the roads preferable to that endured by a peasant farmer. His most recent expedition, at the beginning of the cold season of 1809–10, had opened successfully; Ujba and his 15 men lured their first victim to a *nullah* – a dried-up riverbed – a short distance from the road,

> and murdered him in the following manner: Ramsooth, inhabitant of Dultua, strangled him with a handkerchief; when he was senseless one of the party inflicted wounds with a knife in both eyes and another wounded him, in the same manner, in his belly so that no person might recognize the body. They then buried the corpse in a nullah about a mile to the left of the road.

The dead man was carrying 100 Benares rupees, two turbans and some other clothes, which Ujba's men appropriated. The gang then left the area, going on by forced marches to evade any possible pursuit, until they met two Afghans, whom they befriended and persuaded to accompany them on the road. Having rested for the night, the gang and their intended victims arose very early the next morning, breaking camp four hours before dawn at a time when they could be sure there would be few if any other travellers on the road.* The little party walked a further six miles, halting for a rest at a spot well away from the nearest settlement. The Afghans were then cut down with swords. The first was run through while he was relieving himself; his friend was hacked to the ground as he attempted to flee, then finished off with repeated stabs to his back and neck. On this occasion, however, the Thugs were almost immediately betrayed to the local police – Hossyn did not explain how this occurred –

---

*Rising early and persuading sleeping companions that the time was much later than it really was, in order to assuage any suspicion, was a common Thug trick – one easily played on poorer travellers in an age when watches were only rarely carried.

and brought back to Shekoabad. So ended the boy's short and unproductive criminal career.

Perry's main concern, having taken down the Thug's initial deposition, was to discover all he could of the methods of the gangs. Hossyn reluctantly obliged, describing in awful detail the manner in which the members of his gang had strangled their victims with cloth strips. Even that was not enough for Perry, who now asked his prisoner to demonstrate exactly how the strangling cloths were put to use. Hossyn called for an example and a dramatic scene unfolded. 'The deponent,' the court clerk recorded,

> takes a handkerchief, being a piece of Guzzy Cloth, about two yards or less in length (which the natives throw over their shoulder), he twists the cloth and makes a knot at one end; a person in Court is called, and he shews on this person how the Cloth is passed twice round the neck of the Victim. The knot remains at the back of the neck, and serves as a kind of handle by which the cloth is screwed to its utmost tightness round the neck.

Why, the horrified Perry next asked, did Hossyn and his confederates stab their victims after strangling them? 'Because,' the boy replied,

> people have been known to recover after strangling partially, particularly a person who was recently strangled by Huittea, who, afterwards recovering, fled with the Cloth, and is now at Furruckabad, where he narrated all particulars . . . We therefore now stab, it was not formerly the practice, we used only to strangle and throw the bodies in to a well.

Perry was disgusted by Hossyn's detailed descriptions of the ruthless methods of the Thugs. But the magistrate was quite certain that their 'atrocious crimes' were not committed out of any sort of blood lust. On the contrary, the gangs' entire modus operandi had been cleverly calculated to maximize their prospects of plunder while minimizing any chance of being caught.

To begin with, the Thugs' technique of befriending strangers on the road disarmed their intended victims, making it a simple matter to take them by surprise. It also allowed skilled murderers to gauge the travellers' likely wealth. Impoverished peasants could thus be discarded in favour of richer merchants, or sepoys travelling home on leave and carrying with them their arrears of pay. Next, Thugs never tackled a party of travellers unless they greatly outnumbered them. This made the killing itself a quick and relatively simple process, and ensured that any intended victims who attempted to escape could be pursued and despatched before they could summon help.

Obtaining evidence against such men was, Perry recognized, almost impossible. Many Thugs, although by no means all, never killed close to home, which made tracing them an unenviable task. 'In this part of the country,' a strangler named Kalee Khan explained, 'we have never murdered, for it is the custom amongst us never to commit a murder within a distance of 100 *coss* [200 miles] round our habitations.' Men from the Jumna ranged as far south as Nagpore and even into the Deccan on occasion, where – having disposed of one traveller – they would move quickly on, often into a neighbouring territory with a different ruler, before murdering again. This, in the fragmented India of the early nineteenth century, meant that pursuit was generally futile and prevented such authorities as existed from realizing just how many victims were being killed. By restricting themselves to despatching travellers who were often hundreds of miles from their own homes, and unlikely to be missed for weeks or even months, the gangs minimized the risk that a hue and cry would be raised while they were in the vicinity; many, in addition, chose to operate in the Native States rather than the Company's territories, not least because it was often possible to bribe a local rajah or his men to permit Thug operations or to release captured stranglers from jail. Finally and most importantly – as Perry reluctantly conceded – the fact that the gangs invariably murdered every member of every party they inveigled meant that no witnesses survived to testify against them. The 'precaution of the Perpetrators of this crime', the Etawahan magistrate remarked, 'by destroying all living testimony to the fact precluded the possibility of any complaints being preferred . . . and consequently in no one of the cases which has been reported to the office has any individual been directly implicated'. Were it not for the occasional confessions, made by captured criminals such as Gholam Hossyn, there would have been no evidence that specific Thugs were responsible for particular murders. 'Had this inhuman offender chosen to have asserted his innocence,' Perry wrote of one captured strangler who had confessed to killing

50 travellers, 'what evidence either direct or circumstantial could have been brought against him?'

Having listened to several days of graphic testimony, the magistrate found himself persuaded of one thing. The Thugs' habits were quite different from those of the dacoit gangs, and apparently unique to India. The Thugs themselves believed that their methods set them apart from other robbers and made them special – an opinion apparently shared by their fellow villagers, who sometimes referred to them by the honourable term *sipahee* (soldier) and described their murderous expeditions as *cakari* (military service). The surest way to anger a captured strangler – at least one of long experience, who derived a good portion of his income from the practice of 'Thuggee' – was to suggest that he was nothing but a common criminal. 'There are many thieves in my village,' one of the Company's prisoners explained, 'but I would not go with them. My father, a Thug, used to counsel me: "Do not join them! They take money without thugging!"'

Not every member of every gang was quite so scrupulous, of course; a few years after Perry interrogated the first captured stranglers, a British traveller heard evidence 'which proves that they conceive themselves to be occasionally justified in robbing from tents'. But many Thugs insisted that they spurned other forms of crime, and were wont to decry other sorts of robber in the strongest terms. Ordinary theft was 'low and dirty' and dacoits 'men of force and violence – they have no science!' 'The Thug is the king of all these classes!' the eminent leader of one gang concluded in great indignation:

A Thug rides his horse! Wears his dagger! And shows a front. Thieving? Never! Never! If a banker's treasure were before me and entrusted to my care, though in hunger and dying, I would scorn to steal. But let a banker go on a journey, and I would certainly murder him. Dacoits and robbers are contemptible. I despise a dacoit. Let him come before me!

Thugs had lived in the district around Etawah for at least a hundred years. If the gangs' own oral traditions are to be believed, their ancestors probably arrived on the banks of the Jumna late in the seventeenth century, some coming from the town of Himmutpore and others from Sursae, to the south of the river. These early immigrants prospered so much in the course of the

eighteenth century that by 1797, when the Marathas had established themselves at Gwalior and could levy taxes on the people of the Jumna valley, they
recorded no fewer than 440 'families of Thugs' in one small area south of
Etawah alone.

It is difficult, if not impossible, to say how closely these early criminals
resembled the men whom Perry interrogated in 1810. The first-hand recollections of the oldest stranglers ever to recount their histories date only to
1760, and contain no hint that these Thugs' methods and habits were not
broadly the same in those days as those encountered in the nineteenth century. Many families, indeed, took great pride in their traditions and lineage,
and could recite genealogies tracing their ancestry back through at least seven
or eight generations of stranglers – which, if true, would place the Thugs' origins somewhere in the period 1650–1700. Gholam Hossyn told his
interrogator that his fellow Thugs believed that their fraternity had existed
since the days of Alexander the Great. A more plausible fragment of tradition,
though, takes the story back no more than another century, for many of the
men living in the first decades of the 1800s firmly believed that their forebears
had lived together in Delhi in the time of the third Mughal Emperor, Akbar
the Great.

In those days – Akbar ruled northern India from 1556 until 1605 – there
were said to have been seven great Thug families. All of them were Muslim
and most had their headquarters in the ancient city, and it was only when one
clan incurred the wrath of the Great Mughal himself by murdering one of his
favourite slaves that 'the whole of the Thugs fled from the capital and spread
themselves about the country'. Some went no further than Agra, while others
scattered hundreds of miles to the south, into the Deccan. A handful – among
them several of the families whose descendants finally established themselves
near Etawah – crossed the Jumna into Oudh, where they lived for several
decades under the protection of the Rajah of Akoopore.

The reliability of these purely oral histories is difficult to gauge. There seems
to have been broad agreement among many Thugs that their ancestors had
come from Delhi, but various traditions – not set down until the 1830s – can
hardly be entirely true. The supposedly 'Muslim' clans of Delhi had Hindu
names, for example; and for all the Thugs' proud boasts that their forebears
had defied the Emperor himself, there were hints that their true origin was
much more humble. At the weddings of one Thug clan, a grizzled murderer

conceded, 'an old matron will sometimes repeat: "Here's to the spirits of those who once led bears, and monkeys; to those who drove bullocks, and marked with the *godnee*,* and those who made baskets for heads"' – an account suggesting that, far from being aristocratic Muslims, the earliest members of this family were actually *khunjurs*, wandering tradesmen who roamed through Hindustan with their herds of cattle. Many Thugs hotly disputed this explanation. 'By no means,' protested one. 'Our ancestors, after their captivity at Delhi, were obliged to adopt these disguises to effect their escape. Some pretended to be khunjurs, but they were not really so; they were high-caste Musulmans.' But even this man admitted that the glorious genealogies he had often heard recited were probably false, and guessed that some early Thugs, at least, had sprung from among the impoverished camp followers of the Mughal army.

That, really, is as far as the available evidence can take us. All attempts to trace the history of the seven clans further back than Akbar's day founder on the difficulty of interpreting earlier sources, for the first incontrovertible use of the word 'thug' to refer to murderers, rather than to thieves and swindlers, dates only to the 1600s. It is interesting – given the Thugs' own insistence that their earliest ancestors were Muslims – to note that 'stranglers and assassins' formed one of the five classes of brigands discussed by the Arabic author Uthman al-Khayyat in a work dating to the tenth century AD.** The seventeenth-century travellers Jean Thévenot and John Fryer, meanwhile, both described gangs of Indian highway robbers whose methods resembled those employed by the Thugs two hundred years later; Thévenot heard of the existence of cunning highwaymen who murdered their victims with 'a certain slip with a running noose, which they can cast with so much sleight about a man's neck . . . that they almost never fail', while Fryer recalled an encounter with a fifteen-strong gang of robbers captured near Surat, who 'used to lurk under Hedges and in narrow Lanes' and possessed 'a Device of a weight tied to a

---

*Needles used to create tattoos.
**This group, Uthman wrote, could be divided into several distinct categories: the *sahib baj* – that is, disembowellers – the *sahib radkh*, 'crushers and pounders', and the early Islamic stranglers themselves. Both the latter groups bore a certain resemblance to the Thugs of India; the 'crushers and pounders' befriended travellers on the road and, having ingratiated themselves with them, crept up on their victims while they were praying or asleep and struck them over both ears simultaneously using two smooth stones, taking care to kill them in order to avert the risk of being identified later. The stranglers' favoured method, on the other hand, was to throw their victims' robes over their heads to disorientate them while they were being throttled, or to lure them into a house where they could be despatched while accomplices drowned out the sound of the murder by playing music or wailing like lamenting women.

Cotton Bowstring made of guts of some length' which they threw over the heads of passing travellers. But references in old chronicles and histories to gangs of stranglers may simply demonstrate that the Thugs had no monopoly on this method of killing their victims. Certainly murder by strangulation was common enough in Mughal times for the Emperor Aurangzeb to draw up a *farman* (law) specifying the punishment to be meted out to those found guilty of the practice. The Thugs, awful as they were, were merely one product, among many, of India's lawless interior.

By the early nineteenth century, moreover, Thug gangs were far from the socially exclusive clans described in their early traditions. Most, the surviving evidence suggests, were thoroughly heterogeneous, recruited from men of all backgrounds, classes and castes. Their members were defined by the manner in which they made a living, rather than by their racial or religious identity. There was no such thing as a typical Thug, and the Thugs of the Jumna valley, whom Perry had stumbled across by chance, were far from the only sort of Thug gang.

There were, indeed, more than a dozen varieties of strangler scattered across much of the length and breadth of India. Almost all were distinguished by their place of residence, a detail that may suggest there was some truth in traditions of a general flight from Delhi. The men of the Doab and Oudh were 'Jumaldahees', from their homes along the Jumna river.* In the northern reaches of the Deccan, the Telinganies, Arcottees and Beraries hailed from Telingana, Arcot and Berar respectively. Other Thugs, however, seem to have taken their name from the occupations followed by their principal leaders. The Lodahas, who came mostly from the province of Bihar, were caravan drivers named for the *lodh* (load) they carried; the Motheeas were 'from a class of weavers'; the Moltanees were bullock drivers who strangled their victims with the leather thongs they used for driving their oxen.

Few outsiders – even the British officers who questioned captured Thugs – ever really penetrated the complex interrelationships that seem to have developed between the various groups. So scanty is the evidence for the mere existence of some classes of Thug that their importance remains largely a matter of guesswork, even today, and some authorities have argued that

---

*An alternative explanation was that these Thugs descended from a strangler named Jumulud Deen.

most of the gangs mentioned in early nineteenth-century sources do not deserve to be classed as 'Thugs' at all. The captured stranglers questioned by Perry and the Company officers who came after him do seem, nonetheless, to have recognized the existence of a number of different groups of Thugs, and were insistent that each saw itself as 'distinct'. 'The Hindu Thugs of Talghat,' for example, 'were admired by all,' one Deccan man explained. 'They are extraordinary men. They have three painted lines on their fore-heads extending up from a central point at the nose . . . They always wear them. They and the Arcot Thugs associate and act together; but they will never mix with us of Telingana . . . They will never intermarry with our families, saying that we once drove bullocks and were itinerant tradesmen, and consequently of lower caste.' The Lodahas, meanwhile, had left their original homes in Oudh around the year 1700 and lived, in Perry's time, along the border with Nepal, restricting their activities to the provinces of Bihar and Bengal. 'They are,' a Doab Thug recounted, 'descended from the same common stock as ourselves . . . Their dialect and usages are all the same as ours, but they rarely make Thugs of any men but the members of their own families. They marry into other families who do not know them to be Thugs, but their wives never know their secrets, and can therefore never divulge them.'

The various bands of Thugs seem, in any case, to have mixed relatively freely amongst themselves. Most gangs were lead by stranglers of long ex-perience who had become acquainted with the principals of other groups and knew a number of their followers. The sheer range and mobility of many Thugs – who thought nothing of walking hundreds of miles in the course of a single expedition – may help to explain how such relationships developed. In the course of a long career, a strangler could expect to fall in with gangs from all over India. Men from Etawah often knew Thugs from Oudh, Bengal and the Deccan, who could be recognized by 'certain signs' that many of the gangs had in common, in much the same way that groups of vagabonds passed information to each other on the roads of rural England. Special phrases, or the particular shape of a purse or a campfire, were among the signals that identified a Thug.* This system, informal though it undoubtedly

---

*Thug 'passwords' were said to include the phrase 'Peace to thee, friend'. 'This,' claimed one British offi-cer, 'to anyone but a Thug would seem a common salutation, but it would instantly be recognised by a Thug. Anyone who should reply in the same manner would be quite safe.'

was, seems to have worked surprisingly well. A captured strangler named Morlee
recounted how

> I was one day walking with some of our party near Jypore by an encamp-
> ment of wealthy merchants from the westward, who wore very high
> turbans. I observed to my friends as we passed, 'What enormous turbans
> these men wear!' using our mystic term *aghassee*. The most respectable
> among them came up immediately and invited us to sit down with them,
> saying: 'My good friends, we are of your fraternity, though our aghassees
> are not the same.' They told us that they were now opulent merchants, and
> independent of Thuggee, the trade by which they had chiefly acquired
> their wealth, though they still did a little occasionally when they found in a
> suitable place a *bunjj* [merchandise] worth taking; but that they were now
> beyond speculating in trifles! We were kindly entertained, and much
> pleased with our new friends, but left them the same day, and I have never
> met any men of the same kind since.

Relationships of this sort were eminently practical. Experienced stranglers
knew full well that they could expect little help from any but fellow Thugs
once on the roads. They were glad to share the knowledge of each other's
crimes, and took pride in the exploits of other gangs. Informal ties were
strengthened when Thug gangs cooperated in inveigling and murdering large
parties of travellers, and it was not uncommon for stranglers from one part
of India to serve with those from another for a while, occasionally out of
sheer curiosity as to the customs and methods of their hosts. Even more
revealingly, the depositions made by captured Thugs often feature striking
instances of gangs sharing the proceeds of their murders equally with others,
even in cases in which one group of Thugs had done far more of the work
than had their companions. The cooperation and the selflessness displayed on
such occasions strongly suggest that the Thug gangs shared a heritage and displayed a degree of mutual trust that simply did not exist between groups of
dacoits or other highway robbers. They were – as Perry and his assistants
quickly recognized – something utterly unique.

CHAPTER 4

Mr Halhed's Revenge

'cheyns – noise, confusion, clamour'

Whether or not the Thugs of the Jumna valley were truly as ancient or unique as they thought themselves to be, the confessions made by Gholam Hossyn and his fellow prisoners soon led to the apprehension of other members of the fraternity. The members of Ujba's band had been arrested in March 1810. By the middle of May, the British had seized a further 70 men, most of them associates of one or other of his original prisoners. Several of the stranglers' most influential leaders did contrive to slip through the Company's net. But, alarmed by the rapid progress of the British campaign, others abandoned their homes along the north bank of the Jumna and fled south, out of the Company's lands, to escape similar fates.

From the Company's perspective, then, this first drive against the Thugs of the Doab seemed to have been a considerable success. The number of bodies discovered on the high roads around Etawah and in the wells of the district fell sharply almost at once, from 67 in 1808–9 to only 14 in 1810. 'As a further proof of the decrease of this species of offence,' Perry added in a report drawn up for his superiors in Bengal, 'it may be necessary to observe that only four murdered bodies have been found during the [last] period of six months.'

It was, in truth, no more than a partial victory. The captured Thugs who had been sent for trial before the *Nizamat Adalat* (the Company's supreme court) in Bengal retracted the confessions they had made in Etawah and were eventually acquitted. The law, as it then stood, required that formal complaints be lodged by the families of the Thugs' murdered victims and that the statements of other witnesses, as well as circumstantial evidence, should supplement the testimony of even admitted criminals if a conviction was to be secured. Perry – who had been unable to establish the identity of the mutilated corpses discovered within his jurisdiction, much less find living witnesses to the Thugs' depredations – was reprimanded for his 'irregular' proceedings. But it was only towards the end of the cold season of 1812, when bodies began appearing once again on the High Road outside Etawah, that the magistrate fully realized his enemies' resilience. The men whom he had driven from their villages north of the Jumna two years earlier had not given up Thuggee. Nor had most fled far from their old homes. Many had travelled no more than a few miles, establishing themselves in the district immediately south of Etawah, on the far bank of the Jumna. There, amid the badlands along the Company's border with the Maratha territories, they continued to practise their familiar trade, secure in the knowledge that their new home was one of the most inaccessible and lawless places in the whole of the Subcontinent, and that the powerful local zamindars who ruled it would protect them – for a price.

The villages that welcomed the fleeing Doab gangs were already home to more Thugs than any comparable district in India. There were several dozen such settlements in all, scattered across three *parganas*.* The northern portion, which lay below the Jumna and the valley of its clear, fast-flowing sister river, the notorious Chambel, fell within the district of Sindouse. This region, nominally part of the Company's possessions since 1807, was as bleak as anywhere in India: a sparsely inhabited wilderness of scrub and naked rock, with 'only here and there a patch of culturable ground', all but impenetrable to outsiders. Its principal feature was a maze of jagged ravines which scarred the land in either direction for as far as the eye could see, twisting and turning back upon themselves so frequently that it was all too easy to become lost. The rest of the district was 'made up of a succession of steep ridges, low sloping hills, deep hollows and winding streams. In places the soil is devoid of all vegetation, while elsewhere it is covered with low scrub jungle.'

A few miles to the south – on the far side of a second tangle of impenetrable

---

*An Indian term used to describe an administrative district of anywhere between 20 and 200 villages.

gorges – British territory butted up against the furthest flung of Sindhia's lands along the rugged banks of the Sindh and the Coharry. These districts, too, had been settled by Thugs in considerable numbers. Contemporary estimates put the number of stranglers living in Sindouse at around 400, while in the Maratha territory there were at least 500 more, many of them living in the large village of Murnae, a mile or two to the west of Sindouse and only a few hundred yards on Sindhia's side of the border.

Dealing with the Thugs of these recalcitrant parganas was no easy matter. So formidable were the inhabitants, and so strong the natural defences afforded to them by the fortified villages they had built in the ravines, that the district had been more or less ignored by the Company authorities at Etawah ever since its acquisition. The local zamindars appeared to be 'almost invincible', and were certainly strong enough to resist the limited British forces in the area. Virtually the entire population was armed, and 'instances of prowess', Perry's assistant magistrate, Nathaniel Halhed, observed, 'are common occurrences. The Sindouse *Sirdar* (headman) can turn out 2,000 armed men and with the assistance of his connections in the Mahratta states can call for 2,000 more.' These irregulars, in turn, could summon reinforcements amounting to another 12,000 men, and though even this combined force would never stand and fight a pitched battle, the ease with which they could retreat over the Maratha border made it almost impossible to defeat them.

It is scarcely surprising, in these circumstances, that Thomas Perry and his colleagues left the inhabitants of Sindouse largely to their own devices. Effective control of the district thus passed from its former ruler, a minor Maratha potentate known as the Rajah of Rampoora, to a group of zamindars whose principal aim was to prevent the British authorities from interfering in their territory. Under the leadership of a certain Raja Madho Singh, these men contrived to obstruct the Company at every turn for several years, while conceding just enough to make British intervention south of the Jumna seem unnecessary and unwise.

Ordinary policing was of no avail in such a district. As late as 1810 there were no Company police in Sindouse at all, and though a detachment 40 strong was sent to the pargana in that year, it proved so pathetically inadequate that the men were soon reduced to cowering within the walls of their half-ruined mud-brick fort in the village of Sindouse itself, on the south bank of the Coharry some 30 miles south-east of Etawah. Over the next two years the police ventured out of their headquarters so infrequently that – Halhed noted with disgust – 'an entire village was only discovered six months ago, even though it was only half a mile from the fort'. Law and order was thus non-existent. Travellers foolhardy enough to wander into the district, the assistant magistrate observed, 'never go out of it alive'.

It was not until late in 1812 that Perry at last received the information he required to disperse the Thugs who dared to make their homes on British territory. Early in the cold season of that year, an argument flared up between the members of several Sindouse gangs and a zamindar by the name of Tejun, who had been their landlord for some years. The dispute soon became so serious that the Thugs decided to move to another part of Sindouse and seek the protection of another zamindar called Laljee. Tejun – who had no doubt claimed a considerable proportion of the profits of his Thugs and so stood to lose a good portion of his income – asked his colleague to force the disgruntled stranglers to return to their old homes. When Laljee refused, an angry Tejun took his revenge by informing the authorities in Etawah of the existence of the Thugs.

Perry wasted little time in acting on such important information. Assembling all the troops at his disposal – 40 sepoys from the Company's 23rd Regiment, Native Infantry, led by a young Irish lieutenant named John Maunsell, and the men of his own guard – he placed them under Halhed's command and ordered his assistant to march south and impose order on the rebellious pargana. The inhabitants were to be disarmed, in so far as this was possible, and the district's zamindars, including Laljee, compelled to observe the Company's regulations. Once that had been achieved, the police would be in a better position to deal with the Thugs and dacoits so prevalent in the district.

Nathaniel Halhed was well suited to the task Perry had set him. He was the nephew of a distinguished Company servant, NB Halhed, who was the author of the first codification in English of Hindu laws,* and he had been in India since 1804. He spoke the local languages so well that – suitably disguised – he could pass undetected among native Indians. Most importantly,

---

*In later life NB Halhed became a long-serving Member of Parliament and, notoriously, the vocal supporter of an eccentric millennial cult.

he was tough. He had already brought order to several recalcitrant districts around Allygurh and had survived at least one skirmish with rebellious locals in the Doab, in the course of which he had been struck full in the forehead by an arrow. He was supremely confident in his own authority and determined to ensure that the zamindars of Sindouse, like those he had encountered elsewhere, yielded to the Company's authority.

Halhed and his men reached Sindouse on the evening of 9 October 1812, their first day in the ravine country. Their march south from Etawah had been without incident. But the magistrate – hearing that 'Laljee and others, principal zamindars . . . had assembled a large force to cut me off in the Ravines' – was determined to approach the village cautiously. He picked up some reinforcements in the shape of Indian troops sent by his friend, the Rajah of Bhurdaweree, stationed a small party in the ravines to protect his line of retreat, and set up his camp outside the village of Sindouse itself.

The local inhabitants proved to be friendly – disconcertingly so. 'The people of the village,' Halhed noted, 'were extremely assiduous in offering milk and flour to the people who came in with me.' But it was not until late that first evening that the magistrate discovered the real reason for this show of cooperation. Shortly after supper had been taken, he and Lieutenant Maunsell were prostrated by sickening stomach cramps, 'and from the violence and suddenness of the symptoms I had every reason to suspect poison had been administered'. A large dose of datura had been added to the milk purchased in the village, and though both officers immediately dosed themselves with violent purgatives, they lay virtually incapacitated in their tents throughout the night. 'I imagine,' Halhed added,

it was their intention in case the poison had taken effect, to have attacked and cut up the whole of the detachment, which they might have done with ease, if it had not been commanded by a European, for during the night they assembled in large bodies in the Ravines, close to the camp, and frequently sent up reconnoitring parties, but the alertness of the sentries prevented an attack being made, and every hope on their part of our deaths had to be given up from our appearance on the parade yesterday, which,

tho' still very unwell, we made considerable efforts to accomplish, to prevent their receiving confidence, or our own people being deprived of it.

The sight of Halhed and Maunsell reviewing their men disconcerted Laljee
and the force of Thugs and armed retainers he had assembled in the ravines.
Rather than launching an attack, the zamindar prudently retreated towards
the Maratha border, leaving the Company's troops in possession of his village.
But Halhed knew that he was worryingly exposed. Thousands of well-armed
rebels lurked nearby, ready to attack, and the pargana could scarcely be pacified until they had been dispersed. Until that could be achieved, Sindouse
itself, with its limited resources, had to be occupied and its recalcitrant inhabitants faced down. It was far from an appealing prospect.

The magistrate's mood – probably not good to begin with – can only have
been worsened by the sight of his new quarters in the village's barely defen-
sible mud fort. The walls were in a poor state of repair, and were unlikely to
resist determined assault. A cursory inspection revealed that there were no
reserves of food. In the event of an attack, Halhed grimly concluded, the
place could hardly be relied on to do more than 'provide [for] the lives of
every soul belonging to the Government for a few hours'.

Halhed and Maunsell spent the first half of October struggling to impose any
sort of order on the pargana. Their attempts to disarm the people of the surrounding settlements were only partially successful. Twenty stands of muskets
were seized in the village of Chourella – 'which has been noted above all others
for obstinacy and violence' – but Halhed's sepoys had only been in the village for
a matter of hours when Laljee and 300 of his men appeared in the surrounding
ravines, 'from which they kept up a smart fire on us for about five minutes'.
Three villagers were wounded and a horse killed before the Thugs and their sup-
porters made good their escape and a worried Halhed retired to his ruined fort.

Worse followed. On the evening of 22 October, Halhed took an evening
ride through the ravines along the Maratha border, accompanied by Maunsell
and a bodyguard of a dozen sepoys and three mounted guides. The evening
had been a quiet one, but as Halhed rode along a dried-up riverbed outside
the village of Bindawa, 'a party of about 500 armed men, headed by Loll Jee
and his son, Suntak Arn, who had it seems laid in wait for us, rushed out'. The
attack was quite unexpected. 'I had no reason to apprehend any such disturbance in our own Territories at that time,' Halhed protested. 'Nor had anyone

the least idea that it was possible to happen. We offered no provocation whatever and were proceeding quietly on our road, and I certainly deemed the protection of 12 horsemen sufficient.' In a matter of moments, however, the British party found itself entirely surrounded and cut off from their base.

Their situation was desperate. 'To move forward,' the magistrate would recall, 'was death, to stand still to prolong our existence for a very short time, to return was equally dangerous, for it is the custom of these villagers to rush on when the opposing or defending party retreat.' Only the Sindouse men's reluctance – common among Indian irregulars at this time – to assault armed Europeans prevented an immediate attack. But, even so, there was no obvious escape and Halhed swiftly realized that his men's one hope was to retreat to the top of the ravines, under cover provided by a desperate rearguard action.

All was confusion as the ascent began. Halhed placed himself with the rearguard and was overseeing the retreat of the last of the sepoys when

> at this instant a shower of Balls assailed us, and the road was so narrow as only to admit of one horse at a time . . . A man was shot just before me by a rascal who had aimed at me; he fell and at this moment the Rebels cried out, 'We have killed a *Ferringee*!*'

Turning, Halhed found that Maunsell was nowhere to be seen. Four wounded sepoys, coming up the ravine after him, confirmed that the lieutenant 'had been shot and cut down, that Manoolah, horseman, was killed, and also one of the mounted guides, and that the villagers were coming up'. There was very little the magistrate could do, but he 'went to the braw of the cliff and fired my pistols at them, which they returned with matchlock balls'.

Halhed's flight brought him and the remaining members of the party to the village of Bindawa, a few hundred yards from the Maratha border. The village zamindars – whom the magistrate 'had every reason to suppose would try to destroy us' – refused to offer any help, and though Halhed was anxious to counter-attack, the most he could do was return to the foot of the ravines to recover Maunsell's corpse. It had been 'cut into pieces . . . stripped and covered with numberless wounds, most of them apparently inflicted after life had left them'.

*European.

Such an outrage could not be left unrevenged. It was more than simply a matter of prestige; the Company was so badly outmanned in India that its entire position could be swiftly undermined if its subjects thought they could kill Europeans with impunity. Within a few days another party of sepoys, this one under a Captain Popham, was sent to Sindouse to reinforce Halhed's men. A battery of artillery capable of reducing the rebels' strongholds was floated down the Chambel. And a reward of 5,000 rupees was offered for the capture of Laljee himself. When news reached Halhed that the zamindar had taken refuge, with most of his retainers, in the village of Murnae, just over the Maratha border to the west, he wasted no time in crossing into Gwalior after them.

Once again, Laljee did not stand and fight. At the first news of Halhed's approach, he fled, accompanied by almost all his men, including a party of well over a hundred Thugs. Murnae, which had been one of the stranglers' principal headquarters for more than a century, was left exposed. And in the second week of November, the Company's troops descended upon it. Their orders were to raze the village to the ground.

Murnae burned, a vivid flare of colour amid the grey of the ravines. Two months after the end of the rains, the grass roofs of the village houses were dry and combustible. It took only seconds to set them alight, and as Captain Popham's sepoys ran from hut to hut, thrusting flaming torches into the thatch, thin columns of smoke began to rise into the air and went spiralling up over the surrounding gorges to scar the cold November sky. Long before nightfall, the settlement had been reduced to little but ash and a scattering of sagging walls, black with soot and still hot to the touch.

Popham did not rest even then. Before he marched away, the captain had asses harnessed to the local farmers' ploughs and sent his sepoys back into Murnae. The smouldering remnants of its mud-brick buildings were ploughed back into the earth from which they had been made, until there was nothing but rutted heaps of black, charred soil where the village had once stood. Maunsell's death had been avenged. The destruction of the Thug headquarters was complete.

By then, of course, the stranglers themselves had fled. At the first signs of Popham's approach, every able-bodied person in Murnae had hastened south or west into the Maratha lands to escape the vengeance of the Company. Some did not go very far. Most of the village's farmers and artisans probably halted no more than a few miles away, fearful for their crops, and some of these men had already returned home by the end of the year to begin rebuilding their village. Laljee himself, accompanied by a band 400 strong, did not venture much further. The zamindar sought refuge in Rampoora, a small town 15 miles to the north of his former home, and hovered for several weeks along the south bank of the River Sindh, hoping for an opportunity to cross back into British territory and seize back the cattle that were the main source of his wealth. This proved to be a serious mistake, for – surrounded by a detachment of Maratha troops despatched at the Company's request, handed over to the British authorities for trial, and swiftly found guilty of complicity in Maunsell's murder – Laljee found himself imprisoned for life in the British jail at Roy Barelly, east of Delhi. Some 140 Sindouse and Murnae Thugs, picked up by the Marathas in nearby villages and towns, fared only a little better. These men were thrown into a grim prison in Gwalior where almost a third of them died, apparently of rheumatic fever.* The survivors had to endure 13 months of incarceration before securing their release by paying the enormous total of 16,000 rupees as security for their future good behaviour. Every one was, in the meantime, 'horribly maltreated', even those with money – which usually purchased good treatment in the prisons of the Native States – for 'those who could not pay' (one of their number recalled) 'were beaten in the hopes that their friends would in time pay; and those who paid, were beaten in the hopes that their friends would be made, in time, to pay more'.

The wisest of Laljee's followers were those who left the district altogether. A number of Thugs fled south into their traditional hunting grounds in the lands south of the Nerbudda river known as the Deccan, and 200 more found sanctuary amidst the mosaic of tiny semi-independent states that made up

*The Thugs themselves firmly believed that these deaths were inflicted by 'a great Demon that every night visited our prison and killed or tortured some one'. One of their number, Thukoree, recalled: 'I saw him only once myself. I was awake while all the rest were asleep; he came in at the door, and seemed to swell as he came in till his head touched the roof, and the roof was very high, and his bulk became enormous. I prostrated myself, and told him that "he was our *Purmesur* [great god] and we poor helpless mortals depended entirely on his will". This pleased him, and he passed me by; but took such a grasp at the man Mungulee, who slept by my side, that he was seized with spasms all over from the nape of the neck to the sole of his foot . . . This was his mode of annoying them, and but few survived . . . This spirit came most often in the cold and rainy weather.'

eastern Gwalior and the province of Bundelcund. Many settled with their families along the south bank of the Jumna in districts ruled by petty chiefs who – like Laljee and the zamindars of Murnae – were happy to extend their protection to men able to pay for the privilege; the remainder headed south towards the towns of Jhansee, Saugor and Bhopal. These men, too, found secure boltholes. Two decades later, one Jhansee official was still lamenting the fate that had brought Thugs into his master's lands in 1812 and prompted them to settle in a score of villages scattered across the district of Khyrooah, where the local chiefs shielded them from all manner of threats:

> The Khyrooa *Thakoor* [local notable] will not give up the Thugs at the order of the Jhansee Chief because he desires a service from them, and pays no attention to the Jhansee Chief's orders. This residence is on a hill, and is a strong castle, and he confides in its strength, and has put two pieces of cannon on it; and has a thousand followers at command. He has never paid any regard to his Chief's order and always takes a fourth from the booty the Thugs bring home with them from their expeditions, and this prevents his giving them up.

The Company's officers in Etawah remained quite ignorant of the fate of these fleeing Thugs. They had little knowledge of events in the Native States of central India, and their concern, in any case, was not so much to catch and try the stranglers themselves as to ensure that Sindouse was pacified and the pargana's rents and taxes paid on time. The dispersal of the Thugs and bandits living in the district had been necessary to achieve this aim. But while Halhed's actions did secure the disputed revenues, and deter the Chambel valley Thugs themselves from operating in British territory, it must be doubted whether they saved many lives. The destruction of Murnae did not even prevent the district from becoming a Thug headquarters again, for by the end of 1813 the village had already been rebuilt. Several prominent families of stranglers soon settled back into the ravine country, and in no more than a year or two the parganas south of Sindouse were once again notorious for harbouring all manner of Thugs, dacoits and rebels. The Marathas tolerated their presence while they paid for protection, and the British took little interest in their activities while they confined themselves to the districts south of the Jumna. No attempt was made to capture them or drive them out again.

The Thugs themselves did curtail their operations in the Company's territories as a result of Perry's efforts. But this did not mean that there were fewer stranglers on the roads, nor that the number of Thug murders actually decreased, even in the immediate aftermath of the attack on Murnae itself. Most gangs were content to direct their attentions southwards, into the central provinces of India and away from Company lands. These provinces were then made up entirely of small, poorly resourced native states, where policing was often inadequate and the Thugs went largely unmolested. During the cold season of 1813, several new or enlarged Thug bands had taken to the roads of southern Hindustan with considerable success. In the course of the cold season several parties of Thugs united to seize 27,000 rupees from one group of travellers outside the town of Rewah, and another 13,500 rupees from a gang of 27 dacoits who were tracked and slaughtered close to Lucknadown. This made the year 1813–14 one of the most successful ever known by the Thugs.

In later years, the Company would come to see the destruction of Murnae as a mistake. 'It is, to me, extremely doubtful whether by this dispersion of the Thug headquarters we performed any real benefit to India,' one senior judge observed two decades later. Yet this was scarcely Halhed's fault. There were, in 1812, already many precedents for expelling undesirables from British territory into the Native States; it was a cheap and simple – if scarcely effective – solution to the problem of tackling crime, and it was still almost unheard of for large gangs to be smashed by the mass arrest and trial of their members. Had the Etawah magistrates wanted to tackle the Sindouse Thugs in this way, there was no prospect of them mustering the resources required to arrest, try and imprison the hundreds of bandits and rebels living in the ravines.

For Company officials such as Halhed and Perry, cast more or less adrift in Etawah, the activities of the Thugs – and indeed criminal justice in general – were little more than unwelcome distractions from more pressing tasks. The idea of pursuing highly mobile gangs of stranglers through central India was certainly impractical. Even the cost of imprisoning the Thugs who were in custody was such that the Company was glad to let others bear it. When news reached Etawah that Maharajah Sindhia had arrested 130 men from Laljee's band, no effort was made to have more than a handful of the Thugs most responsible for Maunsell's death transferred to British jails, though Halhed and Perry must have known that the rest were unlikely to spend long in a Maratha prison. There was a simple reason for this failing: no one, in 1812, was greatly concerned to discover the fate of the unknown number of travellers who vanished on the roads of the Subcontinent each year. Even after Murnae had been razed to the ground, most of the Thugs who had lived there felt quite safe in their new homes in Bundelcund.

CHAPTER 5

'The Infamous System of Thuggee'

'tupjana – changing direction'

Even as the Murnae and Sindouse Thugs vanished into the patchwork of independent and semi-independent states that made up Gwalior and Bundelcund, the East India Company was forgetting them. Halhed left Etawah for a better position at a larger station within a few weeks of his return from Sindouse at the end of 1812. Perry, who remained in the town until the early 1820s, concentrated more and more on other work, and though Etawah's new magistrate, George Stockwell, took up the task of harrying any Thugs bold enough to settle within the Company's borders, he was very much alone. Few other British officers in India knew or cared about the stranglers.

A scant and scattered body of knowledge concerning the Thugs did exist, had Perry only known it. British officials had first encountered organized bands of stranglers a full quarter of a century before Halhed ventured into Sindouse, and, even before that, there had been indications that such gangs, or something very like them, were roaming India. But the almost total lack of communication between the Company's three Presidencies – each of which maintained its own administrative system, its own army and its own police – made it difficult for anyone to draw together the few reports that did exist. News of Perry's activities in Etawah barely penetrated further than the Jumna at first; the proceedings of magistrates in Madras were filed in the archives of that Presidency and forgotten. And so long as Thuggee was perceived as a local problem – with officers expelling criminals from their territories without worrying too much where they would settle next – the situation was unlikely to change.

The first unequivocal description of an Indian strangling gang had been composed nearly a thousand miles from Etawah, in the vicinity of Madras. Writing home in 1785, more than a century after John Fryer had witnessed the execution of what may have been a gang of Thugs outside Surat, a Company administrator by the name of James Forbes reported that

> several men were taken up for a most cruel method of robbery and murder, practised on travellers, by a tribe called *phanseegurs*, or stranglers . . . Under the pretence of travelling the same way, they enter into conversation with the strangers, share their sweetmeats, and pay them other little attentions, until an opportunity offers of suddenly throwing a rope round their necks with a slip-knot, by which they dexterously contrive to strangle them on the spot.

The arrests that prompted Forbes to compile this brief account can no longer be traced in the records of his Presidency. But his letter is important for several reasons. It is the first British account to mention the word 'phanseegur' (Phansigar), which the Emperor Aurangzeb had used to describe the stranglers whom he condemned in his farman of 1672, and which would henceforth be applied to all Thug-like bandits living south of the River Tapti. It is the first, too, to describe one of the Thugs' most distinctive tactics: the practice of inveigling their way into their victims' confidence and awaiting the perfect moment to murder them. And its mention of the Phansigars' favoured weapon – the noose – is a useful reminder that the gangs' habits and methods evolved over time, for only a few decades later this weapon was superseded by the strangling scarf or cloth, which, while less effective, was far less conspicuous. The noose (often made of catgut and sometimes mounted on a stick) seems not to have been employed after about 1810, and even experienced Phansigars questioned on the subject in later years had no recollection of ever seeing it in use. This they attributed to the danger of being stopped by police and found with such a compromising object in their possession.

No more was heard of the stranglers of the Deccan for two decades after Forbes wrote his report, although some sources suggest that, in 1799, a large

gang of suspected Phansigars was detained outside the southern city of
Bangalore during the Company's war against Tipu Sultan of Mysore. The fact
that such murderous bands existed was recognized outside the borders of
Madras, for a dictionary published in Bombay in 1808 defined the word
'Phanseeo' as 'a term of abuse in Guzerat,* applied also, truly, to thieves or
robbers who strangle children in secret or travellers on the road'. But the
Phansigars and their methods were certainly not widely known, nor discussed in newspapers or journals during the first decade of the century. The
great majority of British officers, it seems safe to say, heard nothing of their
activities. Nor, apparently, did the Indians themselves, for 'among some 2,000
fragments of oral tradition' collected from the central provinces, one historian searching, many years later, for evidence of the stranglers' existence
found 'many stories about robbers, but none specifically about Thugs'.

It was not until 1807 that first-hand reports of the Phansigars' activities
began to appear. In that year, purely by chance, several stranglers 'belonging
to a gang that had just returned laden with booty from an expedition to
Travancore' fell into the hands of William Wright, the British magistrate of
the district of Chittoor, 75 miles inland from Madras. These men were thrown
into jail and, confronted with the prospect of lengthy prison sentences, several
of them confessed to playing minor roles in a number of murders. Their
crimes included the theft of 2,500 pagodas – the property of a Company officer – and the killing of five of the officer's servants at Coimbatoor in 1805; the
throttling, two years later, of seven men carrying 1,000 pagodas for a
Lieutenant Blackston of the Engineers; and, most spectacularly, the murder,
on the coast south of Madras, of three men who had been escorting treasure
valued at 160,000 rupees. There seemed little doubt that the same band had
murdered other victims, including many whose disappearances had never
been reported to the police. Wright soon became convinced that gangs of
Phansigars were active throughout the Deccan, killing hundreds, if not thousands, every year.

The Chittoor magistrate's reports, which were the first to describe the
stranglers' activities in any detail, would have proved invaluable to Perry, for
the Phansigars of southern India were practically identical to the Thugs
of Hindustan. By careful questioning of a number of informants, Wright

*That is, Gujerat, a province in northwest India.

discovered that most Phansigars lived under the protection of local land-holders in his own district (which had been an independent territory until it was ceded to the Company in 1807), and that their gangs were active chiefly during the cold season. Like the Thugs of Etawah, many Deccan stranglers worked on the land for the remainder of the year, apparently because few derived large incomes from banditry. Phansigars played a full part in village life, and the loot they acquired in the course of their expeditions ensured that they were welcomed, rather than feared, when they returned to their homes. 'They and their families,' the magistrate was told, 'lived peaceably with their neighbours, whom they never attempted to molest.'

Wright's evidence also revealed something of the gangs' methods for the first time. The Chittoor magistrate was the first official to draw attention to the defining characteristic linking the Thugs and Phansigars – the fact that 'they never commit a robbery unaccompanied with murder'. He determined that the Deccan stranglers generally travelled in bands 30 to 50 strong, seldom disposed of any victims within 30 miles of their own homes, and frequently used aliases or changed their names, so that 'it may generally be said there is no discovering Fauseegars while travelling' – all information that might have aided Perry in his interrogation of Gholam Hossyn. Wright also noted that the members of several Chittoor gangs were well known to one another, and that they often combined forces on the roads to overwhelm large parties of travellers, dividing into groups of about a dozen men in order to cover more ground and arouse less suspicion in the minds of their intended victims. They had their own slang or argot, impenetrable to ordinary travellers, and their method of killing was generally the same as that practised in Hindustan:

It is customary for the Fauseegars to pretend friendship for travellers, and going with them a short distance, to strangle them with their Dhoties. When the cloth is thrown round the neck, the travellers are seized by their legs, and kicked upon their private parts, and their dead bodies are cut open, and the limbs divided, to prevent their swelling and emitting a smell through the crevices formed in the ground . . . It is also the custom of the Fauseegars to select a man especially to cut the corpse so, and to give him an additional share of plundered property.

Like their counterparts in the north of India, the Phansigars were careful never to kill the people of the districts they passed through, preferring to attack travellers whose disappearance was unlikely to be noticed for some time. Other than that, though, Wright found them to be indiscriminate. 'They murder,' he wrote, 'even Coolies, Palanqueen boys, Fakirs and Byragees* – no one escapes whom they have an opportunity of murdering – the chance is that every man has a rupee or two about him in money or cloths, and with them the most trifling sum is a sufficient inducement to commit murder.'

Gradually, Wright learned enough about the Phansigars to arrest the leaders of some other gangs. Large groups of stranglers were tried at Chittoor in 1809, and as late as 1812 at least 40 alleged Phansigars were still being held in the Company prison there, although they had been acquitted in the district court. Wright refused to release them until they lodged substantial bonds, called 'securities', to guarantee their future good behaviour – a ruse commonly used in India to detain prisoners whom the authorities suspected might be dangerous. The magistrate remained untroubled that supposedly innocent men were languishing in prison. 'Of their guilt,' he insisted, 'not a shadow of doubt exists.'

Wright's reports received scant attention when they were first compiled. Probably they were initially restricted to a small group of administrators in Madras, and there is certainly no evidence that Thomas Perry was aware of them as he struggled with the mystery of the Thugs. From these small beginnings, however, the Company's knowledge of the strangling gangs did gradually expand. In the second decade of the century, word of the Thugs' existence spread slowly east along the Jumna. This was probably a consequence of the pursuit of the Murnae gangs. After 1810 the new Superintendent of Police for the western, or inland, provinces of northern India became the first British officer to be formally charged with responsibility for combating Thuggee. From then on the forms used to compile crime statistics in the interior included a space for listing 'murders by Thugs', and the addition of this category allowed Calcutta to estimate, however incompletely, the incidence of Thug crime. The essential details of Wright's reports became known in the Bengal Presidency by 1811–12, when they were at last circulated to local magistrates. Information gleaned from

*That is, labourers, litter bearers, wandering ascetics and cattle drovers – the poorest of the poor.

Perry's interrogations of Gholam Hossyn was also copied for the use of other magistrates and the police.

These early bulletins were still very much provisional. Thuggee was not formally defined for several years; nor was there as yet any tendency to see all stranglers as practically identical, or as members of a single, rigidly controlled fraternity. George Stockwell, writing from Etawah during the monsoon of 1815, was of the opinion that 'the Thugs who have been in the habit of infesting this part of the Company's Provinces may . . . be divided into three classes, entirely unconnected with each other.'*

The most important reason for this upsurge of interest in India's stranglers was the Company's belated recognition that large numbers of its sepoys were falling prey to Thugs. Soldiers were – as we have seen – favourite targets of the various Thug bands. Not only did they travel home on leave each year taking large sums of money to their families, their disappearance was unlikely to be noticed until the expiration of their leave. The first general warning that gangs of stranglers were active in the interior was issued in April 1810, just a month after the Company's first encounter with Gholam Hossyn, by the officer commanding the British armies of Bengal. In an Order of the Day, Major General William St Leger not only drew his men's attention to this hitherto unknown danger but detailed what was known of the Thugs' appearance and methods. He described the manner in which their inveiglers contrived to fall in with strangers on the road, and sepoys were urged not to partake in conversation with other parties whom they might meet on the roads. The men were particularly warned not to leave their camping grounds before dawn or allow others to lead them to 'some solitary spot', and ordered never to accept food or drink from strangers and to stay together on the road. Attempts were also made to end the soldiers' habit of setting out for home carrying their arrears of pay. A new system, involving the issuing of what amounted to cheques that could be cashed by applying to the British Residents at Delhi and Lucknow, or to various Collectors of Revenue, was introduced. This, it was hoped, would reduce the sepoys' reliance on cash and make them less appealing targets.

*Stockwell's categories were the predominantly Muslim Etawah and Allyghur Thugs, who lived on large landed estates under the protection of various rajahs; the more numerous Hindu Lodhee Thugs of Cawnpore; and the gangs formerly based in Sindouse and Gwalior, who were the most numerous of all and who travelled together in larger numbers than the other Thugs.

Thus by the year 1812 knowledge of the Thugs was at last growing within the ranks of the Company and its army. However, civilians in India, as well as newspapers and magazines in Asia or at home, still paid little attention to the stranglers. The honour of introducing Thuggee to this broader audience fell to another Madras magistrate – an acquaintance of Wright's – by the name of Richard Sherwood, who, adapting his friend's various reports, produced a highly influential article titled 'Of the murderers called Phansigars' in the year 1816. This paper's first appearance, in the pages of the obscure *Madras Literary Gazette*, aroused little comment. But in 1820 the same article was reprinted in *Asiatick Researches*, a respected academic journal produced in Calcutta. *Asiatick Researches* had a larger circulation than the *Literary Gazette* and its readers included some of the most senior men in the Company's service and a significant number of subscribers in Britain itself. This time Sherwood's information was noticed.

A few other officers had taken an interest in the subject. John Shakespear, the Superintendent of Police for the Western Provinces, published a short description of Thugs and dacoits, based on one of his official reports, in the same issue of *Asiatick Researches*. A paper describing 'The habits and character of the Thugs', and based on the statements made by three stranglers arrested on their way across Gwalior, was sent to the then Governor General by the Resident at Sindhia's court in the same year. And John Malcolm, one of the most able British officers stationed in the central provinces of India in the mid 1810s,* encountered a group of Thugs in the course of his service in Malwa and wrote an instructive account of them in memoirs that he published in 1823.

None of these new sources of information added greatly to what was already known. The Resident at Gwalior confirmed that 'the race of Thugs' travelled in large gangs – the three men captured had been members of a group of 300 murderers – and 'employed both the sword and the noose' in the course of excursions that took them from the Ganges into the Deccan. They were thorough; it was by now 'well known' that Thug gangs 'act in parties and scour all the parallel and cross roads on the route which they take. These parties bring in and give account of their respective acquisitions, after which a fair distribution of the whole is made.'

*Although known as 'Boy' Malcolm for his infectious high spirits and rumbustious enthusiasm for hunting, shooting and all manner of outdoor pursuits, Malcolm proved to be an able administrator and was among the principal architects of a settlement imposed on the Maratha lands in the year 1818.

The Thugs' 'principal residences', added Malcolm, were still in the Chambel ravine country, where they 'usually maintain a connexion, or at least an understanding, with the manager of the district'. His estimate of Thug numbers was quite low; there were, he thought, no more than 300 stranglers at large in the central provinces, selecting wealthy victims when they could, and killing by strangulation or by using datura. 'Some of them have horses, camels and tents, and are equipped like merchants; others are dressed like soldiers going under a leader to take service; some affect to be Mahommedan beggars . . . or holy mendicants: they assume, in short, every disguise.'

Perhaps the most interesting fragments of new intelligence, however, emerged from the depositions of the Thugs captured in Gwalior. These revealed a picture of men driven by extremes of poverty to join Thug gangs. The first prisoner, a man named Heera, was nominally a cowherd but, 'forced by hunger', he had left his village in search of a better living and been lured into the company of a group of stranglers by a jemadar who 'said he would feed me if I accompanied the Thugs'. Heera's statement also painted a revealing picture of the gang's dependence on the zamindar of their home village, a man whose protection cost these Thugs no less than half of all the plunder they took on every expedition.

The slow accumulation of information on the Thugs had one important effect. It was not until about 1820 – as Shakespear pointed out in his report on the subject – that the existence of Thug gangs became generally accepted by Company officers whose duties had never brought them into contact with such men. As late as 1815, Shakespear said, 'much scepticism [had] still prevailed regarding the existence of any distinct class of people who are designated "T'hegs"'. He himself, he would admit, had long supposed that they were no more than highway robbers who occasionally employed brutal tactics.

Even after 1820 a number of Company magistrates shared Shakespear's early doubts. As the men most directly concerned with the quality of the evidence that could be mustered against supposed Thugs, they found it particularly hard to accept prosecutions based upon circumstantial evidence and the confessions of informants whose motives were seldom entirely praiseworthy. The sceptical magistrates' position was perhaps most clearly put by Thomas Ernst, of the Hooghly court, who protested vigorously at plans to recruit 'spies and common prostitutes' to inform against suspected stranglers. Such evidence, Ernst asserted, could never be reliable, and his own investigations led him to believe that magistrates such as Wright were exaggerating the threat posed by the Thugs and overstating the uniqueness of their methods.* A similar scepticism remained prevalent in other towns. In Gorruckpore, on the far eastern border of Oudh, a persistent informer named Khodabux Khan attempted to bring charges against the members of a local gang of stranglers on no fewer than three occasions over the course of nearly a decade, only to have the depositions he had sworn rejected out of hand. In 1814 Khan was imprisoned for three months for giving false evidence, and a year or two later he was murdered by the men he had informed against. It was another dozen years before the unlucky Khan was vindicated by the conviction of the very Thugs he had offered evidence against as early as 1809.

The use of Thug informers – 'approvers', they were called at the time, because they confirmed the tentative identification of captured stranglers – provoked controversy for years. Magistrates convinced of the existence of the Thugs, endlessly frustrated by the lack of living witnesses, favoured the employment of approvers. An officer named William Wright – not the same man as the Madras magistrate – appears to have been the first to make systematic use of such prisoners; with their help he rounded up nearly 200 Oudh and Doab Thugs and sent them to Bengal for trial in 1814. But the results were the same as they had been two years earlier, when Perry had sent his prisoners before the Nizamat Adalat; much of the approvers' testimony was struck out, and the remaining case collapsed for lack of evidence. After that, interest in the use of informants lapsed for several years.

Few magistrates had better luck than Wright. For years, all sorts of problems bedevilled attempts to bring suspected Thugs to trial. A magistrate named Gregory was dismissed from his post in Madras in 1819 after arresting nearly 200 suspected Phansigars, together with their families, when it emerged that his conduct towards the prisoners had been 'marked by great injustice and violence'. A few years later, in the northern town of Patna, an

*Ernst was removed from his post shortly after registering this protest — not for his views on Thuggee (though they were emphatically dismissed by the Governor General, Lord Minto, himself), but because he had dared to suggest that British rule in India was 'selfish, exploits natives, and will not last for ever'.

approver recruited by a British civil servant, JA Pringle, came up before the local commissioner, John Elliot. Elliott was another disbeliever in the Thugs, and more difficulties ensued as the trial began. As one of the prisoners involved in the case recalled:

The property of the murdered [man] was produced in Court, and his wife came forward to recognise it. Mr Elliot told her that if she did not speak the truth she would be punished, upon which she took fright and would say nothing, although she knew the property to be that of her husband . . . There was no [other] evidence but the depositions of the approvers, and the case was not proved, and the approvers were sentenced to 15 lashes, five years' imprisonment, and to be taken round the City mounted on asses for five days. The rest of the Thugs were released. Mr Elliot told the Nazir of the Court who had arrested the Thugs that he was ruining the country by seizing innocent people, and sentenced him to 14 years imprisonment; when in confinement the Nazir swallowed some piece of diamond by which he caused his death.

Even Pringle, the magistrate, did not escape from the case unscathed. His 'own conduct was visited with the severest censure, and both the Government and the Nizamat Adalat were led into a belief that there was no such gang of Thugs, and that the crime, if it existed at all, was very limited in its extent'.

It is not surprising, in these circumstances, that British officers rarely found it worthwhile to pursue Thug gangs, and that most of the encounters between British magistrates and Thugs in the first quarter of the century occurred by chance. Either a gang of stranglers would be arrested on general suspicion by authorities alarmed at the discovery of murdered bodies in their districts, or one or more of a gang's own members would betray the group as the result of some quarrel. There were several such incidents. Thug bands were detained at Jhalna in 1821, at Seonee in 1822, and at Mozuffurpore in 1826. At Jhalna, British officers in a nearby cantonment mounted a search after hearing reports from local villagers of murders committed in the area. At Seonee, nearly 60 Thugs were detained after a chance discovery. In the Mozuffurpore case, a gang of 15 robbers who had strangled a party of travellers fell out over the ownership of a coral necklace and one, 'in a passion', turned the others in to the local police.* Success in cases of this sort owed nothing to any concerted effort on the part of the Company authorities. There was no particular pattern to the encounters, nor any attempt by senior officers to draw lessons from what had been learned or to coordinate further action against the gangs.

Little or nothing, then, was done in the years that followed Halhed's assault on Murnae to build on Wright's and Perry's pioneering work. British knowledge of the Thugs, their methods and their plans remained partial at best, and clues that might have led to the gangs' destruction were undoubtedly missed. Had the magistrates and district officers scattered through the mofussil understood the stranglers better, they might have enjoyed greater success in tackling them. As it was, however, some of the darkest secrets of the infamous system of Thuggee remained known only to the Thugs themselves.

*'Syfoo and Gheena Khan had married two sisters, and Syfoo gave himself airs, and demanded a coral necklace that was taken from one of the travellers. Gheena refused to give it; a quarrel ensued, and Syfoo . . . went to the Thanadar [police sergeant] at Durbhunga, brought him and his guard down upon them at night, and seized the whole gang. But Syfoo had not seen the grave, and he made the Thanadar tie up his cousin, Peerbuksh, a boy, throw him down, draw his sword, and pretend to be about to cut his throat. The boy got alarmed, confessed, and pointed out the grave. The bodies were taken up . . . the four men who had strangled them were hung.'

CHAPTER 6

Scarf and Sword

'sosalladhna – strangling a victim in favourable circumstances'

The flight of the Sindouse and Murnae Thugs from their homes in the Chambel ravines was not unprecedented. For many, perhaps most, of the stranglers who infested the lands south of Etawah, precipitate departures were a fact of life, for the Thugs' earliest datable tradition – the hasty abandonment of Delhi by the seven Muslim clans during Akbar's reign – was merely one example among many of gangs falling foul of the rulers who had protected them and being forced to seek sanctuary elsewhere. In the course of the seventeenth century, the Thugs' oral histories suggest, their gangs left Delhi for Agra, abandoned Agra for Akoopore, and then quit Akoopore for Himmutpore. Their appearance in Sindouse was a consequence of a falling out with the Rajah of Himmutpore, who 'became in time too exorbitant in his demands for a share of the booty', and though they seem to have lived largely unmolested for the next hundred years, several of their villages (including Murnae itself) were razed to the ground by Maratha troops seeking payment of rents and taxes in the first years of the nineteenth century. Others were seized, in 1800, by the Rajah of Rampoora, whose exactions forced the Thugs of the district to flee west into Sindhia's domains.

Forced migrations of this sort continued for as long as there were Thugs, and were probably more common after 1812 than they had been before, as men fleeing into Bundelcund were forced to establish new and no doubt sometimes uneasy relationships with the zamindars and rajahs of their adopted districts. Certainly Thugs frequently quarrelled with their protectors over the division of their spoils, or attracted so much unwelcome attention that their protectors were forced to expel them from their lands. Yet another flight, from the town of Jhalone into the Deccan, took place in 1823, and others again occurred wherever Company officials took up arms against the gangs.

The Thug gangs were, thus, of necessity, far more mobile – geographically, and also socially – than most Indians of their day. At a time when the great majority of peasants lived their entire lives in a single village, clinging stubbornly to whatever plots of land they could obtain the rights to farm, it was not at all uncommon for a Thug to dwell in six or seven different places in the course of a long life of crime. This was, on the whole, an advantage to the gangs. Individual stranglers became familiar with a variety of districts within the territories in which they operated. It was more difficult for the authorities to track them down, not least because many Thugs also employed a variety of aliases. And the members of each gang undoubtedly recruited novice stranglers to their ranks as they moved from place to place.

The establishment of good relations with the zamindar or rajah of their chosen homes was nonetheless of critical importance to the Thugs. In addition to offering protection, a cooperative zamindar could be approached for loans of the cash or goods required to fund an expedition. Laljee had certainly financed the Sindouse Thugs, advancing capital that the gangs used to pay their way through India in return for interest at the exorbitant rate of 25 or even 50 per cent, and making what amounted to personal loans to members of the gangs in exchange for loot. 'If we have nothing to eat,' explained Budloo Thug, an Afghan who had lived in the pargana for well over a decade, 'he feeds us, in lieu of which he takes a horse, or money, or anything else – whatever he finds, he takes.'

The relationship between the members of a Thug gang and their protectors was, of course, an unequal one.* Fear of incurring a landholder's displeasure led some stranglers to pay as much as fifty times the going rate to rent land in their villages, and all were regularly forced to part with their choicest plunder in return for protection. It was highly risky to upset

---

*'These were not well-oiled complicities,' one writer on the subject observes, 'but ruthless relations of force that at every moment were renegotiated and could swing in favour of one or other of the parties.'

a zamindar in this respect. 'Our chiefs give a part to our village chiefs before giving us our part,' explained one Thug, and generally it was 'the handsomest horse, sword or ornament' that was 'reserved for the most powerful patron of the order'. Any attempt to make do without the support of a local notable of this sort, or to cheat him, led swiftly to the Thugs' arrest or imprisonment at the hands of men more anxious to extort their dues from the captured bandits than they were to render justice. Even the fiercest Thugs, so formidable on the roads, cowered in the presence of their zamindars.

The men responsible for dealing with the petty notables whose patronage was so vital to the Thugs were the leaders of the various Thug bands. Each of the 200 or more gangs scattered across India was organized along broadly similar lines, being recruited and commanded by leaders known as *subadars* and *jemadars* – titles that aped those awarded to native officers in the Company's armies. But it would be a mistake to imagine, because of this, that Thug gangs were rigidly obedient to their leaders or subject to military discipline. They were much more loosely organized than that.

The members of a Thug gang were never simply ordered out onto the roads; each man made up his own mind whether or not to join an expedition, and the depositions of captured stranglers are full of accounts of Thugs who decided to remain at home, working the land, for months or even years at a time, or who had to be talked into joining some planned foray into the Deccan. It was equally common for Thugs to break off an expedition and return home when they thought they had garnered enough loot, and for gangs to join together for a few days before breaking apart again. Similarly, rank-and-file Thugs were not beholden to any particular commander for more than a few weeks at a time; men only ever agreed to serve a leader for the duration of a single expedition. There were, certainly, cases of Thugs working together in the same band for decades on end – but jemadars who failed to accumulate sufficient plunder to pay adequately for the services of their men soon found their followers abandoning them to join more successful gangs.

The size of the band commanded by a given Thug thus offered an accurate reflection of his status and ability. The smallest that we have records of numbered as few as 5 or 10 men, but most were between 15 and 25 strong. This was a practical number; any more and the cost of maintaining the gang for a period of several months would be excessive; fewer, and there would be insufficient men to tackle more than a moderately sized party of travellers. Thus while a handful of the richest and most successful Thugs were capable of mustering as many as 50 or even 60 followers, gangs containing more than 25 men were considered to be noticeably large, and the Thugs had a special vocabulary to describe them.

The title of subadar was the grandest to which a Thug could aspire. It seems to have been awarded by general acclamation, and was only bestowed upon the most respected and experienced Thugs – men capable of leading and coordinating the actions of several gangs. A jemadar, on the other hand, was simply the self-appointed leader of a single band, or even the head of a small group of Thugs absorbed into a larger gang commanded by several leaders. The rank was not perceived as an especially distinguished one. Experienced Thugs sought many different qualities in their jemadars, but it was not necessary for a would-be leader to possess more than one or two in order to gather a small gang around him. The most important qualification, certainly, was to be 'a man who has always at command the means of advancing a month or two's subsistence' to his men, either from his own resources or in the form of a loan from the local zamindar. But

a strong and resolute man, whose ancestors have been for many generations Thugs, will very soon get the title, or a very wise man, whose advice in difficult cases has weight with the gang; one who has influence over local authorities, or the native officers of the courts of justice; a man of handsome appearance and high bearing, who can feign the man of rank well – all these things enable a man to get around him a few who will call him jemadar; but it requires very high and numerous qualifications to gain a man the title of subadar.

The members of the Thug band itself were divided according to their duties and paid according to their skills and seniority. Some worked as scouts. The best dressed, most plausible and eloquent were employed as inveiglers, the men responsible for befriending parties of travellers and luring them into the clutches of the gang. The victims were actually murdered by designated stranglers, who were invariably Thugs of long experience and considerable strength, assisted by 'hand-holders' who restrained a victim and prevented their escape.

Some gangs also contained specialist grave-diggers, responsible for the disposal of the bodies. Camp followers, in the shape of older Thugs past their prime, children and, in many cases, ordinary labourers and other villagers who were certainly not hardened murderers, but had been recruited on a more or less casual basis in order to swell the ranks of the gang as a whole, generally took no part in the killing of victims, serving instead as lookouts or guards.

Scouts seem to have been employed by only a few Thug bands, and then only occasionally; in most cases a gang's victims consisted of parties of travellers unlucky enough to fall in with a jemadar and his men on the road. There were, nonetheless, obvious advantages to employing men to scour the countryside for potential targets. For one thing, a single gang could cover a far wider stretch of countryside with the help of scouts; for another, an experienced spy might be expected to distinguish between wealthy groups of merchants or treasure bearers and poorer travellers, thus greatly increasing the chance that his gang would seize a substantial quantity of loot.

A jemadar who had decided to use scouts would usually halt the main body of his gang in some convenient grove near a large town or an important crossroads, sending out 'men chosen from among the most smooth-spoken and intelligent' members of his band. On rare occasions, when hunting for some known consignment of great value, Thug pickets might travel up to three or four days' journey from their temporary headquarters. It was more usual, though, for scouts to 'parade the bazaars of the town near which their associates are encamped, and endeavour to pick up intelligence of the intended despatch or expected arrival of goods'. Frontier *chokies* and customs posts were also favourite places to intercept parties of potential victims, since travellers were forced to unpack and display their wares and possessions at such places.

Sometimes scouts would double as inveiglers and begin the process of luring a chosen group into the clutches of their gang:

> Inquiry is also made for any party of travellers who may have arrived; every art is brought into practice to scrape an acquaintance with these people; they are given to understand that the [scout] is travelling the same road, an opportunity is taken to throw out hints regarding the insecurity of the roads, and the frequency of murders and robberies, an acquaintance with some of the friends or relations of the travellers is feigned, and an invitation given to partake of [a] repast . . . The result is, that the travellers are inveigled into join-

ing the party of Thugs, and they are feasted and treated with every politeness and consideration by the very wretches who are also plotting their murder and calculating the share they shall acquire in the division of their property.

In general, however, the tricky job of seducing a victim was left to men with the experience and subtlety to attempt it successfully. Soothing the suspicions of wary travellers – many of them fully alert to the dangers of the road, if not to the existence of the Thugs themselves – required a considerable degree of charm and cunning, and only the most intelligent members of a gang were permitted to attempt it.* In many cases a gang's jemadar would himself act as inveigler; being better dressed and wealthier than his men, and often mounted on a tattoo, or pony, he would find it easier to effect an introduction to the leader of another party. On other occasions, the task would be allocated to a specialist known as a *sotha*.

Most gangs of any experience possessed a variety of tried and tested stratagems for deceiving a traveller, and which was used depended largely on the destination, the job or the caste of the unfortunate men selected as victims. Probably the most common method was to overtake a party of travellers on the road and enquire as to the purpose of their journey. Once the strangers had disclosed that they were heading for Meerut, say, or for Benares, it was a simple matter for the Thugs to declare that they were travelling by the same road, and to suggest the two groups should join forces as a protection from dacoits and thieves. Other Thugs adopted appropriate disguises. 'When going south towards the Native States,' one explained, 'where many native soldiers found service, I used to assume the disguise of a native sepoy, and wear a sword, shield and carry a matchlock, pretending I was going to service. I had a large horse with me, and used to ride with English spurs; this disguise enabled me to deceive sepoys . . . On returning from the south, I used to assume the apparel of a table attendant of a rich man, or I gave myself out as the *darogah* [police officer] of some Raja. In short I suited my disguise to the traveller I had to inveigle, so as to blind him and disarm his suspicion.' On the whole, however, Thug gangs cultivated an unremarkable demeanour that the Company officials responsible for hunting them down plainly regarded as

*'My companion Hyder,' a strangler named Ramzan deposed, 'was a staunch Thug, fearing nothing, but he was not a good inveigler. To inveigle a man is no easy matter, to answer all his questions and act upon them.'

more terrifying than the more bloodthirsty appearance of the dacoits. 'There was nothing to excite alarm or suspicion in the appearance of these murderers; but on the contrary they are described as being mild and benevolent of aspect, and peculiarly courteous, gentle and obliging.'

The great majority of men and women murdered by the Thugs fell prey to a device of this sort. But the best inveiglers were capable of even greater subtlety on occasion, and when in pursuit of a particularly rich prize the most skilled displayed a cunning and determination that Company officials came to regard as practically diabolic. It was, for example, common for a large gang to split into several smaller groups, strung out across several miles of road, in order to render its members inconspicuous and assuage the suspicions of any party met along the way. The various portions of the gang would move at different speeds, those in the lead pausing for a while so that their comrades could come up, those at the rear overtaking one another as they went. Then, if 'the travellers show any signs of disliking or distrusting the inveigler of one [group] . . . the inveigler of the one in advance learns of it by signs from the other as he and the travellers overtake him. The new inveigler gets into conversation with the traveller and pretends to dislike the appearance of the first, who, in turn, pretends to be afraid of the new one and lags behind, while the new man and the travellers congratulate each other on having shaken off so suspicious a character.'

Possibly the most extraordinary example of the successful inveigling of a suspicious victim was related by a group of Thugs imprisoned at Lucknow, the capital of Oudh, whom a sepoy officer overheard discussing their most memorable expeditions. These men had once encountered

a stout Mughal officer of noble bearing and singularly handsome countenance, on his way from the Punjab to Oudh . . . mounted on a fine horse and attended by his butler and groom. Soon after crossing a river, he fell in with a small party of well-dressed and modest-looking men going the same road. They accosted him in a respectful manner, and attempted to enter into conversation with him. He had heard of Thugs, and told them to be off. They smiled at his idle suspicions, and tried to remove them, but in vain. The Mughal was determined; they saw his nostrils swelling with indignation, took their leave, and followed slowly.

The next morning he overtook the same number of men, but of a different appearance, all Musalmans. They accosted him in the same respectful manner; talked of the danger of the road, and the necessity of keeping together, and taking advantage of the protection of any mounted gentleman that happened to be going the same way. The Mughal officer said not a word in reply, resolved to have no companions on the road. They persisted – his nostrils began again to swell, and putting his hand to his sword, he bid them all be off, or he would have their heads from their shoulders. He had a bow and quiver full of arrows over his shoulders, a brace of loaded pistols in his waist-belt, and a sword by his side, and was altogether a very formidable-looking cavalier.

In the evening another party, lodged in the same inn, became very intimate with the butler and groom. They were going the same road; and, as the Mughal overtook them in the morning, they made their bows respectfully, and began to enter into conversation with their two friends, the groom and butler, who were coming up behind. The Mughal's nostrils began again to swell, and he bid the strangers be off. The groom and butler interceded, for their master was a grave, sedate man, and they wanted companions. All would not do, and the strangers fell in the rear.

The next day, when they had got into the middle of an extensive uninhabited plain, the Mughal in advance, and his two servants a few hundred yards behind, he came upon a party of six poor Musalmans, sitting weeping by the side of a dead companion. They were soldiers from Lahore, on their way to Lucknow, worn down by fatigue in their anxiety to see their wives and children once more, after long and painful service. Their companion . . . had sunk under the fatigue, and they had made a grave for him; but they were poor unlettered men, and unable to repeat the funeral service from the holy Koran – would his highness but perform this last office for them, he would, no doubt, find his reward in this world and the next.

The Mughal dismounted – the body had been placed in its proper position, with its head towards Mecca. A carpet was spread – the Mughal took off his bow and quiver, then his pistols and sword, and placed them on the ground near the body – called for water, and washed his feet, hands, and face, that he might not pronounce the holy words in an unclean state. He then knelt down and began to repeat the funeral service, in a clear, loud voice. Two of the poor soldiers knelt by him, one on each side in silence. The other four went off a few paces to beg that the butler and groom would not come so near as to interrupt the good Samaritan at his devotions.

All being ready, one of the four, in a low undertone, gave the signal, the handkerchiefs were thrown over their necks, and in a few minutes all three – the Mughal and his servants – were dead, and lying in the grave in the usual manner, the head of one at the feet of the one below him. All the parties they had met on the road belonged to a gang of Thugs of the kingdom of Oudh.

In most cases, an inveigled victim would be despatched relatively quickly – typically the night after he fell in with the Thugs, or early the next morning. But, in special circumstances, the members of some gangs were capable of displaying inhuman patience in order to disarm the suspicions of a large party of potential victims, or when no good opportunity arose to dispose of their prey discreetly. 'They will travel,' one British officer discovered in the 1830s, 'with a party of unsuspecting travellers for days, and even weeks together, eat with them, sleep with them, attend divine worship with them . . . and live with them in the closest terms of intimacy till they find the time and place suitable for the murder of the whole.' The most striking example of such persistence, dating to 1820, concerned a gang that accompanied its intended victims for 'about twenty days, on the most intimate terms', covering a total of 200 miles, before putting the entire party to death.

The business of murder itself fell to a Thug band's stranglers and hand-holders. These two positions were interchangeable, the hand-holders in one murder acting as stranglers in another, and vice versa; but, even so, only a minority of the members of any one gang actively participated in the killing of victims. Those who did so were invariably the strongest and most experienced men available – stranglers who were hardened to their grisly duties and well practised in the surest techniques for despatching even well-built and sometimes suspicious travellers.

The Thugs' preference for murder by strangulation needs some explanation. Throttling a victim is no easy task; as well as requiring considerable strength and coordination, it is also an appallingly intimate method of killing. To despatch a man in such a way requires the murderer to close with his intended prey, to stand over him and physically restrain him, to feel him lose his struggle for life. Strangulation places no distance between the killer and his victim in the way that a firearm does; no weapon acts as an intermediary; even a murder committed with a sword or a knife is less immediate than one carried out with a man's own hands. Few murderers experience the sensation of the last breath leaving their victim's body in the way that a strangler does, and killing in this manner requires a ruthless, cold-blooded and protracted determination that comes naturally to few if any men. The Thugs themselves found it difficult to get used to. When other members of his gang were squeezing the life out of their victims, one deposed, 'I always stood at a distance and trembled.'

Some Company officials, baffled by the appearance of murdered bodies in their jurisdictions, supposed that Thugs chose to kill by strangulation in order to leave no evidence of their crimes, and it is true that men who throttled the unfortunate travellers whom they had marked for destruction would not be splashed with blood in the way that a man who stabbed or hacked at travellers with swords would be. But the Thugs had no compunction in shedding blood once their victim was dead, as they showed when mutilating the corpses of those they had killed prior to disposing of their bodies. The truth may well be much simpler. Owing to a peculiarity of Islamic law, murderers who killed by strangulation were not liable to the death penalty in Mughal India.* Convicted stranglers were merely flogged and imprisoned until they repented and paid blood money to their victim's family. It seems possible that the earliest Thugs chose to throttle travellers in order to avert the risk of capital punishment.

The swift and efficient murder of a chosen group of travellers was crucial to the success of any gang, and able stranglers possessed considerable prestige within the closed world of the Thugs. 'Do you look up to or think more of those associates who have strangled many victims?' one group of captured jemadars was asked. 'We respect the expert Thug the most,' came the reply. 'He has his attendants from among the tyroes, several of them wait on him as servants. [Others] carry his bundles. He often rides upon his horse, whereas the tyro is held in no estimation amongst us.' Attaining the rank of *bhurtote*, or expert strangler, might take years, and 'the office', another Thug explained, 'in these gangs is never allowed to be self-assumed but is conferred with due ceremony after the fitness of the candidate in point of firmness, bodily strength and activity has been ascertained'.

---

*As one historian of law in the Subcontinent explains: 'According to the Hanafi school of jurisprudence favoured in Mughal India, capital punishment could be awarded only if the homicide involved a weapon usually associated with the shedding of blood, and whether a particular weapon met this requirement was the subject of much legal debate.'

Would-be stranglers were encouraged to acquire the necessary skills 'by long sham practice of the process among one another', and promotion to the ranks of those employed to murder travellers was neither automatic nor inevitable. A good many Thugs never achieved it; Henry Bevan, a British officer who spent three decades in the Subcontinent, talked to one 18-year-old Thug who 'stated that he could never acquire the requisite dexterity' and was 'frequently punished for his want of [it]'. Those who displayed some promise were – another Company man was told – given the chance to dispose of one of the gang's more weak and helpless victims:

> Favourable opportunities are given to the *buttoats* to make their first essay in the art of strangulation. When a single traveller is met with, a novice is instructed to make a trial of his skill: the party sets off during the night, and stops while it is still dark, to drink water, or to smoke. While seated for this purpose, the jemadar inquires what time of night it may be, and the Thugs immediately look out to the stars to ascertain, this being the pre-concerted signal; the buttoat is immediately on the alert, and the unsuspecting victim, on looking up to the heavens in common with the rest of the party, offers his neck to the handkerchief, and becomes an easy prey for his murderer.

Further assistance was available to even the most expert murderers in the shape of one or more *shumsheeras* (hand-holders), Thugs whose duty it was to help the stranglers to overcome their victims. It was this 'ganging up' on doomed travellers that perhaps most outraged the British officers charged with pursuing the Thugs, offending as it did any sense of fair play. 'Two Thugs, at least, are thought necessary for the murder of one man; and more commonly three are engaged,' one Company officer asserted, although almost all surviving depositions mention the presence of only a single hand-holder at the murder of each victim. In most cases a single shumsheera would perform precisely the role suggested by his title, seizing a traveller's hands to prevent him from struggling or loosening the cord around his neck. Where two were present the second man would kick the dying man's legs from under him and grasp him around the calves or thighs to stop him from thrashing about. In some cases, it appears, a shumsheera would also place a well-aimed kick 'in that part of a man most endowed with sensitivity' in order to further disable his victim.

It was very rare for any Thug to attempt to murder a victim on his own. Those who proved themselves able to kill without any assistance 'attained a distinction that was conferred not only upon themselves, but on several successive generations'. But this did not mean that bhurtotes lacked either skill or determination. There were many cases of Thugs strangling travellers as they walked along a road, or even tackling a man on horseback.* The one thing they invariably avoided was strangling a sleeping man, for it was difficult to apply a cord to someone whose head was resting on the ground. In cases where a gang found it impossible, for whatever reason, to murder their intended victims in the course of the evening, the unfortunate travellers might be woken at a very early hour in the morning 'with an alarm of a snake or scorpion' and promptly throttled.

Bhurtotes were well rewarded for their efforts. Jemadars always received the largest share of their gang's loot, usually claiming between 10 and 15 per cent of all the cash and precious metals taken from their victims, and 'a tithe of all pearls, shawls, embroidered cloth, brass and copper pots, horses &c'. But stranglers were paid considerably more than the remainder of their fellows. When the proceeds of an expedition were divided up, each received not only the share that was due to every member of the gang, but an additional half-share for their services as killers. Typically this might amount to a half-rupee bonus for every murder committed in the course of an expedition – a considerable sum.

In the first third of the nineteenth century the bhurtotes' favoured weapon was the *rumal*, the 'scarf' they used to strangle victims. 'This implement,' one Company official explained, 'is merely a piece of fine strong cotton cloth about a yard long; at one end a knot is made, and the cloth is slightly twisted and kept ready for use, in front of the waistband of the person carrying it.' The knot prevented the strangler from losing his grip at a critical moment,

---

*'We strangled travellers on horseback in this way,' the notorious Thug Ramzan explained. 'It requires three men, each being at his post. One Thug . . . walks near the horse's head, ready to seize the reins – another Thug, the decoyer, walks by the side of the horseman, engaging him in conversation – the strangler, all ready for his office, walks a little to the rear by the flank of the horse. The decoyer in the course of conversation offers the horseman some tobacco, or anything else. When he puts out his hand to receive it, the decoyer seizes the victim's hands, at the same instant giving the signal for the others to perform their offices, he himself dragging the horseman down. The strangler, the moment the hands are seized, and with the horseman's neck within his reach, seizes him firmly by the throat and falls with him to the ground, where he completes the strangulation. The third Thug, having at the signal seized the bridle of the affrighted horse, secures him as a prize.'

and practised assassins might also tie a small coin into the cloth halfway along its length. This pressed against their victims' windpipes, expediting the act of murder, but the coin made the rumal more difficult to handle and it was probably not often used. It was difficult, in any case, to master all the various methods of strangulation. Strike too soon and the cloth would tighten around an intended victim's face rather than his neck; too late, and he might have time to scream or struggle. The correct technique, if it might be termed such, was to take the knotted end of the rumal in the left hand, to twist the cloth and hold the other, in the right hand, a few inches higher than the first, to throw the rumal over the victim's head from behind and then to cross the hands as the man was throttled, thus exerting greater pressure on the windpipe. Done properly, this gave the victim no time to speak or utter any sound; indeed, the ability to murder in complete silence was esteemed highly among the Thugs.

The rumal was a very inconspicuous weapon, and there are hints that it may have been a relatively late addition to the Thugs' arsenal. One of its great attractions was that it could be readily disguised, as a scarf, handkerchief or sash, thus 'answering the atrocious purpose in view as well as a regularly prepared noose, and having the additional recommendation of exciting no suspicion'. It was, in any case, easy enough to add a slip knot to an ordinary length of cloth and so turn it into a makeshift noose, and some stranglers did so on occasion, tying the knot around their own knee or thigh in order to simulate the dimensions of a human neck. This made it an easy matter to finish off a victim who had been brought to the ground. At that point, one Thug informer explained, the strangler 'makes another fold of [the rumal] around the neck; upon which placing his foot, he draws the cloth tight, in a manner similar to that . . . of packing a bundle of straw'.

Long years of practice enabled an experienced bhurtote to bring the ignoble art of strangulation to a pitch of perfection. Death, wherever it occurred, usually came swiftly. 'In how short a time,' one group of Thugs was asked, 'do you despatch and bury a band of travellers after reaching your ground?' 'When we have reached the appointed place,' came the reply,

> we get the travellers to seat themselves. The inveiglers who have deceived and conducted them to the spot, when they have seated them summon the stranglers and the holders of hands to their posts by calling out in the

Thug slang in the ordinary way. The travellers think it means an ordinary enquiry. If the stranglers are all ready they reply and the inveiglers see that all the murderers are at their posts near their respective travellers . . . Before the signal is out of the mouth, quick, like the pulling of a trigger, every man is strangled! Thus! [Here the assassin Ramzan, smiling, showed with what energy it was done.] Jhut! Instantaneously are the whole party strangled, though there should be 20 of them. I have with my own eyes seen seven travellers thus dispatched! It is the work of an instant! You are long in writing it – but in reality it is instantaneous.

'Such is the certainty with which the act is done,' added one Indian army officer, '[that] the T'hags frequently declare, that before the body falls to the ground, the eyes usually start out of the head, and life becomes extinct.'

Gangs evolved a variety of stratagems to make the work of murder easier. Where possible, they preferred to strike in the evening, when travellers were tired and less alert than they had been earlier in the day – 'generally before the twilight is completely over and night has set in; and always while the business is going on, the hand drum is beat and singing commenced to drown any noise that might be made by the victims'. Often travellers would be seated when they were attacked by Thugs approaching from behind; this ensured that the stranglers enjoyed all the advantages of height and mobility, and made it far more difficult for their victims to resist. A favourite trick was for the Thugs to call their companions' attention to something above them, in the sky; when they raised their heads to look, they exposed their necks for the rumal. A more subtle variation on the same technique called for one member of the gang to feign a sudden illness; other Thugs would cluster around the stricken man, taking his pulse and offering water, until one of their number would announce that the only way of saving him was to invoke a charm. The group's intended victims would then be asked to sit, uncover their necks and count the stars above their campsite. 'And in this state', the account concluded, 'the rumal is thrown around their necks and they are strangled.'

From the various depositions that survive, it seems that most Thug gangs developed their own modus operandi of proven efficacy, and employed it whenever they could. 'Into whatever part of the country we went, we murdered and committed the acts, always in this manner,' one man prefaced a description of his gang's methods, and the techniques of murder developed by gangs in different parts of India were broadly similar, as might be expected given the loose ties that existed between them. The details varied, nevertheless, from time to time and place to place: there was no one method favoured by all Thugs. One captured strangler described stamping on his victims once they had been throttled. Others stabbed the bodies of the men they had just killed, either to prevent the bodies bloating after burial or simply to ensure that they were dead.

Descriptions of this sort fly in the face of the belief, commonly held at the time, that the Thugs' only weapon was the rumal and that they killed solely by strangulation. This was far from the truth. Certainly almost every gang killed by stealth where possible, and most favoured the use of the cloth so extensively that more than nine-tenths of the Thug murders recorded between 1800 and 1840 involved the use of the rumal; but even the keenest stranglers were capable of using other weapons when they had to, and of varying their methods according to the circumstances. One class of Thugs used lengths of rope, weighted with lead, to murder their victims; others preferred the leather reins with which bullocks were led. It seems to have been relatively commonplace for men to kill using a dhoti, or cotton loin-cloth, rather than the rumal.

There were, indeed, distinct differences between the methods employed by men from various parts of India. In the first two decades of the nineteenth century the Thugs of Sindouse were said to kill 'like banditti', and far more openly than those of Oudh, who were already confining themselves almost exclusively to the rumal. In at least one case, a victim was beaten to death 'with fists and elbows', and another shot. There were also occasional reports, from the earliest times, of gangs who poisoned their victims with datura, which was commonly used by many Indian highway robbers to stupefy their victims. It seems to have been used only intermittently. One Thug described this technique of using the drug as the tool of 'mere novices', implying that an experienced strangler should have no need of such an aid to murder.

Swords, on the other hand, were carried by most gangs. It seems likely that they were widely used by Thugs during the turmoil of the late eighteenth century, when the roads were full of parties of armed men seeking military service and even the most peaceable travellers carried weapons for protection. But by 1810 the advent of the Pax Britannica meant that most

Indian roads were safer than they had been for some time, and it became cor-
respondingly less usual for men to travel armed. By 1819 the mere possession
of a sharpened sword, rather than the blunt one usually found in the possession of a poor traveller, was cause for suspicion, and from about this time
Thug gangs 15 or 20 strong felt it wise to carry only two swords, or perhaps
three. When they were used, it was now generally to murder travellers who
could not be safely lured to the rumal – small parties of armed men,
or treasure carriers under orders not to fraternize with strangers on the
roads – and then frequently in conjunction with staffs and knives. Many Thug
jemadars also took the precaution of stationing guards armed with swords
at any spot where murder was planned, to prevent the escape of victims
who had somehow torn themselves free of the stranglers and hand-holders
attacking them.

The one certain thing in the whole process was that those travellers
marked for death by Thugs would die. Treasure bearers and merchants,
nobles and sepoys all fell to the grim efficiency of the stranglers, befriended
and lured to a favoured spot, their suspicions assuaged, then seized and murdered so swiftly that few even had time to cry out. A practised and efficient
gang was capable of disposing of as many as 7 or 10 travellers at once, sometimes more, and the number of victims ascribed to individual stranglers
occasionally ran into three figures.

All these bodies had to be disposed of, and the Thugs employed a variety
of techniques to hide the remains of those they murdered. Some corpses
were buried, others thrown down wells. Yet others were concealed under
rocks or brushwood. But what distinguished the Thugs from dacoits and
highway robbers was that they only rarely abandoned their victims where
they fell. Stealth and security were important to them, not least because,
proceeding barely armed, they could ill afford confrontations with the local
militia or police.

The method chosen for the concealment of the dead depended on the circumstances and habits of the gangs themselves. Some were exceptionally
well organized. When there was plenty of time, or a real risk of discovery, a
grave pit might be prepared well in advance so that corpses could be disposed
of quickly, and even the shape of the graves themselves was carefully considered. Many Thugs favoured what they called *gobbas*, circular pits dug
around a narrow pillar of compacted earth, believing that scavenging animals

were less likely to find and dig up bodies buried in this way. Careful Thugs would also take precautions to disguise the patch of disturbed earth that betrayed a freshly dug grave, building a fireplace over the remains of their victims and cooking, eating and even sleeping at the spot in order to hide the traces of their crimes. If forced to hurriedly conceal the bodies of their victims by the threat of discovery, the same men might send back a burial party to inter the remains properly a day or two later.* A properly constructed grave would escape detection in most circumstances, and was sometimes difficult to find even when informants who had been present at a murder were called on to locate it.

For all this, however, deep, well-dug graves remained a rarity in Hindustan. The depositions of the Thugs themselves abound with cases in which gangs disposed of their victims much more casually – most frequently, it seems, by hurling them into the nearest watercourse. Outside the monsoon season, these were frequently little more than dried riverbeds, in which cases the bodies would be 'slightly buried' or concealed under a pile of stones and leaves. Corpses might also be thrown into ravines or over cliffs where the terrain allowed. In general, it was thought enough to prevent the immediate discovery of the murder. Thug gangs moved so swiftly, and the men themselves dissembled so convincingly, that they had little fear of being captured a day or two further along the road.

Another reason for the less-than-scrupulous disposal of some bodies lay in the difficulty of preparing a secure grave, a problem often remarked upon by Thugs. Sometimes the terrain was simply unsuitable for a gobba, for 'in some place where the ground is stony', as one strangler explained,

> the [soil] can only be about knee deep. In such cases the dead bodies must
> be cut to pieces and buried, otherwise the body would smell and lead to dis-
> covery. I remember being much alarmed at the first burial of this kind that
> I saw . . . I expressed fear at such a sight, for the blood flowed on the
> ground! But [the grave-digger] said: 'Unless we cut them to pieces we shall
> be discovered!'

---

*It should be mentioned that the Thugs' methods of burial would have been highly distasteful to their Hindu and Muslim victims alike. Hindus were cremated after death, the only exceptions being those who died of cholera or smallpox. Muslims believed that the dead should be buried with their heads facing Mecca, and then only in coffins; the touch of earth was thought to cause torture in the afterlife.

The grave-digger was right. Human remains did not long stay hidden if such precautions were not observed. Animals that found dead bodies generally tore them to pieces, scattering odd limbs and lumps of flesh about, and this – or the cadavers' stench – would attract a passing villager. But it was rare, even then, for the authorities to be alerted, for those who had discovered a body knew all too well that the appearance of the police was likely to mean trouble, and might even lead to the accusation that they themselves had committed the murder.

Wells were also popular with the gangs of Hindustan, for there were thousands of them close to the roads of northern India, making it a simple matter to dispose of several bodies quickly and surely. Nearly nine-tenths of the bodies discovered around Etawah in the years 1808–11 were hauled from wells. Some sites were so popular with certain gangs that they yielded a huge quantity of bones when dredged; one was found to contain more than 100 skulls. Cautious Thugs would hurl the carcasses of dead animals into the wells after their victims, in order to disguise the source of the awful stench of rotting flesh, and a number avoided the deep, permanent wells found in many parts of the northern provinces altogether. 'We change the wells,' one Thug explained. 'They are usually temporary and fall in after a year or two so that no great number of bodies will be found in one well.'

It must have taken time for the stranglers to develop these techniques. A hundred years of experience, and probably more, had burnished the gangs' skills until few travellers who fell in with a party of Thugs had any chance of escape. Cannily assessed by scouts, flattered into carelessness by the inveiglers, surrounded at dusk by well-drilled stranglers and hand-holders, they met their deaths with an inevitability that was all the more terrible for being so utterly remorseless.

It was a system of murder without parallel: an industry of death. By the end of the first decade of the nineteenth century, Thug techniques were being practised in most of the provinces of India, from the Punjab to the far reaches of the Deccan. As many as three thousand men derived a living of a sort from Thuggee. Now one would bring it to a pitch of perfection.

CHAPTER 7

Feringeea

'burka – a leader or chief of the Thugs, or one thoroughly instructed in the art. The Thugs consider a burka as capable of forming a Thug gang out of the rude materials around him in any part of India'

The most celebrated of all the Thugs was born, in 1800, in suitably melodramatic circumstances: in the midst of a desperate assault on his home village, surrounded by smoke and fire and without the benefit of beds, blankets or midwives.

He was called Feringeea, which means 'European' – a name that commemorated the destruction of Murnae, 12 years before it was burned to the ground by Nathaniel Halhed, by one of Maharajah Sindhia's regiments under the command of French and British officers. His father, Purusram, was one of the great Thug leaders of the Chambel valley. His uncle, Rae Singh, was the richest man in the pargana, having used the proceeds of his expeditions to purchase the right to farm the district's taxes. His mother, who gave birth to him while fleeing from the sepoys, was the daughter of a Maratha noble. Theirs was an influential and wealthy family. But it was influential because of the sway Purusram enjoyed over the gangs of Murnae, and wealthy thanks to the wages of Thuggee.

Feringeea was born a Brahmin. He was descended from the clans that ruled the arid lands to the west of the Chambel river – a race of people known throughout India for their military prowess – and was a member of the highest Hindu caste. The Brahmins were India's hereditary priests and scholars; as well as being *dvija*, or 'twice-born' (once physically, and for a second time through an initiation ritual), they were generally well educated, and the members of other castes deferred to them. Some Brahmins earned a living as soldiers or farmers rather than as priests, but none would stoop to manual labour, and it was held to be a sin to shed a drop of their sacred blood.

Purusram's ancestors had lived in Murnae for more than 100 years. If the family's own traditions are to be believed, they had first appeared in the ravine country towards the end of Aurangzeb's reign, probably at some point during the last two decades of the seventeenth century. The first members of the clan to dwell in Murnae itself were two brothers, Seeam and Assa, who married sisters from a local Brahmin family whose own ancestors had been – so later legend said – 'initiated into the mysteries of Thuggee' during a sojourn at the Mughal court at Delhi. Seeam and Assa consequently became Thugs themselves, and though Assa died without issue, Seeam's descendants continued to lead the Murnae gangs for well over a century. Purusram himself could trace his ancestry back through five generations of stranglers. All six of his brothers travelled with the village gangs, as did more than 30 cousins, and in each branch of the family, so it was claimed, 'every male, as he became of age, became a Thug'.

Feringeea himself took part in his first Thug expedition some time before his fourteenth birthday. If he was introduced to the Murnae gangs by his father, he must have begun to Thug at the age of 10 or 11, for Purusram was hanged at Gwalior in 1812 with a number of his men. This is far from impossible; the sons of active Thugs often joined the gangs at a very early age. There are records of boys aged eight or nine participating in expeditions.

Children took no part in the killing of the gang's victims, and were taken on the road largely in order to increase their family's income, since each member of a Thug gang, whatever his age, received an equal share of the loot. 'If you love your sons,' one strangler was asked, 'why do you teach them to be Thugs?' 'How [else] could they be supported?' came the reply.

Fathers are glad when their children accompany them – why should that not be? They get a share; they instruct their sons in Thuggee and the mode of inveigling travellers; and they are glad when their children become proficient and expert. If the family be in no pecuniary want, the father will tell their sons to remain at home. But when in want, they take them with them.

Children were generally introduced to the Thug's way of life quite gradually. 'At first they know nothing of what we do,' one strangler explained. 'They accompany us and are allowed a pony, and soon become fond of the wandering life. At the end of the first year they know that we steal, and some suspect that we do more. At the end of the second year all know we murder, and in the third year they will see it.'

This careful introduction to the ways of Thuggee seems to have been intended to ease the shock that novice Thugs inevitably felt on witnessing murder for the first time. Such caution was necessary. Feringeea himself told the story of a nephew who was so terrified by the sight of the men of his gang falling on a party of travellers that he collapsed in shock and never properly recovered.

Although it seems entirely probable that older Thugs instructed their sons in the methods and tactics employed by their gangs, many Thugs insisted that 'a father does not initiate his son in strangling'. This duty fell to a 'Teacher of the Duties of a Thug', or *guru*, usually a man of considerable experience. The novice murderer, one Thug explained,

> proceeds to the fields, conducted by his Gooroo previously selected who carries with him the Roomal or shred of cloth, and anxiously looks out for some favourable omen, such as the chirping of certain birds or their flight past the right hand. He knots the Roomal at each end the moment that either occurs, and delivers it to the candidate imploring success upon him . . . It is the seniors only who confer this office, generally old Thugs held in some estimation.

Some Thug informants made a great deal of the relationship between a novice strangler and his guru, insisting that a strangler would betray his own family before he allowed any harm to come to his mentor. There is no trace of such strong and mystical relationships in the surviving records of Thuggee. But if the depositions made by captured stranglers can be believed, the appointment of a guru may have been intended to benefit the teacher as much as it did his pupil. 'The preceptor who initiated a novice,' one jemadar explained, 'is afterwards looked up to by the Thug so initiated, who through life will always give part of his spoil to the teacher.' Other Thugs described how elderly stranglers of this sort, too old to be of any use out on the roads, were maintained into their old age by donations made by grateful former pupils.

It was the guru who presided over the feast, or *tuponee*, at which a boy was accepted into the fraternity. A key feature of this feast was the ritual consumption of unrefined sugar, or *goor* – a sacrificial meal that the Thugs also consumed after each successful killing. 'The leader of the gang and the other bhurtotes sat on a blanket with the rest of the gang around them. A little sugar was dropped into a hole and the leader prayed for the gods to send them some rich victims. The remainder of the sugar was divided among all present.' This ceremony – unlike the majority of the religious trappings associated with the gangs – seems to have been unique to the Thugs, although the members of many other castes and professions celebrated with ritual feasts at which other foodstuffs were consumed.

Novice stranglers attached particular importance to their first taste of goor. They were told that the consecrated sugar they consumed during the tuponee would prepare them for the grisly work they undertook in the course of their expeditions. Feringeea was no exception. His own initiation ritual, he firmly believed, changed his character fundamentally and for ever.

'We all feel pity sometimes,' he explained two decades later.

But the goor of the tuponee changes our nature. It would change the nature of a horse. Let any man once taste of that goor and he will be a Thug though he know all the trades and have all the wealth in the world.

I never wanted food; my mother's family was opulent, her relations high in office. I have been high in office myself, and became so a great favourite wherever I went that I was sure of promotion; yet I was always miserable when absent from my gang, and obliged to return to Thuggee. My father made me taste of that fatal goor when I was yet a mere boy; and if I were to live a thousand years I should never be able to follow any other trade.

The gangs led by Purusram and Feringeea were made up mostly of men who lived with them in Murnae. These Thugs came from a variety of backgrounds. Some were Purusram's close relatives – uncles, brothers, cousins, sons – who belonged to the same extended family and had these bonds in common. A few were old and trusted associates who had served the same jemadars for decades; Purusram's gang included one aged Thug named Lalmun, whose grandfather had arrived in Murnae early in the eighteenth century and Thugged with

Purusram's ancestors for years, 'adopting their notions on all points of Thuggee'. Others had married into families that practised the trade, as Purusram's own family had themselves done generations earlier, but others again were ordinary villagers with no ties to the jemadar or his family. These men became Thugs because they needed money or found it easier to make a living from murder than from the back-breaking work of farming the poor local soil. There are numerous examples of men who did not become Thugs until they were well over 20 years old, and some of stranglers who had never ventured onto the roads of India until they were 40 or even 50. Some of these men worked on the land for years at a time before being tempted back into service with the gangs. A good number had once been soldiers, and were forced to resort to Thuggee by the sharp fall in the demand for military service that occurred in the last years of the eighteenth century and the first years of the nineteenth. But other Thugs had been labourers or drovers. One, seized in central India in 1829, turned out to be a former elephant-keeper for the Rajah of Jhalone.

Many gangs, perhaps most, included a fourth variety of Thug. These men were the children of parents who had been murdered by Thugs years earlier, and whose lives had been spared because they were too young to escape or give evidence against the killers. Children as old as six or seven were often forcibly 'adopted' in this way, which meant that many of them grew up remembering their mothers and fathers and the manner of their parents' deaths. They were, in effect, treated as a form of capital by their abductors. The boys were made to serve their adoptive fathers until they were old enough to be inducted into the Thug gangs; initiation made them eligible to receive a share of the loot, which added to the wealth of their adoptive family. Girls stayed at home, assisting the Thugs' women with domestic work until they could make a profitable marriage. The interrogations of captured Thugs preserved by the Company sometimes refer to such adopted children as 'slaves', which no doubt says a good deal about the way in which they were treated after the murder of their parents. Even so, the stranglers' life was all these children knew, and virtually all the males, when they grew up, became murderers themselves; many were eventually hanged for the same crimes that their adoptive fathers had committed against their natural parents. The gangs, indeed, depended heavily upon adoptive children to augment their ranks. Almost one in 10 of the Thugs known to the British were men whose families had been murdered by their own associates.

Ghoolam Hossyn, the very first Thug captured by the Company, was one of the many men adopted in this way. He was about four years old when, in 1798, he left the town of Rampoora, just south of the Chambel ravines, with his father and uncle to sell horses. The party came to a well where a group of 15 Thugs were resting. The Thugs killed all the adults on Ghoolam Hossyn's party and took the boy back to their own village, where 'in the evening I cried and called for my father. They told me my father had sold his horses to them and had gone away but would return. They also gave me sweetmeats and told me to remain quiet.' After three days, the child was taken to another village and presented to the local zamindar, who treated him kindly. But when, a month later, Ghoolam Hossyn asked the man to 'carry me to my father, he told me in reply that if I ever again made such a request he would kill me . . . [and] moreover suspended me in a well for two days with a view to deterring me from mentioning the subject, and I have never spoken of it since.' Ghoolam Hossyn instead grew up to be a Thug himself.*

There was, then, little homogeneity among the ranks of a Thug gang. The leaders of many bands were in effect hereditary Thugs, coming from families in which the trade had been practised for generations and among whom sons followed their fathers and served alongside brothers, cousins and uncles. These men were sometimes known as *aseel*, or well-born, Thugs, and it seems likely that a good number of the most influential Thug jemadars came from such a background, and that these men passed on the skills and tricks of the Thug trade to newer members of their gangs. But even in the most eminent Thug families men did not become stranglers either automatically or inevitably. Some sons followed other professions; others Thugged only occasionally, at times when money was short. There were many cases of men leaving off the trade for years or sometimes even decades at a time, only to be lured back to it by need or the importuning of a passing gang.

Careful study of the surviving records of Thuggee nevertheless suggests that blood ties of one sort or another lay at the heart of every gang. In one

*It was generally impossible to treat older children in this way. When, in 1809, a gang of 360 Thugs fell in with a mixed party of 31 men, seven women and three children on the road near Nagpore, Punchum Jemadar wished to spare the life of one beautiful girl 'as a wife for his son Bukholee. But when she saw her mother and father strangled, she screamed, and beat her head against the stony ground, and tried to kill herself. Punchum tried in vain to quiet her, and promised to take great care of her, and marry her to his own son who would be a great chief; but all was in vain. She continued to scream, and at last Punchum put the roomal around her neck and strangled her.'

case, from the Deccan, 25 members of a gang of 31 stranglers were related to other members of the band, the gang's jemadar alone being accompanied by his father, a son, four nephews and a son-in-law. No single instance has been found of a gang composed entirely of men unrelated to one other. But, equally, there are no records of any gangs in which every member was related to at least one of his comrades by blood.

Hereditary stranglers – if the expression can be used – made up a good proportion of most Thug bands met with up to 1835 (the situation is a good deal less certain after that date). Among the 25 members of one gang brought to trial in 1829, 13 had fathers who had practised Thuggee. A table listing their names, castes and homes shows that one was the 'son of a noted leader, and has followed the trade since his boyhood' and another 'a very noted Thug lately taken on a Thug expedition (his ancestors Thugs)'. But the remaining dozen members of the gang were new to the trade, and had come to it in a variety of ways. One had 'followed [Thuggee] for many years since his connection with the Thugs by marriage'. Another was the son of a mere pickpocket, but 'has followed the trade of Thuggee from his youth'. A third 'seized on Thuggee lately after the murder of some men near Cawnpore, [joining] a gang of seven Thugs'.

No sharp distinctions seem to have existed between the hereditary Thugs and those who had only recently taken up the trade. Half of the newcomers in this particular gang were described by the Company authorities as 'noted Thugs'. Nor is there any suggestion that *burkas*, the most respected of all Thugs, and the only men thought capable of successfully forming a new gang made up entirely of novice stranglers, were required to be, or were usually, the sons or grandsons of Thugs.

Feringeea's first Thug expeditions were made in the company of just such a mixed gang of murderers. In 1813 he joined a large band of some 150 men on an expedition to Kotah in the North Western Provinces, and it was there that he helped to inveigle what may well have been his earliest victim, a wandering mendicant whom he encountered bathing in a river. A few years later the young Thug was not far from the town of Seonee when he and a gang of 60 men killed no fewer than 14 travellers in a single night. On both occasions, Feringeea's companions included not only Brahmins and Rajputs, whose status was roughly equivalent to his own, but also bullock drivers, weavers and ordinary peasants with whom he would never usually have mixed. Still more surprisingly, perhaps, both gangs included a substantial proportion of men who did not even practise the same religion as the young Thug.

The make up of the Thug gangs puzzled many of the British officers who encountered them. Most gang members professed to be Hindu, though a good number – perhaps a third – were Muslim. 'The castes chiefly to be met with are Brahmans, Rajputs, Sodhis and Kolis,*' one Company official calcu-lated, but – given the suspicion that the earliest Thugs probably were low-caste men from wandering tribes – police officials speculated, no doubt correctly, that low-caste Thugs often appropriated fine clothes and horses from their vic-tims in order to pose as high-born men. There were certainly practical advantages to travelling in mixed groups. It was difficult for men of different castes to meet and mix in India, and a gang composed solely of high-caste stranglers would find it impossible to strike up any sort of friendship with most of the people they encountered on the roads. Islamic Thugs, who were uncon-strained by the requirements of the caste system, must have found it easier to inveigle potential victims, and several Company officials – discovering that many Thugs possessed a wide variety of aliases – became convinced that Hindu stranglers often passed themselves off as Muslims.

Each gang, then, contained members drawn from a variety of back-grounds. Thugs did have many things in common – not least a shared history of murder – but because most came together for only a few months at a time, they often lacked a strong sense of community and felt less loyalty to each other than the Company's officials anticipated. The British, influenced by their own preconceptions concerning India's religion and society, often assumed that the gangs they encountered were tight-knit groups of heredi-tary murderers, sons following fathers into a profession that was both exclusive and preordained. But the reality was rather different.

Feringeea's Thug career seems to have been a success almost from its outset. He claimed the title of jemadar at the very early age of 12, perhaps by using his late father's money to fund an expedition. But the testimony of the boy's companions suggests that he possessed a talent to match his inherited wealth. He was a handsome young man of youthful appearance, well spoken and of

*Priests, soldiers, farmers and herdsmen.

high caste – ideally suited, in short, to impress any wealthy and high-born travellers whom he encountered on the road. Indeed, some of his companions began half-jokingly to refer to him as 'subadar' because, one explained, 'He was a charming young man of noble appearance, and so useful to us.'

Feringeea's activities in his earliest years remain obscure. He certainly Thugged between the years 1813 and 1817, and was present, with the other members of his gang, at the murder of a party of treasure bearers and a passing buffalo driver near the village of Sujaina in 1814, an affair that yielded the 40 Thugs involved an impressive 4,500 rupees. Shortly thereafter, however, he abandoned Thuggee for a while and sought service in the Company's army, a decision that he himself claimed was taken after he fell out with his cousin Aman Subadar on a Thug expedition, but which possibly owed something to the endemic disorder afflicting central India between 1814 and 1818, when the Company renewed its war with the Marathas and it was far more dangerous to seek a living on the roads. The four years that Feringeea spent in British service demonstrated, nonetheless, the jemadar's evident charm and talent, for by 1821 he had risen to the post of chief of the messenger service controlled by David Ochterlony, the powerful British Resident at Delhi. He might even have remained among Ochterlony's entourage had not a friend, the captain of the guard, not been caught 'in an awkward position' with one of the Resident's maidservants, prompting Feringeea to flee ahead of Ochterlony's retribution and resume his Thug career.

For all the attractions of the central provinces, newly restored to peace under the Company's rule, Feringeea did not return immediately to his home in the Maratha lands after leaving Ochterlony's service in the early 1820s. If the Resident really did want to extract vengeance from his young Rajput servant, he would seek him in his village in Khyrooah first, and Feringeea found it expedient to spend the years after 1821 working with the Thug gangs of Rajpootana, to the west, and Telingana, in the Deccan. Living 'among these clans . . . for years together' offered certain advantages to an ambitious but still relatively inexperienced jemadar, for a man who spent the cold season with the men of Telingana could remain active during the monsoon by shifting his base to the arid lands of Rajpootana, where the rains rarely fell, and so avoid having to wait out the six or eight months that otherwise passed between expeditions. A number of comrades already Thugged in this way. One, an Oudh bhurtote named Ramzan, boasted of being 'at work for nine years without returning to my home'.

It was while making their way into southern Rajpootana at the very end of the cold season of 1822–3 that Feringeea and the men who now made up his gang fell into the company of the girl who would become one of their most notorious victims. She was a Mughalanee – a young Muslim woman of high birth – who was travelling alone, protected by only the lightest of escorts ('an old female servant, mounted upon a pony, one armed manservant, and six bearers for her palanquin'), because she had, rather impulsively, taken leave of some friends and decided to go on to her destination near Agra without them. She was also 'very fair and beautiful', and apparently somewhat flirta-tious, too, for she quickly took a great liking to Feringeea. The Thug jemadar, who was by now 'a handsome young man, [who] looked like a man of rank', evidently enjoyed her attentions. He and the Mughalanee spent the next few days together, deep in conversation.

In other circumstances, the girl's advances might have provided welcome proof of Feringeea's prowess as an inveigler. As it was, he had no interest in strangling her. His gang had decided, almost as soon as they had fallen in with the girl's party, that she was carrying too little money to be worth murdering, and so the Mughalanee's growing affection for their leader was not merely embarrassing, but deeply inconvenient. Several attempts to shake off her party failed, and the Thugs were just beginning to despair of enticing more worthwhile prey when the girl turned to Feringeea and told him she would like him to escort her to her home. Sensing his reluctance, she added slyly that she would 'get him into trouble' if he refused.

This threat sealed the Mughalanee's fate. Feringeea knew all too well that he had already been compromised by his friendship with the girl; as a Brahmin, he could not enjoy intimate relations of any sort with a Muslim woman, and should they be accused of 'improper intercourse', he could even be turned out of caste. His men were still reluctant to murder her – 'We were very averse to it,' insisted one, 'and often said that we should not get two rupees apiece, and that she ought to be let go' – but the jemadar held firm, and the members of the gang were searching for an appropriate spot to kill the Mughalanee's men when their scouts lost their way in the early hours of a March morning. There was a moment's confusion; 'the young woman became alarmed, and began to reproach us for taking her into the jungle in the dark', and Feringeea had just been summoned to quieten her when, 'dreading that some of her party might make off, the signal was given', and the girl and her servants were all strangled on the spot.

The Thugs, when they recalled this sad affair at all, did so because their gloomy forecast of the likely profit proved only too correct: each man received, as his share of the loot, the sum of only four rupees. Feringeea, too, dismissed his brief friendship with the girl, believing that the unusual circumstances fully proved 'it was her fate to die by our hands'. But the murder would eventually attract more attention than any of the jemadar's other crimes – not because of the Mughalanee's position, or even her youth and great beauty, but because she should never have been a victim of the Thugs at all.

There can be little doubt that the first decades of the nineteenth century were marked by a deterioration in the discipline maintained within many strangling gangs. The reasons for this decline were complex, though they evidently owed at least a little to the appearance of large numbers of novice Thugs with few ties to old families such as Feringeea's and little respect for their established practices, and more to the difficulty many bands experienced in making a decent living from their murders. One consequence was that rules that had been followed by the gangs were increasingly flouted, and a number of the customs and proscriptions that had guided the Thugs for years began to be ignored. The Mughalanee and her travelling companions were merely a handful among many hundreds of the gangs' victims who died as a result of this sea change.

The Thugs, like almost every Indian of the time, were highly superstitious. No strangler was supposed to kill a woman. Nor a fakir. Nor a musician, a dancer or a bard. Indeed, the list of those whom the gangs were prohibited from harming, by custom or superstition, was a lengthy one. It included the maimed and the leprous, as well as the members of several specific castes or professions, such as elephant drivers, oil vendors, washermen and sweepers. Anyone travelling with a cow was to pass unharmed, and Sikhs were also spared, at least in the province of Bengal.

The laws that guided the choice of the first victim of every expedition were, if anything, more complex still. Many Thugs invoked what was known as 'The Rule of the Bones', which forbade them to kill any victims accompanied by a horse, an ox or any other quadruped until some other traveller had first been strangled. Men wearing gold ornaments were likewise to be spared until another victim had been murdered, as were Brahmins and Sayyids, the most holy members of the Hindu and Muslim faiths.* It was also considered unlucky to select a poor man as the first victim of an expedition, no doubt for fear that every other traveller met along the way would be similarly impoverished.

Yet more rules existed to govern special situations. *Kawrutties* (the carriers of sacred Ganges water) could only be killed if their pots were empty, while blacksmiths and carpenters – who could be strangled if they were encountered separately – were to be spared if they were travelling together.

Most of these proscriptions were firmly rooted in the folk religion and the superstitions practised in the main Thug villages. Oil vendors and sweepers were generally thought to be unlucky, while seriously ill or physically disabled travellers were (as one strangler explained) spared on account of their misfortune: 'These, God has afflicted; we may not touch them.' Criminals who harmed women had been singled out for particular punishment in even the most ancient Hindu texts. The Thugs' superstition concerning the killing of travellers accompanied by beasts of burden, meanwhile, probably reflected the sanctity accorded to those conveying the remains of their deceased parents to be consigned to the Ganges.

This mass of laws was, in any case, not scrupulously observed. Most jemadars were simply too pragmatic to be entirely bound by customs that so limited their prospects of inveigling worthwhile victims, and though the most successful Thugs did indeed pass over members of the forbidden groups and castes, poorer stranglers were sorely tempted to kill any travellers whom they were certain had money on them. Others struggled with the practical difficulties involved in sparing some members of a party, while contriving to strangle others. Even if it were possible – and the Thugs certainly did employ considerable ingenuity on occasion to separate those they could not kill from those they fully intended to** – it was horribly dangerous to leave witnesses

*The title 'Sayyid' denotes a Muslim claiming direct descent from the Prophet Muhammad; that of 'Sheikh', a man of Arab (rather than native Indian) stock – a descendant, in other words, of an invading Muslim soldier, rather than the offspring of a later, local convert. Numerous Thugs laid claim to these distinctions, among them the great strangler Sayeed Ameer Ali and the fêted leader of the Arcottee Thugs, Sheikh Ahmed.
**When one gang of Thugs encountered a group of 14 men near Hattah, in Bundelcund, they were dissuaded from murdering them by the fact that they were travelling with a cow. An inveigler persuaded the animal's owner that he had made a vow to present a cow to a local priest. Unwilling to stand in the way of such piety, the travellers agreed to sell the animal, which was indeed presented to the Brahmin. All 14 were then strangled forthwith.

capable of identifying the members of a gang alive, and there were, thus, numerous cases in which victims who should have been safe from attack were killed. In particular, women accompanying large parties of travellers were frequently murdered because the alternative would have been to allow the entire group to escape.

Captured Thugs invariably lamented this development and a good number believed that their gangs had lost the divine protection that shielded them from capture when they first defied the old proscriptions. Reverses or misfortunes of all kinds were commonly attributed to failures to observe the sacred laws, and when the jemadars Punchum and Himmut strangled no fewer than 6 women in the course of disposing of a group of 40 travellers near Nagpore in 1809, the awful deaths suffered by many of their men were widely attributed to divine retribution. 'How was Punchum punished?' Feringeea asked. 'Did he not die before he could reach home? And was not his son, Bughola, hung the November following . . .? And was not Bhugwan hung with him? And what a horrid death did Himmut die! He was eaten alive by worms.'*

Probably it had once been easier to obey the various proscriptions that bound Feringeea and his men than it eventually became. Most of the customs followed by the Thugs seem to have come into existence before the British appeared in central India, at a time when comparatively few stranglers were active and the countryside was peaceful and prosperous enough for highway robbers to make a decent living on the roads. Certainly most Thugs dated the earliest lapses from their informal code to around the year 1800, when there was great disorder, fewer travellers and a good many more men trying to eke out a living from Thuggee. The first woman murdered by the gangs of the Chambel valley was said to have been the Kale Bebee, the wife of a prominent Maratha officer, who was killed, together with the 12 men of her bodyguard, by Feringeea's father Purusram around the year 1801. Purusram and another Thug jemadar attempted to atone for the crime, and restore their ritual purity, by hosting a feast for all the Brahmins of their district, and this, the other members of their gang believed, would have been enough to conciliate their gods, had they not given way to temptation once again and strangled other

---

*This was not the only indignity suffered by the unfortunate Himmut. 'He died,' another Thug named Punna recalled, 'barking like a dog.'

women in 1805, 1809 and 1813. This repeated flouting of the old proscriptions was sometimes said to have led not only to the jemadars' own deaths but to have doomed their relations as well. It was, Feringeea said, 'from that time that we may trace our decline':

> Our family was never happy; not a year passed without [Purusram] losing something, or being seized; he was seized every year somewhere or other. Ghasee Subadar was another leader, and he suffered similar misfortunes, and his family became miserable. Look at our families; see how they are annihilated.

The gangs led by Purusram and Feringeea may have been among the first to stoop to killing women. In the years that followed their flight from Murnae in 1812–13, the men of the Chambel valley were often harshly denounced by Thugs from other districts for killing indiscriminately and even for corrupting their fellow Thugs. The Lodhees of Bengal and Bihar were proverbially strict, for 'no prospect of booty could ever induce them to kill a woman'. But three Doab jemadars, accused of strangling some girls in the central provinces, protested that they had been led astray by 'the Bundelcund and Saugor men', and insisted that such things never happened north of the Jumna, where 'we do not even murder a person that has a cow with him'. The Phansigars, or stranglers, of the Deccan were also loud in their denunciation of the 'Hindustani heresies' that they believed had brought bad luck down upon the heads of their compatriots.

The tendency to shift blame for the failure to observe the old Thug customs existed even within the ranks of the Chambel valley gangs themselves. The Hindu members of Purusram's band insisted that they were sometimes forced, against their will, to agree to the murder of women by the more numerous Muslims in the gang, who did not feel bound by customs based on ancient Brahmin texts. Feringeea's men were adamant that no Hindu took part in the Mughalanee's murder, and possibly some were sufficiently religious to be genuinely disturbed by the forbidden practice. But there were other Thugs who – while never stooping to kill a member of one of the proscribed groups themselves – were happy enough to let unscrupulous or low members of their gangs flout custom in the convenient belief that they themselves were not defiled by such objectionable practices. 'Among us,' one strangler explained, 'it is a rule never to kill a woman; but if a rich old woman is found, the gang sometimes get a man to strangle her by giving him an extra share of the booty, and inducing him to take the responsibility upon himself.' This practice eventually became common even in Oudh, whose Thugs considered them-selves more scrupulous than those of Hindustan. One Oudh gang included a bhurtote by the name of Jubber, who could often be persuaded to strangle inconvenient victims 'for the love of four additional annas'.*

The Thugs were, in short, strikingly inconsistent in their interpretations of old customs that seem to have been common to all the gangs of northern India. The outcome of an encounter between a Thug band and travellers from one of the proscribed groups and castes could seldom be predicted; it depended upon the circumstances, the character of the jemadars involved, and the proportions of Hindus and Muslims in a gang. This was a consequence of the absence of any sort of central leadership or hierarchy among the gangs. In most cases, the Thugs' leaders were free to act as they saw fit, and that meant that need, chance and – on rare occasions – even compassion all played their parts in determining the outcome of an expedition.

Compassion was a subject seldom touched on by hardened stranglers. Most Thugs felt little sympathy for the people that they killed, such feelings as they possessed having been, as we have seen, squeezed from them in the course of their first few expeditions. The business was also the only way of making a living that many stranglers knew. 'The love of money makes us kill them,' a Thug named Dhoosoo once explained, 'we care not for their life.'

Yet even the most ruthless stranglers did feel compassion on occasion, sometimes when it was least expected. In about 1830, for example, a gang of 40 men working near Lucknow met

a very handsome youth, a native officer of rank, upon horseback in the King of Oudh's service, who had a camel with him, and six sepoys, and some ser-vants, and some one or two thousand roopees. We inveigled him and . . . every Thug was ready for the destruction of the youth and his whole party – stranglers being all ready – [when] the light of the fire fell upon the hair and handsome countenance of the young man, doomed to death, who was the

*This Thug was eventually captured by the British authorities, one officer noting, 'This Jubber, now in jail here, is a poor, wretched-looking being, whose head continually shakes from palsy . . . 6 Feb. 1837: Jubber died in jail this day; his skeleton is to be preserved as one of the most relentless and notorious assassins in the world.'

head of the party, and as he sat upon his horse he looked so very beautiful that we all felt compassion. I was appointed to seize the reins of his horse . . . but so beautiful was he as the light fell upon his face that we could not find it in our hearts to kill him, so we let him and his whole party pass on their way, though it was a rich prize! A camel and many roopees and much property! It often happens that we thus let men off from pity.

Most such cases occurred when Thugs were confronted with the need to murder women or young children. Feringeea, the year after killing the Mughalanee, was once again working his way through Rajpootana when he and his men fell in with the handmaid of a Maratha ruler, 'on her way from Poona to Cawnpore'. The fact that she was a woman would not in itself have been enough to save her, 'for she and her escort had a *lakh* and a half of property and jewels and other things with them'. But 'after having her and her party three days within our grasp', the Thugs eventually let her go, 'for she was very beautiful', as well as being – presumably – less likely than her Muslim predecessor to cause trouble. It was not an unprecedented incident – 'We all feel compassion sometimes,' the jemadar concluded. But such sentiments were generally rare.

One reason for the Thugs' flouting of ancient proscriptions and their ruthless despatch of victims who might once have been spared was an increasing fear of arrest and punishment.

Feringeea, whose Thug career had proceeded more or less without incident for the best part of a decade, was one of a number of prominent stranglers to fall foul of either the British or the Indian authorities in the early 1820s. No more than a year after he had left Ochterlony's service, the young jemadar was nearing the town of Kotah with his men when the gang was waylaid by a patrol of sepoys. Feringeea's band had enjoyed recent success, having strangled 'four men with bundles of clothes' less than a week earlier and killed a Hindu chief and his retinue of servants four days later, and they were carrying a considerable quantity of incriminating plunder. In consequence, no fewer than 28 Thugs were arrested, Feringeea himself escaping only because he chanced to be bathing when the troops appeared and was able to flee, naked, into the countryside and then evade pursuit. His followers were also fortunate on this occasion; the local rajah baulked at the cost of imprisoning so many men, and released them after only a day, having 'blackened their faces' with a dye in order to give warning to other travellers of their character. But two other gangs of Thugs were not so fortunate: 40 men whom the Kotahan patrols chanced upon while chasing Feringeea were jailed for the best part of four years, perhaps because the evidence against them was stronger.

In these changing circumstances, fewer and fewer Thugs could afford to be scrupulous about their choice of victims. At roughly the same time that Feringeea's men were arrested at Kotah, for example, another band of stranglers under a certain Khimolee Jemadar was committing what came to be regarded as one of the most atrocious of all Thug murders. This, the so-called 'Beseynee affair', began in a temple at Kamptee, just outside Nagpore, with the killing of three men working for a local merchant and the seizure of a bag of valuable spices and another containing silks. Khimolee's men then fell in with a party coming north from the Deccan. This group was led by a man named Newul Singh, a disabled soldier who had lost one arm in the Nizam's service and was travelling with two daughters, aged 11 and 13, the girls' intended husbands – two youths of about their ages – and a son aged seven. Both Singh and the girls thus belonged to classes of travellers forbidden to the Thugs, and several of Khimolee's men refused to have anything to do with the murder of a disabled man, splitting from the main party. The jemadar himself, however, successfully inveigled his way into Newul Singh's confidence and became a great favourite of his daughters 'from numerous acts of kindness and attention on the roads'.

This attachment served the Thugs well when, stopping for the night in a village called Dhoma, the house in which most of the gang were staying caught fire and the occupants were arrested on suspicion of arson. Newul Singh was vocal in protesting his new friend's innocence, and was able to call upon a relative serving with the British forces in nearby Seonee to secure their release. By the time the party reached Jubbulpore a few days later, the two groups had become so close that Newul Singh laughingly rejected several warnings from acquaintances in the town that the men he had fallen in with were dangerous characters. He was, he said, more than happy to remain in their company.

Some Thugs, owing so much to a party of intended victims, might have searched for other prey. Khimolee and his men, however, chose to avail themselves again of the attachment of Newul Singh and his daughters only a day or so later, when messengers from Nagpore reached the town with news of the robbery at Kamptee and the Jubbulpore authorities began a search for the missing bags of silk and spices. Singh's daughters were persuaded to sit down on the bags of loot 'and to say that their companions were friends of theirs, and honest men', while the police searched their lodgings. Nothing was found, and a few days later, at the village of Beseynee, Singh and all the members of his party were murdered and robbed, the Thugs having accompanied them 'a distance of more than 200 miles, and were with them about 20 days on the most intimate terms, before they put them all to death'.

The growing danger of arrest had other consequences. Many Thugs became, for example, much more cautious regarding the disposal of their victims' bodies during the third decade of the nineteenth century. Hitherto, as we have seen, the stranglers had only roughly concealed many of the men they killed, abandoning their corpses in dried-up riverbeds or close to roads with only leaves, branches and stones to cover them; the burial of victims occurred more rarely, and then chiefly in densely populated districts – scouts would be sent ahead of the gang to find a suitable murder-spot, or *bele*, within a day's march. After about 1820, however, the use of beles and well-dug graves became more common and greater efforts were made to conceal the evidence of murder.

Feringeea was among the jemadars who began to take precautions at this time, and it is possible that his lucky escape at Kotah inspired him to take greater care whilst on the road. Certainly he and his men very carefully buried the bodies of 16 men whom they had murdered west of Seoni in 1820; two years later, near Jypore, they concealed the remains of a Company subadar-major named Akhbar Khan and eight other travellers 'under the wall of a building' to guard against a chance discovery. It helped, in cases such as these, to find a place 'where the ground is soft for the grave, or the jungle thick to cover them, and where the local authorities [take] no notice of the bodies', but really anywhere secluded sufficed. The temple of Kamptee outside Nagpore, where Khimolee Jemadar and his men had murdered three travellers, was a good example of a well-appointed bele – it was ruined and deserted, but offered welcome shelter; it retained gates that could be closed to prevent intended victims from escaping; and its earthen courtyard made it a simple matter to dispose of bodies within the grounds without risk of discovery.

More usually, however, Thugs made use of a ready-made network of potential beles – groves and orchards that flourished a short way outside many villages and towns in the central provinces of India. These groves had long been favoured resting-places for weary travellers. They often contained around 400 trees; hardy mango saplings were favoured, but 'orange, pomegranate and other small trees that will always require watering' were almost equally commonplace, and so most groves were planted close to a stream or well. Many had never been intended as commercial ventures, though it was usual for the rights to harvest their fruit to be leased out by the owners. Instead they were often planted as acts of charity on the part of wealthy local notables, who hoped to earn religious merit by providing sanctuaries for travellers. As two merchants encountered by a British officer observed:

> We hope that those who enjoy the shade, the water and the fruit will think kindly of us when we are gone. The names of the great men who built the castles, palaces and tombs at Delhi and Agra have been almost all forgotten, because no one enjoys any advantage from them; but the names of those who planted the mango groves we see are still remembered and blessed by all who eat of their fruit, sit in their shade, and drink of their water.

It was thus particularly unfortunate that the prospect of excellent cover, ready access to a *nullah* or a well, and soil deep enough for graves combined to make the groves and orchards planted with such good intentions irresistible to Thugs.

In certain circumstances it remained unnecessary to dig elaborate graves. One of the Thugs' *matarbur beles* (favourite murder-spots) was a stretch of dense jungle on the road between Chupara and Jubbulpore; another was near Punna, in the hills of Oudh – 'a secret place where no tidings of our victims transpired. Hundreds of travellers were there strangled; we concealed their bodies under stones and the tigers devoured them'.* High ground was

---

*'Travellers in that wild country used from fear to go in small bodies through the Ghat,' added the Thug who described this bele, 'lest the tigers or Thugs should fall upon them. Those who escaped the tigers fell into the hands of Thugs, and those who escaped the Thugs were sometimes devoured by the tigers.'

favoured, presumably because the Thugs were less likely to be caught there unawares by the police or passing troops; but the most important duty of the scouts charged with locating a bele was to find a spot near the end of a stage, where the Thugs' inveiglers could easily persuade their companions to stop for the night.

The increasing importance attached by most gangs to the proper disposal of their victims can be glimpsed in accounts of the numerous rituals and super-stitions associated with the burial of a corpse. The most common of these, and the one most often mentioned by Thugs themselves, was the consecration of the pickaxe with which they dug their victims' graves. This ritual was regarded as so significant that many gangs performed it prior to every expe-dition as a way of seeking the favour of the deity under whose protection the gang was placing itself. It was most usual for an appeal of this sort to be made to Kali, the black-skinned, six-armed Hindu mother-goddess of destruc-tion, venerated by many low-caste Hindus and Indian criminals, and for the consecration to be attended by every member of the gang and presided over by their jemadar, or some other strangler judged 'most skilled in cere-monies'. So important was the ritual that it was performed inside a house or tent 'so that the shadow of no living thing might fall on or contaminate the sacred implement'.

Accounts of such ceremonies, given by Feringeea and a number of his fellow jemadars, suggest that the Thugs' pickaxe was simply an ordinary agricultural implement – typically consisting of a curved blade forged from wrought iron about 10 inches long, sharply pointed at one end and mounted on a long wooden shaft – but one usually made in such a way that it could be easily disassembled so as to avoid detection. Once taken to pieces, one man would be entrusted with the haft, and another – the gang's most experienced gravedigger – would conceal the blade within his clothing so that it could not be seen by casual passers-by. Reassembled, the implement would be brought out as the ceremony began; a pit would be dug in the ground and the pickaxe held over it and washed, successively, with water, a sugar solution, sour milk and alcohol. Finally it would be marked seven times with vermilion, symbol-izing the blood of future victims.

According to the testimony given by one Thug, a cow-dung fire – made fragrant with incense, sandalwood and coconut – would then be lit, and the blade of the pickaxe passed through it seven times. At the height of the ceremony the gang's jemadar would take a coconut, place it on the ground and ask the members of the assembled band, 'Shall I strike?' Receiving a positive response, he would break open the coconut with the butt of the pickaxe amid 'a loud cry of devout approval' and share pieces of the flesh amongst the principal stranglers. Finally, the blade of the pickaxe would be placed on a piece of clean white cloth and the assembled Thugs would bow to it. The expedition, suitably blessed, was ready to begin.

Elaborate rituals of this sort have always been common in rural India, and similar ceremonies – appealing, for example, for protection from danger on the roads – would have been conducted by many of the travellers who would eventually fall prey to the wiles of the Thugs. But the stranglers' superstitions regarding their sacred burial tool were so extensive that they went far beyond the consecration of the pickaxe. Thugs recounted numerous tales concerning their veneration of the implement. Once properly blessed, one said, it could only be carried by the member of the gang 'most noted for his sobriety, shrewdness and calm', and it was believed to be practically a living thing. When in camp, it was buried in a secure place with its point facing in the direction that the gang intended to go, and it was sometimes believed that Kali would move the point around in the course of the night if another route were likely to be more propitious. Some elderly Thugs added further and more mystical details, alleging that in earlier times the pickaxe had been thrown into a well whenever the gang halted for the night, from which it would rise of its own accord when summoned with due ceremony. A handful even claimed to have witnessed the feat, one recalling a time when several gangs had camped together 'and at the call, the pickaxes of the various gangs came up of themselves and went to their respective bearers'. Similarly, the Thugs insisted that as long as the implement was cleansed after each use, the sound made by it in digging a grave could not be heard by anyone but a member of their gang. The pickaxe was so sacred that it could never be allowed to fall to the ground; if such a calamity occurred, the bearer was instantly deprived of his office, and the gang-members either returned to their homes to begin a fresh expedition, or chose a fresh route, consecrating the implement anew.

The tool's most important property, however, was neither its supernatural silence nor its ability to prophesy good fortune. It was the security it was believed to offer to the Thugs under its protection. Properly consecrated, scrupulously maintained and treated with reverence, the pickaxe was believed to protect the members of a gang from detection or capture.

This protection was not absolute. A great priest, or a man so favoured by the gods that his *iqbal* (good fortune) was superior to that of the stranglers themselves, could overcome the powers of even the most sacred symbols of Thuggee. Admittedly the very oldest Thugs, men whose memories stretched back halfway into the eighteenth century, could never recall encountering such a man. But, in fact, one did exist. His name was William Sleeman, and he had only recently arrived in India. Sleeman knew nothing whatever of Thuggee. But he was about to learn.

CHAPTER 8

Sleeman

'dhaundhoee – a hunter of Thugs'

Sleeman was a Cornishman. He was born, in 1788, in a wild stretch of countryside, as unlike India as it is possible to imagine. His first home, the hamlet of Stratton on the coast north of Bodmin Moor, was bleak and grey and blasted by fierce sea winds that howled in from the north, sending waves crashing in against the cliffs and stunting and bowing the handful of trees that clung to the heights. This was smuggling country, and the Sleemans themselves had once been heavily involved in the importation of illegal cargoes. But the family had grown respectable. Many of its sons now served in the army or the navy. Sleeman's father, Philip, was the Supervisor of Excise for his stretch of coast, charged with catching the smugglers his ancestors had once employed.

Philip Sleeman had a large family: eight boys and a girl. It was scarcely possible, on an exciseman's salary, to provide liberally for so many sons, and when the old man died in 1802 his wife was reduced to comparative poverty. Her two eldest sons had already been set up in business and a third was studying medicine, but the younger children were forced to seek less expensive careers. Three brothers became sailors (two were to drown at sea), and William himself – the fifth son of the eight – was forced to set aside his ambition of becoming an officer in the British Army, which in those days required a man to have a private income sufficient to make a good show in the mess. With his family's approval, he determined to make his career in India instead.

The East India Company had long been a popular refuge for the sons of impoverished British gentry. The vast sums seized by Robert Clive and his colleagues in the 1760s were still vivid in many people's memories, and even though government regulation had put an end to the prospect of building a substantial private fortune, there was still plenty of money to be made and honours to be won in the Subcontinent. The 20 or 30 'writerships' that provided entry to the Indian civil service every year were so highly sought after that nominations occasionally (and illegally) changed hands for as much as £1,300. Service with the Company's three armies – one in Bengal, another in Bombay and the third in Madras – was less lucrative, and the 100 or 120 young cadets recruited annually to fill the vacancies within their ranks joined regiments that were neither so grand nor so socially exclusive as those of the King's Army. But there were advantages to a military career in India nonetheless. Not the least of them, in Sleeman's eyes, was the fact that officers without private means could survive there on their pay alone.

There was, of course, still a good deal of demand for the handful of cadetships available each year. But open examinations and formal competition were half a century away. In Sleeman's day, recruits were still drawn almost exclusively from the ranks of the English gentry, and 'influence', in the form of an acquaintance with one of the directors of the Company, was all that was required to secure one of the coveted nominations. The Sleeman family possessed the necessary connections, and in 1809 William – by then aged 20 – was gazetted as an ensign in the Bengal Army. He sailed for India that same March, and disembarked at Calcutta six months later after a long sea voyage around the Cape.

Sleeman was old for a newcomer to India. A good proportion of his fellow cadets had gone out to Calcutta at the age of 16 or 17 to enrol at the military college established at Basaret by Richard Wellesley. The college was so close to the temptations of the city, so badly staffed and poorly disciplined, that it soon acquired an evil reputation. It was peopled with rambunctious cadets who took little interest in their lessons and remained (one contemporary observed) 'in a continual uproar, blowing coach-horns and bugles, baiting jackals with pariah-dogs, fighting cocks, and shooting kites and crows'. Students learned 'drinking, coarse language, vulgar amusements and gaming' rather than Indian languages, and Sleeman – an ambitious, serious-minded boy – had chosen not to enrol there, remaining at home and hiring a private tutor instead.

The education Sleeman thus received was mixed. He displayed a considerable talent for languages, which would stand him in good stead throughout his Indian career. He picked up a fair knowledge of Hindustani, once the lingua franca of educated men throughout the Mughal Empire and now the language spoken in the Bengal Army. He also read, with some attention, the handbook supplied to each cadet during the long voyage out. This manual dealt copiously with the importance of behaving as a gentleman and proffered advice on the treatment of servants in Calcutta. But it contained nothing whatsoever about a cadet's military duties and did not discuss the qualities or habits of the soldiers he would soon command.

Sleeman therefore arrived in India with at best a merely theoretical grasp of military affairs and no first-hand knowledge of Bengal. These deficiencies could only be remedied by practical experience.

If even the callowest novice in the Company's service knew one thing about India, it was this: the Subcontinent was a dangerous place in which to live.

Mortality among British officers stationed in the cities of Bombay, Calcutta and Madras had long been staggering. In the seventeenth and eighteenth centuries it was not uncommon for half the Europeans scattered through India to die of fever, drink or heatstroke in a single year. In Bombay, in 1692, nearly 90 per cent of the British population succumbed to disease in just three months; in the same city, 15 years later, a mere seven men were fit for duty, and an ambassador from Persia, arriving unexpectedly offshore, had to be refused permission to leave his ship 'lest he should relate to his master the nakedness of the land'. Even a century later, in Sleeman's time, an officer joining the Company's army 'said goodbye to his family in England knowing that there was only a slender chance that he would ever see them again'. Statistics show that six out of every seven British officers despatched to the Subcontinent between 1800 and 1825 never returned.

The principal difficulty was surviving long enough to develop resistance to India's main diseases. In any given year the great majority of those who died were comparatively recent arrivals; fatalities were most common in men under the age of 30 and women aged 25 or less. As late as the 1830s, when Emily Eden studied the gravestones filling the European cemetery at Meerut, she failed to discover 'any one individual who lived to be more than thirty-six'.

Those who did survive the dangerous first years might well enjoy long careers. It was not unusual for an officer to serve in India for 20, 30, even

50 years. But none emerged unscathed from the experience. Repeated bouts of illness left them prematurely aged, with yellowed skin, peppery tempers and greatly reduced stamina. Protracted confinements, followed by lengthy convalescences, were normal in this period; in the course of his own 45 years in India, Sleeman would be absent on sick leave for almost all of 1825–6, the whole of 1836, and much of 1855.

The Subcontinent could kill in many ways. Dysentery, often carried on the wind in dust laden with organic matter, was one of the most common illnesses; typhoid was another; smallpox and plague were common, too. But cholera, the fever carried in the water, was the most feared of all diseases. This was not merely because it was generally lethal (nine out of ten of those infected with the bacillus died, the linings of their intestines eaten away, voiding as many as 25 pints of diarrhoea in a day), but because it struck with awful speed. The interval between the first emergence of the symptoms and the victim's death might be as little as two or three hours, and corpses decomposed so rapidly in the damp heat of India that they had to be interred almost immediately. 'We have,' one Company officer noted in 1805, 'known two instances of dining with a gentleman [at midday] and being invited to his burial before supper time.' It was all profoundly depressing, particularly during the monsoon season, when all sorts of fevers raged unchecked. One Company wife, writing a few years after Sleeman's arrival in India, confided in her diary: 'Here people die one day and are buried the next. Their furniture is sold on the third and they are forgotten the fourth . . . O lord! Preserve my husband and me!'*

The unforgiving Indian climate contributed its own share to the difficulties confronting Sleeman and his fellow cadets. Those fortunate enough to reach the Subcontinent during the cold weather, between October and March, found the place delightful; the days were warm, the evenings cool and sometimes frosty, and it was possible to indulge in all manner of outdoor activities. But the hot season, which followed, was a different matter. For the best part of three months, newcomers and old India hands alike sweated as the temperature rose to levels never experienced in northern Europe. Merciless sun, tight woollen uniforms and – all too often – choking dust combined to make life all but unbearable for British officers, and though the first rains were

---

*Her entreaty was in vain. The author's husband died five years after this entry was made, during the monsoon of 1828, and she followed him only a month later. 'The kingdom of Bengal' – as the contemporary saying went – 'has a hundred gates open for entrance, but not one for departure.'

invariably refreshing after months of searing heat, it was difficult to bear the monsoon humidity for long.

Sleeman, disembarking in September, was unlucky enough to reach India at 'the worst time of the year'. The wet season was drawing to a close, and there were now long and oppressive intervals between the cascades of torrential rain – lasting, one British officer observed, 'often for 10 days. The heat and the humidity became very trying. This was the time when people got boils and probably felt most run down.' The heavy pall hanging over Bengal drained men of all their energy, rotted furnishings and ruined clothes. Heavily robed judges, sitting in the central court, had to change their soaking vestments as often as four times a day, and their wives knitted with silver needles instead of their usual iron ones, which turned to rust in the damp air.

Not even the worst extremes of weather, though, could suppress the cadets' high spirits. Calcutta, where Sleeman would spend three of his first four years of service, was a bustling, raucous city, not much more than a hundred years old. It had been founded, in 1690, as a mere trading post in the interior of Bengal. But it had been the capital of the British administration for almost 50 years and by the early nineteenth century was, if not the largest, then certainly the richest and the most important city in the entire Subcontinent.

The place had changed a good deal since the 1750s, when it had been described by Robert Clive himself as 'one of the most wicked places in the Universe'. The Calcutta of 1809 might not even have been recognized by Mrs Sherwood, the chronicler of the latter half of the eighteenth century who lived in the city before the stinking marshes that surrounded it were drained, and scathingly described 'the splendid sloth and languid debauchery of European society' at a time when 'great men rode about in State coaches, with a dozen servants running before and behind them to bawl out their titles'. Since then, thanks in large part to Wellesley, Calcutta had grown considerably and had acquired its share of monumental architecture. It was now 'the City of Palaces', and the government district was so splendidly laid out along the banks of the Hooghly river that William Hunter, a newly arrived Company writer, could observe: 'Imagine everything that is glorious in nature combined with everything that is beautiful in architecture and you can faintly picture to yourself what Calcutta is.'

The public portions of the city were, however, merely one of Calcutta's several faces. The back streets seethed with taverns and bordellos, where youthful ensigns and clerks – freed for the first time in their lives from adult supervision – frittered away their pay and contracted venereal diseases. And outside the European quarter squatted 'Black Town', a vast Indian settlement where the streets were filthy and unpaved, dogs and rats picked through piles of refuse, and houses that were little more than hovels piled up crazily against each other. Europeans never went there, but the thousands of Bengalis who scratched a living within its walls endured extremes of poverty and misery that were considered shocking, even at the time.

All this seemed very strange to newcomers to the Subcontinent. Novice writers and cadets freshly out from England – they were always known, for obscure reasons, as 'griffins' – were stock figures of fun in British India. The griffin 'fell off his horse, he shot the wrong birds, he speared domestic pigs [rather than wild hogs], he produced comic situations by using the wrong words and by misunderstanding Indian customs.'* Naive young officers of Sleeman's type were taken advantage of by nearly everyone they met.

A griffin's ordeal generally began the moment he stepped ashore, to be met by a collection of the rascals, touts and criminals common to ports throughout the world. Unwary novices were easily persuaded of the need to hire throngs of porters to carry their baggage, and a dragoman to command them, and the better-off might be tricked into paying over the odds for a fine horse or an unwieldy carriage. Such purchases were, of course, well beyond the means of all but the most affluent, but it did not take the new arrivals long to make the acquaintance of a moneylender who would be pleased to advance the necessary funds. So considerable were the loans, and so great the rate of interest, that it was common for Company men to remain in debt until they reached the rank of major, some 20 or 25 years after first stepping ashore in India.

Nor were the griffins' problems over once they were ensconced with their regiments. New men would be offered, as a 'particular favour', the opportunity to hire whatever useless servants their brother officers were anxious to be rid of, and the really unfortunate were taken in by some roguish major-domo, bearing apparently impeccable references, who would at once arrange for numerous friends and relatives to join the young man's household at inflated rates of pay.

In fairness to the unfortunate griffins, most officers arriving in India found

*A typical anecdote, told by Sleeman himself, concerned a British officer who asked the rajah of the district he was passing through to procure six bags of coffee (*kahwa*) for the mess. Next morning the man was disconcerted to be approached by a large party of the rajah's servants, who salaamed profoundly and laid at his feet six bulging sacks full of dead crows (*kawa*).

it difficult to make sense of the sheer quantity of servants they were expected
to employ. Indian households were anywhere between four and 10 times the
size of those at home in Britain. In part, this was because servants were cheap
in the Subcontinent, and there was a tendency to ostentation among the
wealthier British residents – in the richest households, according to one lady
who lived up-country from Madras, every horse had not only its own groom,
but a grass-cutter as well, and every dog a boy. ('I inquired,' the woman added,
'whether the cat had any servants, but found that she was allowed to wait upon
herself, and, as she seemed the only person in the establishment capable of
doing so, I respected her accordingly.') But the real problem, as those anxious
to economize quickly discovered, was caste, the Hindu social system that prevented servants from performing tasks that were properly the business of
another group. Maids could not be told to sweep, sweepers would not make
beds, and many officers employed men whose sole duty was to manage their
master's hookah. A British family living in Malaya in the first half of the nineteenth century, and employing Muslim servants, found that two or three staff
could do the work of a dozen or more of their equivalents in India.

The most senior officers were, of course, expected to employ the largest
retinue of servants. Somewhere between 30 and 40 was considered a mere
minimum,* enough for the officers concerned to be washed and shaved and
clothed and horsed and, when the time came for dinner, to be surrounded by
a 'living enclosure' of bearers flicking constantly at flies. But even Sleeman, as
a newly arrived ensign, was expected to allocate approximately half his
monthly salary of 100 rupees to pay for the most essential half a dozen servants. By the time he had reached the exalted rank of lieutenant and drew
three times that pay, he would have a retinue of a dozen.

The great majority of British officers soon grew used to the plethora of
servants and relied on them implicitly. This was, in part, because cadets
remained almost invariably single. Few Indian officers married before the
age of 40, the age when most could expect promotion to the rank of major
and with it the increase in pay that would at last enable them to support a wife

---

*Lord Minto, who succeeded Wellesley as Governor General, famously complained that on 'the first night
I went to bed in Calcutta I was followed by some 14 persons in white muslin nightgowns. One might have
hoped that some of these were ladies; but on finding that here were as many turbans and black beards as
gowns, I was very desirous that these bearded housemaids should leave me . . . which with some trouble and
perseverance I accomplished, and in that room I [now] enjoy a degree of privacy, but far from perfect.'

and children. The 'spins' (spinsters) of 'the fishing fleet' – as the single women, mostly plain, despatched each year to Bengal by their families in search of husbands, were cruelly known – understood this, and rarely displayed much interest in even the most dashing youths. 'India,' the lady of Madras explained, 'is the paradise of middle-aged gentlemen. When they are young they are thought nothing of; but at about 40 when they are "high in the service", rather yellow and somewhat grey, they begin to be taken notice of and called "young men". These respectable persons do all the flirtation too in a solemn sort of way, while the young ones sit by, looking on.' The perhaps inevitable consequence was that marriages between teenaged girls and men aged somewhere between 40 and 65 were commonplace.*

Freed from the responsibility of family life, the daily routine followed by most Company cadets varied only according to the season. Outside the cold weather, officers slept in string cots, with thin cotton rugs thrown over them, 'since a mattress would not only be unpleasantly hot but might breed fleas', and under a thick mosquito net. They rose at dawn in order to make the most of the few hours they had before the heat of the day. A plethora of servants helped their masters to wash, shave and dress. One soldier described how he was roused each morning by the sound of his valet making

> an oration by my bed . . . I wake, and see him salaaming with a cup of hot coffee in his hand. I sit on a chair and wash the teaspoon till the spoon is hot and the fluid cold (others less delicate, or perhaps disdainful of even so trifling an effort, hand the cup to the butler, who blows vigorously on it till the coffee is cool enough to drink) while he introduces me gradually into an ambush of pantaloons and Wellingtons. I am shut up in a red coat and a glazed lid set upon my head, and thus, carefully packed, exhibit my reluctance to do what I am going to do – to wit, my duty – by *riding*.

Morning exercise complete, Sleeman and his fellow officers took breakfast, and then went on parade or tackled administrative duties from 9 till 12; in the cold season office hours were from 10 until 1.30. Afternoons were spent sprawled in their cots, attempting to escape the awful temperatures; then, in

---

*One Bombay newspaper of the late eighteenth century announced the marriage 'at Tranquebar, [of] H. Meyes Esq., aged 64, to Miss Casina Couperas, a very accomplished lady of 16, after a courtship of five years.'

the early evenings, Company men and their wives emerged to take the air and promenade in their carriages along the wide boulevards of Calcutta's government district. Evenings were given over to balls and other entertainments, or to elaborately staged visits to each other's homes.

The working day being so short, there was plenty of time to devote to dining. Native dishes, widely consumed and appreciated a few decades earlier, were rarely eaten now. Instead, Indian cooks attempted traditional English favourites – Brown Windsor soup, cutlets and roasts, plum pudding – with varying results. Appetites, in Sleeman's day, were not quite so gross as they had been 10 or 20 years earlier, when one griffin was 'shocked to see one of the prettiest girls in Calcutta eating some two pounds of mutton chops in one sitting', and a peculiar craze for food fights was at its height. ('Formerly,' one veteran officer recalled, 'instead of drinking a Glass of Wine with a Gentleman, it was usual to throw a chicken at his Head – while the ladies pelted with Sweetmeats and Pastry. This was thought Refinement in Wit and Breeding.') Even so, breakfast generally consisted of a considerable profusion of 'rice, fried fish, eggs, omelettes, preserves, tea, coffee, etc.'. Tiffin – lunch – was taken 'at two o'clock in the very heat of the day . . . A soup, a roast fowl, curry and rice, a mutton pie, a forequarter of lamb, rice pudding, tarts, very good cheese, fresh churned butter, excellent Madeira . . .', and a similar but even larger array of dishes appeared at dinner. It was then that the most serious drinking took place, and again the quantities consumed were staggering. Even ladies typically finished off at least a bottle of wine every night. Gentlemen would drink more than that and then – after the women had withdrawn – dispose of as many as three bottles of claret apiece with their pipes and cigars. Such conspicuous consumption (which proved fatal to many an Indian career) was more or less compulsory. Any officer attempting to leave the table before his companions had finished their drinking 'would be pursued with cries of "Shabby fellow", "Milk sop" or "Cock tail".'

It is difficult to know how the peculiarities of Calcutta society affected Sleeman himself. Probably they repelled him. He was an austere man at heart, more serious and much more academically inclined than most of his colleagues. Social life, particularly the ostentatious conviviality of Calcutta, held little interest for him; letters to his family at home never mentioned women and satirized the conventions of the time, remarking on how ridiculous it was for men posted to distant stations to pay elaborately choreographed social calls upon each other during the heat of the day. Colleagues seem to have regarded him as sober, able, perhaps a little dry, but there was no suggestion, at this early date, that he was in any way exceptional. A routine Company assessment, dating to 1817, was neither effusive nor overtly critical, describing him as 'able, impartial and satisfactory'.

Sleeman's first decade in India was comparatively uneventful. His three years in Calcutta were broken by a short period of service in Bihar, followed by a posting to Mirzapore, a city on the Ganges. From there, his regiment marched north to Nepal, where it fought in the Gurkha Wars of 1814 and 1816. Sleeman was fortunate to survive these conflicts; half of the officers serving with him died, mostly of disease, and he himself contracted a severe case of 'Nathpore Fever' – malaria – that was to trouble him for the remainder of his life. But by 1817 he was in Allahabad, at the junction of the Jumna and the Ganges, stationed in a substantial cantonment with all the social obligations that entailed. There was little prospect, apparently, of further active service, and less of rapid promotion. It was there that the young lieutenant decided to apply to the Company's political service.

It had become obvious, even in the first years of Sleeman's service, that he was best suited to life up-country, in some little station where his talents would stand him in good stead, where officers worked longer hours than was the case in Calcutta, and where fewer social demands would be made upon him. Obtaining such a position was, however, far from easy. With few exceptions, the Company's military officers could expect postings to major cities dotted along the most important routes through the interior, or to large cantonments where substantial bodies of troops were concentrated. Positions up-country, offering greater responsibility and more scope for initiative, were largely the preserve of the political officers employed by the civil administration. And it was to this branch of the East India Company that Sleeman now transferred.

Sleeman was, by Indian standards, now in the prime of life. He was 29 years old, tall, stocky, with a round, open face and red-gold hair that was beginning to recede. His languages were by now so much better than those of the vast majority of his peers that he would be described, later in his career, as 'probably the only British official ever to have addressed the King of Oudh in correct Urdu and Persian'. His service in Nepal had helped him to add at least the elements of Pushtu and Gurkhali to his fluent Hindustani. Like many intelligent men born late in the eighteenth century, Sleeman was interested in almost everything: agronomy, ethnography, political economy, palaeontology – even the contentious subject of 'wolves nurturing children in their dens'. Politically a liberal free trader who once refused to commandeer private stores of grain to relieve distress during a famine, he was otherwise an eminently practical man. Later in his career he supervised the introduction of new varieties of Mauritian sugar cane to India, taught himself the art of printing, and even installed a small press in the parlour of his home so that he could print his own copies of the numerous reports and books he wrote.

Most significantly of all, Sleeman possessed a passionate interest, most unusual in any British officer of the time, in the lives of the 'respectable peasants' of India, among whom he found 'some of the best men that I have ever known'. This fascination with the local people dated to around 1816, when his service in Nepal had taken him into the foothills of the Himalayas to question landholders and farmers. From then on, Sleeman made a habit of talking to the people of all the districts through which he passed. He was insatiably curious about their customs and habits, their lands and rights, and their opinion of the East India Company itself. In time he developed a pronounced sympathy with the lot of peasant farmers prey to the exacting financial demands made by rapacious rajahs and zamindars, and indeed by the Company itself. Nor were these enthusiasms limited to mere conversation. They formed the bedrock of numerous official reports remarkable for their detail if not for their conciseness. The 800-page journal that Sleeman produced, during the 1840s, on the state of the Kingdom of Oudh was so much more detailed than any equivalent work that it remains, even today, the most complete source of information on the condition of that province in the early nineteenth century.

The love Sleeman professed for India and the Indians had its limits. He never doubted the superiority of European civilization, that the British soldier was innately superior to the sepoy, or that the Company's rule, for all its many exactions, was a considerable improvement on that of most native princes. He believed that the British system of justice, founded though it was on ideas (such as the private ownership of land) that had no direct parallel in India, could and should be imposed throughout the Company's territories. And he despised the peculation and corruption that were an established and inevitable part of government in India. But he never referred to his servants or his sepoys as 'blacks' or 'niggers', as did many of his contemporaries; he opposed the annexation of any state that had showed itself capable of ruling its people moderately and justly; and he was genuinely determined to improve the lot of the ordinary people of the Subcontinent.

This unusual agglomeration of skills and interests made Sleeman peculiarly well suited to the life of a political officer. The scattered members of this group, whether revenue collectors or magistrates,* were the men who actually ruled Britain's Indian empire. Each was placed – often in his late twenties or early thirties, and without any special training – in charge of a district that was home to several hundred thousand people. 'Politicals' were required to be conversant with rural India and well versed in its customs and languages; self-confidence and self-sufficiency were necessary and highly prized. Help, in the shape of the nearest military force, could be several days' ride away, and the work was physically arduous. Officers toured throughout their districts, calling on Indian notables, inspecting the land, hearing legal cases, and – in the absence of British clerks – writing out their own reports in longhand and in duplicate. One, serving a few years later in the Maratha country, described a routine of almost constant work:

> Up at 5am, and go out about the survey of the roads. In by 8 o'clock and answer letters, English and Mahratta, till ten; bathe and breakfast over at eleven. Then to cutcherry [court] work, trials, etc. till 6pm, without stirring – often, indeed, until seven. Dine and sit an hour or so with Palmer, if he is there, or with some native friend, by way of a rest, which brings up the time to half-past eight or nine. Then to my room, and work at translations and other business till eleven or twelve. Count up all this and you will see there is no time for anything except hard work.

What made the job worthwhile, of course, was the enticing prospect of freedom of action. Unlike an army lieutenant, whose every duty was ordered from above, political officers possessed 'broad and broadly undefined' powers that made them little princes in their own districts. The best used their

*Promotion, in either branch, followed an established pattern. Revenue officers advanced from the rank of assistant to collector and eventually commissioner of revenue. Those who – like Sleeman – belonged to the legal and administrative branch started as assistants and were promoted to joint magistrate, full magistrate, and – after perhaps 20 years' service – to the rank of judge or commissioner.

influence to improve the administration and the infrastructure of their territories – and, by extension, the lives of the Indians who lived within them. The
worst rode roughshod over local feelings, cowed the notables of their districts,
and extracted the maximum in rents and taxes. Either way, the very nature of
the job ensured that a political officer's actions 'were almost invariably high-
handed and independent, lacking precedent, and – given the unavoidable
delays in communication – without the endorsement of "higher authority"'.

The work suited Sleeman perfectly. It was also a real step up. The Company's
civil servants saw themselves as far superior to their military brethren. They
certainly took more responsibility and were significantly better paid, being
known to the avaricious women of the fishing fleet as 'three-hundred-dead-
or-alive men' because most earned a salary of about £300 per annum and the
same sum was payable, once they had accumulated a few years' service, to
their widows should they die. The soldiers, whose jobs were – if not as
taxing – certainly more dangerous, resented the politicals and found them
arrogant. Before long they were calling them 'The Heaven Born', a derisive
reference to the Brahmins who comprised the highest Hindu caste and considered themselves 'twice-born'. The lady of Madras recalled that one
evening, at dinner, an army officer turned to her and said: 'Now I know very
well, Mrs ____, you despise us all from the bottom of your heart; you think
no one worth speaking to in reality but the Civil Service. Whatever people
may really be, you just class them all as civil and military – civil and military;
and you know no other distinction. Is it not so?'[*]

Sleeman's first posting, as a freshly minted political officer, was to the town of
Jubbulpore in central India. The job was scarcely one of the administration's
plums. The beauty of the surrounding countryside did make it perhaps

> the pleasantest of Indian stations; situated in a green hollow among low
> rocky granite hills always covered with verdure; with tidy hard roads and
> plenty of greensward about them . . . remarkable for the delicacy and abun-
> dance of its fruits and other garden products, including the pineapple,
> which will not grow anywhere else in Central India.

---

[*]To which the lady replied, 'with some spirit': 'No; I sometimes class them as civil and uncivil.'

But Jubbulpore itself was of little intrinsic importance, being merely a collection of neat, low houses and listless markets, built amidst ponds and lakes, clustering in the lee of a second-rate Maratha fort and sustained by traffic passing through on the main road leading from Poona to the Ganges. Even 50 years after Sleeman's time, when another British officer posted to the central provinces enquired about the town, he found it was a station 'of which few who had not been there knew anything, except that it was situated somewhere in the wilds . . . I remember when we first got our orders to march there from Upper India, no one could give us a route to it.'

Life in Jubbulpore was harsh. Although the climate was by no means so severe as that of northern India, temperatures still rose precipitately during the hot season, and many of the whitewashed bungalows dotted across the district were provided with not one but two thatched roofs, one over the other, to help keep out the sun. During the hot weather the windows and doors could be covered with screens of dampened *khas-khas* grass, which cooled and perfumed such gasps of wind as could be made to enter, but relays of servants were still required to labour inside the buildings, tugging lazily at *punkahs*, the thick cotton mats that swung to and fro from all the ceilings to circulate currents of air.*

The most unpleasant single aspect of existence around Jubbulpore was undoubtedly the plague of insects, and it was remarked upon by many visitors. 'Moths, flying ants, beetles – besides creatures which leap or crawl' were all attracted to lights left burning after sunset; and they appeared in such profusion that, one disgruntled officer complained, 'Sometimes dinner is a difficult task, as they may even make the tablecloth more black than white, so numerous are they . . . They settle on the food as it is being passed from one's plate to the mouth, and the fork and spoon has to be

---

*The *punkah* (ancient) and the *khas-khas* screen (introduced in the 1780s) were the most advanced technologies available for cooling homes when Sleeman arrived in central India. Not until 1830–2 was anything better invented: this was the fearsome-looking thermantidote, 'a wooden machine nine feet long, four feet broad and seven high', which sat on the verandah outside a window. The window was removed and in its place a khas-khas mat was fixed. A hole was cut in this to take a funnel projecting from the thermantidote. Inside were four fans turned by hand which drove the air into the room. To cool the air, two large circular holes were cut in the sides of the machine in which grass mats were fixed. Water was dripped from perforated troughs above onto these mats, and the surplus water fell into other troughs below to be used again in the troughs above. The thermantidote's chief defect was that it required at least six coolies to work it, not to mention reserves.

shaken to drive them off before the mouthful can be taken.' Worse still were the swarms of ants; the red and black varieties found their way into stores of food, or dropped from the ceilings into bowls of marmalade or sugar, while the even more voracious white ants attacked clothes and paper, 'sometimes eating important documents and small articles of clothing so quickly as to destroy them in a single night'. Dining tables stood in bowls of water, and uniforms were stored in sealed tin boxes, to deter attack.

For all these reasons, Jubbulpore was little visited by British officers. The town's only real significance lay in the fact that it had been chosen as the administrative capital of a district bounded to the north by the town of Saugor and to the south by the valley of the Nerbudda river, and known accordingly as the Saugor & Nerbudda Territory. This province, which had been British for only two years when Sleeman arrived there in 1820, was in a ruinous state. It had been acquired as a result of a campaign waged by the Company against vicious bands of freebooters known as Pindaris, whose ranks were filled with former soldiers and armed retainers thrown out of work by the British-imposed peace that had descended upon India since Wellesley's day. For more than a decade, Pindari bands with a combined strength of as many as 50,000 men had looted and raided their way across the district, often at the behest of one or other of the rival Maratha princes. Most of the villages of Saugor & Nerbudda were sacked and plundered at least once during these years; many of the inhabitants were killed or compelled to abandon their homes. It was only in 1818, with the final destruction of the marauders and the defeat of their Maratha overlords, that any sort of order was restored.* Even then, it took years for the territory to recover. Sleeman thus reached Jubbulpore to find the surrounding districts still in turmoil and his task by and large a thankless one.

To begin with, Saugor & Nerbudda was unusually isolated. It was the only British possession in the central provinces, being completely surrounded by at least nominally independent territories. The district itself was tableland,

---

*One Pindari leader, Chitu, remained defiant. Refusing to surrender, he and a dwindling band of followers were at large for more than a year. At length, when even the most loyal of his retainers had deserted him, the Pindari sought sanctuary in the jungle near Asigurh, where, some time later, his horse was discovered grazing by a track, its saddlebags stuffed with coins. Chitu's pursuers followed his trail into the forest, discovering, first, bloodstained clothing, then pieces of bone, and finally their quarry's crudely severed head. It was concluded that this most feared of mercenaries had been ambushed by a lurking tiger.

largely flat and fertile, but much of the highest ground was nothing but bare rock, and to the north 'it appears to a traveller as if hills, small and great, have been sown broadcast over the face of the country'. Much of the countryside had been depopulated and in many places jungle was encroaching on once-flourishing settlements. Then there was the matter of the Company's rents and revenues, which were falling well below Calcutta's expectations.

It took Sleeman two years to learn to meet this challenge. He had been sent to Jubbulpore as assistant to Charles Welland, the Company's political agent in the new province, and served what was effectively an apprenticeship. Only in 1822, after two years in the town, did he at last receive orders to proceed to the village of Nursingpore, 50 miles to the south, to take charge of a district of his own.

Nursingpore was Sleeman's first independent command, and his responsibilities were considerable. His predecessor's attempts to increase the district's revenues had ended in 'disastrous failure', there were few records to show what rents and taxes had been paid, and it was in the landholders' interests to deceive the new district officer as to the true figures if they could. It took months of touring, and many long hours of compiling and copying reports, to even begin to set matters straight. The three years that Sleeman spent in Nursingpore were, he would later recall, 'by far the most laborious of my life'.

In these difficult circumstances, as the newly qualified political officer would freely admit, the presence of a Thug gang in a nearby village entirely eluded Sleeman. He expected ordinary crime – the spate of assaults and petty burglaries and the occasional acts of dacoity that so inevitably occurred in the aftermath of the Pindari wars – and he tackled this as vigorously as he could: 'No ordinary robbery or theft could be committed without my becoming acquainted with it; nor was there a robber or a thief of the ordinary kind in the district, with whose character I had not become acquainted.' But Thuggee remained very much a mystery.

'If any man had then told me,' Sleeman confessed more than a decade later,

that a gang of assassins by profession resided in the village of Kundelee, not 400 yards from my court, and that the extensive groves of the village of Mundesur, only one stage from me, on the road to Saugor and Bhopaul,

[were] one of the greatest Beles, or places of murder in all India; and that large gangs from Hindustan and the Deccan used to rendezvous in those groves, remain in them for many days together each year, and carry on their dreadful trade along all the lines of the road that pass by and branch off from them, with the knowledge and connivance of the two land holders by whose ancestors those groves had been planted, I should have thought him a fool or a mad man; and yet nothing could have been more true. The bodies of a hundred travellers [lay] buried in and around the groves of Mundesur; and a gang of assassins lived in and about the village of Kundelee while I was Magistrate of the district, and extended their depredations to the cities of Poona and Hyderabad.

Sleeman's failure to appreciate the threat posed by Thuggee was, of course, far from unusual, even in the early 1820s. More than a decade after Perry and Wright had first made their discoveries, few British officers knew much about the stranglers. Their depredations were still seldom reported, and most British soldiers and administrators were simply too busy in their towns and cantonments to spare much thought for the dangers confronting anonymous travellers passing through their districts. But that did not mean the Thug gangs were not active; most, indeed, became bolder and more deadly once the Pindaris were suppressed and travel through India became safer once again. Out there, out in the mofussil, the subjects of the Company still lived and died in ways that men such as Sleeman barely understood.

CHAPTER 9

'A Very Good Remuneration for Murdering a Man'

'bunjj – merchandise; the wealthy travellers craved by Thugs'

North of Bombay and west of Indore, a group of two dozen men came hurrying along a narrow track. They were Bundelcund Thugs, 'the stoutest and most active' members of five gangs that had joined forces to scour the countryside around Baroda, and they were in an ugly mood.

Their expedition had opened well. They had strangled 30 people in ten separate affairs, and taken a fair quantity of loot, including the best part of 2,000 rupees' worth of gold from a group of sepoys whom they had killed a month or so earlier. Since then, however, the gangs had been casting about for other travellers with very limited success. Scouts had been despatched to all points of the compass while the main body loitered, waiting for news, but in the last fortnight their only victims had been three unlucky passers-by who had blundered into their camp. Their bodies had not yielded much, and – even more frustratingly – when at last a group of spies did hasten in with news of a potential haul, it was already almost out of their grasp.

The prize was a party of treasure-bearers, heading west. There were four of them, carrying their goods in bulky packs slung over their shoulders. But it had taken the scouts several days to return to camp, and by now the bearers were, they guessed, at least six days' travel away. The only hope of catching them was for a group of the fastest men to set off in pursuit at once, travelling by forced marches until they overtook their quarry.

Thus it was that 25 exhausted Thugs found themselves a stage or two east of Baroda, having covered nearly 80 miles in no more than two days. There they at last sighted the bearers and, falling in with them, walked on a little way until they came to a deserted spot where all four were set upon and murdered. As soon as the bodies were safely concealed, the Thugs turned to rifle through the packs, fully expecting to find a horde of jewels and silver. But, one recalled later on, 'to the great disappointment and chagrin of us all, no property was found upon them, for they turned out to be common stone-cutters, and their tools tied up in bundles . . . [had] deceived the spies into the supposition that they were carrying treasure'.

The arduous pursuit of the Baroda stonecutters demonstrates just how precarious life could be for a Thug. Even the members of a successful gang – killing regularly, escaping unmolested, and stumbling occasionally across a substantial prize – seldom made so much money that they could afford to remain idle for long; and the Thugs' habit of banding together into groups 50 to 100 strong, which made it possible for them to tackle large parties of travellers, also meant that the loot they did seize tended to be divided among so many men that only the gangs' leaders saw an appreciable return. Successful subadars and jemadars could certainly become wealthy men – there are accounts of such men spending thousands of rupees on weddings and family celebrations – but the lesser members of their gangs had to be content with a great deal less.

Estimating the value of a typical Thug haul is difficult, for it was generally partly or wholly made up of the victims' goods or possessions, rather than cash. But the gangs involved in the Baroda affair split 2,150 rupees between nearly 80 men that year, and in another case a Thug who scrupulously listed every murder he had been involved with over a 24-month period came up with a total of 1,300 rupees, taken from 61 victims and split between about 20 men – an average of less than 33 rupees per man per year. Even this meagre income had to be set against the protection money demanded by the Thugs' landlords or the police, not to mention the expenses of a typical expedition, largely borne by the jemadars, which one witness put at around 500 rupees for a single gang. Supplemented though it was by the sale of loot – sundry items of cloth and cooking utensils were the most common booty – it is evident that many Thugs barely scraped a living from their trade.

For this reason, most gangs were careful in their choice of victims when circumstances allowed. Thug scouts became expert in calculating the value of each potential prize; a favourite tactic was to loiter at rural customs posts while the officers there searched travellers' baggage for contraband. Potential victims with no money would occasionally be spared, though there were also cases of gangs savagely mutilating the corpses of men who had failed to yield the expected plunder. Individual Thugs described hauls of 10 or 12 rupees as 'trifling', and one of a single rupee – the equivalent of a week's wages for the meanest Indian labourer – as 'paltry', though when they were desperately short of cash gangs would gladly kill for even the tiniest amounts. Eight annas – not much more than half a rupee – 'is a very good remuneration for murdering a man', a Thug named Shumsherah thought. 'We often strangle a victim who is suspected of having two pice.' But Shumsherah was a weaver who Thugged only occasionally, and he seems to have been more easily satisfied than many of his comrades. Experienced men, and particularly those who came from a long line of stranglers, had more ambition, and they were far from indiscriminate.

The greatest of all Thug hauls seems to have been the enormous sum of 200,000 rupees, seized in Candeish early in the nineteenth century by 'Bowanee the Soosea and his gang of Rajpootana', and consisting of remittances on their way from Bombay to Indore. Another strangler, named Jhora Naek, was greatly venerated by generations of Thugs for the honesty he displayed after killing a man found to have 160,000 rupees' worth of jewels on him. Although he had committed the murder accompanied only by a servant, Jhora took the booty back to his village and divided it among the members of his gang as though all of them had been present. The saintly reputation he acquired suggests such steadfastness was unusual, and though many Thugs prided themselves on their honesty (at least when it came to dealing with colleagues) it was certainly not unheard of for men who chanced upon really substantial quantities of loot to keep it for themselves. The largest sum ever taken by the Murnae Thugs – a haul of about 130,000 rupees, seized south of the Nerbudda in about 1790 – caused huge dissension among the members of the gang, for Rae Singh, Feringeea's uncle, purloined a gigantic diamond worth 65,000 rupees from the loot and, in the ensuing fracas, was stabbed in the belly by a rival, 'causing his bowels to burst out'. A sheet of beaten silver was quickly pressed over the wound, and Rae Singh survived to sell his diamond and become a great man in the district, but he was 'for a long time obliged to wear the silver plate'.

Hauls of such magnitude were, however, very unusual. In the first two decades of the nineteenth century, only one other group of Thugs seized a lakh of rupees in a single affair, and most gangs seem to have been fortunate to realize as much as 1,000 rupees in the course of an entire expedition. There were, of course, exceptions; what became known as the 'Sixty Soul Affair' – the strangling of a large party of Muslim men and women in 1805 – yielded 26,500 rupees, and the 'Murder of Forty' near Nagpore in 1809–10 another 17,000 – but the men who committed these crimes had to work hard for the money. In the Sixty Soul Affair, several gangs of Thugs travelled with their intended victims for about two weeks, 'winning more and more upon their confidence every day', and covered upwards of 160 miles while awaiting the right moment to strike. The booty, moreover, was once again divided among a large number of men. As many as 600 Thugs were involved in the Murder of Forty, which must mean most saw less than 30 rupees from even this enormous haul.

The difficulty experienced by the many stranglers who struggled to make a living from Thuggee was not in itself surprising. More and more men were being driven to join such gangs by desperation and grinding poverty, for the 1820s were a poor time for much of central India. There was famine every year from 1824 until 1827, and between 1827 and 1832 a new and strange disease blighted the wheat crop in central India. These misfortunes, together with the fierce rents imposed by an East India Company anxious to recoup the vast expenses of its Pindari and Maratha wars, reduced thousands of peasants to misery, and badly depressed the economy. Yet, paradoxically, the indigenous bankers of Bombay, Poona and Indore had rarely been so busy, and had never sent so many huge remittances to and fro across the central provinces. Their businesses were booming; profits were up. This success, and their great wealth, was based largely upon the trade in a single product: opium.

Opium was one of India's biggest exports. Manufacture of the drug was legal at this time – contemporary medical opinion held that it was considerably less harmful than alcohol or tobacco – and the poppies from which opium is harvested were grown across great swathes of the Company's territories, particularly in Bengal and Bihar. They were also the most important crop in Malwa, a fertile plateau to the north-west of the Saugor & Nerbudda Territory. The profits on the Bengal trade alone were enormous – around two million rupees a year at the beginning of the nineteenth century, and as much as eight million fifteen years later. The trade in Malwa opium, which remained in Indian hands, was perhaps less lucrative, but it was nevertheless substantial. Hundreds of private traders from Bombay and the central provinces were involved in manufacturing the drug.

Opium had been known in India since the eighth century, when it was introduced by Arab invaders, and its properties as both a narcotic and a painkiller were widely recognized by the time the first English traders arrived in the Subcontinent. Morphine – which is its main ingredient – dispels cares, dulls pain, and induces sensations of weightlessness and, eventually, lassitude. Taken as a pill (this was the 'opium-eating' famously described by De Quincey) or smoked in a pipe, the oriental way, it is also highly addictive. John Company's greatest general, Robert Clive, died of an overdose of opium in 1774; William Wilberforce, the anti-slavery campaigner, was prescribed it as a young man and remained an opium-eater until his death. The drug was even more popular in China, where it was known as 'foreign mud'. By the late 1820s, more than 2,500 tons of processed opium were being shipped from India to Canton each year, and the money the Company made from its sale, together with the duty it levied on private traders, made up one-seventh of its revenues.

The opium trade was, indeed, so lucrative that the government in Calcutta did everything it could to keep it to itself. The Company maintained a strict monopoly on the cultivation of poppies in its own territories; landowners had to obtain permission to grow the crop, and heavy fines were imposed on unlicensed production. Similar restrictions also applied in Malwa, for most of the tableland was divided between Holkar and Sindhia, two of the Company's princely allies, and they were bound by treaty to uphold the monopoly in their lands. Malwa opium should – the government insisted – be shipped only to Bombay, and purchased solely by the Presidency's agents.

The Indian response to this edict was entirely predictable. Illicit opium production increased, and cargoes were diverted to native ports along the western coast to avoid the swingeing duty at Bombay. Shipments were sewn into saddles or hidden inside bales of cotton, and smuggled out of Malwa along unfrequented jungle paths. Efforts to curtail this illegal trade were fruitless, for the princes themselves connived in it, and in 1819 the Company grudgingly accepted that the monopoly was unenforceable. Attempts to suppress smuggling were curtailed, and by 1830 an estimated 10,000 chests of Indian-owned opium were being shipped to China from the west coast ports each year – three times the total despatched by the British from Bombay.

The Company had, in short, underestimated the ingenuity of Indian merchants and bankers determined to profit from the trade in drugs. But, ironically, this native success presented the Thugs of the central provinces with opportunities they could scarcely have dreamed of when the monopoly was in force. Throughout the 1820s Thug gangs occasionally chanced upon and seized small consignments of smuggled opium. The rapid growth of the Malwa trade, moreover, required substantial investment, and increasingly large sums of money began to make their way to and fro between the landowners and merchants of the district and the great financiers of the central provinces.

The transfer of funds on so large a scale was not unusual in India, which had an ancient and sophisticated economy. The existence of bankers – *seths* – had been recorded as early as the sixth century BC, and by the time the first Europeans reached the Subcontinent the industry had grown deep roots. 'In India,' the French traveller Tavenier noted in the 1670s,

> a village must be very small indeed if it has not a money-changer who acts as a banker to make remittances of money and issue letters of exchange . . . All the Jews who occupy themselves with money and exchange in the empire of the Grand Seigneur* pass for being very sharp; but in India they would scarcely be apprentices to these Changers.

These village bankers, he went on, did more than exchange the coins issued by the Company and the many Native States – a profitable business until the British imposed the Madras rupee as the single Indian currency in 1835. They were mainstays of their local economies, advancing money to villagers who wished to buy tools and seed, and the Frenchman was deeply impressed by their parsimony and intelligence. A village money-changer would, for example, discount the value of a rupee according to its age, since a silver coin lost an infinitesimal amount of precious metal each time it was handled. In the same way, Tavenier observed,

---

*The Sultan of the Ottoman Empire – the greatest of powers in Tavenier's day.

of all the gold which remains on the touchstone after an assay has been made, and of which we here make no account, far from allowing such a thing to be lost, they collect it with the aid of a ball, made half of black pitch and half of wax, with which they rub the stone which carries the gold, and at the end of some years they burn the ball and so obtain the gold which has accumulated.

The village money-changer's methods were not, in fact, too far removed from those employed by the greatest of the city bankers. They, too, diversified and took care to account for every pice, though the greatest of them – such as the famous Jaggat Seths of Calcutta, whose money underpinned the business of the East India Company itself – were fast becoming huge concerns. The seths faced little competition from the British, whose own Indian banking operations were geared to the overseas trade, and by the 1820s many had become prominent dealers in both cotton and grain. Opium, which was far more profitable than either, naturally attracted them.

Most of the seths of central India had their headquarters in Poona, Bombay or Indore. The majority were members of the Marwari caste – famously clever businessmen who learned mathematics and accounting from the age of 12. Young seths soon achieved a mastery of mental arithmetic that astounded Europeans. 'To give an instance of their efficiency,' one Indian writing early in the last century observed, 'while an English-educated graduate may take five minutes to work out on a piece of paper the compound interest on a given sum, the Marwari boy will get an answer correct to the nearest pice mentally, without the aid of pen and paper, in less than half a minute.'

This expertise struck visitors as all the more remarkable when they saw the cramped establishments from which many of the seths did business. Even the grandest Indian banks bore little resemblance to the monolithic temples of commerce found in European capitals, and a British traveller calling at the office of a Poona seth early in the nineteenth century discovered that

this bank, in which large sums are deposited and extensive business transacted, was nothing but a mud house plastered over within and without. The counter was an inclined platform reaching from the front to nearly the whole length of the building; on it squatted, cross-legged, surrounded with

bags of all kinds of money, a Mahratta banker with his handsome countenance and keen piercing black eyes, talking to his customers, discounting
bills, and counting money with astonishing rapidity and ease.

In this establishment, too, the seth's young child was a centre of attention.
The banks of central India were invariably family concerns, whose histories
could be traced in the names they gave their houses – the firm of Mahanand
Ram Puran Mal, for example, had been established by a Mahanand Ram and
passed to his son, Puran Mal. The Poona seth, too, must have had hopes of his
child, for

the bank was managed, in the absence of his father, by a young Hindoo boy
who could not have been over 12 years of age. This youthful cashier astonished us with his accuracy and quickness in counting and discounting
money. His only account-book, as far as I could see, was a flat board covered
with fine white sand. On this primitive slate he made all his calculations,
writing them down with his forefinger. When he had finished he blew
away the sand and handed over the amount due, with interest for odd days,
etc., all calculated with the nicest accuracy down to the smallest fraction.

It meant something, of course, to be heir to such a business. Like modern
banking conglomerates, Indian seths often operated branches in a number of
towns. The largest firms might have as many as seven – the house of Bhyaram
Gopal Das, headquartered in Benares, also operated in Calcutta, Nagpore,
Poona, Bombay and at least three other cities. Some even maintained agencies
overseas, in Japan, Aden or Abyssinia. The banking houses of central India
tended to be more modest concerns; the majority had no more than one or at
best two local branches in addition to their headquarters, run by agents known
as *gomashtas* who took care of business in the provinces. But even these firms
thought nothing of sending remittances totalling tens of thousands of rupees
to and fro, and it was small wonder that the bankers' agents were closely
supervised and expected to report to their seth master on a regular basis.

By the mid-1820s, a good part of many a gomashta's task was to facilitate
the flow of cash into the central provinces. A large part of this money was
advanced to the landowners who grew the poppies from which Malwa opium
was made. The manufacture of the drug was a difficult and time-consuming

business, and it required substantial capital. Every mature poppy in a field of several thousand had to be scored, by hand, with a special three-pronged implement resembling a fork. At night a sticky residue oozed from each incision, and when morning came a host of men, women and children flocked into the fields to scrape this raw opium from each flower. This process was repeated daily for about a month, until the poppies no longer yielded the residue; then the drug was mixed with linseed oil, to prevent evaporation, patted into cakes three or four inches in diameter, and left to dry in the shade. Next, the cakes were taken to a local opium factory – most likely financed by the same bankers – where the oil was drained away and they were crushed together into 3lb balls. Each ball was coated with leaves gummed together with an inferior grade of poppy juice to form an inch-thick protective shell, and this processed opium was then packed into cases, 40 balls to a chest, ready for sale and shipment to China.

The growth of the opium trade was so swift and so considerable that it changed the pattern of banking in central India. It was this, in turn, that presented new opportunities to the Thugs and drew men who normally based themselves along the Jumna and in Bundelcund into districts such as Nursingpore. In normal circumstances, only a small portion of the funds sent by one seth to another was remitted in cash. Large payments were normally made in the form of *hoondees*, 'bankers' cheques written on a thick country-made paper, rolled up and fastened with gum-water'. Each hoondee carried 'a secret mark or sign that renders forgery difficult', and could only be cashed at the designated branch of a certain bank; like modern cheques they were useless to thieves, and when the Thugs found one on the body of a murdered traveller, they would generally burn it. But since dealing in opium without the sanction of the Company remained illegal, traders preferred to deal in cash, and native bankers also began to send treasure to Malwa and Indore to take advantage of the favourable exchange rates prevailing there. Before long, huge quantities of gold and jewels were passing through central India in the care of special parties of treasure-bearers.

These bearers played an important part in the economy of central India. They were generally implicitly reliable men of superior caste, proficient at concealing treasure, hiding gold in their baggage and jewels in their hair. Most preferred to travel in disguise, and in small groups, because trusting to an escort – even an armed guard – merely attracted the attention of dacoits and thieves. This reliance on subterfuge, however, made them all the more desirable to the Thugs, who generally refrained from tangling with large parties of armed men.

Certainly it was not long before the Thug jemadars such as Feringeea realized that their best hope of seizing a substantial sum was to take it from a party of treasure-bearers. Identifying the seths' men was, of course, a tricky business. Every few years, however, a courier would prove careless, or the Thugs' spies too adept, and one gang or another would chance upon a huge quantity of booty. In 1807 a party of 17 bearers were murdered on the road between Jubbulpore and Saugor, the Thugs rifling their corpses so thoroughly that they left 'nothing but naked bodies lying in the grove, with their eyes apparently starting out of their sockets'. Another group was strangled on the Nerbudda, at Jhansee Ghat, in 1820; and three years later a group of Deccan Thugs seized 14,000 rupees from another party of five bearers. Luck, too, played its part, as it did when, on one notorious occasion, a filthy, raggedly dressed and fly-infested fakir attached himself to Feringeea's gang on the road to Hyderabad. The man was evidently absolutely destitute, and the Thugs were reluctant to kill him and tried three times to shake him off. On each occasion, however, the obdurate mendicant returned to beg for their protection. When the gang at last lost patience and strangled him, they were startled to discover he was a treasure-bearer in disguise, carrying no fewer than 365 strings of pearls.

It was the gomashtas' job to arrange such shipments of cash, to hire bearers, agree a route, settle on appropriate disguises, and pursue and recover any remittances that might be lost. Assignments of this sort, difficult though they were, were nothing new to them. Most were 'invested with very wide powers; they are not highly paid, but their industry, integrity, and efficiency are remarkable and proverbial'. Their resourcefulness was sometimes severely tested – when the bankers of the central provinces had first begun to invest in opium, their gomashtas were sometimes charged with smuggling the drug to the coast, bribing the local authorities and protecting the shipments from theft and seizure along the way – but they were seldom found wanting. And when the Thugs tangled with the firm of Dhunraj Seth Pokur Mal, a substantial bank with its headquarters in the far north of Hyderabad, they found the bank's agent in Malwa fully their equal – not merely in resourcefulness, but in savagery as well.

CHAPTER 10

The Devil's Banker

'bunar – a bad road for Thugs'

Thug gangs had begun to stumble upon Indian bankers' treasure parties with increasing regularity in the mid-1820s. One of the earliest groups of bearers to fall into their hands was a body of 13 men and a single woman from Poona, murdered near the Tapti river in 1826. A Thug jemadar named Budloo and his men had fallen in with the bearers nearly a week earlier, and walked with their intended victims across much of the province of Candeish, waiting for the chance to strangle them. Their victims were leading a number of horses piled with baggage which, when searched, proved to contain not only a good quantity of merchandise but also the enormous sum of 25,000 rupees in cash and gold bars. But even this great loss was little more than a foretaste of the disasters of 1828 and 1829, when a further 135,000 rupees' worth of cash and jewels were seized in the course of another three affairs and 19 more bearers were killed.

The first of these robberies was carried out five miles outside the town of Malagow in the division of Nasik. The district, together with its northern neighbour, Candeish, was still a 'disturbed and deserted' area and had only recently been ceded to the Company and incorporated into the Bombay Presidency; 'in order to prevent sudden and extensive changes', it had been administered directly by the Governor General in Calcutta until 1827. Northern Candeish, and the far western portions of both divisions, were relatively wealthy areas. But the remainder of the district, which included

Malagow and the land around it, was bordered in the north by the wild Satpuda hills and in the south by long stretches of desolate ridges. Within these bounds, Candeish and Nasik consisted mostly of 'rolling broken ground . . . much of it, from fear of wild beasts, waste or covered with brushwood'. Towards the west lay expanses of 'wide, stony, thorny plains, rising in broad ridges, or sinking in rich valleys studded with mango groves and large prosperous villages'. To the south, around Malagow itself, the land was flat and treeless – a substantial plain surrounded on three sides by a horseshoe of low, steep, flat-topped hills.

At least half the land here was either abandoned during the Maratha wars or had never been cultivated, and much of the remainder had been devastated in the course of the Pindari campaign. The weather, though not hot by Indian standards, was humid and notoriously unhealthy, for visiting Europeans required time to acclimatize; and the roads were terrible. In 1828, after a decade of Company rule, almost all were – a government official later recalled – still mere tracks, 'ill-appointed and deficient in everything but discomfort and danger. Few and far between were the miserable hamlets, and the mountain passes were as rugged and impracticable as their fierce possessors.' Even the main route through the district, the Bombay to Agra trunk road that ran through Malagow to Doolea and beyond, was scarcely maintained before 1850. It was ideal territory for the Thugs. The Company's authority was weak, there were plenty of travellers on the great trunk road, and so many ill-frequented tracks that it was easy to escape the scene of a murder.

It was at Malagow itself that Feringeea and his men first encountered the seths' treasure-bearers. There were four of them, going from Poona to Indore with 22,000 rupees in gold and jewels, and they were accompanied by three other travellers and no fewer than six other Thug gangs, 225 men in all. The first of these gangs had fallen in with the bearers on the road four stages from Poona, and the others – alerted to the discovery of the treasure – had joined up with the party further along the way. They had hoped to kill the bearers at the river crossing outside the town, and been frustrated by the appearance of some of the Company's cavalry. Now they were planning to murder the men as they made their way north into Candeish.

The arrival of Feringeea's group brought the number of Thugs trailing the seths' party to 250. Most were experienced men, but one gang, led by a man named Omrow, was less reliable, being 'composed chiefly of fellows of all castes whom he had scraped together, to make up a gang for this expedition'. Worried by the sheer number of Thugs who had been drawn to the bearers like flies to freshly butchered meat, and sure that these novices would be more trouble than they were worth, Feringeea and the other jemadars sent 30 of the rawest men on ahead, 'that they might not, by their blunders, frustrate our designs upon the treasure-bearers', and ordered a second group to remain in Malagow. The remaining gangs, now 125 strong, watched the bearers from a distance until the men packed up their belongings and left town an hour before dawn next morning. The Thugs followed, trailing their doomed victims at a distance, and – being unable to shake off the Company messenger and two cotton-cleaners who still accompanied the bearers – killed all seven only half a mile along the road shortly before daybreak. The treasure they had been carrying was found to consist of golden coins and jewellery, and once they were well clear of the vicinity, the Thugs set to haggling over the division of their haul.

This proved to be a tricky business, for Omrow claimed – as was the custom – a full share for his novice followers even though they had played no part in the killings. After considerable wrangling it was decided to split the money equally among the gangs involved, and leave the members of each to decide how best to share their loot with those of their men who had been elsewhere. Each of the Thugs actually involved in the murders thus received between 80 and 125 rupees, as much as 35 rupees more than they would have expected in normal circumstances; and two of the gangs did indeed adhere to their own code of honour by dividing the money they had received with those who had been sent elsewhere.

Early the next year, 1829, four Thug gangs were making their way south through Candeish once again when they chanced upon an even larger consignment of treasure. On this occasion, perhaps as a consequence of the grievous losses of the previous years, the number of bearers had been increased to eight, armed with matchlocks and provided with camels to carry their baggage. This group gave the Thugs a good deal of trouble: 'They went fast,' one strangler explained, 'and, afraid to appear near to them in a body, we several times lost all trace of them.' The seths' men were cautious, too; they laid false trails, telling the people of the bazaars where they rested that they were heading for a certain town, then taking a different road. At least twice the Thugs were themselves deceived, and had to send out scouts in all directions, promising rewards of 100 rupees, over and above their share of the booty, to the men who relocated the treasure party. On the second occasion they were extremely fortunate to stumble across the bearers on the Indore road, more than 60 hours after losing them.

The triumphant scouts hurried back to their gangs. There was no time to rest. The Thugs – all 112 of them – set off at once after the treasure, 'although we were much tired', finally catching up with their intended victims at midnight on the third day of the chase and making camp close by. Both parties rose early the next morning, and the Thugs followed the bearers over the Nerbudda river at Burwaha Ghat, where customs men detained the members of the treasure party. As they passed by, the Thugs had the grim satisfaction of hearing the matchlock-men protest bitterly at 'the hardship of being obliged to expose the value of their charge in an unsettled country'; and they went on only a short way before stopping for the night in 'a small deserted village in the midst of a jungly waste'. They would wait for the bearers there.

'It was about nine o'clock in the morning when they reached the place,' one of the Thugs recalled.

The party consisted of eight men, mounted on camels, and a merchant, by name Futteh Alee, who had joined them on the road in the hope of being more secure in their company than alone . . . The signal was given; we rushed in upon the camels, seized them by their bridles, and made them sit down by beating them with sticks. The men were seized and killed; some were strangled, some stabbed with spears, and some cut down with swords. Futteh Alee was pulled off his pony and strangled. We transferred the treasure to our ponies, threw the bodies into a ravine, and went on for three days without halting anywhere, as we knew we should be immediately pursued.

It was only when the Thugs stopped to rest at last, more than 50 miles from the place where they had slaughtered the bearers, that they realized the true extent of the treasure they had seized. The packs they had taken from the camels' backs were cut open with knives and swords, and out tumbled 15,000 rupees in coin, a quantity of silver bullion and a small brass box that, forced open, disgorged 'four diamond rings set with jewels, eight pearls, and one pair of gold bangles'. This plunder was valued at a total of 40,000 rupees. Each man in the party received about 150 rupees and a small quantity of jewels as his share.

The Burwaha Ghat affair showed the Thugs at their most resourceful. Not only had they tracked a suspicious, highly mobile party of bearers across well over 100 miles of difficult terrain; they had also abandoned the practice of inveigling their victims, knowing that the cautious matchlock-men would never willingly travel with a large body of strangers, so that the murders were actually more like a highway robbery than a typical case of Thuggee. They had trusted to swords and spears, as well as their rumals, and shown that they were willing to draw blood when the potential prize warranted it.*

The gold and jewels seized at Burwaha Ghat took the total plundered from the seths of central India in a mere three years to more than 90,000 rupees, split between as many as 500 Thugs. It was an enormous sum, and the gangs, well satisfied with their efforts, turned at once for home. They made their way north 'by regular stages' along the main roads, anticipating – it seems fair to guess – a warm welcome in their villages. But the wiser heads among them were apprehensive. They knew the seths would never let the theft of so much of their property go unrevenged.

Few Thugs were deterred by the fear of imprisonment or execution.

For some, this was a matter of necessity. These men either regarded murder as their trade or could find no better way to feed their families. But most Thugs believed, in any case, that they ran scant risk of conviction. Before the mid-1820s, the handful who had found themselves in court had generally been betrayed by disgruntled colleagues or been caught in possession of some item of loot that they could not account for. It was rare for the police, in either the Company's territories or the Native States, to actively pursue a gang, much less for them to catch one.

The failings of the Indian police dated to Mughal times. In the seventeenth and eighteenth centuries, the police had been little more than a militia, employed to keep the country's zamindars in check, and there were never many of them. A pargana of perhaps 200 villages would be policed by a detachment of 40 or 50 matchlock-men stationed in a special compound, called a *thanah*, from which they issued periodically to overawe recalcitrant

---

*Ambush was, indeed, a technique the Thugs used frequently enough to have a slang expression for it. The term *khomusna*, meaning 'to rush upon travellers when there is no time for the ordinary ceremonies of murder', was employed to describe such incidents.

landholders. By acting as a brake upon the powers of a district's zamindars, the police played a vital role in keeping the peace and ensuring the smooth flow of taxes from the provinces. But they were not equipped to solve complex crimes.

Policing, in the modern sense, remained largely the duty of the village *chaukidar*, or watchman. Every Indian community had at least one, hired by the local zamindar to guard fields and deal with the minor thefts and robberies that could plague any community. But the chaukidars, too, had their deficiencies. They were so poor that they were vulnerable to bribery. Their responsibilities ended at the edge of their villages, and since there was more often rivalry than cooperation between the watchmen of neighbouring settlements, few rural policemen had much success in catching criminals from outside their own communities. The village chaukidar was neither trained nor a part of any hierarchy; he had few if any resources to draw on, and rarely shared such information as he might possess concerning criminals living in his district with any higher authorities. There was no reason for him to pursue suspects beyond the borders of his village. Worse, each man was so beholden to his zamindar that he naturally felt compelled to connive at any breaches of the law committed by his master.

The Company's solution to these problems had been to transform the men of the old thanah system into a modern force that combined the responsibilities of the militia with many of the duties of the village watch. From 1793, its magistrates were required to divide their districts into 'police jurisdictions' some 400 square miles in extent, and to recruit an Indian police officer, known as the darogah, to take charge of each. The notion of police compounds was retained, each thanah being manned by 10 or 12 militiamen, paid for by a special police tax to ensure that they were free from the zamindar's control, and charged with patrolling a substantial swathe of countryside. The darogahs themselves were also given responsibility for solving major crimes, such as murder and cases of banditry, and were required to tour their districts constantly. They possessed the power to decide all but the most serious cases without reference to their magistrate, handing down the appropriate sentences and fines. In order to end the plainly unsatisfactory lack of cooperation between adjoining districts, Company darogahs were also permitted to pursue wanted criminals into neighbouring territories – though not, of course, into the Native States.

British Superintendents of Police were appointed to oversee the efficiency of the entire scheme.

This new system did tackle some of the problems endemic in Mughal times. But it had drawbacks of its own. Each darogah's territory was so large that it was almost impossible to police properly with the handful of men available. The responsibilities – and thus the income – of the chaukidars, meanwhile, were so severely curtailed that most watchmen became implacably opposed to the darogah and his men, actively hindering their investigations. All in all, the Company scheme placed so much power and responsibility in the hands of the new police that it could only work if the darogahs themselves were outstandingly honest and efficient. Most, unfortunately, were neither.

The principal difficulty was a simple one: the pay of a darogah was so low that respectable men could rarely be enticed into the ranks of the police. To make matters worse, many magistrates delegated the task of finding a suitable officer to their court clerks, themselves poorly paid and frequently corrupt officials willing to appoint any coarse, ill-educated man who would part with a substantial bribe in order to secure the post. Since these clerks generally possessed the ear of their British masters, and could have an officer dismissed as quickly as he had been recruited, many darogahs found themselves forced to hand over some or even all of their monthly salaries to the clerks simply in order to keep their jobs. The inevitable consequence was that most were not merely badly paid but also fully aware that they could be dismissed at any moment. It is hardly surprising, in such circumstances, that many took up their posts determined to make as much money as they could as quickly as was practicable.

By the mid-1820s, the excesses of the Company's police were already legendary. It was common for darogahs arriving at a village to charge the local people for both their services and their travelling expenses, to insist that food and lodging be provided for their entourage, and to solicit payments from both parties in each case. In many districts, each local watchman was forced to pay his darogah three rupees a year – a good sum in itself, but one that amounted to a substantial income when multiplied by the number of villages in a typical jurisdiction. All in all, the total realized by a successful policeman in the course of a single year could amount to as much as 2,400 rupees – a very handsome sum, particularly when it is compared to the policeman's nominal annual salary of a mere 300 rupees.

Nor were innocent villagers the only source of a darogah's wealth. Many officers accepted bribes from criminals who lived within their districts in return for concealing their existence from the magistrate, and as early as 1807, one British district officer discovered that every darogah in his jurisdiction 'entertained on a small salary an agent whose duty it was to attend the Magistrate's Court and communicate to his employer all the happenings there'. The information was then sold to criminals who lived within the darogah's territory so that 'the principal dacoits and others have pretty good information of any orders that may be passed respecting them'. The upshot was that malefactors were able to live relatively unmolested in British territory, while Company magistrates themselves had 'no local knowledge of their districts, nor can they have much information of what passes in the mofussil beyond what the darogahs think fit to report'.

Abuses of this sort had severe consequences for the efficiency of the Company's police. In many districts, villagers who discovered that some serious crime had been committed would do almost anything to prevent the authorities getting wind of it, believing that a visit from the police would be a far worse catastrophe than the crime itself. Murders were particularly likely to be covered up, for in the absence of any obvious suspects many darogahs would not only take the opportunity to ransack a village in search of 'evidence', taking bribes from those able to pay to escape the attentions of their constables, but would seek to pin the blame for a murder or a robbery on some unfortunate local rather than admit to their superiors that they could not solve the crime. Innumerable Thug crimes were concealed in this way. Terrified villagers preferred to dispose of bodies that they stumbled across in wells or shallow graves, and only rarely reported them. 'The police,' one Indian concluded as late as 1833, 'is as dangerous as any fierce and grotesque creature in this universe, and resembles the frightful description of the hell in legends . . . It is death to come into contact with.'

Even the Company's darogahs, though, took notice when treasure-bearers disappeared. Most of the Thugs' victims might be travellers without influence or powerful friends, had no particular itinerary, and were often not missed for weeks or even months after their deaths. But the seths' treasure parties followed predetermined routes, and were expected at their destinations by a certain date. Their disappearances were quickly noticed, and the bankers lost little time in alerting the local authorities. They insisted on thorough investigations, and because they were wealthy and powerful men the police were anxious to oblige. The sums of money involved were so substantial that most seths did not hesitate to commit their own resources to the hunt as well, despatching search parties to track the missing bearers down.

By an extraordinary chance (or, one is inclined to suspect, thanks to the presence of a Thug spy somewhere in the bank concerned) all three of the great consignments of treasure lost between the years 1826 and 1829 were on their way either to or from the house of Dhunraj Seth. Dhunraj, who came from the town of Oomroutee, on the road from Jhalna to Nagpore, was a man of substantial means. His bank had agents in Bombay and Indore, correspondents in Poona and Nagpore, and ambitions to expand into Saugor and beyond, and he was wealthy enough to finance his own search for his missing bearers. He was also – at a time when even Maharajah Sindhia of Gwalior had no treasury of his own, since 'all the cash is in the hands of the bankers of the bazaars, on whom the Government obtains credit for certain sums by negotiating loans' – so important to the native princes of the central provinces who depended on his funds that the Thugs could not rely, as they had always done, on the protection of the petty rajahs and landlords who usually shielded them. In this sense, at least, Dhunraj had greater power than the civil authorities, whether British or Indian, whose interest in Thugs and dacoits ceased at the borders of their own territories.

The seth's search for the gangs who had robbed him and killed his men properly began in 1828. Enquiries had evidently been made into the disappearance of the dozen or more men strangled near the Tapti river in 1826, but the Thugs who murdered this party of bearers seem to have buried their victims with some care; their bodies were never found and the circumstances of their deaths remained a mystery. The seven men killed two years later in the Malagow affair, however, were disposed of hurriedly, as frequently occurred when the stranglers were anxious to leave the scene. 'Some of the bodies,' Feringeea recalled, 'were thrown into [a] tank, and the others were slightly buried in a field close by.'

The consequences were predictable. Only a few days after the murders had been committed, the stench of decomposing corpses drew a peasant from a nearby village to the spot, and he chanced to return home with news of his discovery just as one of Dhunraj's search parties reached the village. The

villagers and the banker's men returned to the river together, and soon uncovered the remains of a long-haired man in a white shirt, which had been
hidden beneath some stones. He was immediately recognized as one of the
missing bearers.

Next day the seth's men explored the murder site more thoroughly. They
were accompanied by several villagers, who joined in with the search. One of
these helpers, a man named Oda Patel, later recalled:

> I saw in a hollow place bodies with stones over them. Animals had
> devoured part of the flesh. We uncovered [them] and took out bones and
> two or three skulls. About 10 cubits [roughly 17 feet] from this pit, we
> found bones of two or three other people, but the skeletons were not
> entire. The hair on the head was about a cubit [20 inches] long, and part
> being cut off showed that they were men.

While the hunt was going on, another of the peasants confided that the
bodies of five or six people, also supposed to be the victims of murder, had
recently been exhumed nearby, close to the road. Malagow lay within the borders of the Bombay Presidency, so the investigation of the scene fell to the
Company's police. But Candeish had long been such a lawless place that the
discoveries were viewed, 'by the native officers, with a great deal of coolness'.
In ordinary circumstances the local darogah might well have calculated that
he was unlikely to profit in tackling such a tricky case. But at the insistence of
the seth's men a formal report was made to the authorities in Bombay
nonetheless.

The murder site at Burwaha Ghat was uncovered even more promptly. The
Thugs involved in this affair had turned the bearers' three camels loose in the
jungle, and their discovery five days after the slaughter of the treasure party
soon led the local watchmen to the crude graves that had been prepared
nearby. The dead men had been interred at the bottom of a ravine. The first
three bodies recovered were, one chaukidar reported,

> under the branches of a Golur-tree, covered with leaves, dry sand, and
> stones. We took them out, and found all their throats cut, apparently with
> swords. On one of the bodies was a black coat; and by that coat he was
> recognised to be Meer Futteh Alee, a merchant of Borhanpore.

The remaining members of the treasure party were lying 50 yards away – two in a second shallow grave, the others in the open on the bank of a stream, their bodies torn apart by vultures – and checks made with the customs post at the Ghat soon revealed their identities. More importantly, the customs officers recalled levying duty on a large group of men who passed through at the same time as the bearers. They had been travelling, the records showed, to Bundelcund, and since they were at once suspected of the robbery, four men set off in pursuit. One was a policeman from the local thanah, another Holkar's agent in the district. The other two were the seth's men – Beharee Lal and Gomanee Ram, Dhunraj's gomashtas in Indore.

Beharee Lal, the senior gomashta, had received specific instructions from his master. His principal duty, it is clear, was not simply to find the men who had stolen the lost treasure, but to recover the whole sum by whatever means were necessary. So, when the Thugs who had fled Burwaha Ghat were at length tracked down to their home villages in the district around Jhansee – a state then nominally an ally of the Company – Beharee went at once to the Resident at Indore for help in securing them. Supplied with an escort of native troops, he seized as many of the men as he could find, and carried them off, together with their families, to a fortress in the town of Alumpore. There they were in effect held hostage while the gomashta negotiated with them for the return of their loot.

Beharee Lal's next step was to ascertain what had happened to his master's property. The Thugs had divided the loot from Burwaha Ghat into 101 shares, so it had been dispersed, but comparatively little had been spent and much was still recoverable. The gomashta secured its return by promising each of his captives their release in exchange for handing over three-quarters of their booty. Others were set free so they could point out places where portions of the cash were hidden. In this way, Beharee managed to unearth perhaps four-tenths of the treasure – the first large Thug haul ever, even partially, recovered.*

---

*Details of the men suspected of the Candeish thefts having been circulated to the Company's officers throughout central India, a further 4,000 rupees (part of the loot from the Malagow affair) was subsequently located by the Company's Resident at Gwalior, and another 1,400 rupees' worth of gold seized from four men arrested at Jubbulpore. This money was returned to Oomroutee.

Next, the seth's man turned his thoughts to ways of securing the 25,000 rupees that remained outstanding from the Burwaha Ghat affair. Much of this money had either been spent or was in the hands of men who were not in his custody. But the gomashta now realized that there were other ways of obtaining reparation – and also making money for himself. Chance had placed him at the head of a gang of able Thugs, who all depended on him for their freedom. Those who would not cooperate with him, or who could not find the money he demanded, risked being returned to jail. Even those who had handed back their share of the banker's property remained vulnerable to blackmail, for Beharee's word – and of course his money – would probably be taken over theirs in any local court of law. The Jhansee Thugs thus became, in effect, the gomashta's subjects, and he now put them back to work.

Beharee's plan was as straightforward as it was brutal. The men who had been released into his custody were, notionally, employed merely to recover the money stolen at Burwaha Ghat. In practice, however, they were sent out to ply their trade of murder once again. A huge share – 60 per cent – of the proceeds of each new expedition was made over to the banker's man, and he kept some of this commission for himself and returned the rest to Dhunraj Seth. The Jhansee men had, thus, in effect, secured their freedom by selling the gomashta an option on the proceeds of their future murders, and they had little choice but to Thug in order to pay him.

It was not long before Beharee Lal began applying the same methods to men who had played no part in the Candeish or Burwaha Ghat affairs. He discovered it was possible to secure the release of other criminals into his custody simply by alleging they had been members of the gangs he sought, and that these men were so anxious to escape jail that they were willing to pay him for their freedom. After a while, he even established a tribunal of his own at Alumpore and began to 'bind and loose at [his] discretion all the Thugs [he] can get hold of without check or control from the Ruler of the country'. Disquieting rumours began to be heard that Beharee had sur-rounded himself with a number of notorious jemadars, turning himself into the 'King of Thugs'. The gomashta was now busily directing the fortunes of their united gangs.

Much of what was whispered about Beharee Lal was true. 'He got,' one of the men involved later recalled, a good deal of money by procuring the release of all the noted Thugs then in confinement at different places. He got nine thousand rupees for the release of Dhurum Khan Jemadar from Gwalior, on the pretence that he was engaged in the affair, when he had been in prison long before . . . Such was Dhunraj Seth's influence that he could get a gang released from prison in any part of India; and for some time his agent Beharee Lal had always half a dozen of the principal Thug leaders about his person, and used to attend all our marriages and festivals. What his master got, we know not, but he got a great deal of our money.

The Thugs' raids on seth treasure-bearers had another consequence. They finally compelled the British to take notice of their activities in the Native States.

For the better part of two decades, the Company's policy regarding Thugs had been alarmingly pragmatic. Magistrates and district officers from Madras to Hindustan had striven to eradicate Thuggee from their territories. But they had made no attempt to destroy the practice utterly. Experience implied that was impossible. Elusive stranglers who slipped easily from one jurisdiction to the next were simply too hard to catch, and imprisonment was costly. On the whole it had seemed enough to drive suspected Thugs into the Native States and out of British jurisdiction, to make them someone else's problem.

The furore that followed the plundering of Dhunraj Seth's treasure parties changed all this. The officers of Saugor & Nerbudda could scarcely fail to notice the frantic activity that followed the disappearance of Dhunraj's men, the search parties and the exhumations. Beharee Lal had made it his business to stay in close communication with the Resident at Indore, and Dhunraj himself appealed directly to the Company authorities at Jubbulpore for help. Before long Francis Curwen Smith, the Governor General's new agent in the central provinces, had found himself involved in efforts to recover the Thug loot, British troops and Company police were alerted to look out for the murderous gangs, and spies were sent into Beharee Lal's encampment at Alumpore to discover what was going on at the gomashta's Thug tribunal.

Still the British kept a certain distance. Burwaha Ghat did not lie within the Company's borders, so the dead treasure-bearers were not really their responsibility. Dhunraj was the injured party in the case, and the citizens of

Jhansee were subjects of the local rajah. Stranglers picked up in Saugor &
Nerbudda on suspicion of the theft of seth remittances were, thus, not commit-
ted to the Company's courts, but sent on to Beharee's tribunal in the Native
States for trial.

Now that British interest had been piqued, however, awareness of the
Thugs' activities increased and officers in both the Bombay and the Bengal
presidencies found themselves drawn into the seths' obsessive quest for
vengeance. Recognition that numerous gangs of stranglers were at large on
roads that led through Company territory was accompanied by acknowledgement that British subjects, too, were falling victim to their stratagems.

This was seen as something of an affront. But it was not until the early
months of 1829 that the capture of a large Thug band – detained by great
good fortune on the Malwa plateau – at last offered real hope that steps could
be taken to end the menace of Thuggee.

CHAPTER 11

Approvers

'karhoo – one who betrays or molests Thugs'

Captain William Borthwick, the Company's Political Agent in Holkar's lands, had been in India for nearly 15 years. He had served most of that time in the Madras Presidency, transferring to the central provinces at the end of 1828. And he had never, in all that time, encountered a confessed Thug.

He had come close to them, without knowing it, on numerous occasions. The gangs travelled far and wide in the course of their expeditions.* Borthwick's position in one of the largest of the Native States significantly improved the likelihood that he would stumble across them. Several bands had boltholes in the vicinity to which they retreated whenever they became aware of unusual activity in the Company's lands, knowing full well that British sepoys were forbidden from pursuing their quarry into the Native States that lay scattered like patchwork across India's central belt.** But Borthwick, who wielded considerable influence around Indore, was less

---

*Syeed Ameer Ali, for example, one of the most prolific of all Thug murderers, lived in Rampoora, near the Jumna. But in the course of just one of his expeditions, the jemadar covered a vast swathe of territory: he committed his first murders around Gwalior, then moved south to Nagpore and criss-crossed the central provinces, finally heading north through Jubbulpore, crossing into Oudh, and concluding his expedition in the vicinity of Lucknow.

**'My district,' wrote Meadows Taylor, a junior officer in the Nizam's lands in Hyderabad, 'was much cut up by private estates, whose owners or managers defied or evaded the orders of the Nizam's executive government, and would only obey their own masters, some of whom were powerful nobles in Hyderabad who jealously resented any interference by the executive minister, while their agents were well-known protectors of thieves and robbers, whose booty they shared.'

constrained than the majority of his colleagues. Defeat in the Maratha wars had not only reduced the once mighty Holkar to the status of an unwilling ally of the Company, but also forced him to accept the presence of small parties of British-officered sepoys within his borders.

Even so, Borthwick had had no prior intimation that a substantial gang of Thugs was crossing his district when, late in the cold weather of 1829, the headman of a nearby village hurried into his headquarters bearing urgent information. A 'band of villains', Borthwick was told, had entered the area two days earlier and encamped in a mango grove some 15 miles away. Men from the village who passed their campsite that same evening had seen a small party of merchants being entertained within the grove. When the same villagers returned the next morning, the merchants had disappeared. But how, the headman wondered, could that be possible, when their horses and two large packs of goods had been spotted in the possession of their hosts?

Borthwick guessed immediately that the mysterious men in the grove were Thugs. But actually securing so large a gang of stranglers was still no easy matter. Their band was, the headman guessed, at least 70 men strong. They had more than a day's head start. And the only force immediately available to Borthwick was a detachment of sepoys numbering fewer than a dozen men.

Borthwick responded to this conundrum with a piece of improvisation that would eventually earn him praise for coolness from the Government of India. Plainly such a small group of soldiers could have no hope of detaining so large a group. His men might well be in great danger if they attempted it. But what if he could make the Thugs come to his camp willingly? Was there perhaps some way in which a gang of practised deceivers might be themselves deceived?

So it was that two days later, outside the village of Dekola, four stages from Indore, a large body of Thugs was overhauled by a small mounted patrol. 'They came upon us,' one strangler remembered,

and said that Captain Borthwick had heard that we were carrying opium out of Malwa, and they had been sent to stop us. On hearing this, our minds were relieved from suspicion or fear that the object of the horsemen was any other than what they professed it to be, or had any reference to our habits or pursuits. We readily consented to return with the horsemen who we thought would of course allow us to depart after searching us and finding we had no opium.

Another member of the band added: 'We were without fear of any mischance befalling us. We gladly accompanied them.' It was only 'after our arrival there', he said in indignation, 'that we learned the true cause of our being arrested – not, however, before the authorities and the inhabitants of the town had joined in aid of the horsemen to secure us and prevent our escape.'

No fewer than 71 Thugs – the greater part of a substantial gang that had strangled and robbed its way from Bundelcund to Baroda over the preceding weeks, killing no fewer than 31 travellers along the way – were taken by 'this subterfuge'. They were carrying only a little of their loot, having sent an advance party back to their villages only a few days earlier with the bulk of their plunder. But enough evidence of their murderous activities – stolen horses, swords, brass pots, cloths and turbans – remained for the most serious suspicions to be affixed to them.

'We of course loudly protested our innocence,' a Thug calling himself Amanoolah continued. And had all the members of the party continued to do so, Borthwick may well have found it difficult to prove that the loot he had discovered in their baggage was indeed the product of murder. Certainly the stranglers themselves knew that persistent denial was their best defence. 'It is not usual,' a second member of the party by the name of Khaimraj explained, 'with persons of our character when apprehended to make disclosures from intimidation or the application of severities; indeed I was firmly resolved to keep silent.' But Amanoolah – a man 50 years of age, but one who had been a Thug for a mere two years – found his resolve wavering. 'Seeing that the horsemen were deaf to all our entreaties and threats,' he confessed, 'I became alarmed and, as the only chance that appeared to me of saving my own life, determined to admit the truth and make a full disclosure of our habits and acts. I accordingly went immediately to the horsemen and offered on assurance of my life being spared to make a faithful avowal of all our doings.'

Seeing what had happened, two other Thugs swiftly followed suit. Even the staunch Khaimraj saw little point in maintaining his silence in such circumstances. 'Finding that two or three of my companions had already told all,' he conceded, 'and had pointed out the spots, and bodies of the different individuals whom we had murdered during the last few days . . . I considered it would be very foolish to abide by my resolution, particularly when I found I might probably save my life by a full and true confession, while remaining silent would not avail me or my companions anything.'

The confessions given to Captain Borthwick by his informants Amanoolah and Khaimraj were lengthy and detailed. They resulted in the exhumation of 12 bodies and the arraignment of the entire gang on charges of murder and robbery – the greatest success the Company had enjoyed over the Thugs in many years. Despite this, the depositions that Borthwick sent to Calcutta would probably have resulted in the conviction of this single gang of stranglers only. But chance, and a certain opportunism, now involved William Sleeman in the budding anti-Thug campaign.

News of the capture of the Malwa Thugs reached Bengal midway through 1829, causing an appreciable stir. Even at this late date, however, the Company's most senior officers still viewed the apprehension of the stranglers as no more than a welcome opportunity to make an example of some guilty men. The correspondence that passed back and forth between Calcutta and Holkar's court over the next few weeks concerned itself more with the details of where and how to try and execute the Thugs than it did with discussion of the opportunities that Borthwick's exploits might have opened up. No one in authority considered that the depositions recorded by Borthwick might provide the tools required to launch an anti-Thug campaign.

It took the intervention of India's new Governor General to take matters further. William Cavendish Bentinck, who had arrived in Calcutta in the latter half of 1828, was quite possibly the most reserved and unpretentious man ever to be appointed to the post. Shyness ran through his distinguished family like a sinew, rendering him almost incapable of showing ordinary human warmth. His long oval face – tending to jowliness now that he was in his fifties – seldom betrayed a flicker of emotion, and his uncommonly lanky legs ('so long that everyone would like to have him as a second in a duel, to pace out the ground') bore him rapidly away from any prospect of confrontation. Yet reserved as he was, Bentinck was nonetheless a driven man, possessed by the need to erase a stain left on his reputation by an earlier sojourn in India.* Unlike his predecessor, Lord Amherst ('a most amiable but imbecile governor', under whose uninspiring rule British India had more or less stagnated since the early 1820s), the new Governor General had thus disembarked in Calcutta implacably determined to leave his mark on the administration.

Bentinck wasted little time in turning on the Thugs. First, he and his advisors recognized that it had become simply too easy for the stranglers to slip from one state into its neighbour to evade pursuit. The best way to dispose of this problem, they decided, was for the British to assume responsibility for pursuing Thugs wherever they operated. If that meant passing out of Saugor & Nerbudda, well . . . the rajahs' ruffled feelings could be soothed or, if need be, ignored. Next, Bentinck authorized Company officers to try captured Thugs, no matter where their crimes had been committed. This was a more serious breach of existing law and customs, for the British had hitherto claimed no right to so much as detain a suspect whom they could not prove had robbed or killed within their borders. But there was, nonetheless, some justification for a change in policy. 'The hand of these inhuman monsters being against every one,' the Governor reasoned, 'and there being no country . . . in which they have not committed murder . . . they may be considered like Pirates, to be placed without the pale of social law, and be subjected to condign punishment by whatever authority they may be seized and convicted.'

The implication of these policies was clear. Thuggee itself was again under attack. But Bentinck was far too busy in Bengal to lead the new campaign himself. Since Borthwick's captives had been picked up deep in the heart of the mofussil, responsibility for their prosecution thus passed down to the most senior British officer in the central provinces: FC Smith, the Company's Agent in Saugor & Nerbudda.

---

*The Governor General had spent the years 1803 to 1806 in the Presidency of Madras, where he had signed into law an edict compelling the sepoys of the Deccan to wear hats instead of turbans and to decorate those hats with leather cockades. This order had been widely regarded as anathema in a country where a hat was the symbol of a Christian convert and leather was not only an abomination to all Hindus but an object of suspicion to Muslim soldiers, who thought that the material in question might be pigskin rather than cow hide. The consequence had been a terrifying mutiny, the most serious to occur in India before the great rebellion of 1857. Bentinck – held personally responsible for the debacle – was recalled to London in disgrace and never entirely recovered from the shame of his early failure.

At first, the anti-Thug campaign made little progress. Smith – a stiff, pedantic stickler of a man burdened, like Bentinck himself, with a vast amount of work – accepted his commission grudgingly, and showed little immediate interest in implementing the new policies. But he did at least ensure that an official print, prepared on the Governor General's orders and filled with excerpts from the statements made by Amanoolah and his friends, was distributed to every British officer within the central provinces. The circular was designed to alert Company officials to the activities and methods of the stranglers and so make it more likely that further arrests would be made; most of the officials who received it, it seems safe to say, scanned it briefly and forgot it, as they did other missives from the government. But one, at least, did not. At his headquarters in the heart of Saugor & Nerbudda, William Sleeman read of Borthwick's exploits and the capture of the Thugs and saw in them unlooked-for opportunity. Here was a chance to take on interesting work. Here, too, was the prospect of doing some good for ordinary Indians. But there was something else as well. Borthwick's achievement in Malwa had won him praise from Bentinck himself. A similar success, Sleeman was quick to realize, could benefit his own career enormously.

Sleeman was working as district officer in Jubbulpore when the Thug circular appeared. The district was larger, more densely populated, and in some ways more demanding to administer than Nursingpore. Sleeman had been burdened by the difficulties of collecting rents and taxes from the district, by a long series of disputes with the neighbouring Rajah of Nagpore, and by a catastrophic drought that struck his town in 1827. He had also been forced to spend a lengthy period of sick leave on the island of Mauritius, a sojourn that resulted, in turn, in marriage, for the island – taken from the French after the Napoleonic Wars – contained (as Sleeman confided to his friend Charles Fraser, who was magistrate at Jubbulpore) 'a vast number of pretty girls [who] all dress better than English girls of the same class in society'. One of them, a certain Amélie de Fontenne, the dark-haired and strikingly intelligent daughter of an exiled French nobleman, appeared a few years later in central India, searching for new strains of sugar cane that might be introduced to her father's plantations. Her enquiries led her to Sleeman; they renewed their acquaintance, fell in love, and married at Jubbulpore in 1828.

It is difficult to be sure how much Sleeman knew about the stranglers prior to 1829. He had been in India when St Leger's order of the day, warning the Company's sepoys to be on guard against the Thugs, was given out in every station in the Bengal Presidency. And since he was well read and loved the Subcontinent, he may perhaps have browsed through the papers that Sherwood and Shakespear had published in *Asiatick Researches*, too. But there is nothing to suggest that such minor brushes with Thuggee stirred any great interest in his heart. Sleeman took no notice of the considerable investigation that took place at Jhalna, 280 miles from his own station, in 1823. And although he most likely did hear, from his superior Charles Molony, of the arrest of a gang of more than a hundred stranglers, caught crossing the Nerbudda valley in that same year, he himself had – in common with almost every other officer in India – never seen a Thug nor stumbled across a Thug band.

Occasionally, during the mid 1820s, the gangs' activities in the mofussil must have come to his attention. Jubbulpore's jail, the largest in the Nerbudda valley, often held a handful of stranglers and suspected stranglers, confined alongside dacoits and highway robbers of all sorts. But usually the evidence against them was not great, and the men rarely came to trial. Only a single case of Thuggee was heard in the town in the course of the whole decade: a gang 32 men strong, arrested as they passed through the district in 1826, was committed for trial later that same year. Two of the men were executed and the remainder imprisoned, mostly for life.

Sleeman's superintendence of Jubbulpore suggests he must have known of this case. His friend Fraser had tried it, and it is quite possible that the two men discussed the hearing then or later. But though there had been a large body of circumstantial evidence to show the prisoners' guilt, each of the imprisoned men denied all knowledge of Thuggee, and there was no opportunity to learn anything of the other gangs at large in Saugor & Nerbudda. Sleeman can have known little more of Thugs when he first read Bentinck's circular than he had a few years previously, when he was wholly unaware of their activities in Nursingpore.

What he had realized, by 1829, was that a full decade of service in the interior of India had earned him little notice. A solitary promotion, from lieutenant to captain, and a modest increase in pay had been his only rewards for ten years' labour, while brother officers lucky or influential enough to command in battle, or fill posts in the Presidency towns, had earned preferment far more quickly. Company men despatched to the mofussil were all too easily forgotten; only those who made it their business to draw their superiors' attention to every incident and each achievement in their districts had much hope of keeping pace with colleagues in Bombay, Calcutta and Madras. Throughout the 1820s, Sleeman had upbraided his friend Fraser for failing to keep the government informed of his progress. Now, with a new wife to support, he was forced to take his own advice. Bentinck's circular suggested one way forward. So when, in February 1830, rumours reached Jubbulpore that another band of stranglers was making its way through British territory, Sleeman wasted little time. He set out immediately in pursuit.

This new gang had been engaged in a series of murders in Gwalior and Bhopal under the command of a jemadar named Sheikh Madaree, plundering more than 2,000 rupees from a total of more than 30 victims. It had evaded the attentions of the local police and disposed of its victims so securely that no sign of its presence had been discovered. In the first week of April, however, a party of six sepoys travelling home on leave was inveigled only a few miles to the north of Saugor. As was their custom, the Thugs waited until their potential victims were settled in camp for the night before the signal for their murder was given. In normal circumstances, the destruction of a small party of this sort would have presented few difficulties. But on this occasion, one member of the gang later explained, 'the affair was mismanaged'. One of the bhurtotes failed to slip his rumal completely over the selected victim's head. The scarf caught on the soldier's nose and, after a brief struggle, the man got free from his assailants and ran off towards the village. The Thug lookouts and guards were quickly after him, but before they could catch up with the fleeing sepoy the Thugs caught sight of another party of soldiers approaching in the distance. Madaree's entire gang turned and ran, leaving their fortunate victim alive to blurt out the story of his comrades' murder.

This one error doomed the group. It was unusual enough for the men of a Thug gang to leave one of their intended victims alive. It was unheard of for them to make such a mistake in such close proximity to a sepoy patrol. The soldiers – who were on foot like their quarry – were not quite quick enough to round up the fleeing stranglers. But they were close enough to Saugor to reach the town in only hours, and so for once the Company received intelligence of a Thug gang in good time to scour the local roads.

With the sepoys' reports to hand, Sleeman was able to send out strong patrols of troops along the main roads leading into the town, and it was not long before one returned leading the 30 members of the gang. Four approvers soon emerged from the ranks of the Thugs, and their evidence was laboriously compiled into a comprehensive indictment that Sleeman presented to Smith. The depositions, as Smith summarized them, offered numerous proofs of the Thugs' guilt:

Heera . . . is the Chief Witness in this case. His evidence has been corroborated by many circumstances of great weight carrying conviction of its truth in my mind –

1st – The free, unembarrassed and consistent way in which he gave his evidence . . . undergoing a long and intricate cross-examination . . .

2nd – The evidence of [the remaining approvers].

3rd – The depositions of several old pardoned Thugs who recognise the prisoners and unanimously agree about their parentage, trade and other points, in which false testimony would assuredly stumble.

4th – The arrest of the prisoners in a gang, and their inability to give a consistent account of themselves.

5th – The nature of the property found upon them . . .

It did not take long to bring the case to court. In only a few months, fifteen members of the gang were sentenced to be hanged, and eight more to transportation. The remainder were imprisoned for seven or 14 years. 'I beg leave to state,' concluded Smith in his report to Calcutta, 'that the gang of Thugs, or Land Pirates, against whose hand no ordinary traveller can stand, stands condemned on evidence not in the least apocryphal. I am satisfied that, thanks to the exertions of Captain Sleeman, this Territory has seen the last of them.' In this last sentiment, however, Smith was wrong. Sleeman had by no means finished with the Thugs. He had, indeed, only just begun.

The confessions made by captured Thugs had hitherto been used solely to convict the other members of their own gangs. Sleeman was the first Company officer to perceive that depositions taken from men with long experience of Thuggee were packed with clues that, followed up, would inevitably lead British officials to other gangs and other jemadars. He was also the first to interrogate and deploy his approvers with penetrating intelligence. The system that he evolved at Jubbulpore in the years 1829–30 would later be applied throughout the Subcontinent with great success.

The real difficulty, in almost every case, lay in obtaining sufficient evidence to secure convictions in courts governed by Islamic law. The Muslim code inherited from the Mughal Empire, and only partially modified since then, frowned on the testimony of approvers when it was unsupported by other evidence. Indeed it was unlawful to arrest, much less convict, a man solely on the basis of the testimony 'of any number of confessing prisoners'. The great majority of captured Thugs knew this and realized that their best chance of acquittal was to flatly deny all the charges brought against them.

Sleeman was anxious, first, to establish some sort of rapport with the captured men. 'In order to make them assent to us to the extent of their ability, we require to raise them a little bit in their own esteem, and make them feel a little exalted as the servants of a state which . . . will always be found to provide for their decent subsistence,' he decided.

> They require to be decently clothed and well fed, and to be kept separate from the mass of Thugs who are arrested by their aid, for these men, like all others who are leagued against the lives and property of their fellow creatures, at first look down with scorn on those who betray them, and we must either take them out of the reach of their odium or place them above it.

That done, each Thug who had indicated a willingness to turn approver would be brought before a British officer for questioning. The prisoner would receive assurances that his life would be spared in exchange for his testimony, but it would be made clear to him that this promise would apply only if he fulfilled a number of conditions, which (since they generally applied to all Thug informants, and help to explain how the Company was able to extract such a flood of information from its approvers) are worth repeating here:

First   He shall make in your presence and before witnesses a full and unreserved disclosure of every Thuggee, murder or Robbery at which he has either aided, abetted, or connived, with the names, residence, caste and descriptions of all the persons engaged in these crimes.

Second   He shall through the means of his followers and his influence assist you with all his might in arresting and bringing to condign punishment all Persons guilty of Thuggee and murder and Robbery, whether they be relations, connections, or associates of his.

Third   On failure of these conditions, or on proof of his having concealed any Thuggee murder at which he was present or aided or abetted or was acquainted with the persons, conditional pardon to be null and void.

Approvers who fulfilled all three conditions received the promised conditional pardons for their crimes, but – Sleeman and his fellow officers were constantly reminded by their superiors in Calcutta – 'it is of the greatest importance that none are led to believe that they will ever be released from prison'. The loyalty of each man was buttressed with the information that 'a small maintenance shall be allowed to his wife and child, who must however for some time to come be kept under surveillance'.

A long period of questioning would follow. 'The mode of proceeding,' a contemporary article in the *Foreign Quarterly Review* informed its readers,

is to take the deposition of those who turn approvers, wherever this may happen to be. These men are then required to give, to the best of their recollection, a full account of every expedition on which they have been, mentioning the dates of every one, and the detail of every murder; together with the names of those who had formed the gangs, their residence, caste, &c., &c. All this is registered in [Sleeman's] office. It is obvious that when depositions, thus taken almost simultaneously from different people hundreds of miles apart, who have no means of collusion, and none of them expecting to be apprehended, agree in describing the same scenes and the same actors, it is next to impossible to refuse belief.

It was a complicated business. Approvers were questioned in Hindustani and their testimony taken down by Sleeman's moonshees in Persian, before being translated into English when required by the courts. Sleeman made a practice of leading each captured Thug slowly through his entire career, concluding only at the moment of his capture. Great pains were taken to note the details of every murder that could be recalled, including the names or the occupations of the victims and the quantity and nature of the loot taken from their bodies.

Sleeman did everything he could to ensure that suspect Thugs were properly identified. Depositions taken from approvers and witnesses all over India were collated and indexed, and whenever a gang of suspected Thugs was captured, its members were placed, one at a time, in an identity parade, and all the approvers at the station were 'sent for singly, and required to point out any individual of the party whom they may know'. For many months Sleeman was never quite satisfied that all the information he took down in this way was accurate, and his superiors, both in Britain and Bengal, feared that captured Thugs would do their utmost to protect their friends and relatives from arrest. In some cases approvers undoubtedly did conceal information in this way. But there is no evidence that any approvers who were confronted with an unknown suspect guessed at or simply invented an identity for the man.

Testimony recorded in this way possessed an eerie fascination that the officers involved in its collation frequently commented on. The Thugs' statements were generally exact and almost always curiously emotionless. One typical deposition, among hundreds collected by Sleeman over the ensuing months, began when the approver who had been brought before him was asked how often he had travelled with his gang before he witnessed his first murder. 'It was on my return from the first expedition which I made with my father to the Deccan, when I was 15 years of age,' remembered the Thug,

and about 35 years ago [1801–2]. We were a gang of about 80 or 90 Thugs, under my father, Hinga, and some of the Deccan chiefs lodged in the mausoleum outside the town of Ellichpore. Two of our leaders,

Gumboo and Laljoo, on getting into the bazaar, fell in with the grooms of the Nawab Subzee Khan, the uncle of the Nawab of Bhopal, who told them that their master . . . was now on his way home. They came back and reported, and Dulele Khan and Khuleel Khan, and other leaders of fame, went and introduced themselves to the Nawab, pretending that they had been to the Deccan with horses for sale, and were now on their way back to Hindustan. He was pleased with their address and appearance, and invited them to return the next day, which they did; and the following day he set out with as many of our gang as it was thought safe to exhibit. He had two grooms, two troopers, and a slave girl, two horses, a mare with a wound in the neck, and a pony. The slave girl's duty was to prepare him his daily portion of *subzee*;* and he told us that he had got the name of Subzee Khan from the quantity of that drug which he was accustomed to drink.

We came on together three stages; and during the fourth stage we came to an extensive jungle on this side of Dhoba, in the Baitool district; and on reaching a nullah, about nine o'clock, Khuleel said, 'Khan Sahib, we have had a fatiguing journey, and we had better rest here and take some refreshment.' – 'By all means,' said the Nawab, 'I feel a little fatigued, and will take my subzee here.' He dismounted, laid his sword and shield upon the ground, spread his carpet, and sat down. Dulele and Khuleel sat down by his side, while the girl was preparing his potion, of which he invited these two men, as our supposed chiefs, to partake, while the grooms were engaged with the horses and the troopers were smoking their pipes at a distance.

It had been determined that the Nawab should be first secured, for he was a powerful man, and, if he had a moment's warning, would certainly have cut down some of the gang before they could secure him. [So] Laljoo also went and sat near him, while Gomanee stood behind, and seemed to be much interested in the conversation. All being now ready, the signal was given; and the Nawab was strangled by Gomanee, while Laljoo and Dulele held his legs. As soon as the others saw the Nawab secured, they fell upon his attendants and all were strangled, and their bodies buried in the bed of a watercourse. On going back to

*An opium-based drink, also known as *bhang*.

Ellichpore, Gomanee sold the Nawab's shield for eight rupees, but it was worth so much more that the people suspected him, and came to our camp to search for him. Our spies brought us timely notice, and we concealed him under the housings of our horses.

'This, the approver added in conclusion, 'was the first murder I ever witnessed, and it made a great impression on my mind. You may rely upon the correctness of what I state regarding it.'

The truth of depositions of this sort was never taken at face value. Approvers' statements would be checked against the testimony of other members of the gang concerned, where that was possible, and Sleeman also devoted considerable energy to obtaining such corroboration as was possible from surviving witnesses. In the case of Subzee Khan – one of the most difficult he had to investigate, given the 35 years or more that had passed since the murder had been committed – he wrote to the Company's political agent at Bhopal for further information; the agent referred the matter to the chief minister of the city's ruler, and he in turn located 'an old resident of Bhopal' by the name of Sultan Khan Afghan who recalled the commotion caused by the Nawab's unexplained disappearance. 'When his son came home,' Sultan Khan's deposition explained, 'he got 200 rupees and, with four attendants, set out in search of him. He went to Nagpore and Ellichpore, and found traces of his father to the last place, but could find no trace of him beyond it.' The evidence of a second elderly resident substantiated Sultan Khan's in every particular.

Approvers employed under Sleeman's system were confined and kept in chains, but many of the more useful men were often released temporarily from prison into the custody of patrols of *nujeebs* – mounted militiamen. Equipped with lighter irons, concealed by a pair of long and flowing trousers, they accompanied Company troops sent in search of Thug gangs in order to identify wanted men. In most cases at least two approvers would be used in the hope that they might confirm each other's testimonies.

Other informants were put to work identifying those already in prison. As always, the approvers were carefully segregated so that their testimonies could be checked against each other. Each suspected strangler was then brought forward in turn, and the approver would say whether he knew him and, if so, which village he came from, and which Thug expeditions, if any, the pair had shared in. Other details – such as the names of the prisoner's associates and family – were taken down at the same time, if known. 'Ormea took part in the murder of 60 on the road to Indore, four years ago,' ran one typical denunciation. 'During this expedition he himself strangled seven men and a woman.'

Even when they were at Jubbulpore, Thug informants had to be housed separately from other prisoners, not least to save them from the vengeance of the men whom they betrayed. No fixed punishment for betraying a gang, it should be said, was ever exacted on traitorous Thugs by their old comrades. But the earliest approvers plainly did fear the vengeance of those whom they betrayed. 'Thugs will strangle a King's Evidence,' one active murderer confirmed, while Syeed Ameer Ali begged earnestly for protection after he was captured:

> All I require, should my life be spared, is permission to live in irons or in any situation where I may be protected from the numerous stranglers who inhabit [these] districts, as they will exert every endeavour to destroy me. I have already undermined all their houses, and have gone too far in my information against them to recede. No person engaged with these people has ever hitherto said so much; as everyone knows how revengeful these stranglers are . . . I have nothing more to ask, but will do all I can in putting a stop to the work of my late friends, the stranglers, as my safety now depends upon their destruction.

Once the system was fully established, new approvers could be questioned almost immediately concerning the whereabouts of their closest associates. This minimized the chance that wanted Thugs would hear of the latest arrests and flee their homes, and sometimes made it possible for captured Thugs to lure their former friends into the Company's hands using much the same cunning they had previously employed in inveigling travellers. When the strangler Ramzan, nominally a revenue collector in Oudh, indicated a willingness to turn approver, he was (he later testified)

> asked if I could point out Buhram Jemadar, a notorious leader of Thugs for whose seizure a reward of 100 rupees had been offered by the British Government. I said, 'Yes,' and that very night led forth an English guard of eight sepoys to the village of Sohanee. I went to the house where Buhram

Jemadar slept. Often has he led our gangs! I awoke him – he knew me well, and came outside to me. It was a cold night, so, under the pretence of warming myself, but in reality to have light for his seizure by the guard, I lighted some straw and made a blaze. As Buhram and I were warming ourselves, the guard drew around us. I said to them, 'This is Buhram,' and he was seized just as a cat seizes a mouse. Buhram immediately confessed that he was a Thug, saying, 'I am a Thug, my father and grandfather were Thugs, and I have Thugged with many. Let the government employ me and I will do its work.'

Some hint of the motivations that led the Thug approvers to serve Sleeman so readily can be found in this statement by Buhram. We have already seen that some Thugs regarded their involvement with the gangs as a form of military service, depending on their jemadars and, ultimately, the zamindars and petty rajahs who protected them for food and money. Thuggee was no more than a form of employment for them, a means of providing for their families. And as Sleeman evidently recognized, at least some of his approvers saw the transfer of their loyalties from the Thug gangs to the Company as no more disgraceful than the actions of a mercenary selling his services to a new master. 'We . . . are become servants of Government,' one explained. Some of Sleeman's prisoners may even have seen their work as a form of salaried employment, for as well as being clothed, housed and fed, their families received a Company stipend and they were even able to send money to their relatives by earning the rewards offered for the capture of leading Thugs. The men of the remaining gangs, announced the approver Rambux, 'are all my enemies now!'

Not every approver was arrested in the course of a Thug expedition. Other tactics, some of them of dubious legitimacy, were tried with some success, as Futty Khan, one of the most notorious stranglers in Oudh, found to his distress. Futty had been an unusually active jemadar for two decades, and had 'just completed, with his gang, the murder of three entire families' when news reached him that his wife and three children had been seized by a party of the Company's nujeebs, the mounted irregulars most often used to pursue the Thugs. Told his own family would not be released until he gave himself up,

I returned home and in about a month after this, my last murder, I delivered myself up, confessing my crime. I at once turned King's Evidence, and within three days pointed out to the guard the following Thugs, who were seized, namely Maigal and Ameer, now in gaol here.

When I went to catch Maigal, he was at his own house and readily came at my call; but when he saw irons on my legs, great was his consternation! He knew that I had come as an approver to seize him! The lamentation which he and his wife made soon filled the whole village with news of his capture. He is a well-known Thug! He confessed on reaching Lucknow.

The initial progress of the anti-Thug campaign was swift. By the end of 1829, Sleeman had around a hundred newly detained stranglers in custody at Saugor and Jubbulpore. That total was almost quadrupled within 12 months, and as the evidence supplied by the approvers was sifted and checked, hundreds of warrants were issued for the arrest of suspected Thugs. Sleeman and Smith occasionally went further, too, from the very start of their campaign, sending their approvers out in the company of nujeeb patrols armed with what were known as 'general warrants' – papers that gave the troops authority to detain any man pointed out by a Thug informer. The use of such warrants soon proved controversial, even in the comparatively lawless central provinces, not least because unscrupulous approvers were suspected of using them to have their enemies arrested. Dozens of other suspects were detained on 'mere hearsay' obtained from spies and prostitutes, and police officers, too, were far from immune to the temptation that the warrants posed. Some used them as instruments of extortion, threatening to arrest men who refused to pay them bribes, and even FC Smith – whose signature appeared on many of the papers – had to admit that general warrants did 'occasionally create great evils'. There were similar problems with the identity papers Sleeman drew up for his approvers, confirming that they were exempt from execution or transportation to a penal colony overseas. On at least one occasion it was discovered that convicted Thugs were loaning such papers to old associates who used them for 'bad purposes'.

The approvers sent out on the roads in search of other Thugs were given one other important task. It became a grim routine for them to prove the truth of their testimonies by supervising the exhumation of their victims'

bodies, and for the identity of the cadavers to be proved, if possible, by articles found on their bodies and identified by relatives or friends. 'Often,' noted
Sleeman, 'I have seen incredulous visitors at my court house, come to seek
information about missing relatives, burst into uncontrolled tears at the sight
of some small possession, which had been taken from the corpse and which
they instantly recognised.'

Sleeman's comment sheds a rare shaft of light on the human cost exacted
by the depredations of the Thugs. In the midst of so much murder, the voices
of the stranglers' living victims are heard only occasionally in the Company's
records. Bereaved relatives can be glimpsed here and there, 'setting up a most
dismal yell' when the bodies of their husbands or children are discovered, or
recognizing an article of equipment or clothing recovered from bodies found
in a nullah or along the road. But their testimonies were seldom put down in
writing, and the grief that they experienced was all too often forgotten then,
and still is now, by those investigating Thuggee.

No account of the Thug gangs is, nonetheless, complete without some
reference to the human cost exacted in the course of decades of brutal
murder. Consider, for example, the experiences of Ruckbur Singh, a Rajput
and brother to a man strangled by Thugs near Ellichpore in 1823. Five weeks
after the murder had taken place, Singh became seriously alarmed at his
brother's non-appearance and set off to search the road on which he had been
travelling. After making fruitless enquiries for several days, the Rajput was
close to giving up the hunt when he fell in with a party of the Company's
sepoys conveying a group of captured Thugs towards Jhalna. These men
'gave me a full account of my brother's murder, and his servant Khooba's
murder', and pointed out the well into which they had pitched the bodies of
a large group of their victims. Investigating the spot more closely, Ruckbur
Singh soon uncovered an horrific sight:

> I found five skulls close to the well, and eight skulls in the bottom of the
> well, into which I dived repeatedly and took up all the bones I could find.
> As it was impossible to distinguish my brother's skull and bones, I col-
> lected all the bones and placed them with the thirteen skulls on a pile of
> wood, which I prepared agreeably to the rites of my caste and burnt them
> all together.

Then there was the case of the Cotwal of Sopur, a Maratha from Gwalior whose 17-year-old son fell into the hands of a Thug gang while on his way to fetch his bride around the year 1828. The boy was expertly inveigled, and disclosed that he was carrying a purse full of gold mohurs to defray his party's expenses. That was enough to seal his fate, and the whole group was strangled, but jackals disinterred the bodies soon after they were buried and the murder was discovered. 'Going back,' one Thug involved in the case recalled, 'we found the uncle of the youth sitting in front of the door, weeping and lamenting the loss of his nephew . . . The father died of grief soon after. He could never be persuaded to eat anything after he learnt of the fate of his only son, and soon died.'

One further example will stand for the myriad of mute testimonies that never found their way into the Company's official records. An Indore merchant by the name of Humeerchund became concerned for the safety of his brother and brother-in-law, who vanished, in 1829, while transporting a large load of English chintz to Sehore. After a long and anxious wait for news, he learned

> that the bodies of some persons had been found about three months previously near the Gola pass . . . A boy observed a number of jackals and vultures near the pass, and had gone there in expectation of finding some dead animal and getting its skin. On reaching the spot, however, he found the bodies of two men which had been buried under a heap of stones so imperfectly that the wild beasts had afterwards dragged them out and almost entirely devoured them. The boy gave notice to the villagers, who went to the pass and buried the remains of the bodies. On hearing this account, I went to the Gola pass in company with the [witness], who pointed out the spot where the bodies had been found. A large stone which lay near the place had some marks of blood upon it, and on removing it I found a shoe, which I at once recognised as having belonged to my brother, and I wept bitterly.

In this case, rather unusually, Humeerchund was able to confront his brother's murderers in court, for some time later a Thug gang was apprehended nearby, and one of its jemadars was found to be wearing a distinctive *ungurka* (jacket), cut from chintz and lined with blue cotton, which had belonged to the strangled man. It had been a present from his uncle, a fellow

Thug, 'and rather than alter so pretty a garment, he ran the risk of wearing it till he was taken'.

Even though he knew his brother was dead, the shock of seeing his jacket produced in evidence was too much for the merchant. When the ungurka was brought out, Humeerchund 'immediately recognised it, and was so much affected as scarcely to be able to speak'. And 'as we had no doubts that our relations had been murdered', his deposition concluded, 'we performed their funeral rites according to the customs of our sect'.

The arrests of two large gangs of Thugs by Borthwick and Sleeman, coming so close together and at a time when the Company was at last receptive to the idea that such bands of murderers existed, caused a considerable sensation.

'Few who were in India at that period,' wrote Meadows Taylor from his cantonment, 'will ever forget the excitement which the discovery occasioned in every part of that country, [though] it was utterly discredited by the magistrates of many districts, who could not believe that this silently destructive system could have worked without their knowledge.' The newspapers were suddenly full of accounts of Thugs. Tales of silent murder became fashionable for a time. The Company's prisons were scoured for captured stranglers and concerted efforts were, for the first time, made to detain more.

'I became very busy,' Taylor recalled a few years later. 'Those famous discoveries in regard to the practice of Thuggee had recently been made at Jubbulpore and Saugor by Captain Sleeman, which made a sensation in India never to be forgotten. By the confessions of one gang, who were apprehended, many Thugs in Central India were brought to justice; and at last the Thugs of the Deccan were denounced by these approvers, and as many lived near Hingolee, they were at once arrested. Day after day I recorded tales of murder, which, though horribly monotonous, possessed an intense interest; and as fast as new approvers came in, new mysteries were unravelled and new crimes confessed.'

Much remained to be done. Progress, even with the help of the first approvers, was slow at first. But Sleeman, whose headquarters at Jubbulpore were ideally positioned to place him at the centre of the great Thug hunt, could see a way forward. What was needed was an informant capable of betraying not just one gang but many, a man so well informed of the plans of his fellow jemadars that he could secure dozens, even hundreds of stranglers in a single season. Feringeea could play this role. But Sleeman would find himself tested to the utmost in his attempts to capture him.

CHAPTER 12

The Omen of the Owl

'jeetae purjana – taking omens'

Feringeea and his companions were not at first particularly concerned by the betrayals of Amanoolah and the other approvers. They could not believe that a single confession, or even the efforts of several turncoats, could eradicate a system so widespread and successful as Thuggee. Both the Company and the native rulers of India had, after all, achieved little in the past other than the destruction of a few isolated Thug gangs, and each successive effort had – as one eminent strangler observed – 'ended in nothing but the punishment of a few'. Why should this new campaign be any different?

In some respects, indeed, the Thugs were stronger in the late 1820s than they had ever been. An extended economic depression had swollen their ranks to the point where it became possible to spread a net of scouts and spies across an appreciable area of country, ensnaring more potential victims than had previously seemed possible and, just as importantly, the return of peace to the central provinces meant an increase in traffic on the roads. Not all of these new travellers were wealthy – many were fleeing precisely the same financial distress that had driven many of the Thugs themselves to crime – but, all in all, more people, and probably more money, had begun to criss-cross India than ever before. The gangs reaped the benefits. 'Before the establishment of tranquillity over the country,' one aged strangler recalled, our excursions were neither carried out to so great a distance as they have since been, nor were so lucrative or certain, for in those days travellers, particularly with much property, seldom ventured to go from one place to another without being well escorted or in large parties, and we feared the Pindaris and other mounted plunderers as much as other classes did.

Feringeea profited from these improved conditions as much as any other Thug. During the cold season of 1827–8, he and his gang of 25 men had travelled south from their homes in Bundelcund, crossing the Malwa plateau into Gujerat and proceeding south into Candeish and the lands that had proved so lucrative for them the previous year. In the course of this one expedition, they had strangled some 105 men and women in 32 different affairs. It is unlikely they would have met so many worthwhile victims even a few years earlier, when the country was still blighted in the aftermath of the Maratha and Pindari wars.

None of the murders committed in the course of this expedition had been particularly noteworthy in itself, and the largest number of victims despatched on a single occasion had been no more than nine, but the gang seized plenty of gold and silver nonetheless. The largest single haul had been a consignment of silver valued at 4,000 rupees, taken from two treasure-bearers killed outside Aurangabad. But an additional 1,100 rupees was discovered among the possessions of a solitary thief whom Feringeea himself cornered in an old graveyard close to Oomroutee and personally strangled.* His gang had also murdered four unlucky drovers and appropriated the two bullock-loads of copper coins they had been conveying north, and added several hundred 'strings of small pearls', 15 of large pearls, a gilded necklace and a quantity of coral from the body of another victim. This loot had to be split with eight other Thug gangs, amounting in all to about 190 men, with whom Feringeea had cooperated at various times during the four months he and his followers spent on the road. Even so, allowing for the numerous small sums and pieces of loot taken from the remainder of the dead, the Thugs' haul must have been worth a total of nearly 6,000 rupees, leaving a most respectable total of nearly 30 rupees for each member of the expedition.

*This money, remarkable as it may seem, was also said to be the property of the ubiquitous Dhunraj Seth, and had been stolen by the ambitious but unfortunate thief as it passed through the nearby town of Parowtee.

The sheer variety of the men and women who met their deaths at the hand of Feringeea and his companions in the course of this one journey says something about the vibrancy of the roads of India after a full decade of peace. In addition to the usual mass of undifferentiated 'travellers', 'Marathas', 'Rajpoots' and 'Brahmins' despatched in the course of the expedition, the Thugs had murdered two dozen sepoys, eight bearers, six merchants, three *pundits* (learned teachers of Sanskrit, law and religion), a messenger, a fakir, two shopkeepers, an elephant driver and a bird-catcher. Their victims also included four women who – travelling with men whom the Thugs wished to murder – had been despatched without any apparent compunction.

Feringeea was by now at the height of his powers. He was still young – perhaps in his mid-twenties – and had yet to accumulate a sizeable number of followers; the gang of 25 men he led in 1827–8 was less than half the size of the largest group of Thugs at large in India that year. Nor is there any evidence that he exercised influence over the movements of gangs other than his own, other than in agreeing with his fellow jemadars, in the loosest terms, the districts most likely to yield returns in the prevailing circumstances. Yet there can be little doubt that Feringeea was one of the most deadly and effective stranglers ever to operate in the mofussil.

His high caste, practised charm and good looks made him a particularly successful inveigler, but he was a consummate leader, too. Year after year, he and his men killed as many, if not more, travellers than any other group of stranglers. Perhaps even more significantly, Feringeea was unusually well connected. He seems to have known, either by name or reputation, virtually all of the most important Thugs of Hindustan, and – in a career that by now dated back the better part of 15 years – had travelled, at one time or another, with most of them. His knowledge of other gangs, their successes, their members and those members' families and homes, was unsurpassed.

The frequency with which Feringeea and his men cooperated with other jemadars on the roads of central India comfirms that loose alliances did exist between gangs quartered close together in the wilds of Bundelcund, or sharing common origins in a village such as Murnae. Feringeea himself often joined forces with a number of other Thug leaders, among them two much older men by the names of Zolfukar and Sheikh Inaent, both of whom were old associates of his family. Zolfukar had taken part, with Feringeea's father, in a Thug expedition that had occurred as long ago as 1801, while Sheikh Inaent,

Three captured Thugs demonstrate their technique for strangling a victim.
This study is attributed to the pioneering photographer Felice Beato, and was
probably taken at Lucknow in March 1858.

William Sleeman (1788–1856), an East India Company officer, led the British campaign to eradicate Thuggee, developing revolutionary new police techniques to do so.

Murderers in India's native states could be sentenced to be 'trodden to death by elephants'. Among those executed in this way were the Thugs Boodhoo and Khumoli, brothers who were put to death at Jhalone in 1814–15.

Thugs about to Strangle a Traveller!

These infamous Assassins in order that the Neck of their unsuspecting Victim may be the more exposed for their Satanic purpose, pretending to see something extraordinary, direct his attention to the Stars or Skies! and when he lifts up his head Strangle him!

Four scenes from a typical Thug murder, sketched by an Indian artist at Lucknow in 1837 under the direction of the leaders of several gangs. *Top*: Thug inveiglers induce an intended victim to bare his neck by pointing to the stars. *Bottom*: the appointed strangler and his assistants, the handholders, despatch their victim, incongruously depicted here as a European. *Facing page (top)*: members of the gang carry the bodies away for disposal. *Facing page (bottom)*: Thugs ensure their victims are dead by stabbing them in the eyes prior to hurling their corpses into a well. One strangler explained that this practice was introduced around the year 1810 after the victim of one attack had recovered and escaped. (British Library)

Thugs Strangling a Traveller

This Sketch was shewn to me by three thug approvers Futteh Khan Jumadar, Sindh who he all detailed at to...

A Gang of Thugs carrying the travellers whom they have strangled, from the Bhaits, to the graves, or wells.

Thugs stabbing the Eyes and bodies of the travellers whom they have strangled, preparatory to throwing them into a Well.

A sketch by the British traveller Fanny Parks showing a British magistrate or judge – possibly Sleeman's superior, FC Smith – hearing evidence against a captured strangler during the Thug trials of the 1830s. (British Library)

Thug prisoners, probably photographed at Jubbulpore, sit on one of the carpets they wove by hand. The most spectacular example of their work, a carpet weighing more than two tons, was presented to Queen Victoria and can still be seen in the Waterloo Chamber at Windsor Castle. (British Library)

Convicted Thugs were tattooed with the details of their crimes, in Hindustani if they were to be imprisoned in India and in English if sentenced to be transported to a penal colony overseas. Tattoos were generally applied to prisoners' foreheads in order to deter attempts to escape. Some men tried to hide them beneath turbans, and this sketch suggests that a few Thugs may have been tattooed beneath the eyes instead. (British Library)

The central courtyard of the School of Industry, opened in Jubbulpore in 1837 to provide useful work for Thug informants and their families. Aside from their celebrated carpets, the Thugs' main product was latrine tents for the British army.

Gibbets on a roadside in the Madras Presidency, said to have been used to display the bodies of executed Thugs. The practice was officially frowned on, but may have endured in rural districts as late as the 1860s.

who was nearly 20 years older than his young colleague, came originally from Sindouse and had fled, with his fathers and brothers, when Halhed invaded the pargana, settling with other Chambel valley Thugs in Bundelcund. Ties of this sort must have proved invaluable when it came to turning several smaller gangs of stranglers into one large group capable of tackling a sizeable party of travellers. But the loose associations that existed between Thug leaders left them ever more vulnerable to the denunciations of approvers. In the course of the cold season of 1829–30, this fatal weakness would at last be fully exploited.

Feringeea left his home in November 1829 determined to atone for the disastrous outcome of his most recent expedition. He and his gang had strangled a further 77 men and three women in the course of the cold season of 1828–9. But a jemadar named Phoolsa, who came from the same village as Feringeea himself, had been seized by the local militia almost as soon as they had killed their first victim, and had to be abandoned. The travellers who had fallen prey to the Thugs were carrying so little cash that the loot hardly covered the costs of the expedition, and the stranglers' frustration had only been increased by a chance encounter with another group of Thugs returning from an expedition to Dhoree, in Candeish, with somewhere in excess of 70,000 rupees of gold and jewels taken from yet another party of treasure-bearers. In this same year, Feringeea himself had spent an uncertain four months in Holkar's prison at Alumpore, placed there no doubt on the orders of Beharee Lal, before contriving to escape. And by then it was so late in the season that most of the jemadar's followers dispersed not long after he rejoined their gang, leaving him with only two companions. Feringeea had been forced to join Zolfukar's band simply in order to remain active on the long road home.

The expedition of 1829–30 opened rather more auspiciously. Feringeea and the 25 men who made up his gang strangled a moonshee, five servants and four Brahmins before they had even crossed the Nerbudda river, and a shopkeeper and three other travellers shortly thereafter, before falling in with Zolfukar and his followers not far from Saugor. The two gangs joined forces, and – now nearly 40 strong – inveigled and murdered another 15 travellers on the roads leading to Bhopal. Sheikh Inaent, meanwhile, was in the adjoining district with his men, working their way along the road towards the town of Sewagunge.

The Company's net was, however, now closing fast around the gangs still at large in the half million square miles of the central provinces. The approvers captured by Borthwick and Sleeman a few months earlier had produced a list of 23 leaders quartered in villages around the town of Jhansee; five of the men named had already been arrested, and the remainder were now being sought in the very districts through which the gangs were passing. The captured stranglers had also betrayed the routes most favoured by their comrades and the dates when they were active in the cold season. With this information to hand, it became possible for Sleeman and his colleagues to station parties of sepoys along the roads frequented by the gangs, and to supply some of them, at least, with informants capable of identifying Thugs whom they encountered along the way.

These tactics were immediately successful. While Feringeea's men were still in the vicinity of Saugor, word reached them that a jemadar named Sheikh Macub had been seized, together with his men, only a few miles away. A few days later, they encountered another Thug who was fleeing back towards his home in Bundelcund. This man bore even more disturbing news. A day or two earlier, the jemadar of another gang had been seized by Company troops between Jubbulpore and Banda. Once again the arrest had been made uncomfortably close to hand. But it was the identity of the gang's leader that particularly disturbed Feringeea. Sleeman's sepoys had captured his old associate, Sheikh Inaent.

Inaent, travelling with five other jemadars and a combined force of 85 Thugs, had been 'intending to operate that season along the great road from Mirzapore to Jubbulpore, and strike off to that between Saugor and Calpee'. He and his men had already murdered two shopkeepers, a pair of blacksmiths and a Muslim sepoy carrying a *churee*, or painted stick – his badge of office – and had just formed designs on a second party of four when they reached a convenient tank and agreed to stop there for the night. 'We were preparing to go on with them after the third watch,' Inaent would recall, 'with the intention of killing them on the road, when we heard the *duheea* (the cry of the hare), a dreadful omen; and we let them go on, unmolested.' Even this observance of ritual, however, was not enough to save the gang, for late that same night, when the Thugs halted in order to burn the evidence of their earlier killings, they were overtaken by a group of Company sepoys, accompanied by two approvers by the names of Doulut and Dhun Singh. The soldiers did not linger for very long, but to

Inaent's horror, the approvers decided to stop and rest by the Thugs' fire. The two men sat down to warm themselves, telling their new comrades that they would catch them up.

It was now a little before dawn, and both groups were in desperate danger. The two approvers were heavily outnumbered; Inaent and his men could easily have killed them. On the other hand, the sepoys were not yet far away, and the murdered soldier's clothes and his churee could clearly be seen blazing away in the fire. Doulut and Dhun Singh could scarcely fail to notice and understand such an obvious clue.

They did not fail. 'We overheard,' Inaent recalled, 'Doulut saying to Dhun Singh: "This stick and these clothes must have belonged to murdered men; and these must be some of our old friends, and a large party of them." And both seemed to be alarmed at their situation, as they were then alone.' But rather than fall upon their former comrades, whose presence they knew would all too soon be missed, the nervous Thugs decided to make good their escape instead. They packed hurriedly and prepared to leave, but were not quite quick enough. Inaent was in the act of mounting his pony when a second party of sepoys appeared on the horizon:

> I had my foot in the stirrup, when [the approvers] saw part of the advanced guard, and immediately made a rush at our bridles. We drew our swords, but it was too late. Both fell upon me, and I was secured. Had Doulut and Dhun Singh called out, 'Thugs!', the guard might have secured a great part of the gang, but they appeared to be panic struck, and unable to speak. By this time the regiment came up, and finding some of the remains of the trooper's clothes on the fire, the European officers found it difficult to prevent the sepoys from bayoneting me on the spot.

While Inaent was being secured, the other members of his gang fled into the surrounding jungle and made off. Even while they were evading probable arrest, however, these men continued to murder the travellers they met. The strangler Rambuksh, heading north-east towards the town of Rewah with 25 men, encountered a party of six on their way to the holy city of Benares. Four were Gosains, wandering mendicants 'remarkable for their wealth' who often engaged in moneylending and were, thus, likely victims; suspecting that the men had jewels concealed somewhere about their persons, Rambuksh and his companions strangled them, a little before dawn, in a mango grove for possessions worth a total of 900 rupees. The dead men's corpses were stripped and left exposed and, when the bodies were found by the people of a nearby village, it was observed 'that their long matted hair seemed to have been opened out and examined; and the only mark of violence that appeared on the bodies was that of a string around the neck, with which they seemed to have been strangled'. Another portion of the dispersed group killed two carriers of Ganges water, a tailor and a woman who were on their way to Banda, and then six more men two days later, the latter murder yielding a further 200 rupees. But Feringeea and Zolfukar were much more cautious. They retreated all the way to Bhopal 'without killing any person' before beginning to murder again, contriving, nonetheless, to strangle another 14 travellers, in five separate affairs, by the time they finally found their way back to the Nerbudda close to the town of Hoshangabad.

The two jemadars had shaken off Sleeman's pursuit. And for all its difficulties, the cold season of 1829–30 had at last begun to produce better returns than they had endured 12 months earlier. The Thugs must have hoped that they could continue unmolested, and be spared the alarms and arrests that had certainly begun to fray the nerves of all their men. But it was now, in the last weeks of 1829, that things began to go still more badly wrong for Feringeea and his followers.

Suddenly and without warning their world was filled with portents of disaster. First, 'to our great surprise and consternation', Zolfukar's mare dropped a foal – a serious matter, since the blood and mucus associated with the birth contaminated the ritual purity of the Hindu Thugs and placed them all 'under the *eetuk*', a religious proscription that made it impossible for the men to continue the expedition.* Then, when the gangs had parted company and begun their long journeys home, something altogether worse occurred. Feringeea's men were resting by a river eight miles from the town of Bhilsa, and their jemadar was bathing in the stream, when all distinctly heard the sound Thugs dreaded more than any other. Clearly – though it was the middle of the day – the hooting call of a baby owl echoed overhead.

---

*No doubt Zolfukar's mare was part of the loot seized from one of the travellers murdered by his gang, and this was one of the unanticipated hazards of life as a Thug. Had the horse really been Zolfukar's own, he would presumably have realized she was pregnant.

Belief in omens and portents was very common at this time. The lives of ordinary villagers could be disrupted or cut short in so many ways – famine, disease, drought, the failure of the crop or the exactions of landlords – that peasants, travellers and merchants alike were only too anxious to place their faith in systems of prophecy and divination that offered guidance to an uncertain future. Farmers watched for signs while they tilled their fields. Townsmen consulted the auguries before embarking on a business venture, and hunters interpreted the cries of wild animals as omens for the success or failure of their efforts.

Superstitious thugs and dacoits – who depended heavily on luck to bring them worthwhile hauls of plunder and who risked capture at every turn – were as susceptible to these omens as any peasant. Some dacoit gangs firmly believed that certain days of the week were luckier than others for committing robberies, and others held that the sound of a bull bellowing, or a man sneezing, was so unlucky that they should abandon whatever dacoity they was planning. The Thugs, similarly, swore by an elaborate array of omens,* which guided them from first to last on their expeditions.

The movements and the sound of wild animals were the most important signs. When the members of a gang first left their village, Sleeman was told by one approver, they would go a little way along the road they planned to take, and wait until they heard a partridge call. If the cry came from the right, the expedition could begin. If it were heard coming from the left, the men would return home and begin again the next day on a different road. The Thugs would also halt at the first river or stream they came to, awaiting guidance as to whether to proceed, and in some gangs further auguries were taken at the start of each new day. A few men threw dice to determine the best time to commence an expedition; others gargled sour milk each morning and spat it out in the belief that this would guarantee them luck; while

> if any Thug is heard to break wind while they are at their resting place, dividing the booty, it is considered a very bad omen. They remove the offender

---

*'Indeed,' the ethnographers RV Russell and Hira Lal observe, 'the number of these was so extensive that they could never be at a loss for an indication of the divine will, and difficulties could only arise when the omens were conflicting.'

from among them, and kindle a fire upon the place where he sat, and quench
it with water, saying: 'As the signs of the water disappear, so the threatened evil
passes away.' Five blows of a shoe inflicted upon the head of the offending
person mitigates the evil to be apprehended, but cannot avert it altogether.

Many portents, naturally, were interpreted as warnings. Some travellers
who had fallen into the clutches of a gang of stranglers were saved from
imminent death when the scream of a kite was heard in the camp and
interpreted as a signal for their would-be murderers to hasten away from
the *bele* immediately. A wolf crossing the road was a signal for the whole
gang to go back and take another road, and the call of a jackal during the day,
or a partridge at night, was a more general instruction to flee the whole district. One old Thug who fell into British hands around this time impressed
the officers who interrogated him with his fervent belief in the dire significance of the latter omen, having once been a member of a party that
heard a partridge call at two in the morning; he and his companions had
made off at once in great alarm, but before they could get very far they were
surrounded and arrested by a party of troops in the service of the local
rajah, and 45 members of the gang were subsequently blown from the
mouths of cannon.*

Each gang seems to have had its own soothsayer – normally a Brahmin –
who bore responsibility for the interpretation of portents. 'The Ass, the Deer,
and the Jackal, are considered the auspicious four-legged beasts,' FC Smith
was told, 'and omens from any of these are more valued than the call of one
hundred of the most auspicious of the feathered tribe.' Even then, however,
the interpretation of the animals' calls and movement depended greatly upon
whether they were seen or heard to the left or to the right. Sounds heard from
the left while the gangs were on the march were generally interpreted as an
instruction to go on, and those coming from the right as warnings to stop or
retreat. When a group of Thugs reached a possible campsite, the omens
were reversed, and a sound coming from the right was regarded as a good
sign, and one from the left as an instruction to go on. To complicate matters

---

*A particularly gruesome punishment favoured in some Native States (and by the British in the aftermath
of the Indian Mutiny). The prisoner was strapped across the barrel of a loaded cannon on a parade ground.
When the gun was discharged, 'the air seemed to split. A head would come dancing across the ground, and
an obscene shower of blood and entrails would cover both gunners and observers.'

further, many gangs believed that it was dangerous to begin an expedition until one sign had been received from the right and a second from the left; this 'signified that the deity took them first by the right hand and then by the left to lead them on'.

For all these complexities, however, the Thugs could be surprisingly pragmatic when it came to interpreting portents. A warning to abandon an expedition and return to their villages might be obeyed if it was received only a day or two after their departure; one heard or seen when a gang was hundreds of miles from home might be dealt with merely by retreating a stage or two or making an offering. Similarly, the firm belief that a turban catching fire was so terrible an omen that disaster could only be averted by waiting seven days before beginning a journey afresh did not apply when far from home: 'If they had travelled for some distance, an offering of goor was made, and the owner of the turban alone returned.' Occasionally a whole succession of portents were simply ignored, and although many Thugs could cite examples of the awful fates that had befallen comrades foolish enough to proceed in the face of such warnings, it seems that only a minority of jemadars would willingly sacrifice a prize that was almost within their grasp in such circumstances.*

Only the direst auguries seem to have been obeyed more or less without exception. The call of the hare, which had prompted Sheikh Inaent and his fellow jemadars to abandon their designs on the four travellers they had planned to murder, was one such omen, possibly because the hare was a sacred animal for many Hindus – in central India women would not eat its meat, and the animal's long ears and exceptional hearing may account for the widespread belief that it could foresee the future. Perhaps the worst

---

*Many Thugs became far more scrupulous in their belief in portents after their arrest, having ascribed their downfall to a failure to interpret and obey such omens properly. 'Even the most sensible approvers,' Sleeman remarked a few years later, 'who have been with me for many years, Hindoos as well as Mussulmans, believe that their good or ill success depended upon the skill with which the omens were discovered and interpreted, and the strictness with which they were observed and obeyed. One of the old Sindouse stock told me, in the presence of twelve others, from Hydrabad, Behar, the Dooab, Oude, Rajpootana, and Bundelcund, that, had they not attended to these omens, they never could have thrived as they did. In ordinary cases of murder, other men seldom escaped punishment, while they and their families had, for ten generations, thrived, although they had murdered hundreds of people. "This," said the Thug, "could never have been the case had we not attended to omens, and had not omens been intended for us. There were always signs around us to guide us to rich booty, and warn us of danger, had we been always wise enough to discern them and religious enough to attend to them." Every Thug present concurred with him from his soul.'

portent of all, however, was the 'low and melancholy sound' of the *chiraiya*, or baby owl, no doubt because it was practically never heard in daytime. This, it was generally agreed, was a sure indication of impending disaster. The gang that heard the chiraiya call was doomed beyond hope of salvation.

As soon as he had emerged from the river, Feringeea consulted his gang's soothsayer, Kuhora, regarding the portent they had heard. Kuhora was 'an excellent augur', whose interpretation of omens the Thugs had found invaluable in the past. But on this occasion his advice was unwelcome. The owlet's call, Kuhora said, was a sign of such dire significance that the whole gang ought to abandon any intention of going on towards Saugor and retreat immediately along the road they had just come by.

This Feringeea was reluctant to do. It was still December 1829, relatively early in the season, and though he and his men had murdered 30 travellers in the few weeks since they had left their homes, none had provided them with a really worthwhile haul. To break off the expedition at such an early stage would mean considerable economic hardship for the members of the gang and, probably, require them to launch another foray into the central provinces almost as soon as they had returned to their homes. Scrupulous though Feringeea had been to the dictates of omens in the past, this was altogether too much to contemplate. He decided to ignore Kuhora's augury, and ordered his men to press on towards Saugor.

Whether or not the owlet's call was truly an omen or not, the jemadar's decision proved to be a critical mistake. Later that same day, and only four miles further along the road, the Thugs halted to rest. Feringeea tethered his pony to a tree and walked alone into the nearest village to obtain supplies. While he was there, the Thug leader 'heard a great uproar and saw my horse running towards the village'. Behind the panicked animal, in the distance, he could see a large party of Company sepoys 'seizing and binding my gang'. Sleeman's men had caught the Thugs unawares, and the approvers who were with them had identified several wanted stranglers among their ranks. There was nothing Feringeea could do to save his men. Only 12 of his 40 followers escaped, and their jemadar himself – who was no more than 'half-dressed' at the time, having left his possessions and the bulk of his clothes in the camp –

had no choice but to flee, alone and on foot, back towards his home in Bundelcund.

The capture of the majority of his gang placed Feringeea in considerable danger. No fewer than seven of the Thugs now brought before Sleeman at Jubbulpore turned approver; worse, several members of the jemadar's own family – including two of his adopted sons and five foster brothers – had been among the men arrested by the Company's patrols. Many of the prisoners had known Feringeea for years, and Sleeman had little difficulty in assembling an impressive quantity of information concerning the fleeing Thug. His most reliable informant was a boy who had entered Feringeea's service two years earlier 'in consequence of some domestic disputes', and been taken on his first Thug expedition shortly afterwards. By the end of January 1830, the magistrate knew of the jemadar's identity, his aliases, his appearance and habits, and a good deal about his Thug career. Most crucially of all, the approvers he recruited from among the captured men had supplied him with one piece of indispensable intelligence: the location of Feringeea's home.

CHAPTER 13

'A Double Weight of Irons'

'bisendee – handcuffs'

Sleeman's information was precise, and he wasted no time in acting on it. Within a matter of days a party of eight nujeebs, led by a *dafadar* (sergeant) named Rustum Khan and supplied with letters of commission addressed to the Company's agent in Bundelcund, left Jubbulpore and headed north in search of the Thug leader. The distance that they had to cover was not great – a little over 120 miles – and before the cold season had reached its end, the Company troops were picking their way across the drab landscape around Jhansee, making for Feringeea's home village of Gorha.

The village was one of at least seven in the vicinity of Jhansee to harbour Thugs, and even though they had taken care to inform the local rajah of their presence, and were accompanied by one of his officers, the nujeebs must have been conscious that they were far from help and heavily outnumbered. They knew that they could hardly hope to catch Feringeea by marching into Gorha openly; but approaching their quarry without being spotted by one of the villagers – most if not all of whom could be assumed to be loyal to the Thug leader and his gang – was impossible during daylight hours. In the end the patrol waited until long after dark, hoping no doubt to catch the jemadar asleep, and crept into the village shortly before midnight, hours after most of the village had gone to bed.

The nujeebs were quiet, but not quite quiet enough. Alerted to their presence just in time by the sound of urgent whispering outside his door,

Feringeea burst out of the rear of his cottage moments before the patrol broke in through the front. The Thug had wasted no time gathering possessions; even so, Sleeman's men missed their quarry 'by only a few seconds', finding his bed still warm, and 'an English blunderbuss and pistol lying loaded upon it'. Feringeea himself, though, had vanished into the night, and since he knew the district so much better than his enemies, his pursuers judged that it would be futile to go after him. Instead, the patrol took the remaining occupants of the house into custody. Among those thus arrested were Feringeea's mother, wife and child. All three, together with one of the jemadar's brothers, were hauled off to the jail at Jubbulpore.

By now the Company's campaign against the Thugs was gaining a significant momentum.

Almost from the instant of his first encounter with the stranglers, in 1829, William Sleeman had thrown himself into the business of destroying them with an implacable energy. The whole idea of the Thug campaign appealed to him. He was thoroughly familiar with the Saugor & Nerbudda Territory, in which much of the work was to be done. His long acquaintance with India, and his unusual affection for the Indian peasantry, meant that he genuinely loathed the stranglers and their ruthless disregard for life. He brought an air of almost religious fervour to his new responsibilities, and it was not long before he was speaking of his campaign as 'the cause'.

There was, nonetheless, another side to Sleeman's devotion to his work. He was an ambitious man, and – for any district officer – promotion, increased salary and honours came most quickly to those who attracted their superiors' attention. It was practically impossible, in normal circumstances, for men stationed far out in the wilds of India to get themselves noticed by the government. Sleeman had spent an entire decade in the central provinces, with little obvious reward, when the advent of the Thug campaign offered him the unexpected chance to make his mark. He seized his opportunity with both hands.

Sleeman's vigour – and his buccaneering determination to harry the Thug gangs wherever they were found – won him the blessing of his seniors. Several high government officials were soon paying close attention to the progress of the Thug campaign. 'The extirpation of this tribe,' confirmed George Swinton,* principal aide to the recently appointed Governor General Lord William Bentinck, 'would, I conceive, be a blessing conferred on the people of India, than which none would be more prized.' A few months later the same official confirmed, in a note to Smith:

His Lordship relies on the approved zeal and activity already displayed by yourself and Captain Sleeman, in bringing to condign punishment some of the most notorious of these inhuman wretches, and if through your instrumentality the abominable race of Thugs should be ultimately exterminated, your services in the cause of humanity would entitle you to the highest meed of applause.

Not everyone shared Swinton's views, of course. Opinion among Sleeman's fellow officers in central India remained sharply divided for years over the merits of the new anti-Thug campaign. Several of the British Residents stationed at Indian courts were appalled by the freedom with which Thug-hunting parties began to sweep across borders in pursuit of their quarries, arguing that their forays into the Native States would seriously antagonize rulers who were at best grudging allies. Certainly many rajahs were unwilling to hand over men who had paid them lavish tribute over the years. Petty zamindars who had for decades sheltered bandit gangs took their own steps to frustrate the Company's pursuit. On several occasions Sleeman's men found the gates of a village barred against them, and one party found itself waylaid within the borders of Gwalior and actually attacked by a detachment of Maharajah Sindhia's troops.

Even rulers who had never knowingly harboured bandits were angered by the nujeebs' intrusions and their treatment of Thug suspects. The arrest of several prominent Indian citizens on the word of mere informers resulted in despatch of a string of strongly worded protests to Calcutta. 'The Government,' the angry Resident at Bhurtpore complained to Swinton after one such incident, 'may be of the opinion that a humiliation of this sort is not felt by a native Prince, but I can take it upon me to assert that it was felt, and deeply too.'

---

*He was secretary to the Government of India, a position equivalent in stature to that of a present-day secretary of state.

The most strident complaints came from Gwalior, a Maratha state long familiar with Thugs. Richard Cavendish, the Company's long-serving Resident at Sindhia's court, consistently deplored Sleeman's willingness to entrust his nujeebs 'with such unlimited power' and proposed that all Thug-hunting parties from Jubbulpore should be accompanied by a British officer to prevent abuse of process. His complaints were consistently rebuffed, Swinton's colleague William Macnaghton noting that 'such a deputation would be impracticable consistent with the secrecy and celerity of movement required', but it took years to overcome such stubborn opposition. In the meantime, Sleeman began angrily insisting, Gwalior remained 'a sanctuary to which, after a glut of murder elsewhere, [the Thugs return] with as much safety as an Englishman to his inn'.

Problems of this sort were seen as mere distractions. Smith, as agent in Saugor & Nerbudda, and even the British government itself, far away in Calcutta, brushed all such disputes aside. 'To check the dreadful evil of Thuggee,' Macnaghton wrote, 'extraordinary measures are necessary', particularly in cases where 'the pursuit is surrounded by too many difficulties'.

Feringeea's wife, mother and infant child had all been seized on one of Sleeman's general warrants, and none had been accused of any crime, although the Company officials felt sure that the women must at least have suspected the source of their relatives' wealth.* Sleeman saw their arrests as a critical breakthrough in his pursuit of Feringeea himself, whose escape was an embarrassment to him. 'I knew,' he told his superiors, 'that Feringeea would not go far while links so dear to him were in my hands.' And if there was no prospect of flight, it was merely a matter of time before the great strangler fell into British hands.

Sleeman was right to suppose that Feringeea would not venture too far from the central provinces while his family languished in the custody of the East India Company. The Thug considered but rejected the notion of fleeing to the inaccessible territories of Rajpootana, where he had spent the early 1820s. But neither could he afford to remain idle after a second financially disastrous cold

---

*Feringeea himself always insisted that he had kept his wife entirely ignorant of his way of life.

season in succession. A few weeks after the Company's attempt to capture him, he slipped back into Gorha, and before Sleeman had the opportunity to send a second party of nujeebs in search of him, mustered another gang – smaller, this time, than his first – and set off again towards Saugor & Nerbudda in the hope of recouping his losses.

It was by now June or July 1830, the beginning of the monsoon season, and very late in the year for a Thug expedition; there were so many fewer people on the roads that this new sortie did not promise much success. Meeting once again with Zolfukar, Feringeea and his men fell upon a party of six near the town of Beseynee, 80 miles north of Jubbulpore. But things quickly began to go wrong. Almost as soon as the combined gangs reached the banks of the Nerbudda, 'Feringeea was taken up on suspicion' by the militia of the local rajah and abandoned by his companions. The jemadar spent only two days in confinement before securing – or more probably purchasing – his release, and was able to join yet another Thug band near Saugor. But there was time to strangle only one more victim, a servant at a police compound, before this gang, too, was detained, this time by the local darogah on suspicion of mere robbery.

It was the third time in less than 12 months that Feringeea had found himself in jail; plainly the whole of the central provinces was becoming a risky area for Thugs to operate in. Once again he enjoyed a lucky escape: 'I was taken to the zamindar . . . in whose presence I chanced to meet a friend who, giving me a good character, caused my release.' But, even so, the jemadar retired to Bundelcund at the end of July with nothing to show for the entire expedition, his arrest having prevented him from sharing in the booty taken by the rest of the gang, which was 'taken off by the [other] Thugs and not divided'.

Chastened by his escape from the Company's nujeebs, Feringeea took elaborate precautions to safeguard himself on his return to his home district. Sleeman was forced to work hard to track him down. After several months, however – no doubt with the assistance of approvers who had friends and relatives among the people of the district – it was established that the fugitive Thug was dividing his time between houses in five different villages, never sleeping in the same bed for two nights in succession. This was a highly effective precaution. Recognizing that it was impossible to determine in advance where Feringeea would be on any given night, and lacking the manpower to raid five villages simultaneously, Sleeman concluded that he had no choice but to search each possible hiding place in succession, arresting and securing the Thug's hosts in every one so as to prevent any warning being given, until Feringeea's hiding place was discovered. Even supposing such a thing was possible, however, there was still an element of risk. The villages stood so far apart that it was impossible to search more than four of them in a single night. If his men had the bad luck to choose the wrong settlements, their quarry would certainly elude them once again.

The Jubbulpore nujeebs were able, dedicated men – spurred on also, no doubt, by the prospect of sharing in the enormous reward of 500 rupees on Feringeea's head. Setting out from the borders of the district at dusk one day in the first week of November 1830, they hurried through the shadows to the first of the Thug villages, Joomaree, eight miles away. Not finding Feringeea there, Sleeman's men arrested his usual host, a man named Chutta, and forced him to guide them to the next hamlet on their itinerary, two miles away. Once again there was no sign of the fugitive, and once again the nujeebs 'seized and bound' the owner of the house they had been ordered to search. This man, a Brahmin, was compelled to escort the party to a third village, Jomun Sagura, another eight miles along the road.

Jomun Sagura was the home of the Thug jemadar Kuleean Singh, who was then in the jail at Jubbulpore. Sleeman guessed that Feringeea was using members of this family to keep in touch with his imprisoned wife and mother, and the nujeebs were not surprised to find Kuleean's spouse and his young son, Soghur, inside the house that their Brahmin captive pointed out to them. Once again, however – to their intense frustration – there was no sign of the fugitive himself.

It was now only a little before dawn. Two settlements remained to be searched, but the next village, Kisrae, a further six miles away, was the patrol's 'last hope, as the alarm would be given before they could reach the fifth'. As it was, the party – accompanied on this occasion by the boy Soghur – did not reach their goal until 'day began to appear', and many of the villagers were already up and about their business. The nujeebs were exhausted (they had covered 24 miles in total darkness), and it was in any case useless for so large a party to enter the village in daylight; if the Thug was about, he would be sure to hear of their approach. So while the guards hid themselves a short distance away, Soghur and a single approver, Dhun Singh, made their way

through the gates and casually approached the fourth of Feringeea's hide-
aways.

This time – at last – they were lucky. The elusive jemadar was still inside
the house. But there was certainly no time for Sogliui and Dhun Singh to
call up the nujeebs. Bravely, perhaps foolhardily, for they were 'only boys',
the pair instead rushed straight through the door, taking their quarry by
surprise.

Even then Feringeea might have escaped. He was, Sleeman later commented, 'strong enough to have strangled both, one with each hand'. But the
Thug simply did not believe that his attackers could have crept up on him
alone, and 'supposing the Guard to be round the house, he suffered his hands
to be tied without resistance'. Only then did the nujeebs appear. By the end of
the day the most wanted man in all the central provinces found himself
securely locked in Jhansee jail, festooned with 'a double weight of irons' to
prevent all possibility of escape.

So important did Sleeman consider his new prisoner to be that the Thug-
hunter travelled as far north as Saugor in order to escort Feringeea back to
Jubbulpore in person – a precaution he was never to take with any other
strangler. The two men finally reached their destination in the first days of
December 1830, some 17 years after Sleeman's captive had set out upon his
first Thug expedition. He would never embark on another.

The ride from Saugor to Jubbulpore took nearly three days. The captured
Thug had been a famous inveigler, famous for his manners and fine clothes
and renowned for the adroitness of his tongue. His powers did not fail him
now. By the time the party arrived at Jubbulpore, Sleeman was certain that his
captive was worth a good deal more to him alive than dead. The prisoner was
a 'great Thugg leader', Sleeman informed Francis Curwen Smith, who had
'exercised so much influence over the gangs, and is capable of giving so much
assistance in their apprehension, that it would be of vast importance to hold
out to him that his life shall be saved if he gives it to the utmost of his ability'.

Much of this information must have come from the jemadar himself.
Exactly what Feringeea had told Sleeman in the course of their ride was
never known. But some flavour of the Thug's claims on his own behalf can
certainly be caught in Smith's exultant response. 'Feringeea,' he wrote,

though so young a man, is evidently at the head of all the gangs of Thugs which infest the countries north of the Nerbudda; is fully initiated in all their plans, secrets, places of resort, and the persons of the members of the fraternities; and, as I have no doubt, is perfectly capable of giving such information as will materially assist in breaking up these bands of atrocious murderers.

On that basis, and although Smith privately thought the Thug 'fully deserving of death', it was decided to accept Feringeea as an approver – principally in the hope that his appearance in the Company's service would demoralize the remaining Thugs, and perhaps make them more wary of crossing into British territory. More senior officials were doubtful, pointing out that Feringeea had practised Thuggee not because he knew no other way to make a living 'but upon a deliberate calculation of the situation and wealth attached to the situation of leader'. In the end, however, Smith's arguments prevailed. This was fortunate, as it subsequently emerged that Sleeman had in any case offered his prisoner a provisional pardon upon their arrival at Jubbulpore.

Feringeea's motives for becoming an approver were never questioned by the Company, but it is possible to hazard a guess at what they were. Like every other captured strangler, the jemadar must have known that his only hope of saving his own life was to turn King's Evidence. Probably he was also encouraged to believe that by entering British service he might hope to see his wife and children once again. Finally, the actions of his fellow Thugs may also have spurred him on. So many men had begun to throw themselves on the mercy of the Company (Sleeman and his colleagues would eventually recruit a total of well over 100 Thug informants) that there was no longer anything to be gained by remaining silent.

Whatever his reasons, Feringeea began his new career anxious to impress his jailers. 'He has,' Sleeman wrote in the first days of January 1831, 'already given me abundant proof of his disposition to be instrumental in the seizure and conviction of several gangs of robbers.' The Thug's intelligence included details of a planned rendezvous of numerous large groups of stranglers in the province of Candeish and news concerning the massing of other gangs near Jypore, in Rajpootana. But Sleeman was not yet ready to place confidence in his newest prisoner. The jemadar's testimony could, after all, be a trick, an attempt to decoy the Company's scarce reserves of troops away from the Thugs' real targets for the coming season. Some proof of his reliability was required.

It did not take much time for Feringeea, with his long career of murder behind him, to convince Sleeman of his trustworthiness in the most gruesomely practical of manners. 'To prove his disposition to tell the truth,' the disbelieving magistrate explained, 'he offered to show me the bodies of about 25 men who had been strangled and buried at different intervals during the last 10 years by Gangs of which he had been a member.' The murdered men had been interred, the jemadar continued, in a favourite spot outside the nearby village of Salohda, 'lying on an open and fully cultivated and peopled plain upon the high road . . . only two stages from the town of Saugor.' The necessary arrangements were swiftly made, and early in January 1831, the magistrate, the approver and a small party of Company troops set out for Feringeea's bele.

The journey was an easy one – pleasant, even, in the delicious chill of the cold weather – and Sleeman's pregnant wife had begged permission to accompany her husband to enjoy the air. The party reached its destination, a small grove of mango trees a short distance outside Salohda, as dusk drew in on the second evening. Sleeman could see no sign of any graves, but it was in any case too late to begin the work of exhumation that evening. The tents were pitched, the guard set, and next morning – the date was 7 January 1831 – the magistrate and the approver rose at dawn to begin the arduous work of excavating the grove.

'He pointed out,' Sleeman would recall,

> three places in which he and his gang had deposited at different intervals the bodies of three parties of travellers, [informing me that] a Pundit and six attendants, murdered in 1818, lay among the ropes of my sleeping tent, a *Havildar* and four Sipahaes, murdered in 1824, lay under my horses, and four Brahman carriers of Ganges water and a woman, murdered soon after the Pundit, lay within my sleeping tent. The sward had grown over the whole, and not the slightest sign of its ever having been broken was to be seen. The thing seemed to me incredible; but after examining attentively a small brick terrace close by, and the different trees around, he declared himself prepared to stake his life upon the accuracy of the information.

My wife was still sleeping over the grave of the water carriers unconscious of what was doing or to be done. (She has often since declared that
she never had a night of such horrid dreams, and that while asleep her soul
must consequently have become conscious of the dreadful crimes that had
there been perpetrated.) I assembled the people of the surrounding villages, and the Thanadar and his police, who resided in the village of Korae
close by, and put the people to work over the grave of the Havildar. They
dug down five feet without perceiving the slightest signs of the bodies or a
grave. All the people assembled seemed delighted to think that I was
becoming weary like themselves, and satisfied that the man was deranged;
but there was a calm and quiet confidence about him that made me insist
upon their going on, and at last we came upon the bodies of the whole five
laid out precisely as described.

My wife, still unconscious of our object in digging, had repaired to the
breakfast tent which was pitched some distance from the grove; and I now
had the ropes of her tent removed, and the bodies of the Pundit and his six
companions, in a much greater state of decay, exhumed from about the
same depth, and from the exact spot pointed out.

The grim process went on for the rest of the day. By the time the corpses
of the Ganges water carriers had been disinterred, and the rotting remains of
the Thugs' victims laid gently on the ground between the remaining tents,
Sleeman was convinced of his prisoner's good faith. Feringeea himself was
not yet finished, even offering to point out graves that still lay hidden in
neighbouring groves, but Sleeman professed himself so 'sick of the horrid
work, and satisfied with what had already been done,'* that the whole party
set off instead to return to Jubbulpore. There was more important work
to do.

From the moment that the first of Feringeea's victims emerged from his
grave outside Salohda, the Thug became Sleeman's favourite approver. In years
to come, other informants, among them some of the jemadar's closest associates, would contribute copious testimony of their own, each new piece of

---

*Upon further investigation, Sleeman discovered that 'the proprietor of the village of Salohda connived at
all this, and received the horse of the Pundit as a present. [The gang] used to encamp in this grove every
year in passing, and remain there for many days at a time, feasting, carousing and murdering.'

information being meticulously recorded and analysed in the hope that it might
lead to another arrest, a further conviction. But of the hundred or more Thugs
made approvers by Sleeman and his colleagues, Feringeea was by far the most
influential. His capture was a critical turning point in the anti Thug campaign.

Feringeea's principal importance lay in the sheer breadth of his knowledge.
Long experience and a prodigious memory (honed, no doubt, by the
jemadar's duty of noting a gang's victims and the loot taken from them so
that the proceeds could eventually be divided equally) combined to make him
an effective witness. He could identify literally hundreds of other stranglers by
name, and his depositions feature more often than those of any other
approver in the Company's records, taking pride of place in the enormous
summaries of evidence assembled by Sleeman as he prepared cases for trial.
In almost all of the surviving files, Feringeea's testimony appears last, as if to
supply final corroboration of the evidence given by other Thugs. The details
of his evidence are placed in columns that have been made twice as wide as
those allocated to other approvers in order to accommodate the sheer bulk of
the information he supplies.

The detail of Feringeea's recollections supplied Sleeman with endless clues.
'I know Badaloo,' he said of one suspect brought in for identification. 'He is
a jemadar of Thugs and has 30 or 40 followers. Last [year] with 40 men he
went to Baroda and murdered four travellers . . . got dollars, gold and pearls
from them. Seven of the gang [have been] taken before. He has been engaged
in hundreds of murders, besides he murdered Gumush Chuprassee, whose
chuprassee* has been found on them.' The Thug Golab was identified with
the comment: 'He is the son of Bukkee Thug. He quarrelled with Jadae in
Lahra, they fought and he was cut in the right shoulder. I was present. He was
at the Murder of Lieutenant Maunsell in Murnae, and he got a coat, pan-
taloons and the Gentleman's horses. He was seized at Etawah but escaped. Mr
Parry offered 1,000 rupees for him.' In a single week, confronted with no
fewer than 289 Thugs captured in a sweep through the villages of Jhansee,
Feringeea was able to identify and name 283, a far greater total than that of
any other approver. In most cases he also supplied comprehensive details of
the men's murderous careers.

The approver's statements proved to be critical in almost every case. In

---

*Stick used as a badge of office.

'Trial no. 6 of 1832', to take only one example, the jemadar was able to identify 13 of the 16 prisoners by name, and all of these men were convicted. In
the next case to be heard, he named 10 of the 18 prisoners in the dock and
supplied details of their criminal careers, explaining that he had Thugged
with several of the accused for as many as 18 years. Unlike most of his fellow
approvers, Feringeea also supplied Sleeman with valuable information concerning the future movements of Thug gangs. Even when word that the
great Thug had turned approver caused other gangs to change their plans and
alter predetermined routes, he continued to track their movements with the
help of members his own extended family – Thugs who remained at liberty
serving under other leaders – still contriving to lead Sleeman to his quarry.*

The significance of Feringeea's evidence can plainly be seen in the growing
numbers of stranglers confined in the Company's jails. Before the jemadar's
arrest, no more than a few hundred Thugs had fallen into British hands in the
course of an entire decade. Afterwards, the number increased swiftly. More
than 700 suspected stranglers were arrested in 1831 and 1832 alone, three-
quarters of them in the central provinces. A substantial proportion of these
men were either betrayed by Feringeea himself, or convicted as a consequence of the depositions he made at their trials.

Before the jemadar's capture, Sleeman's knowledge of the Thugs, their
numbers, their leaders, their plans and their methods had been only partial.
With Feringeea in custody, the Company's understanding of the strangling
gangs was far more complete. And the destruction of those haunting the central provinces of India was now only a matter of time.

---

*Feringeea's value seems only to have been questioned once, in 1832, when he was sent into the Doab –
an area he evidently did not know well.

CHAPTER 14

Sleeman's Machine

'beelha – a great enemy of Thugs'

'Have you ever heard of Captain Sleeman?' one eminent Thug was asked when he was captured by a party of the Company's nujeebs in Oudh. 'Yes,' came the reply. 'We heard that he was hanging and banishing Thugs, and that he had made a machine for torturing Thugs and for breaking our bones.' 'Some said,' added one of his companions, 'that Thugs were ground to death in this machine!'

The captured stranglers were wrong, of course. The Company possessed no infernal contraption for maiming and dismembering guilty Thugs. Yet in one sense there was a shred of truth in this strange rumour. William Sleeman had indeed constructed a machine capable of detecting and destroying the Thug gangs. It was constructed not of grindstones and gears but of books and papers, and armed not with racks and whirling knives, but with maps and piles of manuscripts and a collection of spidery genealogies that the captain had sketched out himself, laboriously, by hand. It was a deadly machine, though, nonetheless, for more Thugs were identified and marked for punishment in the record office that Sleeman established in the Saugor & Nerbudda Territory than were ever picked up by mere chance on the roads.

The meticulous collection of documents and indexes assembled in the course of long months of listening to and noting testimony was what made the swift progress of the Company's campaign against the Thugs possible. Had the effort not been made, dozens of stranglers would have slipped through the British net, and some, no doubt, would have continued to haunt the roads of India, throttling unwary travellers until they were eventually caught. Sleeman's machine may be dry and dusty now, and lying in pieces in the libraries of London, Delhi and Bhopal. But it was a marvel in its day, saving hundreds, perhaps thousands, of lives.

The men of the East India Company had long been enthusiastic record-keepers. Even today, the vast sprawl of their musty archives, assembled in the course of three and a half centuries in India, fill mile after mile of shelves. So tremendous was the amount of business transacted by the Governor General and his council at Calcutta that the documents relating to a single day's business could run to well over 150 closely written pages, and the central records of the Company's three Presidencies alone filled more than 34,000 substantial volumes.* They covered almost every subject: revenue, administration, relations with Indian rulers, court cases, the police. But, until Sleeman began to work towards the suppression of the Thugs, there was no sizeable archive relating to crime or criminals. He was to be a pioneer in this field, and not merely in India. Some of the techniques that he developed in the early 1830s presaged methods that would not come into common use in police departments at home in Europe for another 50 or 60 years.

The creation by Sleeman of several vast databases packed with information concerning wanted Thugs was a necessary response to the back-breakingly difficult work of bringing captured stranglers to trial. The officers charged with prosecuting the anti-Thug campaign faced almost insuperable difficulties. Police investigating a case of murder will generally possess at least a body, from which they can deduce the time, the manner and perhaps the place of death. In the great majority of cases they will also know the identity of the corpse. The killer they are seeking will often prove to be someone who knew the victim well; husbands or wives, friends and business partners are all likely to be suspects. Sleeman and his associates, on the other hand, did not always have a body, and when they did, they rarely had any idea of its identity. Nor did they have the slightest clue – unless some approver told them – which gang had been responsible for the crime, let alone which Thug, among

*William Bentinck was one of those who complained about this. The transactions of the Bengal Presidency alone, he pointed out to his superiors in London, were so vast as to occupy his full attention; he did not believe that a single man was capable of ruling the whole of British India.

many, had actually committed it. Yet convictions could only be secured in cases in which the fact of murder could be proved and the identity of the murderer himself demonstrated to the satisfaction of a judge.

Only by the most meticulous accumulation of every scrap of information let slip by the approvers could Sleeman hope to glimpse the true nature of Thuggee; only by painstaking cross-referencing and the assembly of detailed files could he know the full extent of a Thug's crimes; and only by patient tracking, careful mapping and the intelligent deployment of his scarce resources could he bring his suspects to trial. All this work, moreover, had to be undertaken at a time when the Indian police force was fragmented, poorly paid and appallingly corrupt; when pen, paper and foolscap indexes were the best available technology; and when the techniques of photography, fingerprinting and forensic analysis were more or less undreamed of. At the time that the Company's campaign against the Thugs first got under way, even the Metropolitan Police, at home in London, was a brand new institution, and one still regarded with the very greatest suspicion by a good number of Britons.

Sleeman's work began, in 1829, with the careful cataloguing of every known Thug crime. 'With regard to the mode of collecting the evidence to convict the Thugs of specific murders,' he wrote to a colleague in the Deccan,

> the first point is to ascertain from the approver present the time, place, and mode of the murders as near as possible – the place whence the murdered persons came and whither they were going – the property they had with them. On these points the approvers are always well informed. You then have to send and have the bodies taken up before the people of the neighbouring villages, whose depositions on oath are taken down by the local authorities of the [pargana] on an official form for the evidences. If they [the bodies] are not found, the people of these villages may have seen them at the time, and their depositions to this point will answer the purpose.

Reports on each case, drawn up by the officer concerned, were sent to Sleeman and combed for as much information as they could be made to yield. The raw data was then entered into a vast register that contained the names of every Thug who could be identified – not merely the handful who had already been arrested, but every man named in every deposition made by every approver. Each Thug was assigned his own unique number, and against this number Sleeman recorded his name, the location of his home, and the details of his associates and of all the crimes of which they stood accused. This was never a simple matter, for many Thugs had the same or almost identical names and none had surnames, most being identified by their tribe, their caste or their role within their gang. A good number, moreover, employed one or more aliases. Sheikh Inaent, for example – the jemadar whose apprehension in 1830 had put Feringeea to flight – appears in the earliest documents relating to his case as 'Khuda Buksh', while Feringeea himself used the aliases 'Deahuct Undun' and 'Daviga Persaud'. To complicate matters further, it was common for Hindu Thugs to adopt Muslim names, and for Muslim stranglers to pose as Hindus, in order to inveigle their way into groups of travellers on the roads.

Undaunted, Sleeman also kept careful records of all the information he could find or deduce about each Thug's family. The names of a man's father, his brothers, his sons, and even his adopted children all appeared against his name. So did any distinguishing marks: 'Persaud, alias Omraw Sing Jemadar, son of Hemmut Sing alias Runna, dark mark on his nose'; 'Khuluk, son of Runna Lodhee, with small finger broken'; 'Holkar, brother of Persaud Jemadar, blind of one eye'. With the great Thug register conveniently to hand, the men of Sleeman's department had ready access to the information that they needed to plot the arrest of the 'most notorious' men when the gangs returned to their homes at the end of each cold season. And 'as soon as an accused was arrested and identified' – as the Thug-hunter himself pointed out – 'a mass of evidence was usually at once forthcoming to secure his conviction'.

Sleeman's register proved to be an immediate success. Some 350 captured Thugs were committed for trial in Saugor in 1832. Two hundred more came before the courts in 1833, and another 170 were arraigned in Indore, Hyderabad, Poona and Cawnpore. The rapid progress of the anti-Thug campaign soon persuaded the Government of India to supplement the staff serving under FC Smith. At the beginning of the cold season of 1832, Lieutenant PA Reynolds, one of the assistant Residents at Hyderabad, was appointed to hunt down the stranglers of the Deccan and JC Wilson was placed in charge of operations in the Doab; each received command of a detachment of 40 sepoys and 20 militiamen, relieving the pressure on

Sleeman's own hard-pressed nujeebs. A year later, a Lieutenant McLeod was given responsibility for Rajpootana, Malwa and the lands around Delhi. By 1835, Smith – 'exercising, as heretofore, a general control over the officers employed in the suppression of Thuggee' – and Sleeman, who was at last formally appointed Superintendent of what was already widely known as the Thuggy Department in Jubbulpore, had a staff of seven assistants spread across the territories from Rohilkhand, to the north of Delhi, all the way to Hyderabad, and command over nearly 300 nujeebs. Seventeen other officers, most of them the Residents or Agents in various Native States, assisted in the pursuit and capture of wanted Thugs in their home villages. For the first time the resources available to Sleeman became adequate to the task in hand.

The newly appointed superintendent's next idea was to map the homes of the known Thugs, the routes they followed in the course of their lengthy expeditions, and the spots where their murders were committed. Sleeman thought that this would help him to position his patrols more effectively, 'for I shall often be liable to direct them upon a wrong road and to lose time by doubts and mistakes as to the jurisdiction of the officers with whom I have to communicate'. But the creation of such a map was no simple task. Even though the Company had established a cartographical office, the Survey of India, in 1785, large portions of the Native States had still not been mapped, and an official request for 'a skeleton map of 10 or 12 square feet, comprising the countries north and south from Madras to Delhi and east and west from Calcutta to Bombay' caused a good deal of head-scratching in the Survey's offices, for no attempt had yet been made to combine all the elements that Sleeman required in a single map showing 'all the principal rulers and lands and roads and principal stages at which travellers halt, and all the ferries at which they cross rivers, together with the seats of our own courts and military establishments'. After an exchange of letters between Sleeman, Bentinck and the Surveyor General, George Everest, however, a cartographer named Ferris Robb was given the unenviable task of producing 'a map of peculiar construction' that suited the Thuggy Department's needs. His completed chart was finally delivered in 1832, and put to immediate use in planning the routes to be patrolled by parties of nujeebs during the coming cold season.

By the middle of the 1830s, then, Sleeman had equipped himself with almost all the tools he needed to apprehend suspected stranglers. Endless streams of letters, instructions, orders and encouragement poured out of his headquarters at Jubbulpore, some seeking information and help from the British Residents at Indian courts, others urging his assistants to follow his lead in compiling yet more files, more lists and tables. At least one member of the new department followed the Superintendent's lead, creating an intricately detailed map of Thug activities within his own districts. Captain James Paton, who had been placed in charge of the anti-Thug campaign in Oudh, obtained a large-scale chart of his territory from the Surveyor General's office and carefully plotted on it the location of as many Thug beles as his 20 approvers could identify. The results were startling. 'As nearly as can be calculated,' Paton observed, 'the whole extent of those roads so thoroughly well known by Thugs, infested by them, [is] no less than 1,401 miles, and in those 1,401 miles there are no less than 274 *bails* [beles]. . . or one bail for about every 5¼ miles.' Paton was soon persuaded that the map was proof of his approvers' worth. 'If false,' he argued, 'the Thugs could not possibly have remembered all their varied positions and localities to repeat, on cross-examination, the same falsehoods.' He had descriptions of each of these murder spots worked up into a manuscript he called the *Thug Road Book* and made plans to circulate it to other Company officials in northern India.

Sleeman's register and maps provided him with the key to tracking down and arresting known Thugs. But that in itself was not enough for him. Firmly convinced, by the evidence of his approvers and his own understanding of Indian society, that Thuggee had become a hereditary profession for numerous large families of criminals, he also devoted long hours to the preparation of complicated genealogies, showing the lineage of more than 80 extended families of stranglers. Most of the information came from the Thug approvers, some of whom appear to have vied with each other to create the longest and most detailed pedigrees, for although some of Sleeman's genealogies show the descent of no more than two or three generations of Thugs, others trace a family's ancestry over as many as eight. Between them they list somewhere between 3,000 and 4,000 men, and in some families as many as 100 brothers, sons and cousins had worked together in the Thug gangs. Read carefully against the voluminous notes describing each approver's family, however, the trees show just how misleading it was to suppose that every male member of every ancient family of Thugs inevitably became a strangler himself. Dotted among Sleeman's grim records of 'noted Thugs' and hereditary jemadars are occasional mentions of men who had eschewed life with the gangs to become farmers, merchants, or even common thieves.

Sleeman's genealogies nonetheless impressed Francis Curwen Smith, who saw in them not only confirmation that the most important Thugs were stranglers by birth, but also a useful tool to assess the statements of approvers. The trees could be used, for example, to place an informant within his extended family and thus deduce which Thugs he might favour or attempt to gloss over in his testimony. And 'they show,' Smith added,

> the connection of the families of the principal Thugs committed for trial since 1830 with the Sindhousee (hereditary) Thugs. The tables were revised by Captain Sleeman often in the presence of the members of the different families . . . and the tables of their respective families have been acknowledged by them to be correct, though framed from information derived from members of opposite parties.

It was not long, then, before the pedigrees became another weapon in the Company's war against the stranglers – 'a blue-print, as it were, of everyone, Muslim and Hindu, linked with Thuggee by blood'. Used in conjunction with the Thug register, they enabled Sleeman and his assistants to note the fate of every known strangler and to keep track of those who remained at large. The results of their plodding clerical work were brandished, almost as trophies, in Thuggy Department papers: evidence – so it appeared – that every last Thug had been named, numbered and accounted for.*

'There is,' William Sleeman once observed, 'one truth that cannot be too often repeated: that if we wish to suppress the system [of Thuggee], we must seek the murderers at their homes, and drag them from their asylums.'

The Company's principal failing hitherto – so Sleeman's approvers assured him – had been its inability to maintain a constant pressure on the gangs themselves. Occasional arrests, rarely followed up, had never seriously diminished the efficiency of the great mass of Thugs, and had little effect on their

---

*To take only one example among many: 'Makun, who was hung at Indore, 1829; Gunga Deen, who was hung at Indore, 1829; Chotee, approver; Maharaj Partuk, drowned himself at Saugor; Sheikh Nungoo, dead; Persaud, hung at Saugor, 1832.'

morale. The stranglers had long known, after all, that they were wanted men, and had grown used over the years to setbacks and even the occasional disaster. They took the resilience of their gangs for granted.

The key to the entire anti-Thug campaign thus lay in the ability of Sleeman and his record office to supply accurate and timely intelligence as to the likely movements of the principal jemadars and their gangs. Without the information supplied by the approvers and painstakingly processed and evaluated at Jubbulpore, the Company would never have acquired the ability to pursue the gangs to the very doorsteps of their own homes. And without that ability, the handful of sepoys and nujeebs at Sleeman's disposal would have proved hopelessly inadequate to the task of hunting down the wanted men.

Perhaps the Superintendent's most important breakthrough came during the first year of the anti-Thug campaign, when a solution was at last found to the problem of extracting consistently reliable information from the Company's approvers. Thug informers had hitherto attempted to cooperate in shielding their own families and friends from arrest. Sleeman's triumph was to set his most important prisoners against each other. The fresh round of denunciations that followed ended any prospect that the prisoners might continue to collude, and Sleeman was soon able to divide his approvers into three main groups according to their religion and caste. Feringeea and six other Brahmins formed one group; Kuleean Singh – the fearsome low-caste jemadar whose son had effected Feringeea's capture – led another; the third was made up of five Muslim approvers. 'The list,' Sleeman commented with no small satisfaction when he reported to Smith, 'may be relied upon, I believe. Feringeea is . . . animated by a deadly spirit of hatred against Kuleean Singh and Kara Khan, once the leader of the Musulman Thugs, in consequence of their having been instrumental in the conviction of Jurha and Rada Kishun, his nearest relations.* Kuleean Singh and Kara Khan are united in hatred against Feringeea and his class, but deadly opposed to each other.' 'Each party,' the Superintendent added elsewhere, 'has caused the arrest, capital punishment and transportation of many Thugs of every other party, and consequently they hate each other most cordially.'

---

*Rada Kishun [or Radakishun] was a survivor of a party of travellers murdered by the jemadar's father, Purusram, and had been adopted into the family. He was executed at Jubbulpore in 1830 and his remains then 'exhibited in chains'. Jurha, Feringeea's nephew, acted as treasurer to his gang and 'received charge of all their affairs'. He was executed on the same occasion.

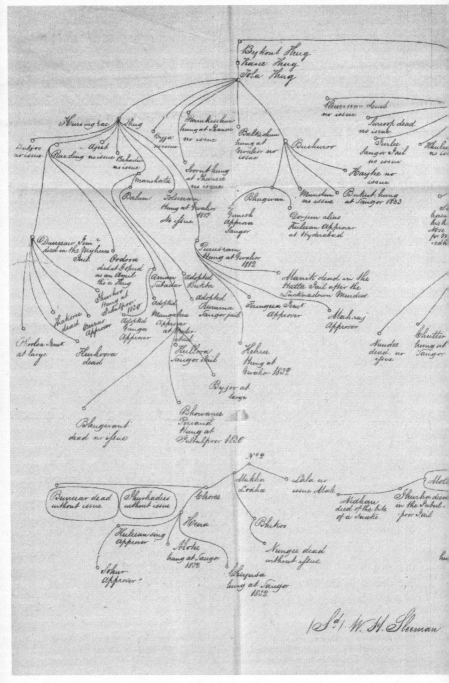

An example of Sleeman's detailed genealogies of the main Thug families, this one extending over eight generations. The name of the celebrated approver Feringeea can be seen towards the left.

A Brahmun.

Seeam and Assa married two sisters the Daughters of a Thug leader, and were the first of their Family that became Thugs.

Assa died without issue

Seeam
Aheen
Khurgolee
Jutha

Reun
Adopted Koroof

Chand
Sister
Dhokul no issue
Hurookia dead
Sehij.

Adopted
Adopted Mihngoo

Bukut no issue
Gholab no issue
Khysroo no issue

Hulaun no issue
Name forgotten
Munsook
Jeswunt
Pruthee

Butun
Naunsook

Durroo

Rampersaud died in the Muttuck Jail after the Lucknadown Murder
A Boy 8 Years of Age

Phuns
Bukun
Hurnagur Approver

Mhurry Jowul hung at Mhain 1831
Phulool Amuldar Approver murdered his Wife Mhain Pul

Chundaloul transported from Saugor 1832

Mahasook transported 1832 from Saugor
Bodhooa shot himself for love
Soorloo approver

Dorjun Approver Saugor

Cheynsa hung Saugor Jail
Bhowanee Saugor Jail

Hindolee
Bhutka

Ponro Sewtal Saugor jail
Muttroo dead
Dan a Boy 14 Years Age

Pucholee
Chotee approver
Malloo approver
A Child

Gunesh 13 Years old

Chidamee hung at Saugor 1832

Adopted Rambuksh Jem'r for whose apprehension 500 Rs reward offered, supposed to be in the Service of the Guikwar at Baroda

Sujanul Amuldar Approver
Futty Approver
Nuthoo Approver

Chubter no issue

Madhoo

Bukara Transported Jubbulpoor 1835
Mhungul Saugor Jail
Oudeea hung at Jubbulpoor 1836
Died aby

Dorjun
Keerue dead no issue Male
Mahadeo Brahmun the Son of the Sister of Jola who adopted him and brought him up to the trade of Murder.

Mohee Saugor Jail
Sewtal dead no male issue
Nundlall dead no issue Male
Heera Sing transported from Saugor 1832

Pursaud

Bhowanee at Jubbulpoor 1830

Ram Buksh at large on Thuggee
Kunhae
Tejun adopted hung at Saugor 1832

Gunesh trans'd from Saugor 1832
Chotee approver
Sultram approver

Adopted Tejuna trans'd from Saugor 1832
Adopted Kunhoea Approver

Pucholee was siezed 1832 & sent with a bag of Pearls of great value found upon him to Hyderabad what was done with him I have never heard. He was siezed by Capt. Moody, Agent Gov. Genl. Bundel. and at the request of M. Molony Agent Gov. Genl. Nerbudda.

Rahma adopted approver now at Hyderabad.

The efficiency and the morale of the patrols despatched to hunt down the wanted Thugs was also high. Service with Sleeman was highly popular among the Company's soldiers and nujeebs, who relished the opportunity to track down 'the Thugs by whose hands so many of their comrades have perished'. The work itself was exciting, and men chosen for the service had good prospects of distinguishing themselves. Their biggest incentive, nonetheless, was money, for the rewards offered for the capture and conviction of leading Thugs were substantial, even when divided between the members of an entire patrol. The largest ever offered for a jemadar seems to have been the 1,000 rupees put on the head of Hurree, 'the notorious Thug leader of Jhalone'. The men responsible for capturing Feringeea shared rewards amounting to 500 rupees, and 200 more were paid for 'Zolfukar, son of Thugs, whose father has just been captured with eight men of his gang in the *jagir* of Poona'. During the six years in which the Company's efforts against the Thugs were at their height, a total of more than 10,000 rupees was distributed among the thousand or so soldiers who took part in the campaign.

The nujeebs sent in search of Thugs were well equipped for their task. Each party travelled in the company of at least two approvers, each representing one of the four rival groups noted by Sleeman – who were weighted down with irons to prevent their escape. By consulting their informants, separately, the Company men were supposed to confirm the identities of the members of any gangs they met on the roads, and each was supplied with warrants giving them the power to arrest wanted Thugs wherever they were found. Most importantly of all, Sleeman's troops received detailed intelligence from the record office at Jubbulpore informing them of the names, aliases and home villages of the Thug jemadars they were pursuing. Provided with definite objectives, the patrols usually achieved what was expected of them.

There were, hardly surprisingly, instances suggesting that parties of nujeebs were sometimes over-zealous. A few of these occasions – Sleeman himself contended – were relatively harmless; on one occasion a patrol passing through Gwalior discovered two known Thugs who had entered Sindhia's service as *sepahees*, and went off to the nearest magistrate to secure an order for the men's arrest. By the time they returned the Thugs, forewarned, had escaped, and when the patrol caught up with them at Bhurtpore a few days later, the suspects were detained while a warrant was secured. 'In this,'

Sleeman added a little piously, 'they exceeded their orders, and have been punished for it.' But there were other instances that suggested some Company
sepoys were corrupt. Sleeman was forced to forbid his patrols from hunting
for Thug loot in the homes they searched; the lure of so much cash and
goods proved too much for some. The leader of one patrol was found to have
accepted bribes from a moonshee known to be an associate of Thugs. On
another occasion, RT Lushington, the Company's Resident at Bhurtpore,
complained bitterly to Sleeman that a party of nujeebs had entered his rajah's
territory and arrested three suspected Thugs on the word of a prostitute and
her pimp. One of the arrested men turned out to be a Brahmin and another
was a member of the rajah's palace guard; none of their names appeared on
any of an embarrassed Sleeman's lists of Thugs. 'On this mere hearsay,'
Lushington protested in a letter sent directly to the Governor General,
'respected members of the community are apprehended as murderers and are
to be sent in chains to Saugor. I beg to ask whether it is consistent with justice
to capture persons on such a charge and evidence, and this, too, without
allowing the prisoners to say a word in their own defence?'

Despite occasional setbacks of this sort, the campaign progressed rapidly.
Most Company officers, including most Residents, supported it. By the
middle of 1832, Sleeman's detachments had swept the roads in a circle
through Baroda and Nagpore in the south, Bundelcund in the north-west and
Jodhpore in the west. Gwalior and Rajpootana had been scoured and scores
of alleged Thugs seized. Sleeman had also sent Major Stewart, the Company's
Resident at Hyderabad, a list of 150 Thugs believed to be at large in the
Nizam's domains with the request that he arrange for their arrest. Similar letters went out to the Residents at Indore and Delhi.

Particular attention was paid to the main routes into Hindustan frequented
by sepoys travelling home on leave from Madras and Bombay in an effort to
reduce the number of casualties inflicted on the Company's troops each year
by the Thug gangs. The Company's nujeebs, Sleeman informed Smith,

> are now provided with approvers well acquainted with the usual movements
> of all the principal Thugs who have hitherto considered the annual leave
> period as a legitimate kind of harvest, so we have a good chance of securing
> some of their gangs . . . Thugs have often told me that the reason why they
> choose the native officers and sepoys of our armies in preference to other

travellers is that they commonly carry more money and other valuable articles about them and are from their arms, their strength, self-confidence and
haughty bearing more easily deceived by the vain humility and respect of the
Thugs, and led off the high roads into jungly and solitary situations . . . where
they are more easily murdered and their bodies disposed of.

By the end of 1832, the Company's patrols were active over an area three
or four times as big as Britain, and the Governor General, Bentinck, had
agreed to nearly double the strength of the troops available to Sleeman.
British efforts were by now being rewarded with substantial success. During
the cold season of 1832–3 Sleeman calculated that only four jemadars
remained at large in the whole of the central provinces, and the number of
suspected Thugs being held in prison at Saugor had tripled to nearly more
than 600. A vast quantity of loot had been recovered from the homes of various jemadars. One Thug leader's home alone yielded 715 large pearls and
1,108 smaller ones, 65 large and 20 smaller diamonds, a large chest crammed
with Spanish dollars and doubloons, numerous gold bangles, and hundreds of
rings, bracelets, necklaces and earrings. On the few occasions when items of
plunder could be identified by relations of the Thugs' victims, the treasure
was returned to its rightful owners. The rest – virtually all of the cash and
goods recovered from Thug homes – was, with a nice irony, banked by
Sleeman himself at Jubbulpore and used to pay the expenses of the sepoys
and nujeebs hunting the men who had first plundered it.

The year ended on the most positive note yet struck in the regular reports
sent by the Thuggy Department to FC Smith. 'Three great results,' Sleeman
observed,

have already been produced by these extensive seizures. First, the roads have
been secured from Thug depredations . . . Second, their confidence in each
other has been so entirely destroyed that in the smallest parties seized there
are some found ready to disclose the murders committed and to point out the
bodies of the murdered . . . Thirdly, there is hardly a family of these wretches
north of the Nerbudda of which we have not some of the members in
prison, and thereby the means of learning what members are still at large,
with increasing facilities of seizing them, and convicting them when seized.

The approvers had done their work. Sleeman had done his. Thuggee had been exposed, its most notable leaders hunted down and arrested, its methods and secrets laid bare – and, in some cases, exaggerated. The next step was to try the prisoners.

'In all my experience in the Judicial line for upwards of 20 years,' wrote FC Smith,

> I never heard of such atrocities . . . such cold blooded murders, such heart-rending scenes of distress, and misery; such base ingratitude; such a total abandonment of every principle which binds man to man, which softens the heart and elevates mankind above the brute creation, were probably never before brought to the notice of a Court of Justice.

Smith and Sleeman and their men had no doubt as to the appropriate response. 'Mercy to such wretches,' the agent wrote, 'would be the extreme of cruelty to mankind.' There was only one way to proceed. 'They must be met in their own ways,' Smith concluded. The guiding principle of the great Thug trials that now began in both Saugor and Jubbulpore would be 'rigid adherence to the law of *Lex Talonis* – Blood for blood.' For too many years the gangs had – in effect – taunted the British administration, exposing its inability to protect its subjects. Now the Company would have its revenge.

CHAPTER 15

In Cutcherry

'khuruk – the noise made by the sacred pickaxe when
digging a grave'

In they came, from Etawah and Gwalior, the Doab and Bundelcund: Thugs
and suspected Thugs, the innocent and guilty, swept up together in the
Company's nets.

There were nearly 4,500 of them in all, so many that they filled the prisons
and threatened to overwhelm the courts available to try them. Most, Sleeman
observed, were Hindus, although about a third were Muslims. They hailed
from almost every part of India and from more than 40 different castes and
tribes; some were high-born Brahmins, others the lowest of Untouchables.
Many, certainly at first, were experienced stranglers, members of the gangs
that had their origins in the Chambel valley or their associates from the
Deccan and Oudh. But there were also hundreds of occasional or novice
stranglers, men who scraped a living in whatever way they could and had few
if any ties with the old Thug families.

The difficulties confronting Sleeman – the man responsible for preparing
cases for trial – and Smith – the judge scheduled to hear them – were enormous. Thugs had seldom been convicted of their crimes before the
Company's campaign began. Many had been arrested, and a good number
had spent long periods in prison – the terrible Syeed Ameer Ali was confined
for 12 years in the King of Oudh's jail at Lucknow, the Sindouse men rounded
up in Gwalior after the murder of Maunsell were held there for more than a
year, and the 115 members of another gang, arrested on their way across the

Nerbudda valley in 1823, spent more than seven years in custody at Jubbulpore. Actual trials, however, had been comparatively infrequent. As late as 1830 it was notoriously difficult to convict suspected Thugs in either British territory or the Native States.

About two dozen cases of Thuggee had, in fact, been heard in the Company's courts between the years 1799 and 1828, but of these no more than four resulted in significant convictions. Forty-nine Thugs were executed in the Upper Provinces in 1813 as a result of hearings held in Roy Barelly and Benares, and of the 16 sentenced at Mozuffurpore a few years later, four were hanged and the rest transported to penal colonies in the Far East. A few years later, 38 more stranglers were convicted in Jubbulpore and Candeish. But these were the exceptions, and it was much more usual for trials to end inconclusively – as they did in 1808 and 1820, when large gangs of Thugs were simply expelled from British territory, a negligible punishment – or even to collapse in disarray. There had been plenty of cases of the latter sort, from the acquittal, in 1812, of the Thugs sent to Bengal for trial by Thomas Perry to the disastrous attempt to bring to trial the murderers of Mr Pringle's servant at Patna in 1827, which had resulted in the imprisonment of several approvers and the jailing of the Indian officer who first brought the matter before the courts.

In the handful of cases in which a gang had been captured, it had proved all but impossible to determine which of its members had committed murder and which had played no direct part in the gang's crimes. To make matters worse, it had long been the Company's policy to return captured criminals to their home states for trial and punishment. Since most Thugs lived among the Native States, this meant that even Thugs who had committed murder in Company territories were rarely tried in Company courts. 'The inconsistent bandying about of prisoners from one distant jurisdiction to another,' thought FC Smith, 'cannot but have proved highly injurious, and the mischief which has been sanctioned or connived at, is most serious and lamentable.'

In the first quarter of the nineteenth century, Company magistrates experienced almost equal difficulty in finding relations of the murdered men willing to press charges in the first place. Only a handful of the Thugs' victims were ever positively identified; many families remained unaware that their fathers, uncles and brothers had fallen victims to the stranglers, and few of the dead had relatives, employers or friends wealthy enough to fund a search for them. Fewer still would risk the inconvenience and cost that summoning a darogah almost inevitably entailed. Even when a case did come to trial there was a general reluctance to give evidence, not least because cases were often heard a hundred miles or more from the spot where a crime had been committed. Giving testimony required witnesses to leave their homes and work and make expensive, time-consuming journeys that ended, all too frequently, in a further lengthy wait for the case itself to come before the court. Although nominally entitled to compensation for lost earnings and the cost of travel, these men often received nothing for all this time and trouble, with the inevitable consequence that many families preferred to 'remain quiet and forgo prosecution than catch a thief or complain about a robbery'.

Justice in the Native States was no better than that on offer in the Company's courts. The assumption, shared by many European officers, that Indian courts were irredeemably corrupt was not correct; some states and some rulers administered the law fairly and well. But the punishments meted out by local rajahs and their officers were very light by British standards. The death penalty was rarely and inconsistently imposed, even on highway robbers such as Thugs, and the lax treatment of Brahmins was a particular concern; members of the caste were exempt from capital punishment until 1817, though in some notorious cases guilty Brahmins were done away with surreptitiously: 'destroyed by poison or by unwholesome food – bread, half salt and half flour, being often used'. Company officials found the methods of execution practised in the mofussil – which included treading to death by elephants, blowing men away from the mouths of cannon, and crushing the condemned's head with a mallet – objectionable, and it was generally (though incorrectly) believed that no Hindu juror could be trusted to convict defendants who were his superior in caste.

The entire Indian justice system was, indeed, based on principles that British jurists found difficult to understand. Most prison sentences involved 'confinement till repentance' and were, therefore, not so much a punishment in themselves as a means of enforcing restitution – the payment of blood money, the return of stolen goods, or the provision of a ransom in the form of cash put up as security for future good behaviour. Few able and experienced stranglers had much difficulty in making such payments, and those who did were often able to borrow the necessary sum from a helpful zamindar or even a local banker – both of whom must have known full well that the Thug in question would most likely discharge his debt with the proceeds of future murders.* Those who were confined to jails often escaped, or were simply expelled from the territory where they had been arrested. Some were permitted to wash away their guilt by bathing in the Ganges and were then released. None of these practices – as the Company had already discovered to its cost – 'carried even the appearance of a punishment' to a hardened strangler.

Francis Curwen Smith and William Sleeman were determined to do things differently in Saugor & Nerbudda. From the moment that the anti-Thug campaign commenced in earnest, preparations were put in train for the trial of captured stranglers. The whole system was centralized. Thugs captured by Sleeman's nujeebs or Company troops now remained in British custody, rather than being sent back to their homes to be tried by their own rajahs. Those detained in the British districts of central India were sent to Saugor for trial. Those captured in sweeps through the Native States could be tried by the nearest British Resident, and as cases accumulated the representatives at the courts of Lucknow, Hyderabad and Indore all began to hold trials of their own.

The great majority of captured Thugs were consigned to Smith's courts in Saugor and Jubbulpore. This decision was nicely calculated to speed up the administration of justice, for the Saugor & Nerbudda Territory had occupied a unique position within the Company's dominions ever since it was ceded to the British in 1818. It was frontier territory and, after its annexation, the government in Calcutta had been anxious not to unsettle its new subjects or add to the chaos left by the Pindaris and the Maratha Wars. For this reason, it had been decided not to impose the comparatively sophisticated but alien law of the Bengal Presidency – informed as it was by many British concepts of justice – on the new districts too swiftly. Instead, the province had been designated a 'non-regulation territory' and was subject to a simplified code of laws. In practice, this meant that the agents and magistrates sent to govern it were permitted a great deal of latitude in imposing the law. So long as they adhered at least loosely to the spirit of the Bengal regulations, their verdicts were unlikely to arouse any great controversy in Calcutta.

---

*The sums involved could be substantial – in Gwalior, in 1818, a Maratha officer known as the Hurda Wallah arrested every jemadar he could find in Murnae and the surrounding district and relieved them of a total of 11,250 rupees.

FC Smith, as the Governor General's Agent in central India, was thus to all intents and purposes a law unto himself. Nominally responsible solely to 'Supreme Government', he did much as he pleased. If the Thug trials had been conducted in an ordinary sessions court somewhere in the Bengal Presidency, the proceedings would have come under the scrutiny of the Company's supreme court, the Nizamat Adalat at Murshidabad. But there was no such appeal process in Saugor & Nerbudda. Smith's verdicts were simply submitted to the secretary of the political department in far-off Bengal to be rubber-stamped, and communication between Saugor and Calcutta took so long that it was impossible for the Company's highest authorities to exercise any real control over his proceedings.* The Thug suspects hauled before the courts of Saugor & Nerbudda thus had only a single chance of obtaining justice. Their fates depended entirely on the care with which Sleeman marshalled his evidence for submission to Smith's court.

The Thug trials, FC Smith once wrote, proved to be a task so arduous that it took no less than six months of 'unremitted labour' to bring each year's sessions to a satisfactory conclusion.

The problem was not the mass of evidence, vast though that was. The approvers' depositions and the statements made by other witnesses, the activities of exhumation parties, catalogues of plunder – all that information was laboriously sifted and compiled by Sleeman before the trials began, which is why, although the anti-Thug campaign commenced in 1829–30, the majority of cases were only heard in 1832. Smith's chief difficulty was, rather, the sheer number of defendants who appeared before his court. The sessions of 1831–2 alone consisted of 26 separate trials; 345 suspected Thugs were arraigned, and because many of them were accused of more than one crime, a total of 847 sentences ('all of more than one page') had to be written out and handed down. Even then, Thugs who might have been involved in hundreds of murders were rarely brought to account for more than one or two, since it would have been utterly impractical to make the indictments entirely

---

*For a while, indeed, Smith was actually permitted to put his sentences into effect without waiting for confirmation from Calcutta. The dispensation was revoked when the court of directors, at home in London, expressed unease that a mere political officer could inflict capital punishment without his sentences being subject to any sort of revision or appeal.

comprehensive. 'These men,' Sleeman explained, 'are commonly tried for one particular case of murder, perpetrated on one occasion, in which case all the gang may have participated, and of which the evidence is most complete. On the average, more than 10 of these cases have been found to occur on every expedition; and every man has, on the average, been on 10 of these expeditions. The murders for which they are tried are not, therefore, commonly more than a hundredth part of the murders they have perpetrated in the course of their career of crime.'

The first stage in the process was to commit the prisoners for trial. These proceedings began at hearings held 'in cutcherry' – that is, in one of Smith's courts of justice in Saugor or Jubbulpore. Fanny Parks, an intrepid British traveller who passed through the central provinces in 1830, sketched the scene in one such court as the evidence against a Thug captive was heard. 'The judge,' she wrote,

> is taking notes. The fat moonshee on his right hand is reading the depo-
> sition, and the native officers of the court are in attendance. The scene of
> the cutcherry is a room in the house of the magistrate. The sergeant stoop-
> ing by the side of the table is putting the seal of office to the paper that will
> consign the criminal for trial. The hookah bearer with his snow-white
> beard, standing beside his master's chair, has just brought a fresh *chilam*
> [charge of tobacco] for the hookah, which the gentleman has laid aside
> during the examination of the Thug. The criminal, who appears to have
> suffered a blow to the head from [an] iron shod club . . . is attempting to
> prove his innocence, and the man to the right, who was speaking in his
> defence to the judge, has stopped in the midst of his sentence, and is cock-
> ing his ear to catch the words of the defendant.

Parks's accompanying sketch, which captures an elderly and balding judge – probably Smith himself – in the centre of his crowded courtroom, wearing a look of surprise, freezes this one moment in time. Over the years, though, there were thousands of proceedings of this sort, each over in no more than a minute or two. A brief capitulation of the evidence – an approver's identi-fication – a 'Not Guilty' plea from the suspected Thug – and the hearing was already over. All that remained was for the judge to pen a summary of his findings, and to refer the case to court.

Huge quantities of evidence had been amassed in order to ensure the conviction of the Thugs.

To begin with, there were the bodies of their victims. Sleeman's approvers had supervised the exhumation of hundreds of corpses, in every stage of decay, from all over the central provinces. As many as 18 were recovered from a single spot, to the great excitement of the local peasantry, who flocked around the investigating officers whenever they stopped to dig. * In several cases the exhumation parties were accompanied by relatives of the unfortunate victims and the bodies recovered from the makeshift graves were positively identified as those of missing travellers. In others, corpses were recovered soon after the murder had taken place, 'very little decayed, and their features were still clear and distinct' – which at least allowed the evidence of the bodies to be tallied against the confessions already made by the approvers. The most impressive confirmation of an approver's testimony was recorded in the Nerbudda valley in 1833, when a spot identified as the burial place of a party of goldsmiths murdered there in 1819–20 was dug up. 'On opening their graves,' recorded FC Smith, 'several sets of goldsmiths' tools were found, which corroborates in the strongest manner the truth of the evidence detailed in this case.'

True, not every set of remains could be positively identified in this way; some were merely skeletons, others so horribly rotten that it was impossible to tell their age or sex. But the officers assigned to supervise the disinterrals were greatly impressed by the accuracy of their approvers' recollections. Several were so successful that the Company men found themselves all but overwhelmed by the sheer quantity of evidence that they revealed. 'I was myself present at the opening of several of these unblessed graves, each containing several bodies,' remembered Meadows Taylor, 'which were pointed by the approvers one by one, in the coolest manner, to those who were assembled, till we were sickened and gave up further search in disgust.'

---

*'I proceeded,' one typical account began, 'to the town of Laikairee. On the 14th November 1832 at a distance of 160 paces from the town gate, at a spot . . . pointed out by the Approvers, the earth was dug up in the presence of the authorities of the mentioned town. Three skulls with the body bones, and the bones of another body without a skull were found under the building at the very place pointed out by the Approver Feereengheea.'

By the time the approvers' work was completed, a good proportion of the victims of the most lethal Thug gangs had been accounted for. Nearly 140 bodies were exhumed in 1831, the first year in which systematic attempts were made to recover the remains of missing travellers, and so efficient did the Company's efforts become that 390 of the 440 victims – well over three-quarters – whose murders were investigated at the sessions of 1834–5 had been disinterred by the time the proceedings began. Whatever the accuracy of the remainder of the approvers' testimony, their accounts of Thuggee were clearly by no means pure invention.

The remains of the Thugs' victims themselves formed only part of the evidence presented to FC Smith. Several of the gangs of Thugs apprehended while travelling the roads of the central provinces were found to be carrying substantial quantities of loot plundered from parties of travellers, and it was often possible, with the help of approvers' testimony concerning the identity of the murdered men, to track down relatives and colleagues who could identify the stolen items. One wife recognized the blue turban worn by her husband; a son identified the patterned slippers of his father. The gang seized by Captain Borthwick as they were making their way out of Malwa in 1829 were carrying swords, turbans and various other items of clothing that had belonged to a party of four Muslim travellers they had murdered; the identifications were made by several of the dead men's acquaintances, but here again attempts were made to check the depositions, Borthwick observing in his report: 'It may be necessary to note here that the persons who came to recognize and claim the property of their deceased friends were in the first instance required to make out lists of the different articles of property which their friends had about them, before they were allowed to see a single article of the things found in the possession of the Thugs.' No fewer than 22 items, belonging to a dozen different victims, were identified in this way.

In the end, however, it was the approvers' evidence that really mattered. The disinterral of a body proved only that murder had been committed; the discovery of stolen property in the possession of a gang was harder to explain away, but it was still possible to argue that the goods might have been purchased from the real murderers or otherwise acquired. Only the detailed testimonies of the Company's informants promised to unravel the facts of the crimes themselves.

Both Sleeman and Smith were acutely aware that each trial would hinge upon their approvers' testimony, and they recognized the dangers of relying

on such evidence in what were by any standards sensational cases. 'The confession of some prisoners,' Sleeman agreed, 'and many other evidences of a
similar kind, have left no doubt as to the fact that the murders had been committed; but to prove the guilt of individuals, the evidence of their accomplices
in guilt alone could be procured. The secrecy with which Thugs act, and
their precaution of never robbing an individual till they first kill and bury him,
render the attainment of any other evidence impossible.'

There can be little doubt that the sheer difficulty of confirming an
approver's testimony, and so overcoming the scepticism that was still sometimes vocally expressed by district magistrates, British Residents, and even the
directors of the Company itself, became a considerable irritation to the men
of the Thuggy Department. Sleeman and Smith were forced to go to considerable lengths to persuade their superiors that their informants' evidence
was reliable. Smith was quick to reassure the Chief Secretary to Government
in Calcutta that the evidence he had heard was 'ample and satisfactory' and
the guilt of the convicted Thugs 'unquestionable'. There were, he added, at
least eight corroborations of the approvers' evidence, from 'the free, unembarrassed and consistent way' in which the original depositions had been
made to the inability of Thugs apprehended on the road to explain why they
were travelling together in such numbers. This evidence could not be
considered 'in the least apocryphal'.

'The following precautions,' Smith added in another letter, 'have always
been adopted:

> First, the Approvers are examined separately respecting their whole life: in
> the course of the narrative of which they pointed out the murders at which
> they were present. They are then made to descend to particulars in each
> case and to state the names of the Thugs who were present at each murder.
> The names of the Thugs are then inserted in [the] Register with the evi
> dence of each approver annexed. The Approvers are then sent out under
> guard to point out the Thugs at their homes and on the roads . . . and the
> guards are ordered most strictly to seize no man who is not named on the
> list furnished by them; to release no man seized by them till they have
> brought them before the authorities of the district; to leave it to the local
> authorities to retain, release or make over to them; and never to allow the
> Approvers to go out of their sight.

Most, if not all, of the Thug informants' testimony was checked with some care. The general reliability of Sleeman's prisoners was well illustrated by an incident that occurred in Hyderabad in the early 1830s, when about 80 Thugs, arrested on the evidence of approvers at various spots throughout the province, were collected into a single party and sent off to Jubbulpore under guard. On their way north, a further party of 11 men was handed over to the nujeebs by a local governor who had 'apprehended them on suspicion' of crimes other than Thuggee. The entire party reached Jubbulpore safely, but upon their arrival the captain of the guard neglected to mention that some of his prisoners were not suspected Thugs, and it was discovered that the documents relating to the supposed Thugs' arrest had been delayed. All 91 prisoners were thus brought before various approvers in the usual way. 'All,' Sleeman concluded, 'were recognised to be Thugs excepting the 11 men, of whom the approvers said they knew nothing. On the receipt of the documents a few days afterwards, these 11 proved to be the party given in charge of the guard by the local governor, with whose arrest our approvers had no concern.'

Plainly, then, the statements of the approvers carried a good deal of weight. Sleeman and Smith pronounced themselves entirely satisfied with their accuracy, pointing out that every informant was constantly reminded that any failure to make a full and true disclosure of everything he knew of Thuggee would result in his return to prison, the withdrawal of all of an approver's privileges, the revoking of the Company's conditional pardon, and hence his own inevitable execution. But the evidence obtained from informants was not always wholly reliable nonetheless – as the captured Thugs protested at the time, and the Company would eventually confess.

The Thug trials held at Saugor and Jubbulpore in the early 1830s were held up as models of efficiency and rigour. By the standards of justice that had long prevailed in the Mughal Empire – indeed, by those usually encountered in courts in Britain at this time – the hearings were scrupulously conducted. But there were, nonetheless, flaws in the proceedings that made it more difficult for suspected Thugs to receive a fair trial than might otherwise have been the case.

To begin with, the trials themselves took place before a judge – Smith – who had been intimately concerned in the progress of the anti-Thug campaign, without the mediation of a jury. Smith no doubt strove to be fair, and a small handful of men – consisting of those who had not been positively identified by any approver – were indeed acquitted in his court. There can, however, be no doubt that the agent firmly believed that the Thugs as a group had committed horrific crimes, nor that he – like almost every other British judge – was of the opinion that 'native defendants lie freely and are undeterred by oaths of truth'. From this perspective it may fairly be said that there was a strong presumption that the accused men hauled before the courts were guilty, and that any statements that the prisoners made in their own defence were unlikely to be believed. The captured Thugs were, furthermore, denied the chance to argue their own cases, a problem typical of Indian courts at this time. They had no lawyers, and their depositions carried little weight with British magistrates and judges.

Nor was the evidence of Sleeman's approvers invariably as reliable as he liked to believe. We know that at least some informants did attempt to conceal their involvement in murders the British authorities appeared to know nothing about. The approver Motee, for example, hid the fact that he had participated in the murder of a party of 10 travellers in central India in 1822. When he discovered that other witnesses had implicated him, 'he was willing enough to give evidence, but it was too late', and he was hanged. Whether or not this unreliability extended to the evidence he offered against specific Thugs in other cases is less clear. The opportunities for approvers to collude were limited at first, and absent later. But even Sleeman freely admitted that he had uncovered cases of Thug approvers settling scores by levelling false accusations against old enemies. If any cases of this sort chanced to escape his scrutiny and came before the courts, the defendant's pleas of innocence were unlikely to be believed.

More serious, perhaps, was the frequent failure of the British authorities to check Thug defendants' alibis with any thoroughness. In some cases the men assigned to obtaining references to the good character of the accused failed even to locate the men's home villages, and when testimony confirming the Thugs' statements was obtained, it was sometimes belittled or ignored. Wilson – Sleeman's representative at Etawah – noted of the testimonies he collected on behalf of a certain Bhugga:

There are seven witnesses to his good character, and did I not know the loose manner in which all depositions are taken in almost every court . . . I should be inclined to think him an innocent man. There is also a letter from the Rajah of Rushdan in his favour. On this I place no reliance whatsoever, as I have a letter of his now in my possession in which he [the Rajah] was guilty of knowingly writing a wilful falsehood.

On other occasions, though, the evidence that was received scarcely helped the prisoners' case. The sole character witness mentioned by one Thug failed 'to come in to depose by reason of his entire ignorance of the character of these persons'. In another case, the Rajah of Gopulpoor 'states that he has ascertained from the zamindars of [the suspect's] village that he has cultivated land for the last five years but they know nothing of him previous to that period'. In a third, a witness testifying to the good character of another of Sleeman's prisoners admitted that the man had absented himself from the village twice in the previous three years; another had quit his home 'when obliged by want of employment'. Plainly testimony of this sort was of limited value to a defendant confronted with statements from a number of approvers that he had been an active strangler.

The sheer volume of the testimony against them nonetheless came as an unpleasant surprise to the Thug prisoners. Most had remained confident that their old tactic of simply denying every charge would serve them well again. Gazing down on the prisoners from the bench, Smith was grimly pleased to note that

the change in the demeanour of many of the Prisoners during the consecutive Trials they underwent during the Sessions was remarkable. At the first two or three arraignments they affected much nonchalance and indifference, some actually laying down to sleep, while others kept spinning balls of cotton in their hands; but latterly their attention was evidently directed with intense interest towards the Proceedings; and especially, whenever a question effected any of them in a more than usual criminatory way, till at last, several pleaded Guilty and begged only to have their lives spared, consenting to Transportation as an inevitable result of the Trials . . . I am therefore, on the whole, inclined to believe that their indifference to the prospect of punishment originates in the known difficulty of their being convicted, and that a great change in their opinion will take place after the result of these Trials becomes known all over India.

There were, even then, few 'Guilty' pleas. A handful of men confessed, caught more or less red-handed or unnerved by the vast mass of evidence assembled against them and hoping no doubt to secure reductions in their sentences. The rest – the vast majority – pleaded 'Not Guilty' instead, though their defences were generally terse in the extreme, consisting of little more than a simple denial or a declaration of good character. 'I am innocent and falsely accused,' a Brahmin named Cheinsah protested, while his companion Bhudalee complained: 'I have always been a cultivator and have never Thugged. Enquire in my neighbourhood.' In a few cases a suspected Thug was able to prove that he had been the victim of a case of mistaken identity, but on the whole Sleeman and Smith were both dismissive of the defendants' pleas. The Thugs, Sleeman pointed out, found it easy enough to produce witnesses from their home villages prepared to testify to their good character and popularity. But that was hardly surprising when they had 'plenty of money, which they spent freely' in their own communities.

The evidence marshalled by Sleeman filled file after thick file. Most defendants were identified by a number of approvers and confronted with a variety of circumstantial evidence. In Trial No. 7 of 1832 ('Government versus Mukka and 17 other prisoners accused of the murder of three men by Thuggee and robbery of 1,000 rupees' worth of property'), four approvers called as 'witnesses to fact' testified as to the course of events and named the Thugs who had actually strangled the unfortunate victims. Another three appeared as 'witnesses to character', and between them these men identified the remainder of the defendants as notorious and hereditary Thugs. The trial did not revolve wholly around such testimony, however. One of the prisoners confessed, and the bodies of the three victims were discovered and exhumed.

The evidence in other cases followed much the same pattern. In Trial No. 10, held during the same sessions to try Thugs accused of the murder of a pair of treasure-carriers, Sleeman mustered three witnesses to fact and three to character, and the court also heard evidence from the merchant who had lost his money, the servant sent to locate the missing men, and the villagers who found their bodies. Trial No. 13, concerning the murder and burial of two soldiers and a boy in Bundelcund, involved four witnesses to fact, three to character, and two confessions made by guilty Thugs. Three bodies had been exhumed, and though they were not positively identified, Sleeman was able to produce a letter from the local British magistrate that stated that the village was a Hindu one in which the dead were never buried. Finally, and perhaps most conclusively of all, seven of the 22 members of this Thug gang had been arrested in the process of dividing up the loot. 'One of the best-proved cases', though, in Sleeman's view, was the murder – at Akola in Malwa – of a sepoy officer together with his wife, her maid, and seven servants. The trial of the alleged killers involved 'no less than four confessions besides the evidence of approvers and ample circumstantial evidence to prove the guilt of the prisoners'. A sari and a saddle-cloth belonging to the murdered couple were found in the possession of the guilty Thugs and identified by relatives, and the sepoy's infant son, who had been spared on account of his youth and forcibly adopted by a Thug family, was found living in the house of a subadar named Dirgpal, 'one of their most influential leaders'.

It is evident, reading through the vast array of trial transcripts still preserved among the Thug archives of Britain and India, that the evidence assembled against many leading jemadars and stranglers was strong – sufficient, in many cases, to secure convictions even today. Khoman, leader of one of the largest gangs ever tried in Saugor & Nerbudda, was picked out at eight separate identity parades by eight different approvers. There were numerous cases of Thugs being caught in possession of items that had belonged to their victims and failing to explain how they had come by them. Nearly a thousand bodies were disinterred, and the depositions given by the Thug informants were so detailed and consistent that they point to a long association between members of the main Thug gangs. Even the directors of the Company, who displayed a constant anxiety to ensure that the prisoners were fairly tried, and 'never convicted upon the mere evidence of accomplices unless confirmed by circumstantial evidence', pronounced themselves satisfied that it was 'beyond the verge of credibility' that six or seven approvers, questioned separately and in some cases bitterly hostile to one another, 'should concur in framing such a story to fix the guilt on an innocent person, as would carry with it the slightest degree of probability'.

The directors were surely correct. Too many dead bodies had been exhumed for anyone to doubt that murderous gangs really did infest the highways and byways of the mofussil. Too many suspected Thugs had been identified by too many informers, and been caught in possession of too much stolen loot, for there to be any question that Thuggee itself was real. But for all Sleeman's labours, some of the most fundamental of all questions concerning the strangling gangs had yet to be answered. Smith's trials no doubt proved the guilt of hundreds of Thug suspects. But they did little or nothing to explain the men's motives and beliefs. From the days of Thomas Perry, most British officials had supposed the Thugs to be little more than common robbers: better organized than most, and uniquely ruthless, to be sure. They killed, it was assumed, for money, and concealed the corpses of their victims to evade arrest. By the last days of 1830, however – only a few months after his first encounter with the Thugs – Sleeman found himself questioning this view. Methodical investigation, supported by his own interrogations of the approvers themselves, pointed to a quite different conclusion. Something far more frightening, he became convinced – and far stranger, too – was going on in the black heart of India.

CHAPTER 16

Demon Devotees

'tuponee – rites'

Few British officers – brought up in Europe, raised as Christians, and sent out to the Company's lands in their teens with no practical experience of the Subcontinent – ever felt truly at home in India. The majority found themselves flustered by the bustle of the cities, disgusted by the poverty in which most of the local people lived, and repelled by the strangeness of the language and indigenous religion. Even William Sleeman, for all his knowledge of the mofussil, rarely met on equal terms with the peasants, merchants and zamindars he ruled. Like his colleagues, he spent much of his time in the company of fellow Britons, adhering resolutely to British dress and manners, and eating what passed locally for European food. Like them, he would never entirely understand the nuances of Indian society.

The increasing isolation of the British community in India was, indeed, one of the principal features of Company history in the late eighteenth century. After 1800, it was perfectly possible – which it had scarcely been before – to serve for years in Bombay, Bengal or Madras while remaining blissfully ignorant of local languages and customs, and of the Indians themselves. A good many officers based in Calcutta were prone to boast that they knew 'just 16 miles of Asia, and no more', that being the distance between the town itself and the headquarters of the Bengal Army at Barrackpore. By 1810 it was no longer admissible in fashionable circles to admit a taste for curry or profess any interest in 'Persian poetry and Hindustani metaphysics', and a Mrs Graham regretted that every British officer she knew 'appears to pride himself on being outrageously a John Bull'. Another lady, asked what she had seen of India and its people since arriving in Bengal, replied: 'Oh, nothing, thank goodness. I known nothing at all about them . . . I think the less one knows about them the better.'

Real friendships between Indians and Europeans – which had been common in the eighteenth century, particularly between Company officers and the Muslim notables of larger towns – were rare in the nineteenth. One reason for this was the increasing size of the British community, which was large enough to be socially self-sufficient after about 1810. The appearance of European women in large numbers in the major Company towns had a decided impact. It became possible to enjoy a full, if very British, social life. But the women themselves were seldom content to leave local institutions as they found them. Those who had arrived in search of husbands naturally resented the arrangements enjoyed by the many Company officers they found contentedly ensconced with local mistresses,* and relationships between European men and Indian women – once so universal that they were considered scarcely worthy of comment – soon came to be regarded as shameful and wrong. This further limited the likelihood of newly arrived officers acquiring a proper understanding of local customs and religion.

The Company's ignorance was especially pronounced when it came to Indian religion. The British were familiar enough with Islam, the faith of the majority of India's ruling class. Hinduism was, however, a quite different matter. Its ancient and magnificent Sanskrit texts had attracted the favourable attention of a small group of scholarly Company administrators, who found much to admire in their literary quality and in the piety and morality of the high-caste Hindus whom they met. But for the great majority of British officers, and almost every Christian minister, Hinduism was a vile and pagan faith. It was generally perceived as a religion of 'prevalent idolatry and indecent ceremonies', one that encouraged 'obscene pilgrimages' and had created and sustained the horrible iniquities of the caste system. It permitted slavery

---

*Even in the eighteenth century, few British men would consider actually marrying an Indian girl. But the fact that most expected to keep mistresses is illustrated by the fact that a demi-official guide to the Company's service – intended for the instruction of young officer cadets freshly arrived on the Subcontinent – contained, as late as the 1790s, a detailed explanation of the costs involved in running a *zenana* (women's quarters).

and repressed women, who in the opinion of many writers on India were treated as little more than 'mere animals' by their menfolk. Its gods and goddesses, with their multiple arms and odd deformities, were dismissed as nothing more than hideous idols, the worst of them all being Kali, the blood-drenched, sword-wielding mother-goddess who – as the patron deity of Calcutta – was especially familiar to British visitors to India.

With very few exceptions, Europeans showed little interest in the complexities of Indian society. They thought of Hinduism as simply a religion, rather than the social system that it was; they saw it as a monolithic and uniform faith, when really it encompassed the religious practices of numerous distinct districts; even the Hindu's fabled tolerance was interpreted as mere passivity, rather than an example of intrinsic good. Most of those who wrote or read about the subject preferred to devote much of their attention to lurid descriptions of the 'excesses' of Indian custom. By the early nineteenth century, these excesses had come to be regarded as somehow representative of both the 'lust, injustice, wickedness and cruelty' of Hinduism itself, and the inhumanity of the Indian people as a whole. Sleeman, who understood the local languages better than the majority of his colleagues, and whose interest in Indian society ran deeper, was better informed than most. But he was not entirely immune to the prejudices of his day, particularly when they offended his very Christian morality.

Many British officials of the period, indeed, took ghoulish pleasure in tales of Hindu barbarism. They were disgusted by the custom of 'swinging' – the ritual practice of inserting hooks into the skin of a man's back, hauling him up on a rope, and setting him circling, at a height of nearly 30 feet, while the suspended devotee 'played a thousand antic tricks' – and utterly appalled by 'the horrid rite of *chundee pooja*', said to involve the deliberate sacrifice of girls of 11 or 12 years of age.* Fakirs, the wandering Hindu ascetics who were a highly visible feature of rural life, were distrusted for their habit of 'endeavouring to stimulate the charity of the multitude by a great variety of ingenious, whimsical, and preposterous devices', and were widely suspected of fostering anti-British sentiment. They were blamed for at least one rebellion against the Company's

*'They dress her up in silver and jewels and sandals,' one Company report explained, 'and having buried her to the waist, her hands are supported by bamboo to which they are tied – she represents the goddess, and after a human sacrifice performed before her in the night she is left in that situation in the jungle (if not dead with fright before) to starve or be devoured by tigers and jackals.'

rule, and defined, in a dictionary published in 1805, as 'a worthless set of villains, who, to obtain money from the credulous Hindoo, put on the appearance of religion, under the cloak of which they commit the greatest excesses'.

In many British minds, therefore, Hinduism became perceived as a barbaric religion. It was a faith that permitted infanticide – specifically, the killing of unwanted female children – and *suttee*, the burning of widows who chose to join their beloved husbands in death, even though both practices were forbidden in its most ancient texts. Suttee was not, in fact, particularly common, and most widows who did choose self-immolation went willingly and calmly to their deaths. But that was not the impression Britons received from their newspapers and books. Prurient reports from India spoke of women being forced shrieking onto their funeral pyres by baying relatives, and dwelled on the agonies of a slow death by fire; a good many readers with no personal knowledge of India certainly believed that this was the common fate of all Hindu widows from Bombay to Bengal. The notion that innocent, healthy and perhaps beautiful young girls* should be made sacrifices to an alien religion profoundly shocked public opinion at home, and when it was learned that the Company – bound by its solemn promise never to interfere in matters of religion – actually endorsed the practice if the woman concerned freely requested it, the howls of outrage that arose from liberal reformers and Christian moralists alike were heard distinctly in Calcutta. Even old India hands commonly believed that, in permitting the two practices, Hinduism made itself complicit in thousands of murders.

Worse yet, in some respects, was the Company's fear of the wild excesses displayed by Hindu devotees. This, too, was largely a product of ignorance, and of the growing distance throughout the Subcontinent between rulers and the ruled. But the concern itself was real enough. From the Himalayas to Cape Cormorin, it was increasingly believed, religious frenzy lurked just beneath the placid surface of Indian society – a frenzy so spontaneous and

---

*The victims described in contemporary British accounts, the historian Amal Chatterjee wryly observes, 'fell into two broadly corresponding groups – officials saw and recorded suttees that involved "mature" women, while non-officials invariably encountered young women, in the bloom of their youth, being tragically destroyed by blind and tyrannical custom.' The latter image was given form by innumerable poems and romances. Mariana Starke's celebrated play *The Widow of Malabar* (1791) featured a beautiful girl driven towards her death by evil Brahmins, only to be rescued by a gallant Englishman at the very moment all seemed lost.

unrestrained that it seemed all too likely it would one day be channelled into actual rebellion. The signs were there for those who wished to see them, not least at the famous temple complex at Juggernaut, on the Bay of Bengal, where every March tens of thousands of chanting pilgrims lined the roads to watch the procession of four gigantic wooden carts, each bearing a 'monstrous idol' in the form of an ancient statue of a major Hindu god. The carts were dragged along by the brute muscle power of the faithful. Each one was 43 feet high, garishly painted, and mounted on 16 enormous wooden wheels, and it was widely rumoured – and generally believed – that pilgrims sacrificed themselves to their gods each year by hurling themselves to destruction beneath the carriages.*

By Sleeman's day, then, India itself – an object of admiration and even envy only a few decades earlier – was increasingly perceived as a 'hideous moral wilderness', and matters were not helped when, in 1813, the British government compelled the Company to allow Christian missionaries into its dominions. Within a remarkably short space of time, even educated Britons, whether in London or Bengal, were condemning the Hindu peasantry as 'universally and wholly corrupt . . . depraved as they are blind, and wretched as they are depraved'.

The Company's discovery, early in the nineteenth century, that Thug gangs were strangling hundreds of travellers in Hindustan, thus fitted neatly into the pattern of British expectation. The belief (which became common later) that India was home to hundreds of secret criminal communities was already beginning to gain ground; the Company had run up against roving groups of dacoits, fakirs and Sannyasis in Bengal, Naga robber-bands in the Rohilla country, north of Oudh, and Kallar cattle-thieves – 'wild Colleries' to the men of the Madras Presidency – in the newly conquered districts of the Deccan. The Thugs were bracketed with such robbers and disturbers of the peace at first. But in the second quarter of the nineteenth century, Sleeman began to think of them as something considerably more dangerous.

---

*In truth deaths of this sort were rather rare, and were generally accidents caused by the sheer press of people along the route; according to the British army officer Thomas Bacon, who wrote about Juggernaut in the early 1830s, there had then been no genuine suicides there since 1821. It was true, he added, that the road leading to the temples was indeed lined with thousands of bleached human bones; but these, he was told, had been deposited not by suicides crushed beneath the wheels of the carts but by hundreds of terminally ill pilgrims who died in their desperate attempts to reach the temples.

Sleeman's interest in his prisoners extended well beyond the determination to catalogue and record their crimes. He was equally fascinated by their methods, customs and beliefs. As early as the cold season of 1830–1 he had composed a letter – published anonymously in the *Calcutta Gazette* – that outlined the stranglers' techniques in such startling detail that its publication aroused 'universal interest' in the Company's capital and prompted no less a figure than Lord Bentinck to enquire as to the identity of the unknown writer who 'appears to possess extensive knowledge of the character and habits of the Thugs'. Gradually, over the next few years, the Thug-hunter teased out further confessions from his approvers. These he set out in a series of detailed 'Conversations with Thugs'.

Sleeman's 'Conversations' recall many of the most notorious and remarkable Thug crimes and describe the gangs' customs and traditions in considerable depth. These interrogations – together with a shorter set of 'Dialogues' set down by James Paton, one of Sleeman's assistants, at his station in Lucknow – supply almost everything that we now know about the Thugs' history and their own beliefs. Their value is enhanced by the care that Sleeman took to question approvers from a variety of backgrounds. Men from the Deccan and Bengal took part alongside those of Murnae and Bundelcund. Hindu stranglers argued with their Muslim colleagues. Approvers who gave one version of events were corrected and upbraided by fellow informers who remembered events differently. Every exchange was taken down, presumably in Hindustani, by the Company's moonshees and then translated into English. The voices of the Thug informers emerge clearly from Sleeman's pages in a way that they never do in the transcripts of their trials.

By his own account, Sleeman's initial purpose was to take down, codify and make available a glossary of Thug slang – an argot known as Ramasee that the stranglers used when in company with a party of intended victims in order to conceal their murderous intentions.* But the 'Conversations' soon strayed

---

*Ramasee has often been described as a 'language'. It was not. It was a form of low-class Hindu cant, full of sly jokes and coarse double entendres. The majority of travellers do not seem to have understood its meaning at all. But there were several instances of some potential victim grasping the true significance of a phrase and hurriedly leaving the Thugs' company in the nick of time.

onto other subjects, and several excerpts, dealing with omens, religious belief and the organization and recruitment of the Thugs themselves, clearly stood out – not merely in Sleeman's mind, but also in the memories of those who read through the captain's transcripts. In these passages, the approvers stressed that the principal Thug gangs were composed of hereditary stranglers, men who could trace their ancestry back through many generations of murderers. And they placed far greater emphasis on the Thugs' religion – in particular their fierce devotion to the goddess Kali – than any earlier source.

We have already seen that Thug gangs took auspices and participated in religious ceremonies before departing on each expedition. Every member of every gang, whether Hindu, Muslim or Sikh, seems to have taken part in these acts of devotion. There was nothing at all unusual in this. Religious ceremonies designed to seek the blessing of the gods were an important part of Indian folk religion and a common feature of village life. Farmers attempted to invoke good harvests; merchants and travellers sought protection on the roads. Thugs – whose livelihood depended so heavily on chance, and whose expeditions were so inherently dangerous – naturally did likewise.*

But there had been no hint, in any of the thousands of pages of depositions and trial documents taken down by Smith and Sleeman and their moonshees, that religion was of any special importance to the Thugs, nor that the beliefs they held influenced the manner in which they practised their grim trade. On the contrary, numerous captured stranglers had implied that their motive for committing murder was financial. The few references to religion that do appear in the statements of ordinary Thugs imply that it was simply a part of everyday life. 'Having performed the usual worship,' one strangler's account of a typical expedition begins, 'we set out towards Sholapoor.'

Sleeman's approvers told a different story. For them, religion was a central feature of their lives and the goddess Kali (who also appears under the names Bhowanee or Davey** in many of Sleeman's documents) was a special protector of the Thugs. Several respected jemadars recounted legends that

---

*Thieves and housebreakers – the Thugs themselves pointed out – performed similar ceremonies. But the stranglers did not think them so punctilious: '[The housebreaker] performs religious rites to the iron instruments with which he breaks through the wall much as the Thugs do to our instruments of murder . . . but they do not worship on every expedition – perhaps only once or twice in the year.'
**A corruption of 'Devi', the female energy force. Neither Bhowanee nor Davey are entirely synonymous with Kali, though Sleeman certainly thought they were.

emphasized the regularity with which the goddess had acted to shield them and their families. Not even the mightiest rulers, they said, could stand against her. The approvers firmly believed that Mahadji Sindhia, one of the greatest of Maratha warlords, had met his death at the Kali's hands after unwisely executing 70 Thugs in February 1794. And 'was not Nanha the Raja of Jhalone made leprous by Davey for putting to death Boodhoo and his brother Khumoli, two of the most noted Thugs of their day? He had them trampled under the feet of elephants, but the leprosy broke out on his body the very next day.'

The Thugs' legends reassured them that they had enjoyed the goddess's protection for many years. As long ago as 1775, the Rajah of Kundul, east of Hyderabad, received repeated warnings that he should release a group of Thugs he had had thrown into prison. But 'he was obstinate, and on the third night the bed on which he and his Ranee were sleeping was taken up by Davey and dashed violently against the ground . . . they were not killed, but they were dreadfully bruised; and had they not released the Thugs, they certainly would have been killed the next night'. Kali was, moreover, capable of wreaking vengeance on lesser enemies as well. The Gwalior zamindars who seized Thugs fleeing from the destruction of Murnae in 1812 'were severely punished for giving us such annoyance', and – at least in the recollection of one of Sleeman's most trusted approvers – their loved ones all died, and 'not a soul of their families are now left to pour the libation at their funeral obsequies!'*

Indeed all of the Thugs' legends concerning the goddess featured exactly the sort of cautionary notes typical of folklore. In some Kali saved worthy stranglers from their enemies, but in others she deserted men who had not been faithful to her commands. A fable told by many Thugs related that they had for many years neglected to bury the bodies of their victims, leaving them lying on the ground so that the goddess could devour them – 'that Bhowanee may have her blood; she delights in blood!' This their protector did with such efficiency that the Thugs were never in any danger of discovery or arrest, and the members of each gang were strictly enjoined never to look back on the scene of the murder for fear of disturbing the deity's feast. But

*It is evident that these stories had their basis in myth and misapprehension. It is now generally believed that Mahadji Sindhia, for example, died after either throwing himself, or being thrown, from a balcony in his palace.

on one occasion a novice of the fraternity disobeyed this rule and, unguardedly looking behind him, saw the goddess in the act of feasting upon a body with the half of it hanging out of her mouth. Upon this she declared that she would no longer devour those whom the Thugs slaughtered; but she agreed to present them with one of her teeth for a pickaxe, a rib for a knife and the hem of her lower garment for a noose, and ordered them for the future to cut about and bury the bodies of those whom they destroyed.

Sleeman's approvers thus used religion not merely to justify their actions but also to explain their failures and their capture. They held that the real reason for the decline and fall of their gangs was to be found not in the Company's tactics, nor in their own faithlessness or poor organization, but in their failure to pay proper attention to the proscriptions they had been ordered to obey. 'That Davey instituted Thuggee, and supported it as long as we attended to her omens, and observed the rules framed by the wisdom of our ancestors, nothing in the world can ever make us doubt,' observed an approver named Nasir. But the gangs of the early nineteenth century had failed to heed the goddess's orders to refrain from killing women and members of the various proscribed classes. 'Our ancestors were never guilty of this folly!' one strangler concluded in disgust. 'We murdered men and women of all classes. How then can Thuggee stand?'

Captured Thugs claimed on many occasions that their crimes were simply a matter of fate; they were destined to commit them. They were 'merely irresponsible agents', no more liable to be held to account for their killings than were the tigers to whom they often compared themselves. This explained how Thugs could – in an admission that plainly baffled Sleeman – 'look forward indifferently to their children, whom they love as tenderly as any man in the world, following the same trade of murder or being united in marriage to men who follow the trade'. Some elaborated further: 'How many men have you strangled?' one notorious jemadar was asked. 'I have killed none,' came the incensed response. 'Is any man killed from man's killing? Is it not the hand of God that kills him? And are we not mere instruments in the hand of God?' But this dispensation applied only to men proceeding on a Thug expedition,

properly consecrated. Those unwise enough to kill when they were not under
the protection of Kali could expect to be punished in the same way as any
other Indian. 'If a man committed a real murder, they held that his family
must become extinct, and adduced the fact that this fate had not befallen
them as proof that their acts of killing were justifiable.'

Sleeman and his associates saw matters differently. 'A Thug,' Sleeman
concluded, 'considers the persons murdered precisely in the light of
victims offered up to the Goddess', and his habits and his actions were all
determined by his devotion to Kali. This faith, moreover, had been fully
rounded and worked out over the course of centuries, and was unique to
the Thugs.

Such views were controversial then. Today, it is generally agreed that the
conclusions Sleeman drew from his 'Conversations with Thugs' were distorted by the prejudices and misinterpretations so common at the time. In
truth, the Thugs' worship of Kali and their veneration of the sacred pickaxe
hardly constituted a religion. The gangs possessed no religious texts, had
no agreed forms of worship, and while they certainly shared in the belief that
their goddess protected them, they held this in common with thousands of
ordinary Indians. Kali was commonly invoked as a protector by all sorts
of Hindus; and at this time she was – later anthropologists have noted –
especially popular among criminals of all sorts and men of lower caste. Pickaxe worship arose merely 'from the common animistic belief that tools
and implements generally achieve the results obtained from them by their
inherent virtue and of their own volition, and not from the human hand which
guides them . . . Members of practically all castes worship the implements of
their profession.'

The Thugs' beliefs, indeed, may be better understood as folklore than as a
distinct faith. This may be seen most clearly in the manner in which members
of various gangs differed sharply in the interpretation of even the most fundamental customs – as Sleeman discovered when he questioned his approvers
regarding their obedience to omens:

Sleeman   When you have a poor traveller with you, or a party of travellers
who appear to have a little property about them, and you hear or see
a very good omen, do you not let them go, in the hope that the virtue
of the omen will guide you to better prey?

Dorgha, Musulman Let them go – never, never.

Nasir, Musulman, of Telingana How could we let them go? Is not a good
    omen the order from Heaven to kill them, and would it not be dis-
    obedience to let them go? If we did not kill them, should we ever get
    any more travellers?

Feringeea, Brahmin I have known the experiment tried with good effect –
    I have known travellers who promised little let go, and the virtue of the
    omen brought better.

Inaent, Musulman Yes, the virtue of the omen remains, and the traveller
    who has little should be let go, for you are sure to get a better.

Sahib Khan, of Telingana Never! Never! This is one of your Hindustanee
    heresies. You could never let him go without losing all the fruits of
    your expedition. You might get property, but it could never do you any
    good. No success could result from your disobedience.

Nasir The idea of securing the good will of Davey by disobeying her
    order is quite monstrous. We Duckun Thugs do not understand how
    you got hold of it. Our ancestors were never guilty of such folly.

Feringeea You do not mean to say that we of Murnae and Sindouse were
    not as well instructed as you of Telingana?

Nasir and Sahib Khan We only mean to say that you have clearly mis-
    taken the nature of a good omen in this case. It is the order of Davey
    to take what she has put in our way; at least, so we, in the Duckun,
    understand it.

Most strikingly of all, the evidence so carefully recorded by Sleeman and
his men makes it clear that Indian villagers did not engage in Thuggee
because they worshipped Kali. Rather, Kali worship was a facet of life as a
Thug – one that could safely be neglected or abandoned by a man no longer
practising the trade. The first hints that this was the case emerge from
questions posed to Muslim Thugs: 'Do Mussellman Thugs continue to follow
the rites of their religion?' Paton asked. 'Or does Bhowanee supercede
Mohammed?' 'What?' exclaimed the approver Allyar. 'Is Bhowanee the equal
of Mohammed? He is the lord of our faith and of our religion.' 'Bhowanee,'
added his colleague Bakh Mohammed, 'is only for Thuggee.' But it was when
Paton turned to the question of the religion practised by the Thugs now they
were in Company custody that the most instructive exchange took place:

Paton   You paid great reverence to Bhowanee, but she deserted you. What do you think of her now?

Futty Khan   God is above, and what do we care for Bhowanee now? We get food from you now.

Dhoosoo, Mussellman   I think now that Bhowanee is a non-entity, for if she were not so, why should I be in trouble now?

Allyer, Mohammedan   If I had the image of Bhowanee now, I would fling it into a well!

Paton   You say so now – but if you ever went on Thuggee again, would you not invoke Bhowanee?

Allyer   Yes. If I went on Thuggee I would still pay my devotions day and night to Bhowanee. She is the chief of that trade.

The emphasis placed by Sleeman and – through him – by the Company authorities on the role of religion in Thug life was thus enormously exaggerated. But in a country such as India, in which most Europeans felt barely at home, such exaggerations were accepted without question. To take only one example, references made by the Thugs to the pilgrimages some made to a temple to Kali maintained in the village of Bindachul, just outside Mirzapore, were built up into suggestions that the temple was itself an important headquarters of Thugs, maintained by Thug priests and funded by the proceeds of Thuggee. Sleeman formed this opinion at an early stage, writing in October 1830: 'Kali's temple at Bindachul . . . is constantly filled with murderers from every quarter of India, who go there to offer up in person a share of the booty they have acquired from their victims strangled in their annual excursion . . . The priests of this temple know perfectly well the source from which they derive their offerings [and] they suggest expeditions and promise the murderers in the name of their mistress immunity.'

Probably this impression of a harsh and murderous cult owed something to Sleeman's own religious beliefs, for he added: 'To pull down [Kali's] temple at Bindachul and hang her priests would no doubt be the wish of every honest Christian.' But the impact of such pronouncements – made, as they were, in the almost total absence of information to the contrary – on British consciousness in India was significant. By 1835 the impression that Thuggee was an alien religion of the most horrible sort was firmly established among the European communities in India. A few years later, with the publication of the sensational novel *Confessions of a Thug*, written by Meadows Taylor, Sleeman's contemporary in Hyderabad, a similar view was introduced to Britain. The consequence was a distinct loss of perspective. The determined criminal, anxious to provide for his family, seeking rich prizes and schooled in the ways of the Thug trade by other members of his gang became 'that fiend in human form, luring his victims to their doom with soft speech and cunning artifice, committing the cold-blooded murder of every man he met'. The murder of potential witnesses became 'the taking of human life for the sheer lust of killing', and 'the plunder, however pleasant . . . a secondary consideration'.

The most unexpected consequence of this perversion of the Thug's religion was the romanticization of Thuggee itself. 'The histories of these men,' the Company magistrate Edward Thornton exclaimed, 'are as romantic as the most ardent lover of Oriental adventures could desire.' Men driven to kill by their beliefs were far more compelling than mere highway robbers, however lethal, and the stranglers were, it seemed clear to Sleeman and his men, no ordinary criminals. Their devotion to Kali could even be perceived as noble. Sharp distinctions could be drawn between the dacoits, who tortured their victims and killed indiscriminately, and the Thugs, who were forbidden – however nominally – from murdering the members of certain classes and castes, and who killed comparatively quickly and cleanly. 'However unscrupulous and treacherous the Thugs were,' Sleeman's grandson concluded, looking back, 'one thing at least stands to their credit, that while they sometimes killed women – though contrary to their faith – they never maltreated them beforehand.'

Seen in this way, the Thugs could appear 'sporting', even chivalrous opponents: men who possessed a code – however obscene – and who lived by it, men to whom faith and honour were important. These were not, of course, the men encountered by the unfortunate victims actually inveigled on the roads, killers devoid of compassion and – at least in the early nineteenth century – more than willing to flout the proscriptions that supposedly governed their behaviour. But it was undoubtedly an attractive image, not least because it elevated and flattered those involved in the pursuit of the Thug 'cult' as well as those engaged in it. The stranglers, one officer of Sleeman's department later wrote, possessed 'noble and chivalrous instincts . . . [there were] specimens who in habitual courtliness and fair faith, were clothed with both dignity and manliness'.

Admiration for the captured Thugs emerged gradually, and was often qualified, at least in print, for reasons of Christian propriety. 'I know not whether most to admire the duplicity with which they continue to conceal their murderous intentions, or to detest the infernal apathy with which they can eat out of the same dish, and drink out of the very cup that is partaken of by the victims they have fixed on to destroy,' wrote Sleeman's assistant in Hyderabad, Lieutenant Reynolds. But prolonged exposure to the approvers – and the destruction of the gangs themselves, which at last rendered the surviving Thugs more of a curiosity than a menace – led some members of the Thuggy Department to become more open. Even James Paton, a stern Presbyterian, whose transcriptions of his Thug interrogations are peppered with disapproving footnotes and Biblical allusions,* succumbed eventually to the romantic lure of his prisoners and 'made positive pets of some'.

Sleeman himself was not immune to the stranglers' allure. He appears to have been not merely puzzled but actually captivated by Feringeea, whose pursuit had presented him with such difficulties. The prisoner was far from being the insensate brute, coarsened by his long career of murder and incapable of any finer feeling that Sleeman seems to have expected, and Feringeea's youth, considerable good looks, firm bearing and unexpected sensitivity took him by surprise. The jemadar, Sleeman discovered, was a paradox, a man who, by his own account, could have escaped the Company's net scot-free were it not for the love he bore for his own family. 'I could not forsake them,' the captured Thug explained, 'and was always inquiring after them, and affording my pursuers the means of tracing me. I knew not what indignities my wife and mother might suffer. Could I have felt secure that they would suffer none, I should not have been taken.' The Thugs' love of their families, remarked upon by several British authorities, became regarded as one of their principal characteristics. 'These common enemies of mankind,' Sleeman wrote after one interview with Feringeea, 'who . . . strangle other people of whatever age or sex without the slightest feeling of compunction, feel towards their relations as

---

*'What a sad but faithful picture of our ruined nature does this present!' Paton scribbled at one point, after setting down an account of murder perpetrated by a vast Thug gang. 'Three hundred sons of fallen Adam leaguing themselves together for the purpose of *murder!*'

strongly as other men. At different times during his deposition, this man had occasion to mention his foster brother, Radha Kishun, and his nephew, Sinha, two of the 11 hung, and every time the tears filled his eyes and ran over his cheeks.'

Other officers found the same contrast between the senior jemadars' murderous behaviour on the roads and the principled lives they led (or claimed to lead) in their own homes a source of endless fascination. 'Mr Wilson,' Sleeman noted, 'describes approver Makeen Lodhee as "one of the best men I have ever known!", and I believe that Makeen may be trusted in any relation of life save that between a Thug who has taken the auspices and a traveller with something worth taking on him.'

Another of Sleeman's assistants, Lieutenant Reynolds, who had charge of the anti-Thug campaign in Hyderabad, was 'quite astounded' to discover that a certain Hurree Singh, whom he had known for several years as a highly respectable cloth dealer in the Sudder Bazaar, 'was the Hurree Singh of the list sent to him of noted Thugs at large in the Duckun'. Singh, a strangler of such notoriety that the reward placed on his head was twice that offered for the capture of Feringeea, turned out to be the adopted son of a Thug subadar executed at Hyderabad in 1816 'for the murder of a party of two women and eight men'. He had, Sleeman concluded, been 'so correct in his deportment and all his dealings, that he had won himself the esteem of all the gentlemen of the station . . . and yet he had, as he has since himself shown, been carrying on his trade of murder up to the very day of his arrest . . . and leading out his gang of assassins while pretending to be on his way to Bombay for a fresh supply of linens and broad cloth'.* Even the Holkar of Indore was greatly astonished when, 'only about two months ago, a party of mine pointed out, as a notorious Thug, a non-commissioned officer who was superintending the drill of soldiers in the very Court Yard of His Highness . . . He was instantly secured and soon after acknowledged that during the whole twenty years that he has been a Sepahee in the service of the Honourable Company or that of different Native Chiefs, he has been himself a Thug or in league with the Gangs that passed up and down the country, and that there was not a Thug of any note in the Hyderabad territories, in the Scindhia, Holcar and Bundelcund

---

*The same small bazaar proved to be hiding three other wanted stranglers: 'Ismail Thug, who turned approver, Mohna alias Ruhman, and Bahleen'.

states, with whom he had not in that time become personally acquainted.'

Sleeman, who hunted game, as did most British officers in India, even seems to have felt some slight stirring of common feeling with a few of his approvers for this reason. 'They all look upon travellers as a sportsman looks upon hares and pheasants,' he wrote, 'and they recollect their favourite beles, or places of murder, as sportsmen recollect their best sporting grounds, and talk of them, when they can, with the same kind of glee!' It is an extraordinary statement, and if the Thugs were being truthful at all (for Sleeman's captives probably dwelled more fondly on their days on the roads of India after their capture – when it was obvious to all of them that they would never be free to wander them again – than they had at the time, when every expedition was, for many of their number, a struggle to provide for themselves and their families), it can only have been true for a handful of the best and most successful jemadars. Yet a few Thug leaders seem to have drawn similar parallels between themselves and the men who had hunted them down. 'Are you yourself not a *shikari*,'* one asked Sleeman,

> and do you not enjoy the thrill of stalking, pitting your cunning against that of an animal, and are you not pleased at seeing it dead at your feet? So with the Thug, who regards the stalking of men as a higher form of sport.
>
> For you, sahib, have but the instincts of the wild beasts to overcome, whereas the Thug has to subdue the suspicions and fears of intelligent men and women, often heavily armed and guarded, knowing that the roads are dangerous. In other words, game for our hunting is defended from all points save those of flattery and cunning.
>
> Can you not imagine the pleasure of overcoming such protection during days of travel in their company, the joy of seeing suspicion change to friendship, until that wonderful moment arrives when the rumal completes the hunt – this soft rumal, which has ended the lives of hundreds? Remorse, sahib? Never! Joy and elation, often!

It would be wrong to overstate the sneaking regard that British officers began to feel for their approvers, nonetheless. Sleeman and his men continued to

*Big game hunter.

abhor their crimes. Nor did their admiration extend to the great mass of
Thugs who served the jemadars they kept in custody; these, the British invariably found, were coarser, crueller and less sympathetic than their more
polished leaders.

In fact, the danger posed by the strangling gangs seemed greater now than
it had done before. Mere murderers were bad enough. But they could be
rounded up and captured and imprisoned, and so the dangers that they posed
could be removed. The evidence uncovered in the course of his lengthy conversations with the Thug approvers hinted at something far more insidious
and much more difficult to eradicate. If Thuggee was a hereditary calling, the
arrest of a single member of a family would do nothing to remove the danger
posed to travellers; the man's brothers would continue his work. Similarly, the
arrest of a Thug who had fathered children neither would nor could deter his
sons from becoming stranglers themselves. Even infants who had never ventured out onto the roads of India themselves would inevitably grow up, join
gangs, and learn the secrets of their father's trade.

Nor, Sleeman became increasingly certain, was it possible that Thuggee
would simply wither and die when the conditions then prevalent in central
India – economic hardship, widespread unemployment and repeated drought
and famine – eased. Men who 'consider the persons murdered precisely in the
light of victims offered up to the Goddess' would never cease to kill in any circumstances, and it was this (the Thug-hunter convinced himself) that
explained how a strangler could cold-bloodedly 'mediate his murders without
any misgivings, perpetrate them without any emotions of pity, and remember them without feelings of remorse'.

Sleeman's conversations with his Thug approvers had other sinister impli-
cations, too. Killing from habit, not from need, seemed particularly perverted.
And the suggestion that a gang's victims were selected more or less at
random, at the whim of some portent or omen, was especially terrifying;
stranglers who were as likely to kill an impoverished pilgrim as the wealthi-
est merchant seemed somehow stranger – and yet more Satanic – than mere
robbers out for plunder.

There is no reason to doubt that the East India Company would have set
out to destroy the Thugs whatever their motives, whatever their beliefs;
sporadic efforts had, after all, been made to do just that for years before Sleeman
began his own enquiries. But there is, equally, no question that his work –

disseminated throughout India in a stream of letters, articles and memoranda – gave the officials responsible for policing India every incentive to pursue their task with grim determination.

If Sleeman's theories were correct, disposing of the last vestiges of Thuggee would be an immense task. And accomplishing it would not only require, but warrant, measures almost as extreme as those employed by the stranglers themselves.

CHAPTER 17

The Last Days of Thuggee

'kondul kurna – breaking clumps of earth and spreading
them on a grave'

'What do you think, Sahib Khan?' demanded Sleeman of one Deccan Thug
brought before him in the cold season of 1835. 'Am I right in thinking that we
shall suppress Thuggee?'

Sahib Khan, a cautious and successful strangler who had served with his
gang for more than two decades, paused to consider his response. 'There
have been several *gurdies** upon Thuggee,' he replied, 'but they have ended
in nothing but the punishment of a few . . . We have heard our fathers
and sages predicting these things as punishments for our transgressions of
prescribed rules; but none of them ever said that Thuggee would be done
away with. [Yet] this seems a greater and more general gurdie than any, and
I do not know what to think.'

This hesitant admission, made nearly six years after the arrest of the
approver Amanoolah, was a symbolic moment in the Company's campaign.
It was the first time that any jemadar had conceded that the Thug gangs
might eventually be crushed.

Captured stranglers had hitherto insisted that Thuggee would always survive, an attitude that owed something to the approvers' understanding of
how easy it was to recruit men in times of economic hardship, and a good
deal to confidence in their own ability to escape detection. 'Suppose all

* Inroads.

our operations against the Thugs were now to be over,' another group of approvers was once asked. 'Do you think it would gain ground again?' 'Yes,' one strangler asserted, 'in five years it would be as extensive as ever.' In this he was probably right, since the Thugs' system was a proven one and many of its practitioners knew no other way to make a living. Their British persecutors naturally agreed. 'Once a Thug always a Thug is their motto and their creed,' wrote FC Smith of his approvers. 'Nothing can or will reform or deter [a Thug] from the practice of his profession. He may for a temporary space retire from business owing to the possession of riches, or other causes, but as sure as a dog returns to his vomit, so will a Thug return to his business sooner or later.'

Sleeman, too, continued to believe that Thuggee had, like some cancer, the ability to regenerate itself while even a handful of stranglers remained free. Hereditary Thugs and Kali's devotees, he was convinced, would inevitably resume their familiar trade if freed from jail or left to their own devices by the government. By the early 1830s he had become so convinced of the need to account for every member of every gang that his registers and records bulged with information drawn from the interrogations of captured men. Suspected stranglers brought to Jubbulpore for questioning were disconcerted by the detailed knowledge Sleeman possessed of their gangs, and this information, carefully deployed, produced confessions that would never have been made earlier, when the Company's knowledge of the Thugs was slight and stolid denials were frequently enough to win a suspect his freedom. From this per-spective, Sleeman's files – which were by now among the most detailed and comprehensive ever assembled by any police force – had become an invalu-able resource, one that kept the Company's Thug-hunting parties supplied with vital intelligence and made the task of tracking down their targets immeasurably easier.

The Thugs responded to Sleeman's accumulation of intelligence by shift-ing their bases with increasing frequency. Most of the stranglers of the Madras Presidency fled to new homes in the Native States, and men who had once based themselves in Bundelcund began to turn up in the wilds of Candeish. But even this tactic was of limited effect while Thugs meeting on the roads continued to talk freely among themselves. Only gangs that recruited selectively and actively shunned the company of others eluded the Company's approvers for long. A group of stranglers in Rajpootana, for example, were 'rarely seized or punished' thanks to their reclusiveness. 'How can their deeds be known?' demanded Sahib Khan. 'They do all their work themselves. They live in the desert and work in the desert. We live in villages and cannot do our work without the convenience and support of . . . influential men; but these men are relieved from all this cost and trouble by forgoing the pleasure of other men's society, and the comforts of a fixed habitation. They are wiser men than we are!'

Even among the gangs known to Sleeman, however, many men evaded capture for a time, and it soon became clear that Francis Curwen Smith had been too sanguine in hoping that the anti-Thug campaign could be concluded in as little as two or three years. The sheer number of suspects, and the ever greater care their leaders took as the Company's men closed in on them, made this an impossibility. 'Two seasons are still required for the work,' Smith admitted late in 1832 after concluding his twenty-sixth major trial of suspected stranglers, though by then well over 600 'notorious Thugs' had been hauled before the courts.

Sleeman, too, occasionally became despondent when he considered the sheer volume of work still left to do. 'There are many leaders and leading members of the old gangs still at large,' the Thug-hunter conceded,

and some of them may perhaps be in situations which enable them to destroy solitary travellers, though they have for the most part I believe found service in the military and police establishments of Native Chiefs. All these persons would return to their old trade, and teach it to their sons, and to the needy and dissolute of their neighbourhood, and thus reorganise their gangs, should our pursuit be soon relaxed. To prevent the system from rising again, it will be indisputably necessary to keep up the pursuit for some years till all these leaders and leading members of the old gangs die, or become too old to return to their old trade. Under the pressure of this pursuit their sons will take to honest industry, seeing no prospect of being able to follow successfully that of their ancestors.

The growing difficulty of securing the remaining Thugs now urged Sleeman and his superiors in Calcutta into a further frenzy of activity. When the anti-Thug campaign had commenced at the beginning of the decade, high standards of evidence were required to secure guilty verdicts in any Company court – even those run by FC Smith in the non-regulation territory of Saugor & Nerbudda. No man could be convicted of murder without the denunciations of several approvers and the support of circumstantial evidence, and after 1833, moreover, it was ruled that the evidence of approvers alone was insufficient to secure a death sentence in any case. In the course of the next few years, however, the ancient legal principle that the punishment should fit the crime began to blur as a stream of new legislation was passed. Each successive act made it easier to convict suspected Thugs no matter what the evidence against them.

This development was directly related to the progress of Sleeman's drive to extirpate Thuggee. The first few years of the campaign had witnessed the apprehension of virtually every major jemadar – men against whom numerous approvers were ready to testify and who could be confronted with a wealth of evidence relating to specific crimes. After 1835, however, the Thug suspects still at large were mostly minor figures. Few had taken a direct part in any murder, and some were guilty of nothing more than being peripheral members of one of the strangling gangs. The conviction of such men was not guaranteed under existing law, and yet the demonization of the stranglers – the suggestion that they were devotees of a perverted cult, and in particular the widespread acceptance of Sleeman's dictum that captured Thugs would inevitably return to their old trade upon release – made it seem imperative that every man among their ranks be detained for life. It was this necessity that drove the changes to the law that characterized the latter stages of the anti-Thug campaign.

The earliest law relating specifically to the crime of Thuggee thus appeared on the statute books some half a dozen years after the first approvers were secured. 'Act XXX of 1836', as it was known, was a sweeping revision of the existing code. It made the simple act of being a Thug, 'either within or without the territories of the East India Company', punishable by life imprisonment with hard labour. A second piece of legislation, Act XIX of 1837, disposed of the criticism (heard from several of the Company's stricter magistrates over the years) that the evidence of admitted criminals such as the Thug approvers could not be admissible in a British court. 'No person shall,' this new law decreed, 'by reason of any conviction for any offence whatever, be incompetent to be a witness in any stage of any cause, Civil or Criminal, before any Court.'

Company officers and magistrates could now charge suspected Thugs in a variety of ways. Men identified by approvers as active stranglers were sent for trial under existing regulations. The lesser members of the gangs – together, quite possibly, with a number of entirely innocent men unfortunate enough to be picked up in the company of Thugs – were charged under the new Act XXX. If there was insufficient evidence to secure a conviction even under the broad terms of the new Act, moreover, an older Company law – Regulation 8 of 1818 – was still at hand, as Sleeman reminded his men. Under the provisions of Regulation 8, Company magistrates were entitled to detain any suspect whom they were 'morally satisfied' was a member of a gang of criminals until the man had furnished security for his future good behaviour. Since British officers were free to determine what security was adequate, the practical result was that many suspected stranglers were held in prison for months and sometimes years, unable to raise the sums demanded. Setting the figure required to obtain bail at some impossibly high level became deliberate policy, for 'to release on security a Thug', insisted FC Smith, was 'folly and ignorance'.

Acts XXX and XIX were not the last pieces of legislation enacted by the Company as it attempted to dispose of the remaining vestiges of Thuggee. Seven years later, Act XXIV of 1843 not only extended the provisions of the existing Thug laws to cover dacoits as well – thus 'affording a security net to convict the prisoner who might escape a specific charge of murder by Thuggee' – but also gave the British authorities power to seize any Thug prisoner still held in the jails of the Native States and send them to a Company jail or to penal colonies overseas. This act ensured that not a single convicted strangler of any importance would ever be released in India.

The general effects of these changes in the law were twofold. Many more Thugs were convicted than would ever have been possible under existing regulations, and this satisfied Sleeman's increasingly determined quest to jail or execute every last strangler in India. But the standards of proof demanded by the courts fell sharply, and this made miscarriages of justice more likely. The second phase of the anti-Thug campaign, which lasted roughly from 1836 until 1840 or a little later, was thus less creditable to Sleeman and to the Company than was the work done in earlier years.

In these changing circumstances the Thuggy Department continued to achieve success. The central provinces were largely clear of Thug gangs after 1832, when their leaders' old strongholds among the Native States of Bundelcund were pronounced 'no longer a secure refuge for them or their families', and even the tenacious stranglers of Madras were believed to be 'completely suppressed' by 1836. Another 50 prominent jemadars were made approvers, and their information made it possible to circulate Company officers in the Upper Provinces with a list of more than 460 Thugs still at large in the Doab, where a good many Bundelcund stranglers had sought refuge. Meanwhile, in the Deccan, the Nizam of Hyderabad offered his assistance in locating the 150 Thugs thought to have fled to his territory from Madras.

There were also new suspects to be added to the register: so many that between 1833 and 1840 the British and their allies in the Native States actually arrested another thousand alleged Thugs, a greater number, by far, than had been captured in the period to 1832. The majority of these men were detained between 1833 and 1835; some 740 prisoners were brought before the Company's magistrates in that time, and all but 12 of them convicted. The number of arrests fell off after that, but, even so, a further 202 suspects were tried in 1836. As late as 1837, 57 additional trials were held at Jubbulpore. These cases involved 160 Thugs who stood accused of the murder of nearly 200 people and the theft of more than a lakh of rupees.

The anti-Thug campaign spread, too, until it encompassed every province in India. Although a good deal of Sleeman's attention was directed away from Saugor & Nerbudda after 1832, it was not until the late 1830s that representatives of the Thuggy Department appeared in Oudh and Malwa, Delhi, Gujurat and Rajpootana in addition to Hyderabad, Gwalior, Nagpore and Indore. These men were expected to track down and arrest any suspected Thugs living in their territories, as well as continuing the work of gathering intelligence and logging the names of suspected Thugs. Their other principal responsibility was to persuade the native princes of their districts to cooperate in Sleeman's campaign, which – thanks largely to pressure brought to bear by the government in Calcutta – virtually all of them now did. The destruction of the gangs' remaining refuges in the Native States resulted in a further spate of arrests. 'Thuggee?' the approver Davey Deen lamented late in 1835.

'Why, it is gone! There are not 50 Thugs of good birth left between the Ganges and the Jumna.'

The last districts to be scoured were those closest to the heart of the Company's own territories. The provinces of Bengal, Bihar and Orissa, which had been in British hands for longer than almost every other part of India, were not cleared of Thugs until 1840. One reason for this was the low priority accorded to the provinces by the Company itself, which believed as late as 1835 that 'the enormities of the Thugs are mostly committed in our newly acquired possessions, or in the Territories of the Native Chiefs of Bundelkhand, Malwa and Rajpootana', and so failed to grant Sleeman permission to extend his operations to the east. But the difficulties in implementing measures against gangs active in Bengal in particular also had a good deal to do with the judicial arrangements of British India, for the system that existed there was more extensive and bureaucratic than that deemed adequate in the Ceded and Conquered districts to the west, and many of the tactics and techniques developed by the Thuggy Department were actually illegal in the 'regulation territories' of Bengal. The Nizamat Adalat, which administered justice in Bengal, cleaved firmly to the Islamic code of law, demanding higher standards of proof than those required in Saugor & Nerbudda. Allegations, made by convicted criminals, that a suspect belonged to a Thug gang were not sufficient in themselves to warrant the man's arrest in the Lower Provinces, and the difficulty of proving that a particular Thug had committed a particular crime – the same problem that had confounded British magistrates throughout India in the past – made it virtually impossible to bring cases there with any prospect of success.

It was only after 1835, when Act XXX of 1836 had come into law and Sleeman had been created superintendent for the suppression of Thuggee throughout the length and breadth of India, that this situation changed. After that date, Thug-hunting parties were able to extend their operations to the east, and the difficulty of bringing captured men before the local courts was averted by the simple expediency of shipping men picked up in Bengal, Bihar and Orissa back to Saugor to stand trial. Armed as they were with information about the Bengal Thugs provided by approvers in the Doab and Oudh, the men of the Thuggy Department made rapid progress in the east. By 1840 Sleeman was stating with some confidence that the only parts of India still infested with Thugs were the foothills of the Himalayas, where some scattered communities survived in villages within easy reach of the border with Nepal.

The Company had by then captured almost all the gangs at large in Oudh and successfully disposed of a group known as the Goolah Thugs, whose men had been 'protected for years by a petty independent rajah on the western borders of the Pooree district'. There were still rumours of 'an isolated colony or two' of stranglers hiding in the countryside near Midnapore, but there seemed to be no evidence they were committing any crimes. Even Sleeman, always vigilant for the faintest whiff of Thugs, was inclined to believe that these colonies did not exist.

So the anti-Thug campaign came to an end. In retrospect, it would appear that the gangs actually posed little threat after 1835. No more than 20 cases of murder by strangulation were recorded throughout the whole of the Deccan in the following year, and the most striking thing about the Jubbulpore sessions of 1837 was that only two of the 57 cases for which the prisoners were tried had occurred after 1832. The remainder of the hearings concerned killings that had been committed as long ago as 1811, and nearly a third of them were 'subsidiary trials' – proceedings brought against individual members of large Thug gangs whose principals had been captured and convicted long before. In most cases, the men arraigned in the subsidiary trials had taken no direct part in the murders for which they were now tried, and were incapable of raising or organizing a Thug gang of their own. Many had been picked up by Sleeman's nujeebs years after they had last ventured on the roads, and had spent the intervening seasons working harmlessly on the land in their native villages. Their limited importance was reflected in the sentences that were handed down during the sessions of 1837 as a whole. Only 19 of the prisoners were hanged, and though a further 69 were transported and 19 sent to prison for life, nine were actually released – one in 20 of the total, a high proportion by the usual harsh standards of the anti-Thug campaign.

Thuggee had in any case faded from the consciousness of British India during the later 1830s. The known gangs were virtually destroyed, and their leaders either imprisoned or hanged. The few jemadars who were still at large were relentlessly pursued, and (largely because they proved incapable of cutting off all ties with their homes and families) the approvers tracked down almost all of them in the end. Their arrests deprived the remaining rank-and-file Thugs of leadership, and they lacked the skills and the determination to continue on their own. Certainly Thug murders became increasingly rare after 1835, when Sleeman was pleased to find that, for the first time in living memory, not a single sepoy had vanished without trace between his home and his barracks while on leave. By 1840, the annual circular that required every magistrate in British territory, and the Company's agents in the Native States, to report on the activities of Thugs showed that no instance of Thuggee had been reported anywhere in India. The gangs, Sleeman declared, had been broken up at last. An ancient menace had been finally extinguished.

CHAPTER 18

The Gallows and the Drop

'lokharna – yelling loudly while being strangled'

The Company's victory was not, in fact, quite so clear-cut as Sleeman's later reports claimed.

A large number of Thugs were never caught – several of the most notorious burkhas, and perhaps 1,000 rank-and-file members of various gangs, simply melted back into their towns and villages to be eventually forgotten. The great majority settled in the Native States, where little effort was made to secure their arrest once it became clear that the Thug murders had ceased. Nevertheless the Thuggy Department did make some attempts to keep track of their whereabouts, and Sleeman's register was kept up to date by his successors. As late as 1879, it contained the names of 340 suspected Thugs who remained at liberty.

It can be said with some confidence that none of these men ever set out again on strangling expeditions, but the many among them who remained poor and desperate may well have turned to other forms of crime. Sleeman's critics have suggested that some cases that would have been classed as instances of Thuggee before the British announced, in 1840, that the gangs were finished were written off as instances of highway robbery or dacoity afterwards – in part to save face, but also because the Company could not believe that Thugs were capable of anything but Thugging. There is some truth in this criticism. Sleeman's men had become so committed to the notion of Thugs as ingrained hereditary stranglers that they refused to see the survivors as little more than common criminals, capable if necessary of adopting different methods. Yet many of them were.

The disappearance of the Thugs did not, in any case, mean that the Thuggy Department had exhausted its usefulness. During the last years of Sleeman's campaign, the Company became increasingly concerned at the discovery of other varieties of thieves and murderers who appeared to share some characteristics with the strangling gangs. Its officers were by now so highly sensitive to any evidence of covert practices and rituals, family ties between members of a gang, or the existence of a predisposition to murder among criminals of any sort that nearly a dozen new groups of 'hereditary criminals' were uncovered in the course of the anti-Thug campaign. Most of them were nothing of the sort, being, rather, loose associations of criminals, sometimes united by bonds of family or origin, whose activities included robbery with violence, poisoning (often with the datura seed), and even a form of fairground gambling. The responsibility for investigating them was assumed by Sleeman's department – in part, perhaps, to justify its continued existence after the Thug campaign had been concluded, but also on the grounds that the victims were travellers who had fallen foul of murderous criminals, at least occasionally.

As it turned out, only one of the newly discovered associations was directly connected to the main Thug gangs. This was a group known as the River Thugs, a collection of stranglers some 300 strong who inveigled and killed their victims on the brown waters of the Ganges. There was, in one sense, nothing particularly special about them; the river was, after all, one of the great highways of India, and tens of thousands of travellers used it to travel from Calcutta to the holy city of Benares and on as far inland as Allahabad, nearly a thousand miles from the sea. Gangs of dacoits and pirates, lured by the prospect of loot, had infested the rivers of the Lower Provinces for hundreds of years. Probably the first River Thugs were stranglers who had worked the busy roads leading to Benares and guessed there was also plunder to be taken from the many pilgrims on the river.

The Ganges Thugs had much in common with their counterparts on land. They killed their victims with the rumal and employed a species of Ramasee that at least some land Thugs found intelligible, though it differed considerably in its vocabulary. Their gangs included inveiglers and hand-holders, and they always killed their victims before robbing them. Like the

Thugs of Murnae, Bundelcund and Oudh, they were generally active only during the cold season, and many evidently derived at least part of their income from farming. They were not particularly wealthy. Most River Thugs did not even own their own boats, hiring them from a compliant boat-builder or from the most powerful of their jemadars, a man named Khuruck Baboo. Khuruck led a group of 50 men and controlled seven craft that were identical to hundreds of others plying to and fro along the waters of the river, being about 20 feet long and equipped with a single cabin, ventilated by a large porthole on either side. Like most boats on the Ganges – where there was often little wind – these craft were towed by gangs of boatmen rather than sailed.

The River Thugs inveigled victims in much the same way as did their brethren on land. Small groups of them would lurk on roads and paths close to the Ganges, seeking to strike up conversations with likely parties of travellers. When they succeeded, talk would soon turn to the discomforts of life on the roads, and the River Thugs would suggest to their new friends that they would all be much more comfortable travelling by boat. If this suggestion was accepted, the inveiglers would lead their intended victims to a craft moored nearby, and – should the travellers be for any reason suspicious – there would usually be two or three more Thug boats tied up nearby, skippered by men who would gravely share the party's concerns and confirm them in their suspicions that they had been lucky to escape from a group of ruffians.

Once aboard one of the River Thugs' craft, of course, the intended victims were practically helpless. Outnumbered by the crew, far away from any help, and in most cases unable to swim, they had no chance of escape. Even a bungled attempt at murder could easily be rectified, and there are no records of any of the River Thugs' prey escaping them, as the land Thugs' victims occasionally did. The principal danger came from searches by suspicious customs officials, and for that reason Khuruck Baboo and his confederates were always careful to dispose of their victims' personal possessions, keeping only money and any jewels they could plunder. Such discipline was necessary to avoid detection, but loot in the form of goods, clothing and cooking utensils was an important part of most Thugs' income, and this no doubt explains the River Thugs' comparative poverty. One Ghazeepore Thug named Shumsheera, who took part in a single expedition along the Ganges, soon abandoned his companions 'as I got very little and grew melancholy, as there were no Thugs of my own clan or district'.

Shumsheera's experience was not unique, for Thugs who worked on land recognized the River Thugs as members of their fraternity, and it seems to have been not uncommon for stranglers from the Doab and Oudh to serve for short periods on the Ganges. Their motive was often simple curiosity as to the methods of the River Thugs, who had no need for beles and were never forced to murder only under the cover of darkness. Victims, too, were easily disposed of, since the Ganges was so filled with the corpses of devout Hindus, set adrift on the holy waters by their families, that a few more bodies attracted no attention.

For these reasons, Sleeman discovered, the River Thugs' murders were

always perpetrated in the day time. Those who do the work of the boatmen are dressed like other boatmen; but those who are to take part in the operations are dressed like travellers of great respectability; and there are no other boats kept so clean and inviting. When going up river they always pretend to be men of some consideration going on pilgrimage . . . [and when victims had been brought on board] they go off into the middle of the river, those above singing and playing and making a great noise, while the travellers are murdered inside at the signal given by three taps.

Corpses were disposed of in a brutal manner, 'the back broken by bending the body backwards and striking the spine with the hand, the most tender parts of the body destroyed, and the corpse thrown into the waters and devoured by the crocodiles which follow the boat'. The practice of snapping a traveller's spine ensured that he was dead, and was the River Thugs' equivalent of the stabbing favoured by the gangs on land. Even on the Ganges it was evidently not a good idea to tip a bloody, mutilated corpse into the water.

Such ruthless efficiency helped the River Thugs to avoid detection for years after the most important of their counterparts on land were captured. So did the location of their bases, which were mostly in the far south of Bengal, hundreds of miles from the districts where Sleeman and his assistants worked. In the end, though, the existence of the River Thugs was betrayed by the Oudh men they had welcomed onto their boats, several of whom were captured and became approvers. Sleeman's subordinates in Bengal destroyed most of the river gangs in 1836, when 160 of their number were at last arrested and arraigned for murders dating back to 1820. Others were picked up by Paton in Oudh. The remainder did not last very much longer, although as Sleeman's men did not extend their operations to the numerous pirates and dacoits on the Ganges, the river was not rendered entirely safe by their arrest.

At around the time that the River Thugs were finally dispersed, Sleeman began to pick up information concerning another group of criminals with similarities to the old Thug gangs. These were the Megpunnas, a loose association of thieves uncovered in the vicinity of Delhi. The Megpunnas relied for part of their living on murdering small parties of travellers – not to rob them of their possessions but in order to steal their children, who were subsequently sold into slavery or prostitution. Sleeman saw definite parallels between their practices and those of the Thugs, although he stopped short of suggesting that the two groups shared a common heritage. The Megpunnas, he wrote in another of his enormous reports, resembled the Thugs in strangling their victims on lonely Indian roads, and invariably killed the adults in the party before seizing their children. Like the Thugs, they consisted of several interrelated bands, travelled in gangs as many as 50 strong, and offered prayers up to Kali.

There were, however, clear distinctions between the two groups. The Megpunnas lacked the stranglers' sophistication, range and numbers, and were involved in a wider variety of crimes than were the Thugs, who rarely if ever concerned themselves with burglary and petty theft as the Megpunnas were compelled to do. One reason for this was the difficulty of locating and inveigling whole families travelling in a group. It is hard to imagine that any large gang of child-stealers could make a living solely from murder, even during the cold season, as a group of Thugs could do. Perhaps for this reason, the Megpunnas rarely struck outside the districts of Delhi and Rajpootana and were never numerous, numbering no more than 200 men and women. The latter (who rarely took part in Thug expeditions) were brought along to mind the children stolen by the gangs.

Sleeman's investigations into the Megpunna gangs nevertheless yielded some intriguing information. Megpunnaism turned out to be a very recent innovation. It had originated, Sleeman was told, in 1826, at the time of the Company's siege of the supposedly impregnable fortress of Bhurtpore. Its practitioners were indigents who probably stumbled across their earliest victims by chance and killed them more or less on a whim. It took some time for them to develop a considered modus operandi, and even in the mid-1830s they were not as well organized or as careful as the Thugs. Their clumsiness, indeed, defined them, for although the first murders definitely known to have been committed by a Megpunna gang – those of three men and two women whose bodies were discovered outside Delhi during the cold season of 1833–4 – were initially ascribed to Thugs, the approver summoned to examine the bodies 'at once disclaimed any responsibility for the dead on behalf of his fraternity. "It was," he said, "altogether too clumsy, and must have been done by men new to the trade and very awkward. For instance, the bodies would never have been left exposed [by Thugs] and in such a position; the strangling cords would not have been left about the victims' necks, nor would such clumsy knots have been tied."'

The Megpunnas were destroyed before they had the chance to refine their techniques or pass them on to others. As such, they offer a revealing glimpse into the likely protohistory of the Thug associations themselves. Probably the forebears of the sophisticated Murnae gangs were much like the first Megpunnas: opportunists who killed sporadically and clumsily with whatever weapons came to hand. Unlike the Megpunnas, however, the first Thugs escaped detection and were able to evolve more deadly and efficient tactics. In time, as they became more expert, these early stranglers no doubt came to rely more and more on murder for their living, and to feel the pangs of conscience less. Had the Megpunnas not been stopped when they were, they too might have evolved into confident mass murderers with their own favourite territories and a well-developed network of fences, informants and protectors.

The remainder of the 'hereditary criminals' exposed by the Thuggy Department in the years 1836–60 proved to have even less claim to kinship with the strangling gangs than the Megpunnas. The so-called 'Tusma-Baz Thugs', for example, found living on the outskirts of Cawnpore in 1848, were little more than Hindu thimble-riggers. Their association had been founded by three sepoys who had been instructed in the tricks of this ancient trade by a Company private named Creagh around the year 1802, and their particular speciality was a deception known as 'pricking the garter',* which

---

*'Played in this manner: a strap being doubled into many folds, the bystanders were requested to insert a stick where the first double took place, which was impossible to do without the consent of the juggler.'

they practised at fairs and bazaars throughout the Native States, having first 'conciliated' the local police with the promise of the usual quarter-share of their profits. They were really professional gamblers, who were bracketed with the Thugs solely because they had, as a sort of speculation, murdered and robbed a few travellers whom they met upon the roads. This was noticed even at the time. 'To call them Thugs was evidently a misnomer,' one contemporary writer observed. 'They were simply organised bands of vagrants of the most worthless character, who preferred fraud to labour and murder to industry.'

The fact that peripheral associations such as the Megpunnas and the Tusma-Baz Thugs could be drawn into the Thuggy Department's orbit (and be widely perceived as threats equal in potential, if not in practice, to the original Thug gangs) is very revealing. The British authorities had been badly shaken by the revelations of the anti-Thug campaign, which had uncovered depredations on a scale that had barely been suspected. The unveiling of apparently respectable stranglers in the most unexpected places had added to the growing feeling of unease.* Evidently, some Company officials now admitted, India remained far from understood. They were more than willing to concede that other criminal bands – some perhaps as deadly as the Thugs – still lurked undiscovered elsewhere in the vastness of the Subcontinent.

All this made it imperative to retain the expertise built up within the Thuggy Department. By the late 1830s, its remit had already been widened to include the suppression of dacoity – a still more difficult task, perhaps, but one that Sleeman himself took on, with his usual vigour, between 1835 and 1847. After that, the department evolved again – first into a sort of pan-Indian police force with overall responsibility for the suppression of a wide range of

---

*A case recounted by several contemporary authors concerned a Dr Cheek, who – at a time when the country around his home was being scoured for a Thug strangler of the most ferocious sort – employed a servant 'who had charge of his children. The man was a special favourite, remarkable for his kind and tender ways with his little charges, gentle in manner and unexceptionable in all his conduct. Every year he obtained leave from his master and mistress as, he said, for the filial purpose of visiting his aged mother for one month; and returning after the expiry of that time, with the utmost punctuality, resumed with accustomed affection and tenderness the charge of his little darlings. This mild and exemplary being was the missing Thug; kind, gentle, conscientious and regular at his post for eleven months in the year, he devoted the twelfth to strangulation.' The Victorians derived a grim enjoyment from this sort of revelation, since it confirmed deeply held beliefs concerning the fiendish deceptions of the Thugs and the unreliability of Indians in general.

violent crimes, and then, in the last years of the nineteenth century, into a central intelligence office, gathering information on Indian nationalist groups and other potential rebels. This was a job its officers – with their intimate knowledge of criminal behaviour in the mofussil – were assumed to be particularly well suited to, and the department thus survived for a further half a century, being abolished, with the empire itself, only in 1947. As late as the latter years of the Second World War, the Government of India's intelligence agency – then based at Simla – was popularly known as the *thagi daftar*: the 'Thug office'.

Sleeman's unique creation – the one arm of the East India Company whose jurisdiction extended across the entire Subcontinent – had been extraordinarily successful. In little more than a decade it had destroyed a menace that the whole vast Indian police system had left unchecked for years. Its officers had developed new methods for suppressing crime; its men had learned the art of tracking down endlessly elusive criminals. Sleeman himself had transformed Indian policing from an almost entirely local affair, dependent on officers with few resources and working, in effect, alone, into a recognizably modern operation, one in which the diligent accumulation of intelligence held sway, and careful record-keeping was as important as drill. He had also abandoned the purely reactive policing characteristic of the time. India's untrained and often inexperienced darogahs, whose jurisdiction and interests were limited to a few square miles, almost always restricted their efforts to solving crimes that had already occurred. Sleeman's men, rather than waiting for their enemies to strike, actively pursued them. In doing so, they created a new template for police work.

These were remarkable achievements, and – for all the excesses of the occasional nujeeb, the exaggerated importance attached to the Thugs' religious beliefs, and the harrying of minor criminals in the later 1830s – they were appreciated by the Company's subjects themselves. A village to the north-east of Jubbulpore was renamed Sleemanabad, and the brass lamp Sleeman himself presented to the temple there was kept burning for more than a century in his honour; it is still there today. Writing in 1840 to the head of the local Thuggee office, a Hyderabadi noble named Hussain Dost Khan, often a vocal opponent of the British, conceded that 'seeing that the best arrangements have been made in this matter, the whole of the inhabitants of this country, and travellers, have been emancipated from the fear of Thugs . . . Where are the murdered men? How can there be any, when you do not hear even the slightest allusion to Thugs? The whole world is giving thanks for this.'

Sleeman, too, felt pride in his campaign. Writing to his friend Charles Fraser, who had succeeded Francis Curwen Smith as magistrate of Jubbulpore, he ended his letter by urging:

Do not I pray you get tired of the duties – neither you nor any other man can ever be employed in any more interesting or important to humanity. I shall look back with pride to the share I have had in them as long as I live . . .

Believe me, Fraser, I would not exchange the share I have had in this work for the most splendid military service that man ever performed in India. I glory in it and ever shall do.

The Thug trials continued with grim regularity throughout the 1830s. It was not long before the prosecutions became a mechanical process, in their way as devoid of humanity as the Thugs' own murders. One hundred men had been committed in 1830, and tried by FC Smith: the first of the great Thuggee trials. A further 389 were dealt with in the sessions of 1831–2, at Saugor and Indore, and another 316 the following year, this time at Poona and Hyderabad as well as at Saugor. By 1835, the number of suspected Thugs brought before the Company's courts had passed 1,500, Smith alone trying three-quarters of that total. By 1840, by which time Sleeman had extended his campaign into Bombay and Madras, the number of committals had reached 3,689.

Of the 4,500 men who eventually stood trial for Thug crimes between the years 1826 and 1848, a total of 504 – or nearly one in every nine – was hanged. Three thousand more were sentenced to life in prison, more than half of whom were transported to penal colonies in the Far East. Most of the rest served either seven or 14 years' hard labour, or died in prison while awaiting trial. Virtually none escaped the Company's wrath altogether. Fewer than 250 were acquitted.

Sentences were passed with reference to guidelines issued by the government in Calcutta. Between 1830 and 1836, at least, these were relatively straightforward:

The death penalty when there was proof that the culprit had strangled or helped or assisted a strangler, or if he had been a jemadar, that is Thug chief.

Deportation for life of the culprit if it was proven that he had been known to be a Thug, but when only one witness accused him of having been a strangler in the course of a single incident.

Deportation for life for Thugs who performed important tasks such as digging graves, convincing victims, helping to make the bodies disappear.

Fourteen years in prison for those who performed lesser tasks such as standing guard.

Seven years in prison for those accused of having been present as the gang perpetrated its crimes, but who did not actively participate in them.

Release on security for young boys taken prisoner.

In the event, almost all Thugs were found guilty of active complicity in their gang's crimes. Shorter terms of imprisonment were imposed only rarely, particularly at first, and almost always involved cases in which the defendant was no more than a boy. And there was never any case in which the initial verdict was overturned on appeal. The willingness of the Governor General to confirm even the harshest sentences seems to have been influenced by the pleas of FC Smith who, having heard all the evidence marshalled for the numerous cases brought before him, became utterly convinced that no Thug deserved mercy.

'They never should recover their unrestricted liberty,' Smith argued,

for numerous proofs exist of the utter impossibility of reclaiming even boys the sons of Thugs from this horrid but apparently irresistible profession. Like tigers their taste of Blood is indelible and not to be eradicated while life exists.*

Men sentenced to seven years' imprisonment or more suffered an additional punishment. Each convicted Thug was forcibly branded or tattooed with the details of his crime, a form of punishment often employed in India at this time, though it had previously been reserved for those who had been handed

*'The case of Kehree,' Smith went on, 'is in point. As a boy he had a hand cut off on conviction of belonging to a Thug association; he witnessed the appalling exhibition of his confederates being blown away from Guns, but so far from abandoning this dangerous profession he is now in his old age condemned to death for the same description of crime he was punished for so severely in his youth.'

life sentences.* The most common formulation specified 'branding on the forehead or on the back, with the word "Thug" marked by the process of the *godna* [tattooing needle] in the Hindee and Persian characters'. Other men received the tattoo 'Convicted Thug', and some contemporary drawings show stranglers with tattoos on their lower eyelids, though there is no written evidence that such markings were actually applied. The principal aim of this punishment was to enable escaping prisoners to be easily recaptured. But it was also seen as a shameful imposition; Muslims were forbidden by their religion to wear tattoos, while Hindus believed that the markings endured after death and would be legible to those who met them in the afterlife.

The Company had planned to execute convicted Thugs in their home villages, where it was thought their deaths might best act as a deterrent to their fellow stranglers. In the end, however, the scheme was rejected on the grounds that it made escape too likely. Those who were condemned to death met their ends in the towns where they had been tried. Most were hanged in either Jubbulpore or Saugor.

Among the first prisoners to be executed were the Thugs of Feringeea's gang, who went to their deaths in Jubbulpore late in September 1830. Betrayed by their leader, they faced their ends with a show of equanimity that impressed the crowd gathered to watch their execution and struck Sleeman as worthy of comment. 'I was,' he wrote to the editor of the *Calcutta Gazette*,

> yesterday present at the execution of eleven Thugs . . . convicted of the murder of about 35 travellers whose bodies were disinterred as evidence against them along the lines of the road between Bhopal and Saugor. A new drop had been constructed of cut-free stone for the purpose of receiving the whole at once, and consisted of three pillars about sixteen feet from each other and twelve feet high, with two beams across them at the top, and two planks as platforms . . . about five feet from the ground. The eleven nooses, suspended at equal distances from the beam, reached down about three feet, so as to give a fall of about two feet; and in order to shorten the duration of

---

*And common, too, in Europe, where French galley slaves were tattooed GAL, English thieves marked with a 'T', and Russian prisoners sent to Siberia branded KAT.

suffering they were made small and formed partly of thongs to ensure strength.

As the sun rose, the eleven men were brought out from the Jail decorated with chaplets of flowers, and marched up to the front of the drop, where they arranged themselves in a line each seeming to select the noose or situation that pleased him best, with infinitely more self-possession than men generally select their positions in a dance or at a dinner-table. When arranged, they lifted up their hands and shouted '*Bindachul Ke Jae, Bhowanee Ke Jae*',* every one making use of precisely the same invocation, though four were Mohammedans . . . They all took their positions on the platform . . . and taking the noose in both hands, made the same invocation to Bhowanee, after which they placed them over their heads and adjusted them to their necks with the same ease and self-possession that they had first selected them; and some of the younger ones were actually laughing during the operation . . . Being directed to have their hands tied to their sides that they might not in their agonies seize the rope, and thereby prolong their sufferings, one of the youngest, a Mohammedan, impatient of the delay, stooped down so as to tighten the rope, either to prevent it breaking with a jerk, or with a view to prevent pain from it, and stepped deliberately one leg after the other over the platform and hung himself, precisely as one would step over a rock to take a swim in the sea.

The platforms were now drawn out from under [the others], and six beside the young Mussulman who had hung himself remained swinging; but, owing to some rains that had fallen during the night and wet the thongs, four of the ropes gave way with the jerk, and the men came to the ground. Spare ropes thicker and stronger were at hand and they were soon again swinging at the side of their companions; and among the people of all religions and all colours that were present, not one, I believe, felt the smallest emotion of pity for their prolonged agonies, in such utter abhorrence are they held by all classes of Society.

Not all convicted Thugs behaved so calmly. Some ascended the gallows still protesting their innocence, and condemning the approvers who had testified against them. One group of men from Borthwick's gang, hanged earlier in

*'Glory to Bindachul! Bhowanee's glory!'

the same year, 1830, 'met their fate with hardened and sullen indifference', and were heard to 'give vent to bitter and unmeasured recrimination of the evidence' as they passed along towards the gallows. But displays of bravado – whether real or feigned – plainly were a feature of a good number of Thug hangings. The British traveller Fanny Parks quoted an observer from Jubbulpore who believed that 'it would be impossible to find in any country a set of men who meet death with more indifference than these wretches; and, had it been in a better cause, they would have excited universal sympathy'. Sleeman's cousin, a Company surgeon named Henry Spry, noted that the night before another mass execution in Saugor 'was passed by these men in displays of coarse and disgusting levity', and that they sang loud songs in the cells. Next morning, under the gallows, 'the air was pierced with the hoarse and hollow shoutings of these wretched men'.*

All in all, about one man in every eight found guilty of Thuggee was handed a death sentence, these being, in the Company's view, the most hardened of all the prisoners brought before its courts. Among them were Feringeea's cousin and his foster brother, hanged at Jubbulpore with the other members of their gang, but on the whole the approver's family did not suffer unduly at the hands of Smith and Sleeman. Of Feringeea's other three brothers, one died in Huttah jail in 1823 and the other two were accepted as approvers. Among his cousins, one died in prison, three turned approver, one fled and remained at large, and three others died natural deaths.

The fate of the executed Thugs varied according to the year and the place in which they were hanged. Some Hindu prisoners asked to be cut down and cremated, in accordance with their faith, but this was not generally granted to them. On rare occasions, the Company authorities permitted the dead men's relatives to erect a rough cairn over their graves. A good number of Thugs, however, were left to dangle from their gallows for weeks or months, as a warning to others – an ancient practice that was not ended until 1836. Even then, several British magistrates made applications to have the rotting bodies

---

*The Thugs were not unique in this; most of the sepoys convicted of mutiny in 1857–8 went to their deaths with similar stoicism. And the Duke of Wellington, as one historian points out, 'had observed long before that in comparison with their European counterparts, Indians were strangely impervious to the prospect of execution'. 'There is a contempt of death in the natives, high and low,' he wrote, 'occasioned by some of the tenets of the religion of both sects, which makes the punishment a joke and, I may say, an honour, instead of what it is in our country.'

of dead Thugs permanently displayed, in gibbets, along the highways they had haunted. This was officially forbidden, but there is some evidence that the practice of 'hanging in chains' continued in the mofussil, at least in a few instances, as late as the 1860s.

Even the corpses that were cut down from the gallows were often subjected to further rituals. It was generally believed in India that men who suffered violent deaths remained on earth as evil spirits called *bhutas*, and the people of Saugor were sufficiently concerned at the prospect of being haunted by dead Thugs to request that Sleeman order incisions to be made in their corpses. A deep cut made above the right ankle, it was thought, would ensure that the dead men's spirits escaped their bodies. Such mutilations had recently been forbidden in an official circular sent out from Calcutta, but Sleeman allowed them to be made anyway, and the bodies of all the Thugs hung at Saugor were given the necessary incisions. Sleeman was never disciplined for this breach of regulations. Smith defended the decision, and the Company accepted it. Circumstances, in the Saugor & Nerbudda Territory in the 1830s, were very far from usual.

Somewhere along the way, and almost unnoticed, there was justice of a sort for the murdered moonshee, Bunda Ali, and his family. The remaining members of the Lucknadown gang, their numbers depleted by the passage of years, were judged at last, in Saugor and Jubbulpore during the sessions of 1830–1. About 90 of the 115 then remained alive, and no fewer than 33 of these were sentenced to be hanged – this being the largest number of death sentences, in proportion to the total of committals, ever handed down by Smith. Another 13 were transported for life, and most of the remainder received long terms of imprisonment. Gubbil Khan, who had tried to claim Bunda Ali's infant child for himself before burying her alive, and had since spent the best part of a decade in jail, was sent back to prison for a further seven years.

Among those who went to the gallows were Bhawanee Jemadar, who had strangled the moonshee, Babur Khan and Sheikh Bazeed, who had between them killed his wife, and Essuree the inveigler – one of the police officers who had lured Bunda Ali to his death by showing him his badge of office and persuading him to travel with the gang. These men were hanged at Jubbulpore in May 1831, and Fanny Parks copied a contemporary account of their execution into her diary. Like their comrades in other gangs, she wrote, the Lucknadown Thugs refused to be executed by a low-caste hangman. Each instead made a show of examining 'with a detached air' the ropes that dangled from the long beams of the gallows. 'There was,' Parks concluded, 'something dreadful in the thought that men, who had so often imbrued their hands in blood, should meet their deaths with such carelessness.' Then, one by one, each man reached out, and took a noose, and placed it around his own neck. And each, when he was satisfied, slid the knot tight under his ear, and launched into eternity.

CHAPTER 19

Across the Black Water

'phur jharna – the process of cleaning a bele to remove
all signs of murder'

On the edge of a lake near the centre of Saugor stood a large stone building.
It was squat and square, made from the rough local bricks, and surrounded
by a high mud wall. This building, with its barred windows and thick wood
doors, was the town jail – the largest in the central provinces, and the main
prison for convicted Thugs.

By the end of 1840, Saugor Jail, and others like it dotted throughout India,
were crowded with more than a thousand convicted members of the Thug
gangs. Hundreds more were still arriving every year. At a time when there
were no more than 30,000 convicts in the whole of British India, this huge
influx of prisoners placed a great strain on the prison system, and posed real
challenges to the resourcefulness of the officers who ran the jails.

Matters were hardly helped by the decrepit state of many of the peniten-
tiaries. Indian prisons were rarely completely secure when Sleeman and Smith
began their anti-Thug campaign. In Saugor & Nerbudda, most – whether run
by the Company or the Native States – were nothing more than thatched and
mud-walled huts, ringed by walls; a few were merely rented bungalows. A
handful of convicts, it is true, were confined within the dark recesses of old
forts, but even here there were few outward signs that they were actually in
prison. The jails of the early Victorian age did not depend on walkways and
watchtowers, or even guards patrolling to and fro inside the building. Instead,
prisoners were confined together in a handful of large, unfurnished living

spaces – male convicts in one room, those awaiting trial in another, perhaps women in a third – each man claiming his own small area of floor and squabbling with his neighbours over space and the handful of comforts they were allowed.

The Company's determination to round up every suspected Thug who could be found soon resulted in serious overcrowding, particularly among prisoners on remand. As early as 1831, Saugor Jail was holding 610 alleged Thugs in buildings meant to house only 200. Sheer lack of space meant that 'a large proportion' were confined not in the main prison, but 'in a kind of building lately erected near the jail without a surrounding wall', an evidently inadequate measure that merely increased the ever present danger of escape.

The sheer press of men in Saugor Jail was unusual, even for the time, but overcrowding had long been a problem in Company prisons and the consequences could be serious. Poor ventilation and the absence of even basic sanitation left jails stinking and unhealthy. The convicts had no access to running water; the bare minimum required for drinking and cooking was brought in by hand from nearby tanks or wells. Little was ever available for washing or flushing drains, and the unsanitary conditions that resulted were at their worst in the disgusting prison privies, which were typically no more than uncovered earthen jars. 'So little care is taken to clean these vessels,' a report on one Bengal jail observed, 'that the whole floor, which is paved with brick, has become perfectly saturated with filth.'

The consequences of this neglect were all too predictable. Repeated epidemics of cholera, malaria and dysentery swept through the prison system, and the mortality rate in Company jails was frequently appalling. More than 40,000 deaths were recorded in Bengal alone during the quarter century from 1843 to 1867, and in the first half of the century it was not uncommon for a quarter of all the men kept in a given prison to die of disease in a single year. Conditions in the central provinces seem to have been rather better – perhaps because most of the jails in the old Saugor & Nerbudda Territory were so small and makeshift that the regimes there were rather relaxed. Even so, one in every 20 of the suspected Thugs imprisoned there died while awaiting trial, and a good many more succumbed to disease while serving their sentences.

The lack of space in Company prisons was exacerbated by the proscriptions of caste, which required most Hindu prisoners to prepare and cook their own meals in order to ensure their ritual purity. This made it impracticable to build a single cookhouse. Instead, the convicts were furnished with an allowance to buy food, and vessels in which to prepare it. The sight of hundreds of prisoners packed into a small, walled courtyard, each man hunched over his own pots and pans, was one of the most common in the prison system.

The staple food consisted of wheat cakes made from buffalo butter and coarse-ground flour, but since little attempt was made, before the 1840s, to regulate the men's diet, prisoners were free to buy whatever they could afford – which was not much. Supplementary purchases included 'bad meat, stinking Fish, musty grain, unripe vegetables and fruit', but also 'the most deleterious spirits and Drugs'. On Sundays, the one day of rest, those who had had sufficient discipline to set aside a little of their ration during the week would prepare modest feasts. Even so, complaints about the food were more common than protests concerning any other aspect of prison life.

Security was, nonetheless, rarely a significant problem in Company jails despite the primitive conditions. The main deterrents to escape were not bolted doors and barred windows but the iron shackles that were worn night and day; and the main purpose of the prisons was neither confinement nor reform, but the infliction of forced labour.

At this time, imprisonment with hard labour was the most common sentence handed down in almost every British court. It was thought to hold particular terror for all the criminal classes, in India as well as at home. 'Nothing,' the Company's Committee on Prison Discipline observed in 1838, 'is so distasteful to a native as hard continuous labour.' It was 'the most powerful engine in the hands of penal legislators in India for making jails as terrible as possible'.

For the first four decades of the century, therefore, virtually all convicts who were fit to work were marched through the prison gates every day to dig and surface roads, which in the Saugor & Nerbudda Territory meant sweating to quarry, shift and shape the bone-hard basalt of the region. Not every observer believed this a harsh enough punishment; it was 'only the semblance of hard labour', thought Henry Spry, and in any case the prisoners worked at it for no more than four or five hours a day. But from the Company's perspective, the policy had several benefits. It kept the prisoners occupied. It forced down the costs of public works. And the common sight of men labouring in fetters had (it was hoped) a deterrent effect on passers-by.

Many convicted Thugs had been in prison before. Some had already served time in native prisons, where they had been forced to work on the local roads until they could lodge the security required to secure release; others had been confined for short terms in British jails, only to be released when the local magistrates found it impossible to make their charges stick. Now, however, things were different. The sheer enormity of the confessions heard in Smith's courtroom, combined with Sleeman's certainty that any escaped Thugs would inevitably return to their old profession, was sufficient to convince the Company that its new prisoners should never be released, even to labour under heavy guard on public works. From the first days of the anti-Thug campaign, therefore, elaborate precautions were taken to secure them from the moment of their arrest. The members of large gangs captured on the roads were chained together in groups of 30, and secured each evening, during the march back to Saugor or Jubbulpore, by stakes driven into the ground through the links in their shackles. Once they had reached their destination – and unlike ordinary prisoners who were released from their irons for at least part of each day – individual Thugs were kept heavily fettered night and day.

There seems, even so, to have been a general perception, in the early 1830s, that confinement to a Company prison was less than such criminals deserved. Dr Spry, who in 1837 reported on the disgusting state of the drains at Saugor Jail, suggested that 'the respiration of prison-air in Hindustan is, in point of fact, the only punishment, after personal restraint, which those in confinement can be said to endure'. It was partly for this reason that, in 1838, the old punishment of work on the roads was superseded by what the government of India described as 'monotonous, uninteresting labour within doors'. This, in Company lands, generally meant either mounting the treadwheel – a sort of convict-powered corn mill – or, more usually, turning handmills for grinding flour. These mills, which were a specifically local innovation, were first issued to prisoners serving life sentences in the inland provinces in 1841, and remained in service for so long that they became one of the defining images of imprisonment in Indian jails.

The increasing numbers of the Thug prisoners raised other issues for the

Company. There was no one Thuggee jail; instead captured stranglers were imprisoned where they had been convicted, and there were Thug wards in the prisons at Aurangabad, Cawnpore and Agra, as well as several more within the borders of the central provinces themselves. Since it was feared that Thugs might corrupt the lesser prisoners, the Company was careful to keep them well apart from the other men. At the same time, the Thugs themselves became deliciously grisly attractions for European visitors to the mofussil, and Sleeman and his men often put their captives on display for distinguished guests. These early tourists had to be escorted and protected when they called at Thug jails, though the surviving records suggest that local officers had so much confidence in their prisoners' behaviour that this responsibility was generally not taken very seriously. The diarists Emily and Fanny Eden – sisters of the then Governor General, Lord Auckland – who visited Cawnpore in 1837, wrote acidly of Captain Paton, 'who is a great Thug fancier – he has a prison full of them'. Paton had, thought Emily, 'by dint of living with Thugs . . . evidently become rather fond of them, and has acquired a latent taste for strangling', which he indulged by encouraging some of his charges to re-enact their old crimes. This demonstration seems to have impressed the gentlemen in the party – though, as Fanny pointed out, 'it is a foolish exhibition and once, they warmed into the play so much, they nearly strangled a sepoy in good earnest'.

Similar re-enactments were a feature of colonial life for years. The Venetian photographer Felice Beato, who went to India in the wake of the Mutiny of 1857, visited one of the Thug prisons of Oudh and was able to secure a portrait of three inmates showing how they disposed of their victims. Altogether more sinister, at least in the eyes of the participants, was the trick played on the Reverend William Butler, an evangelical clergyman, during a visit to Agra at much the same time. Butler and his party had just enjoyed a sightseeing tour of the Taj Mahal when their guide, a Colonel Williams,

> casually remarked, as we crossed the road from the Taj, 'Come, I will show you something else.' So he turned down an ominous-looking portal, and we followed him through a guarded gate into a square with high walls, and thence by a gloomy passage into another inclosed court, where were a group of the most awful-looking men that I had ever seen. The Colonel

coolly remarked, 'These are some of my pets.' In a moment we realised where we were standing, three gentlemen and a party of ladies unguarded in the presence of nearly two hundred Thugs! It made one's flesh creep. The feeling was dreadful, and the situation was not at all relieved when, in retiring again through the long, dark passage, a number of these wretches came clanking close after us, to plead in the outer court for some concession from the Colonel. The ladies of the party could hardly forgive our gallant escort for the trick he played upon them in leading them into such a presence, and that, too, after coming out of the Taj. It seemed like leaving paradise and descending into hell.

Nevertheless, the practice of visiting the Thugs continued a while longer. It probably persisted into the early 1880s. Only the increasing decrepitude of the diminishing bands of survivors, and the British decision to move their jails away from town centres, where they had been easily accessible to visitors, put an end to the practice.

This is not to say that the Company ever viewed its prisoners as harmless. From the late 1830s, when suspects brought into its jails were classified according to the seriousness of the charges that they faced, suspected Thugs were ranked as the most dangerous of all native criminals, one category above men accused of 'heinous crimes' against property or the person, and two above those charged with theft, forgery, fraud or receiving stolen goods. Sleeman and his successors were always concerned that some might escape, and teach their methods to a new generation of Thugs; this was a constant worry, particularly given the large concentrations of stranglers in the jails of the old Saugor & Nerbudda Territory. Saugor itself was, of course, not particularly secure. The position was a little better at the central jail in Jubbulpore, where the men convicted in the sessions there had been locked away, but even this prison was not proof against every attempted jailbreak. In 1834, a group of more than a dozen Thugs sliced through their cast-iron shackles using twists of thread coated with oil and a little powdered corundum stone – an abrasive sold in local bazaars and used to cut gems and polish steel. Having freed their legs, the men used the same technique to saw through the bars across their window, a job that took them only half an hour. After that, they scaled the walls and made off into the night.

Sleeman was astonished at the audacity of this escape. 'The iron was cut through as it were with a knife,' he wrote, 'and in a manner so perfectly smooth as to be almost incredible . . . The bar was so finely cut it would escape detection by the naked eye even at a distance of a few feet, and could only have been detected by sounding the bar with a hammer.' Over the years a handful of stranglers escaped from other jails. Most were, in the end, recaptured; the Company set its approvers on them, and since the majority had returned to their old haunts they were swiftly hunted down. 'The narratives of these pursuits,' Sleeman recalled

> were, many of them, exceedingly interesting. [The approvers] knew the homes of the most remote relations or friends of the fugitives, and, in one disguise or another, led the pursuing party to every one of them, until they had gratified their revenge by recapture.

Nevertheless, in the course of the nineteenth century at least 14 convicted Thugs escaped from prison and eluded all pursuit – presumably by fleeing to parts of the country where they had not been previously known. The only consolation for the British was that these few seem to have been convinced they would be foolish to resume their former careers. There is no evidence that any of them ever killed again.

The fifteen hundred or so convicted Thugs imprisoned in central India may have been housed in poor conditions, and kept hard at work, but their fate was far less terrible than that of the men sent to penal colonies overseas. Well over 1,200 of Sleeman's captives had been sentenced to transportation for life, and these prisoners were shipped, in chains, to a desperate existence in the Malayan swamps. Theirs was a two-fold punishment, for the transportees endured not only unremitting hard labour, but also separation from everything and everyone they knew.

The idea of transportation was an old one. The British had been banishing 'rogues, vagabonds and sturdy beggars' from their shores since 1597 – at first to the tobacco plantations of Virginia and then, when the American War of Independence put a stop to that, to Australia, where the convicts of the First Fleet made landfall at Botany Bay early in 1788. These men were transported

because it was then generally believed that the criminal classes were irredeemable, and Britain would be better off without them; because English
prisons were increasingly overcrowded; and also because the free colonists of
both the New World and New South Wales required a cheap supply of
labour. The practice of shipping convicts out from Britain did not cease until
1868, and by then a total of 40,000 British and Irish felons had been sent to
America and the Caribbean, and about 165,000 to Australia.

Large numbers of Indian prisoners suffered similar fates after transportation to the East Indies was introduced in 1787. In all, perhaps 100,000 were
sent overseas from Bombay, Bengal and Madras, and for much the same reasons as their British counterparts. They went at first to Bencoolen, a ragged
collection of half-built huts sweltering on a mud flat on the south coast of
Sumatra, then to Penang, an island off the Malayan coast, and later to Burma,
Aden, Malacca, the Straits Settlement (today Singapore) and the sugar plantations of Mauritius. These were places where the British had established
footholds of sorts, and where labour was desperately needed to help build the
new colonies. Some were not much more than clearings in the midst of fever-
ridden jungle – desperately unhealthy places, even by the standards of the
time – and the work that the convicts were put to, which included clearing
mangrove swamps and cutting back great swathes of rainforest, ensured that
mortality among the prisoners was always high.

From the Company's perspective, the penal colonies of the east were a
useful resource. They made it possible to remove convicts from British territory far more certainly than the old practice of deportation to the Native
States. They made it difficult for the men to return, since even those transported for a term of years, rather than life, were generally forced to remain in
their new homes as free settlers once their sentences were served. And they
made escape all but impossible, which meant that even Thugs could usually
be put to work outside the prison walls. In both Sumatra and Singapore, the
penal settlements were surrounded by hundreds of miles of impenetrable
jungle filled with tigers and home to hostile natives, whom the prisoners
were encouraged to believe would kill and eat men on the run.

Perhaps most significantly of all, the punishment of transportation was
believed to be a terror to Hindu convicts, whose religion forbade them to
cross open water on penalty of losing caste. 'The belief was that transportation would be polluting,' writes one historian. 'It was thus commended as

"a weapon of tremendous power" . . . and the effect of transportation on the whole community was believed to be greater than the death sentence.' Sleeman, like most British administrators, was certainly convinced that he set a severe example of the Thugs whom he sentenced to be shipped to settlements 'across the black water'. Whether there was any truth in this belief is debatable; it was certainly no deterrent to Muslims, and since Hindu prisoners risked sacrificing their ritual purity in jail in India, where they could not always be sure of choosing their companions or the food they ate, some prisoners actually found the prospect of transportation preferable, and pleaded to be sent overseas. Nevertheless, British magistrates continued to make liberal use of their right to banish prisoners to Malaya well into the second half of the nineteenth century.

The majority of these men – certainly the majority of Thugs – went to the largest of the new settlements, Penang. Prisoners were sent, in irons, from Saugor and Jubbulpore to the coast, and there held in jail, along with other convicts, until a ship became available. A British army officer named Gould Hunter-Weston, who encountered a group of 97 Thug transportees on the Bombay waterfront in 1840, noted that the entire party had been tattooed on their foreheads with both their names and their offence, and that all were heavily shackled to prevent escape. Hunter-Weston asked one what he had done to deserve such punishment. 'The reply was that he did not know, for he had only strangled six men.'

The tattoos were generally effective in marking out Thugs from other prisoners once they arrived at their destinations. The stranglers detested them and took no pride in this visible identification of their status as members of a notorious fraternity; when they could, they hid them by wearing their turbans 'inconveniently low down on their brows'. Such deceptions were, however, difficult to maintain in the confined conditions in which the men were held. In the early years of the Penang settlement, for example, convicts were crowded together inside a small stockade, and went out to work in gangs each day – at first on the roads, and later, in the 1850s, making 'lounging chairs' for sale to British officers. The area was malarial, and since the medical wisdom of the time suggested that fevers were borne by a 'noxious effluvia' that rose from the surrounding jungle, the transportees slept in cramped dormitories raised on wooden stilts. Charcoal braziers burned day and night in every room to drive off diseased air, and the men contributed to their own well-being by coating the floors each morning with a fresh layer of cow dung mixed with water, a common Indian prophylactic.

In some respects, in fact, conditions in the penal settlements were better than they were in India. The leg irons worn by most felons were much lighter than those used on the Subcontinent, and so confident were the authorities that their prisons were secure that even these were generally discarded once the men had served a probation of three months. Such liberal regulations did not, of course, apply to convicted Thugs, who were made to work in heavy fetters and forbidden to cook their own food. The most notorious among them, in common with other 'irredeemable' criminals, were not allowed out of the stockade, where they 'were confined in the refractory ward on severe task work, such as making coir* from the rough husks of cocoa-nuts'.

The knowledge that the penal colonies dotted about the Indian Ocean were full of Thugs only added to the frisson that many Britishers felt when confronted by groups of transportees, whom they were already inclined to see as implacable villains. The shiver that ran down the spine of a Mrs Bartrum, who encountered one gang of prisoners in Mauritius in the 1830s, seems to have been entirely typical. 'I remember being struck with the appearance of the Hindoo convicts, at work on the roads,' she recalled. 'They had a most ferociously scowling aspect. The dark, malignant glance, the bent brow, the turban of dirty white or dusky red; the loose drapery, only half clothing the body, gave them a wild, picturesque appearance, to which mountain scenery added still greater effect.'

Yet the warders responsible for the penal settlements had – or at least professed to have – no fear of the Thugs. Prison officers thought of their charges as cowards, who had relied on the force of numbers to commit their crimes and were harmless when kept isolated from the other members of their gangs. In this they were apparently correct, for despite the casual violence that was commonplace in many jails, there are no records of convicted Thugs strangling either fellow prisoners or civilians. According to JFA McNair, the officer who commanded the penal colony at Singapore until its abolition,

---

*A tough fibre used to make ropes and matting.

It is worthy of remark . . . how signally these men often fail when they attempt to act alone. Amongst our Thugs we had one (a strangler) who, coveting a pair of gold bangles on the wrist of a fellow-convict employed at the General Hospital, one night tried the handkerchief upon him, but missed his mark, and got away without being detected. Later on, the convict authorities examined the warrants of all the men in the hospital, and this gave them a clue, which they followed up successfully and caught the 'Thug'. He was punished, and then confessed, saying, 'Bhawani was unkind, and I could not do it by myself; I missed my companions.'

The contempt that British officers felt for individual Thugs left them determined to prevent any resurgence in Thuggee. Though the authorities occasionally showed mercy to other long-term prisoners with exemplary jail records, no Thug lifer was ever paroled. Even when the convict settlements at Penang and Singapore were closed down between 1867 and 1873, and many of the prisoners freed, the 250 Thugs found there were simply transferred to a brand new penal colony being established in the Andaman Islands. There they passed the remainder of their lives in the uniquely harsh environment of what became the most feared of all Indian prison settlements: a jail built in a jungle on islands that lay two hundred miles out in the Bay of Bengal and were scarcely ever visited; a place whose 'utter unfamiliarity – a deliberately maintained vacuum of knowledge and experience – was expected to make the Andamans a kind of black hole in the imagination of the Indian criminal'.

Those Thugs who survived to be sent to the Andamans found themselves confined, as they had always been, to separate quarters, arranged so that they could not corrupt the lesser prisoners who made up the remainder of the prison population – habitual thieves, occasional murderers and rebellious sepoys rounded up after the Mutiny of 1857. Nevertheless, by the 1870s the tides of penal reform were at last shifting in the Thugs' favour. By now the centuries-old certainty that such criminals could never be redeemed was at last giving way to belief in the potential for reform. Isolated as they were from the mainland, the remaining Thugs posed little danger to society, and – safe in the Andaman Islands – it was at last agreed that they might be rehabilitated within the confines of the settlement. To mark the great Imperial durbar of January 1877, at which Queen Victoria was created Empress of India, a number of the Thugs, dacoits and poisoners on the islands were granted conditional and local releases, and allowed thereafter to live and work with the free men in the island capital, Port Blair. The chance of a return to India was still denied them; but for the time that remained to them, these minor Thugs – men who were, in British eyes, less evil than those who had been hanged, and less useful than those made approvers – were returned to society of a sort.

The approvers themselves, who had proved their usefulness to the Company and atoned – in some small measure – for their crimes, were treated rather differently.

Feringeea's fellow informants remained out on the roads long after he himself was returned to jail in 1832, travelling about with their escorts of nujeebs and chasing the diminishing bands of Thugs of whom they had personal knowledge. This information was the key to their temporary freedom, for they could only avoid confinement for as long as they remained of service to their new masters, and it was certainly suspected – then and now – that a few, at least, levelled false allegations against innocent men in the hope of appearing useful. Even so, 56 approvers had been returned to prison by the late 1830s, where they were, naturally, widely hated by the men they had betrayed. The only way to guarantee their safety was to keep them in isolation from the other convicts, and so they were confined together in a lock-up just outside the gates of Jubbulpore's Central Jail.

This state of affairs endured until 1837, when a new model prison, called the School of Industry, was opened in the town. It was specially designed to house the approvers in relatively comfortable conditions, and unlike the other prisons and penal colonies to which convicted Thugs were sent, it served two purposes, being not merely a prison but a reformatory as well. The approvers themselves were, of course, regarded as beyond salvation; the commutation of their death sentences to life imprisonment, in exchange for their services to government, was the most they could expect. But their sons – those who had never been on a Thuggee expedition, and were (it was thought) too young to have been fully exposed to the full horror of their fathers' lives – were also imprisoned, to be educated and, if possible, brought up as useful citizens. They, too, were forcibly confined, over a good number of protests, for the Company remained convinced that they would take up strangling if they were released. Because they were as yet innocent of any crime, however, they were permitted much more freedom than their fathers could enjoy.

The Jubbulpore School of Industry did not look much like a prison. It was located in the centre of the town, and was close to, but not a part of, the central jail. It was long and low and built of brick, with tiled and sloping roofs to drain the monsoon rains, and it enclosed a large dirt quadrangle, where the inmates ate and exercised. The approvers themselves were housed nearby, alongside the soldiers assigned to guard them, in what were called the 'Thuggee Lines'. The Lines were, in effect, a model native village, built by the prisoners themselves with Company help, in which the informers lived with their wives and children. This was a particular indulgence. The British always took great pains to prevent their other Thug prisoners from breeding, for fear that any children would turn to Thuggee. But here, in what amounted to controlled conditions, the practice was tolerated. By 1870, the village had grown to a substantial size; in that year it housed 158 Thugs (the great majority of them men arrested in the 1840s and 1850s) and 202 of the approvers' dacoit counterparts, together with their wives and more than 1,500 children.

Sleeman's approvers were not, of course, permitted to be idle. The School of Industry was, as its name implied, a place of work – not of numbing toil, like other jails, but of useful labour. This, it was believed, would help to develop the inmates' self-respect, and thus contribute to the process of reform. It was an advanced notion for the time, and also helped the School to become self-supporting, for successive governors sold the products made there on the open market, thus covering the costs of upkeep.

The central provinces, indeed, turned out to be a first-rate market for the goods turned out by the School of Industry. The cost of importing anything from Bombay or Bengal – much less Britain – was prohibitive, and there was little in the way of local manufacturing. The School's first products, bricks, were soon in great demand, and from then on the reformatory paid its way, and even made a net contribution to government funds.

The greatest difficulty that the warders faced was to make the inmates work. The Thugs themselves regarded the whole idea as degrading, and though many of their sons were less reluctant, their fathers prevented them from labouring. It was only when the School's first governor, a Captain Brown, explained that the prisoners would be paid for their work that these objections were overcome. 'The approvers,' wrote Brown, 'are all very fond of money, and when they see they are to share in the profits of the manufacture, they will cheerfully join in the work.'

By the early 1840s even Thugs who had previously lived almost entirely on the profits of robbery and murder were doing manual work to set examples for their sons. The approvers next petitioned for their children to be taught to read and write – a request that was at first refused, on the grounds that superior education would leave the children dissatisfied with their drab existence in the jail – and when Sleeman's successors decided to turn the School into a tent- and carpet-making factory they proved eager to learn how to use the new machines that were brought in. Tent-making was taught by artisans from the Doab town of Futtehpore, and the art of carpet-weaving by men from Mirzapore, the great centre of that trade; by 1847 the men and women of the Thug village were turning out more than 130 tents and 3,300 yards of Kidderminster carpet a year. Revenues for that year exceeded 35,000 rupees, and the School of Industry had placed itself firmly in profit.

The School was not unique in specializing in a certain sort of manufacturing. Other Indian prisons did the same; the maximum security jail at Alipore had a noted print shop that sold more than 200,000 rupees' worth of books and pamphlets in the year 1861 alone. But the superior quality of the Thugs' work was widely recognized, and by the 1850s, the carpets woven at the School of Industry were noted as the best made anywhere in India. An example of the Thugs' work was shown at the Great Exhibition of 1851, and a few years later the men of the School wove a huge, seamless carpet, 80 feet by 40 feet in size, for Queen Victoria herself. It weighed more than two tons and found its way to the Waterloo Chamber in Windsor Castle, where it remains today – still, by repute, the largest that has ever been hand-woven. By then the Thugs had also become one of the main suppliers of tents to the Indian Army, their products – notably latrine, or 'necessary', tents – finding their way to every cantonment from the Himalayas to Cape Cormorin. In time, successive superintendents turned the School into a fully commercial concern, improving capacity by bringing in prisoners from the Thuggee jail in Jubbulpore and even free labourers from the surrounding districts to work alongside the approvers from the village. The most important portions of the annual reports compiled by these officers became the figures for turnover and profit, and the records of the School contain far more about the problems of accounting for the cost of tent-cloth woven, cheaply, in other prisons, than they do about the process of reform or the lives of the prisoners themselves.

The School of Industry did succeed, even so, in turning the sons of Thugs away from a life of Thuggee. By the early 1850s, the children born to the approvers were working as soldiers, porters and even shopkeepers in Jubbulpore itself; and for all Sleeman's fears, none seems to have shown any inclination to take up his father's profession. In time, the School's warders came to trust their prisoners completely. The families in the Thug village, it was noted in 1878, 'have entire liberty to come and go as they like'; indeed, by then even the surviving approvers themselves were 'subject only to certain mild restrictions'.

The Thugs' evident disinterest in either escape or further killing seems to have taken the officers of the Thuggee & Dacoity Department by surprise. Yet it is not hard to explain. One reason, evidently, was the fact that the men and their families were so well provided for that they no longer had any need to steal or kill. Another was the increasing age of the prisoners themselves. Fewer than half of the Thugs arrested in the 1830 and 1831 would have still been active by 1857. Those swept up in the later stages of the anti-Thug campaign were themselves growing old by 1888, when the quantity of tents and carpets made in Jubbulpore was already in steep decline and it was observed that the School of Industry remained profitable only because the cost of feeding approvers who were too old and feeble to work was not set against its revenues.

More important than mere decrepitude, however, was the disapproval of the Thugs' own children. It was here that the benefit of establishing a School of Industry was most apparent, for unlike their old comrades in Agra and Cawnpore, whose enthusiasm for recreating their past exploits remained undimmed for more than 20 years, the Thugs of Jubbulpore proved increasingly reluctant to gratify British visitors' interest in their crimes.

Sleeman himself – who continued to visit the School even after he was given additional duties in Gwalior and Bundelcund – charted the decline in their enthusiasm for murder in a letter composed shortly before his final departure from India. In 1843, he noted, the approvers still liked to talk of the old times with curious European visitors, and would do so without prompting, mulling over

> their old trade, its scenes and excitements, and in showing them how they had perfected its various operations. At the second visit [1844], I found that they were not anxious to do this, though willing, when encouraged;

but at the last visit [1848], I found that they were very averse to answer any questions on this subject, and quite ashamed to look back on the events and incidents of these past lives. They no longer talked among themselves of the scenes of early days. Their sons, who had never seen any of these scenes and incidents, were now become able, industrious, well-behaved young men, who felt no interest in what their fathers could tell them of a trade so abhorrent to the rest of mankind, and were evidently ashamed to see their fathers asked any questions about it by European visitors. All had learned to read and write and were proud of the thought of their independent condition.

William Sleeman's long involvement with the Thugs and dacoits continued almost to the end of his lifetime's service in India. Though he was recognized as one of the most able of the Company's administrators, and repeatedly promoted and asked to assume additional responsibilities, he retained charge of the old Saugor & Nerbudda Territory well into the 1840s, was promoted to the rank of colonel, and remained General Superintendent of the Thuggee & Dacoity Department as late as 1849. These duties – combined with the new roles he assumed as Agent in Bundelcund and later Resident at Gwalior – exhausted him, and although some were discharged by subordinates, he nevertheless tired in his later years.

In truth, Sleeman had no one but himself to blame for his mounting exhaustion. He was 'altogether too willing a horse', as ambitious as ever and as ready to take on the tasks that the government in Calcutta pressed on him as he was reluctant to relinquish his many outside interests. In addition, he wrote several books – his best-known work, *Rambles and Recollections of an Indian Official*, still ranks among the most important memoirs of the Victorian Raj – and, with Amélie, produced five daughters and two sons.

By 1845, indeed, Sleeman was responsible for well in excess of 100,000 square miles of India, if Gwalior is included. Inevitably, he spent a large part of each year on horseback, touring his district – an arrangement that suited him admirably, for he had never been happiest behind a desk. But he tried, nevertheless, to make a home for his growing family. His niece, who visited his new headquarters at Jhansee in the late 1840s, noted at the end of one cold season that with infinite care and at great expense, Colonel Sleeman has made a beautiful garden and in this we are used to walk every evening, regaling ourselves with oranges and loquats, both of which fruits are now in great perfection . . . There are, besides, numerous citron and lime trees, looking extremely pretty with their rich, ripe fruit and dark green leaves. The pomegranate, with its brightly scarlet flower and its beautiful fruit in every stage, and the vine, the fig, the custard apple and the pombello giving promise of delicious fruits during the next three intolerable months of heat, mosquitoes and monotony. Of a morning we used to ride on a high rocky common over which my uncle has cut a nice, wide road and covered it with sand and gravel. We were never early enough to accompany him in his ride, but we used to gallop out and meet him just as he turned homewards when, with the sun behind us and a delicious westerly breeze in our front, we cared not how long we lingered on our homeward path . . . Books, of which Colonel Sleeman has a greater number than I have ever seen in a private collection, work, chess, and visitors agreeably occupied the rest of the day.

Such pleasant domestic interludes were, however, rare in Sleeman's later life. Two of his children died in infancy, while the remaining five suffered so much in the climate that they were sent home one by one to be educated in England – a voyage so lengthy, expensive and taxing, in the days before the building of the Suez Canal, that their father never saw them again. Sleeman himself continued to suffer from recurring bouts of the Nathpore fever he had contracted in Nepal. He spent much of the year 1836 on sick leave, and his wife's health was so precarious that she and her younger children had to absent themselves for a good part of every year to one of the fashionable hill stations built in the shadow of the Himalayas for those Company officers and wives able to escape the suffocating heat and dust of summer. So disillusioned did he and Amélie become with their prospects in the country that they began planning for a retirement to the United States. For a while Sleeman had one eye on a new life in the Mississippi valley, which he considered the most suitable place for a large family such as his own to settle. 'It is a noble country,' he observed, 'were it not deformed with that horrible system of slavery. If it can only shake that off, its institutions will make it a model for the world.'

The government of India was, however, anxious to retain Sleeman's services, and his continued loyalty was eventually secured in 1848 with the offer of the Residency at the court of Oudh. This was the most coveted post available to a political officer of the Bengal Presidency. The position brought with it not only huge influence – Oudh, strategically positioned between Delhi and Benares, was the richest and perhaps the most important Native State north of the Nerbudda – but also a good salary and substantial perquisites. It was part of the Resident's job to impress the king and court with the power of the Company, and the holder of the post was provided with the means to live and entertain lavishly. Sleeman's own entry to the capital, Lucknow, was made at the head of 300 elephants and camels.*

It was, nonetheless, a difficult appointment. The king, Wajid Ali Khan, was a notorious eccentric, 'whose sole ambition was the puerile one of becoming the finest drummer in Oudh'; and the day-to-day administration of the king- dom had been placed in the hands of a courtier named Wasir Ali, whom Sleeman found to be the 'greatest knave' in the country. Under these men's inefficient rule, the once-rich province had slipped so close to bankruptcy that the Governor General in Calcutta had begun to threaten annexation. Sleeman – whose views of the Company's proper role in India were shaped more by the eighteenth century than the nineteenth – strenuously opposed this policy, and he endured five miserable years in Lucknow, increasingly frus- trated by his inability to persuade the court there to accept reform. 'Such a scene of intrigue, corruption, depravity and neglect of duty and abuse of authority,' he wrote,

I have never before been placed in and I hope never again to undergo . . . Had I come here when the treasury was full, I might have covered Oudh with useful public works, and much do I regret that I came here to throw away the best years of my life among such a set of knaves and fools as I have had to deal with.

The Resident's sympathies remained, as ever, with the Indian peasantry, who suffered most under Wajid Ali's rule, and he became so angry at the injustices he saw that at least one historian has suggested he became

*Sleeman had been offered the Residency once before, in 1841, in succession to a Colonel Low, but when he heard that Low had been left destitute by the unexpected failure of his bank, he had insisted that the colonel continue in the post.

dangerously obsessed with the swirling intrigues of the court. He was also, at last, in physical decline. 'Mentally,' wrote one young British officer who encountered him in Oudh, 'he was in his prime in this period, but physically he was far from that: short of stature though somewhat muscular and robust in frame, he appeared shrunken and aged.'

Matters were not helped by the three separate attempts that were made on Sleeman's life between 1842 and 1853. Two were the work of disgruntled local people, but the third was apparently perpetrated by an escaped Thug in Lucknow. The one account of this incident comes from the recollection of Sleeman's daughter Elizabeth, who as a little girl

> was in his study one day when her father suddenly had a premonition of evil, drew aside a curtain concealing an alcove, and disclosed an Indian standing there armed with a dagger. Unarmed as he was and not expecting such an attack, Sleeman had spent too much of his life in the midst of danger to be perturbed by anything like this, and, pointing a finger at the man, he said, 'You are a Thug.' The man promptly dropped his dagger and said, salaaming profoundly, 'Yes, sahib'

before allowing himself to be disarmed.

In any event, the general strain of life in Oudh eventually proved too much for Sleeman, whose health had been severely weakened by his repeated bouts of fever. Although the government wanted him to stay, he was forced to relinquish his position late in 1855, at about the time his old enemy Feringeea also died, and – a sure sign of just how severe his illness had become – even make preparations for a return to Britain, which he had not seen since 1809. Sleeman and his wife reached Calcutta early in January 1856 and sailed for home on the first of February. But the fever suddenly worsened. On 10 February, off the coast of Ceylon, Sleeman died, and was buried at sea. Amélie survived him for a quarter of a century, spending the remainder of her life not in her birthplace, Mauritius, but close to her children in the genteel if less exotic surroundings of Southsea, on the English coast.

Sleeman thus left India before the government's final annexation of Oudh, which took place four days after he had sailed and undid most of the work of his later years. He also died a year before the outbreak of the great Indian Mutiny of 1857. This was perhaps fortunate, for his contemporaries in the

Indian civil service were among those most distressed by the Company's increasingly high-handed treatment of its Indian subjects, which became one of the main causes of the uprising. The Mutiny's great epic, ironically enough, was the rebel siege of Sleeman's old residency at Lucknow, which was grimly defended for six months by a tiny force of soldiers and political officers. When they were finally driven from it, in November 1857, one officer risked his life by going back, through the mutineers' lines, to rescue a portrait of Sleeman that had been hung inside. It was carried to safety wrapped around a soldier's musket, the last relic of the old Thug-hunter's final years.

Sleeman's real legacy, of course, was something more than that. In less than a decade, he and Francis Curwen Smith and their various associates had stamped out Thuggee, a crime that had persisted, in all likelihood, for several hundred years. They had arrested nearly 4,000 men and, by hanging or imprisoning the vast majority of them, made the roads of central India safe for the first time in living memory.

Sleeman's methods have attracted increasing criticism in recent years. Today we can see, rather more clearly than was possible in the 1830s, that the evidence against some of the convicted Thugs was far from compelling. Sleeman himself admitted that his men sometimes arrested people guilty of nothing more than being found in the company of Thugs, though he always remained sanguine that such mistakes would be uncovered by the courts.

It is also no doubt true that the Company men charged with eradicating Thuggee held (as historians have charged) rather a simplistic view of the Thugs themselves. Once the original work of suppressing the Thugs was more or less complete, moreover, the men of the Thuggee & Dacoity Department did cast around for other tasks to justify their existence, and though the department might with some justification claim that its campaigns against the Megpunnas, the Tusma-Baz, and other supposed varieties of Thug did result in the arrest of a large number of professional criminals, they had unfortunate consequences. The tendency to classify whole tribes and castes as inevitably and irredeemably 'criminal' was given additional impetus by the Thug campaigns. Sleeman's department thus helped to create the climate in which what was known as the Criminal Tribes Act of 1876 became law, effectively criminalizing entire communities – and that was one of the most discreditable of all pieces of Imperial legislation. The Superintendent's own growing obsession with exterminating the entire 'race of Thugs' became, eventually, unhealthy, and there can be little doubt that a number of innocent men were tried and found guilty of Thuggee, particularly after 1835.

Yet Sleeman himself was not to blame for all his department's failings. He had as detailed an understanding of the Thugs' methods and organization as any Company official, and made it clear, in both his official correspondence and his published works, that there was indeed a difference between hereditary and occasional Thugs, and between those who murdered out of desperation and those who killed because they had grown up doing so. Nor should it ever be forgotten – as Sleeman's critics do forget – that the suppression of Thuggee did save thousands of lives. Because of him, husbands who would once have been strangled for a rupee returned home safely to their wives, and fathers lived to raise their children.

The Thugs of the School of Industry lived on long after Sleeman's death: almost, some of them, to the opening of the twentieth century.

However impeccable their behaviour and industrious their sons, they could never be released, and one by one they died in jail. The number of men whose age and declining health forced them to give up work and stay within the confines of the Thug village rose steadily for two decades after Sleeman's death. There were 100 of them in 1854, and more than 122 by 1872. After that, the totals of the infirm began to fall as the old Thugs simply expired. In 1874, the British knocked down nearly 60 vacant huts in the Thuggee Lines, and deaths among the remaining Thug and dacoit prisoners were running at as many as 30 men each year. The old Thuggee jail in Jubbulpore, where prisoners other than the approvers themselves were kept, was closed in 1872 and turned into a lunatic asylum; the surviving handful of inmates were transferred to the village, where the last of them died in 1882. By then there were only 71 of the old approvers left, where once there had been more than 200. Three-quarters of those were gone a decade later, leaving so few – no more than 20 – that the School of Industry was finally shut down and its buildings turned over to the city for use as a juvenile reform school.

The approvers' sons were long gone by this time, encouraged or in a few cases forced to leave in search of gainful employment. The surviving Thug and dacoit prisoners were scattered. A few of the younger ones were sent to the prison at Jhalna, and a large proportion – almost half – of the remainder begged to be allowed to end their days in the Thuggee village. They were too late; the plans for the reformatory had already been approved. The mens' petition was rejected, and on 31 December 1892 the last handful of imprisoned Thugs were forcibly evicted from their homes. They had lived there, some of them, for more than half a century. Now they were too old to earn a living, and had no relatives who could help them adapt to a world where they no longer belonged.

While they had been confined, India had changed so utterly that they did not recognize it. Their old cart-tracks were now railroads; the mango groves where they had murdered their victims had been uprooted to make way for ever expanding settlements; and where once it had taken weeks for a man to travel from town to town, and months for him to be reported missing, it was now possible to make the same journeys in a day and for policemen hundreds of miles apart to communicate instantaneously by telegraph. These innovations, which would have doomed Thuggee without the intervention of William Sleeman, could not be resisted.

Thus, for what was certainly the last time, a band of Thugs took to the roads of India. They were very old, and several walked only with the aid of sticks; they hunted not for victims, but for homes; and dreamed not of murdering and plunder, but of coming to a place where they themselves could die.

How Many Dead?

'tubae dalna – killing, being killed'

It is all but impossible to know, even approximately, how many men, women and children lost their lives to the Thugs.

The estimates that do exist vary wildly. Richard Sherwood, writing in 1816, supposed that all the stranglers of the Deccan between them murdered no more than a few hundred travellers a year. Lieutenant Reynolds, 20 years later, interrogated Phansigars who spoke 'of having put their tens and twenties to death daily' in the course of expeditions that lasted for four months at a time. The latter boast implied a number of victims so vast that even Syeed Ameer Ali – who spoke of being 'directly concerned' in the throttling of 719 victims – and Ramzan, an Oudh Thug who (aged 38) claimed that he had witnessed more than 1,800 murders, seemed mere dilettantes in comparison. Certainly the *Sumachar Durpan* (a contemporary Indian newspaper 'of great respectability') concluded in 1833 that the 'Thugs slaughtered on an average *eight hundred persons in a month*', and in 1920, when Sleeman's grandson James reviewed his ancestor's papers in an attempt to arrive at a definitive figure, the estimate he produced was higher still. The gangs, together, he wrote in his book *Thug*, probably killed somewhere in the region of 40,000 people every year.*

---

*This – since Sleeman accepted that the Thugs had practised their trade ever since the Muslim conquests of the thirteenth century – implied a staggering total of some 20 million victims in all, throttled in the course of five centuries of unchecked brutality.

Was such a death toll possible? Sleeman insisted that it was, pointing out that the population of India was somewhere over 250 million, and that more people were killed each year in the Subcontinent by snakes. And it is true that some of the testimonies given by the Thugs themselves do support his calculations. Paton's approver Futty Khan, for one, estimated that a well-frequented bele might witness as many as '10 or 15 murders yearly' – which, given that a total of 274 such spots had been mapped in the Kingdom of Oudh alone, certainly implied that a vast number of murders were committed every year. Paton also questioned his approvers as to the number of killings in which they had been involved. Their responses show that individual Thugs did indeed admit to having strangled dozens, and often hundreds, of victims over a period of years.

According to depositions taken down at Lucknow during the year 1837:

Futty Khan	estimates that he has been at					508	cases of murder		
Buhram	"	"	"	"	"	931	"	"	"
Dhoosoo	"	"	"	"	"	350	"	"	"
Alayar	"	"	"	"	"	377	"	"	"
Ramzan	"	"	"	"	"	604	"	"	"
Sheodeen	"	"	"	"	"	119	"	"	"
Sirdar	"	"	"	"	"	42	"	"	"
Teja	"	"	"	"	"	103	"	"	"
Muckdoomee	"	"	"	"	"	264	"	"	"
Salar	"	"	"	"	"	203	"	"	"
Danial	"	"	"	"	"	195	"	"	"
Bukthour	"	"	"	"	"	294	"	"	"
Khunjun	"	"	"	"	"	117	"	"	"
Hyder	"	"	"	"	"	322	"	"	"
Imambux the Black	"	"	"	"	"	340	"	"	"
Rambux	"	"	"	"	"	28	"	"	"
Imambux the Tall	"	"	"	"	"	65	"	"	"
Bught	"	"	"	"	"	81	"	"	"
Adhar	"	"	"	"	"	153	"	"	"
Ungnoo	"	"	"	"	"	24	"	"	"

Some of these figures are certainly remarkable. As Paton himself pointed out, if a mere 20 approvers could take part in 5,120 murders – 'an average of

256 involving each Thug' – then the death toll exacted by the Thug gangs as a whole must have been enormous. Of course, these killings were committed over many decades: Futty Khan was an active Thug for 20 years, and Buhram thugged for 40, which would mean that each was present at an average of no more than two murders a month. But this – Paton believed – made his approvers' claims more rather than less believable. Certainly there are accounts from elsewhere in India of other stranglers who matched them; Syeed Ameer Ali's 719 murders were the result of 30 years spent on the roads, and also represented an average of two deaths a month – a figure that the Thug himself was perfectly aware of, since he reminded Meadows Taylor: 'Ah! Sir, if I had not been in prison twelve years, the number would have been a thousand.'

Paton's figures, which found their way into print a few years later, were to prove highly influential. In the absence of any similar document from Sleeman or Smith, the manuscript pages of his 'Dialogues with Thugs' make up one of the very few pieces of evidence produced during the anti-Thug campaign that purports to show the number of murders committed by individual stranglers. In 1901 the *Quarterly Review* used the list to estimate that the average Thug killed three victims a year. Two decades later, James Sleeman based his estimate of 40,000 Thug murders per annum upon it.

Yet it is very dangerous to extrapolate a death toll for the whole of India from the confessions of a few approvers. For one thing, Futty Khan, Buhram and Syeed Ameer Ali were hardly ordinary Thugs; their testimonies place them at the head of their profession, and it cannot be assumed that other stranglers enjoyed equal success. For another, the claims they made were never tested in a court of law and were not even broken down and enumerated month by month and year by year, much less cross-referenced against any register of murders suspected to have been committed by the Thugs. In these circumstances, there was nothing to prevent Paton's men from lying in the hope of pleasing their captors, or simply to seek notoriety. Approvers were useful only while they had fresh information to impart, and claiming involvement in a large number of murders may well have struck some of Paton's Thugs as a way of increasing their value to the Company.

It is apparent, from other depositions preserved among the Paton papers, that their testimony could be highly inconsistent. Buhram, for one, who claimed in 1837 to have taken part in more than 930 killings, had told a very

different story only a year earlier. In his first deposition, he confessed to involvement in a mere 275 murders ('I may have strangled with my own hands about 125 men, and I may have seen strangled 150 more'), a discrepancy that neither he nor Paton ever bothered to explain. The lower total, spread over the four decades of his career, equates to no more than seven killings every year.*
Similarly, Ramzan, who figured prominently in Paton's table with the claim to have participated in 604 murders, once deposed that he had actually 'seen between 80 and 90 men strangled yearly' during his 22 years as a Thug, the latter estimate producing a death toll three times greater than the former. Once again, Paton failed to comment on the inconsistency. The best that can be said of his approvers' testimony is that it requires corroboration. Certainly no policeman and no court would take it at face value.

The value of Paton's data is further undermined by the fact that he under-states the frequency with which his approvers would have had to kill in order to reach the totals he attributed to them. The idea that a successful Thug might help commit two murders a month does not seem utterly outlandish – but when it is remembered that even the most ruthless gangs were rarely at large outside the cold season, the requirement triples to 24 deaths in only four months, or one murder every five days. This is a much harder figure to credit, not least because it was comparatively rare for the Thugs to despatch large parties of victims. The number of victims killed in the average affair turns out to be four, and each of these groups had to be encountered, inveigled, taken to a suitable bele and strangled before the next could be pursued. The depo-sitions assembled for the various Thug trials suggest that this whole process often took more than 20 days to complete.

Finally, there is the matter of the Thugs' modus operandi to consider. All attempts to produce a total death toll by multiplying the number of killings confessed to by one man by the number of Thugs at large is fatally flawed by the fact that few members of most gangs actually committed murder. Perhaps no more than one Thug in every 6 to 10 was a strangler or a hand-holder. His companions – scouts, lookouts, inveiglers, grave-diggers and mere hangers-

---

*While Paton himself made it clear that his informants were describing murders committed by their gangs as a whole – 'Futty Khan estimates that he has *been at* 508 cases of murder' – most writers who cite his figures assume that the various approvers personally strangled the victims concerned. This is a vital point, for there is all the difference in the world between suggesting that a single Thug could average two murders a month and attributing the same figure to an entire gang.

on – never personally disposed of a single victim. Thus, when a man such as Syeed Ameer Ali spoke of taking part in 719 killings, he was referring to the murders committed by an entire gang, on average at least 25 men strong and frequently numbering 100 or more Thugs, over the course of three decades. Even if Ameer Ali's claims were true, the number of victims despatched by his gang in the course of a typical expedition turns out to be no more than 24: an average of at most one murder per man per year.

The evidence assembled by Smith and Sleeman and presented at the trials of Thugs arraigned in the central provinces supports the view that few Thugs killed huge numbers of travellers. Plenty of depositions make it plain that victims were very often hard to come by. Some men spoke of being forced by sheer destitution to murder travellers whom they doubted bore so much as a rupee. Others referred to expeditions that saw whole gangs of Thugs go for weeks, and even months, without committing murder. Thus, while the number of victims claimed by a gang could vary dramatically according to their location, luck, and the skill of their inveiglers, only a few enjoyed conspicuous success. We know that Essuree and the 150 men of the Lucknadown gang killed 37 victims in six different beles during the cold season of 1822–3, and that Feringeea, at the head of gangs totalling anywhere from 25 to 220 men, confessed to the murder of 105 men and women in 1827–8, another 80 in 1828–9, and 48 more up to the moment of his arrest in 1830 – a total of 233 victims in a mere three years. But these were Thugs at the height of their powers. A good many gangs accounted for no more than 10 or 12 travellers a year, and some murdered even fewer. Sleeman told of one group of 30 men – led by a subadar, no less – that killed only nine people in the season 1827–8. One of his assistants, a Captain Vallancy, described a group of low Thugs that experienced similarly modest success, for though the members of this gang 'were most inveterate murderers, sparing neither sex nor age; nor did they pay any respect to those castes which other Thugs thought it a heinous offence to murder', their lack of discrimination was evidently offset by a lack of skill, and they accounted for a mere 80 victims in the course of 11 years. Many Deccan Thugs struggled, too. Sheikh Dawood Newly, one of Reynolds's informants, recorded that 17 gangs, working together for two seasons, had committed only slightly more than 60 murders, and his colleague, Sayeed Ally, informed on 10 more jemadars who had inveigled no more than two dozen travellers over the same period. Between them, then, these two approvers supplied evidence against 27 gangs – a grand assembly of stranglers who had, between them, accounted for only 50 travellers a year.

Most of these less able Thugs, it might be conjectured, were mere novices, forced onto the roads during the grim years of the 1820s and the 1830s with little idea of how to go about their task. But even the most capable jemadars rarely matched the success enjoyed by Feringeea and his men. The Arcottee Thugs, a gang of Deccan stranglers 60 strong reckoned by all who knew them to be particularly ruthless and skilful, killed no more than 150 victims over the course of 13 years, an average of fewer than a dozen travellers a year. The gang of an approver known as Rama Jemadar the First murdered 46 men and women in four years for a similar average. Perhaps the most startling statistic was produced by Francis Curwen Smith, who calculated – based on the interrogation of thousands of stranglers at dozens of trials – that the 584 Thugs expeditions that criss-crossed the central provinces and Upper Provinces between 1827 and 1834 had accounted for a total of just 1,803 victims.

The truth seems to be this: even in the 1820s, a single Thug gang 25 men strong would be fortunate to murder more than a dozen travellers each year. A similarly sized group of novice stranglers, in this same period, might well account for half that number. Since no more than 200 jemadars of Thugs appear to have been active at this time, each with his own small group of followers, it might be estimated that in 1829, when the Company's campaign began, the Thug gangs committed somewhere between 1,200 and 2,400 murders a year across the length and breadth of India. The real total, given the Thugs' habit of banding together in large and inefficient groups, was most likely closer to the lower figure than the higher.

This is a revealing analysis. The 1820s were, after all, the great days of Thuggee. The economic hardships of that harsh decade, together with the break-up of the Pindari bands and a sharp decline in the size of the Maratha armies, meant that there were probably more Thugs on the roads in that decade than there had ever been before. Even the great famines of the late 1700s, which were more destructive than the great depression of the 1820s, probably forced fewer men into a life of banditry, for there were then abundant opportunities for the unemployed to seek military service. Perhaps – this can be no more than a guess – the number of gangs active in the worst years of the eighteenth century was between a quarter and a third of the total that existed in 1829. These groups probably did contain a high proportion of ruthless and experienced Thugs, and may well have been more efficient and successful than their successors. But, even so, it seems unlikely they accounted for, between them, more than 1,000 deaths a year. In times of war or plenty, the total would have been less.

Assume, then, that Thuggee came into existence when the oral histories of its practitioners suggest it did, around 150 or 250 years before its ultimate suppression, and that it was indeed distinct from other forms of highway robbery for the whole of that time. What might its true death toll have been? Probably no more than 50,000 or 100,000 men, women and children seems to be the answer, and twice that number at most. This is a far cry from the millions proposed by James Sleeman or the hundreds of thousands suspected by other writers. Yet even 50,000 murders is an inconceivably large number – not many deaths, perhaps, when set against the toll of war, famine and pestilence during the same period, but a vast total nonetheless. And when it is remembered that each of the unlucky travellers inveigled by the gangs left family behind them, and that so far as these loved ones were concerned their husband, wife, brother or child simply vanished from the earth with neither warning nor explanation – leaving, in many cases, their relatives quite destitute – the sum total of human misery inflicted by the Thugs remains beyond computation.

NOTES

Abbreviations used in the notes

Add.Mss.	Additional Manuscripts series in the BL and CUL
BC	Board's Collections, OIOC
BPC	Bengal Political Consultations, OIOC
BCJC	Bengal Criminal & Judicial Consultations, OIOC
BL	British Library
CUL	Cambridge University Library
IESHR	*Indian Economic and Social History Review*
NAI	National Archives of India, New Delhi
OIOC	Oriental and India Office Collections, British Library
Sel.Rec.	Anon. (ed.), *Selected Records Collected from the Central Provinces and Berar Secretariat Relating to the Suppression of Thuggee, 1829–1832* (Nagpur: Govt. Print., CP & Berar, 1939)
SB	Satpura Bhawan, State Archive of Madhya Pradesh, Bhopal
T&D	Thuggee & Dacoity Department files, NAI

Notes on the sources

Primary sources

A vast mass of primary source material relating to the East India Company's government of India survives in archives in the UK and India. The India Office records kept in the Oriental and India Collections (OIOC) at the British Library in London alone fill approximately nine miles of shelving, and a similarly extensive collection of material has been retained by the National Archives of India (NAI) in New Delhi and by regional depositories elsewhere in the Subcontinent. Many of the volumes preserved in India are filled with duplicates of originals that still exist in London, but thousands of letters and reports deemed unimportant at the time were never copied and sent home. Accurate histories of British India thus require research in both countries.

The proportion of the Company's records that relate to Thuggee and the anti-Thug campaign is of course relatively small, but the files that do survive are so considerable that it is probably fair to say that no historian has ever read his way through every document available. I would estimate that the Thug records held in London alone comfortably exceed 60,000 large pages, many of them written in cramped and sometimes virtually illegible hands.

The most accessible of the British Library's records consist of what are known as Board's

Collections. These volumes consist of selected material of particular importance that was copied and sent home from India to London for the attention of the Board of Control, the body with overall responsibility for the government of India. The Collections contain around 80 large files primarily or wholly devoted to Thuggee, many of which consist of copy depositions made by various Thug informants and the transcripts of Thug trials. A good deal of administrative correspondence relating to the anti-Thug campaign was also included in the selections prepared for transmission home.

Once received, the Board's Collections were bound up in enormous volumes, containing on average well in excess of 1,000 pages of manuscript apiece. Virtually all of these volumes contain several individually paginated files. Thus a reference in the notes to, say, 'BC F/4/1898 (80685) fos. 66–188' refers to folios 66 to 188 of file number 80,685, which can be found in volume 1,898 of the Collections.

The broad mass of material from which the Board's Collections were drawn also survives, and very often includes material of considerable importance that for some reason or other was never selected for presentation to the Board. This material originally formed three distinct archives maintained by the Company Presidencies of Bengal, Madras and Bombay, which have been combined to form the bulk of the OIOC. Although I have searched for relevant material in the archives of Madras and Bombay, virtually all of the most important files were produced by the Bengal Presidency, which had responsibility for the districts in northern and central India where the anti-Thug campaign began and was prosecuted with the greatest vigour.

The great majority of this material can be located in two series, known as the Bengal Political Consultations (BPC) and the Bengal Criminal Judicial Consultations (BCJC), which record the weekly transactions of the Governor General in Council as he and his colleagues worked their way through huge piles of correspondence and reports sent in by political officers, magistrates and judges stationed all over the Presidency. A week's work on either might typically produce somewhere between 25 and 60 separate 'Consultations', or written summaries of the decisions taken regarding the lengthy submissions received in each category, most of which include copious extracts from the submissions themselves. Unlike the Board's Collections, the Consultations were, unfortunately, not paginated and have to be referred to by the number and date of the relevant discussion. Thus a reference to 'Consultation No. 46 of 18 Jan. 1811, BCJC P/130/27' is the best that can be done to guide the interested reader to important extracts from the records of the Court of Circuit, Bareilly, Zillah Etawah, for the second Sessions of 1810, as preserved in volume 27 of the Judicial Consultations of the Bengal Presidency – a document that, as it happens, runs to the better part of 40 outsize manuscript pages.

Several lesser series of India Office papers were also consulted. In London, letters relating to Thuggee sent by the Court of Directors of the East India Company to the Governor General and the Governors of the various Presidencies are preserved in series E/4, 'Correspondence with India: Court of Directors despatches, judicial, 1795–1858', and reports relating to the Indian prison system in series V, 'Official Publications'. The Records of the Office for the Suppression of Thuggee and Dacoitee (T&D) in the National Archives of India (NAI) cover the period from the late 1820s to the 1840s and beyond, but most of the Office's holdings for the vital years prior to 1835 are duplicated in London. More than a thousand pages of William Sleeman's official correspondence have also been preserved and are currently to be found in the Satpura Bhawan in the State Archive of Madhya Pradesh in Bhopal, alongside a peculiarly organized collection known as the 'Appa Sahib and Thuggee papers' (peculiar in that Appa Sahib, the fugitive Rajah of Nagpore, had absolutely no connection to Thuggee or the anti-Thug campaign). Again, a large portion of the material in Bhopal is duplicated elsewhere: Sleeman's correspondence after 1832 in the T&D papers in the NAI, and the Appa Sahib and Thuggee papers in one of only two significant printed collections of documents relating to Thuggee – an anonymously edited 1939 volume entitled *Selected Records Collected from the*

Central Provinces and Berar Secretariat Relating to the Suppression of Thuggee, 1829–1832, printed in Nagpore.

Two significant private manuscripts relating to Thuggee survive. Letter-books once belonging to Thomas Perry, magistrate at Etawah in the first years of the nineteenth century, can be found in the Department of Manuscripts at Cambridge University Library, while the 'Collections on Thuggee and Dacoitee' made by one of William Sleeman's assistants, James Paton, in Oudh in the later 1830s are preserved among the Additional Manuscripts series in the British Library. The former collection contains some of the earliest surviving British papers relating to Thuggee; the latter, transcriptions of a fascinating series of 'Dialogues with Thugs' together with a number of illustrations, drawn under the supervision of various informers, showing the members of Thug gangs going about their work.

Documentation concerning the British response to Thuggee is thus relatively complete. What is sorely lacking is material presenting an Indian perspective. Neither the independent states of the Subcontinent nor the Thugs themselves compiled any notable collection of contemporary documents. This omission is only partly remedied within the pages of the single most important book published on the subject, William Sleeman's two-volume *Ramaseeana*, which incorporates a considerable quantity of roughly edited primary material. Sleeman's own collection of official papers, published in the second volume, is an important supplement to the surviving manuscript sources discussed above. More illuminating by far, however, are Sleeman's own 'Conversations with Thugs', published in the first volume, which consist of transcriptions of several lengthy interrogations of a number of Thug approvers, during which Sleeman's prisoners discussed many of their most celebrated crimes as well as recounting traditions, customs and beliefs that go entirely unreported elsewhere. *Ramaseeana* is far from an ideal source; the 'Conversations' have been translated and perhaps edited, losing nuance in the process, and the Thug prisoners answer only the questions Sleeman saw fit to pose, which are not always those we might wish to ask today. Nonetheless, the material – containing as it does numerous repetitions, contradictions and even statements that fly directly in the face of opinions that Sleeman himself put in print – does seem to have been published in a more or less raw state. The 'Conversations' offer the most fascinating and compelling insight into the thoughts and motives of the Thugs themselves.

Books

Among secondary sources, the most important contemporary works are probably Edward Thornton's *Illustrations of the History and Practices of the Thugs* – a book that, while cribbed largely from Sleeman, does include some material not featured in *Ramaseeana* – and Sleeman's own *Report on the Depredations Committed by the Thug Gangs of Upper and Central India From the Cold Season of 1836–37*. This book, despite its title, actually concerns itself with events going as far back as 1827–8.

Modern scholars have contributed enormously to a full understanding of Thuggee and have done much to place the subject in its proper context – something contemporary writers conspicuously failed to do. Among their works, I have found those of Christopher Bayly, on Indian society and British colonial intelligence, Ranjan Chakrabarti and Basudeb Chattopadhyay, on crime and policing, and Radhika Singha, on criminal justice, the most illuminating.

Author's note

'Small editions' Máire Ni Fhlathúin, in 'The Travels of M. de Thévenot Through the Thug Archive', *Journal of the Royal Asiatic Society* series 3, 11, 1 (2001) p. 34, notes that the print run of William Sleeman's *Ramaseeana* (1836) – by far the most influential single book on the subject – was only 750, and that no more than 100 of these copies were sold privately in the five years following publication. The remainder were distributed to East India Company stations in India itself.

Meadows Taylor and Confessions of a Thug See Nick Mirsky's preface to the Oxford paperback edition of 1986, particularly pp. vii–viii.

Number of murders exaggerated This point is dealt with in detail in the appendix.

James Sleeman See his *Thug, Or A Million Murders* pp. v, 235–6.

Gustav Pfirmann See his 1970 PhD thesis *Religiöser Charakter und Organisation der Thag-Brüderschaften.*

Hiralal Gupta In 'A critical study of the Thugs and their activities', *Journal of Indian History* 37 (1959).

Stewart Gordon See particularly 'Scarf and Sword: Thugs, Marauders and State-Formation in 18th Century India', *IESHR* 4 (1969).

Christopher Bayly See particularly *Empire and Information: Intelligence Gathering and Social Communication in India 1780–1870.*

Radhika Singha See particularly her *A Despotism of Law: Crime and Justice in Early Colonial India.*

Parama Roy See her 'Discovering India, Imagining Thuggee' in *The Yale Journal of Criticism* 9 (1996), and also Amal Chatterjee, *Representation of India 1740–1840: The Creation of India in the Colonial Imagination.*

'What made the Thugs unique . . .' A secondary characteristic was the fact that the Thugs invariably posed as inoffensive travellers and almost always attempted to lure their intended victims into a false sense of security before attacking them.

'A small core . . .' Gordon, p. 429.

'The existence of band lore . . .' Singha, pp. 183–4.

'A new generation of historians' The most important study promises to be Kim Wagner's *Thuggee and the 'Construction' of Crime in Early Nineteenth Century India* (unpublished Cambridge PhD thesis, 2004), access to which has, however, been restricted until January 2007.

Prologue: The Road to Lucknadown

Chupara and its environs RV Russell, *Central Provinces District Gazetteers: Seoni District* pp. 169–70.

Bunda Ali's party Deposition of Deena, 25 Mar. 1823, BC F/1/1404 (55517) fos. 224–5; deposition of Chutaree, BC F/4/1309 (52131) fo. 264; deposition of Motee, ibid. fos. 296–300; William Sleeman, *Ramaseeana, or a Vocabulary of the Peculiar Language Used by the Thugs* I, 169–71. There is some confusion in the primary source material as to the number of children in the party, one witness, Deena, saying there were two of them, while Chutaree and Motee stated there was only one; but *Ramaseeana's* detailed description of two girls – one an infant, the other one of marriageable age – appears definitive.

. . . he was a moonshee . . . Sleeman, *Ramaseeana* I, 167, mentions the service of a moonshee named Bunda Ali with Sir John Doveton, then the commanding officer of the Fourth, Prince of Wales's Own, Regiment, Madras Light Cavalry, stationed at Jhalna. The Thugs who encountered him there were not completely certain that their Bunda Ali was the same man as the one murdered by a different gang at Lucknadown, but Jhalna was a possession of the Nizam of Hyderabad, and the primary sources consistently refer to the Ali killed in 1823 as 'the Hyderabad *moonshee*' (cf. Smith to Prinsep, 19 Nov. 1830, *Sel.Rec.* 47). All in all, therefore, it seems very likely that the two men were one and the same. The explanation for the presence of a native of Hindustan in the Deccan, incidentally, must be that the Fourth

recruited almost exclusively from the Carnatic, where Tamil is spoken. Presumably this made it necessary to send north for a properly qualified teacher of Hindustani, the Indian language most commonly taught to British officers. William Wilson, *Historical Record of the Fourth 'Prince of Wales's Own' Regiment Madras Light Cavalry*, pp. 57, 64, 92.

A moonshee's work For most Britons arriving in India, the moonshee was an unwelcome visitor whose services were necessary but seldom appreciated. East India Company officers were supposed to arrive in the country with a working knowledge of the native languages, and tuition in Hindustani and Persian was a compulsory feature of the curriculum at Fort William College in Calcutta, where, from 1800, cadets received instruction before receiving their first posting. Nevertheless, an increasing number of officers made the point of remaining virtually ignorant of the local tongues, even though very few of the men they were expected to command spoke any English at all. Albert Hervey, who arrived in India in 1833 and was one of the more conscientious cadets in the Madras army, in which Bunda Ali served, wrote of his own experiences: 'I fagged hard with the *Moonshee*, who used to come to me every day for four hours. I held conversations with my teacher in English; every sentence uttered was put down on paper in Hindustanee, and the next day what I had written down in Hindustanee, was brought to me fresh written by the *Moonshee*, and those sentences I re-translated into English, so that I not only gained a knowledge of the words, but was able to read the common writing, which was of the greatest assistance. I fagged thus hard for three months, working away without relaxation, except for meals.' Albert Hervey, *A Soldier of the Company* pp. 23–5.

Daughter's age Deposition of Sing Rae Wasilhakee, 19 March 1823, BC F/4/1309 (52131) fo. 251. Sing Rae was a member of the party that exhumed the moonshee's grave, and his statement was based on an examination of the girl's remains.

Condition of the local roads See any contemporary gazetteer. Chitnis, in *Glimpses of Maratha Socio-Economic History* pp. 79–83, comments that in the old Maratha territories that came to form the bulk of the central provinces 'there were few good roads, but many pathways or tracks'.

Nagpore territory Edward Thornton, *A Gazetteer of the Territories Under the Government of the East India Company* II, 279.

Thieves recalled by Harriet Tytler Anthony Sattin (ed.), *An Englishwoman in India* p.25. Greasing or oiling oneself to evade capture seems to have been commonplace among the thieves of this period; see Thankappan Nair (ed.), *British Social Life in Ancient Calcutta (1750 to 1850)* pp. 31, 76.

Interrogation at Jhalna Sleeman, *Ramaseeana* I, 167–8. Sleeman, who recorded this evidence in 1835–6, gives no exact date for the incident, and the Thugs concerned dated it to around 1822–3. In fact the meeting must have occurred after Ali's appointment as moonshee, which cannot have been earlier than 1818, but before the Fourth was posted to Seroor towards the end of 1819. The regiment did not return to Jhalna until 1822, by which time Doveton – whose presence is mentioned by the Thugs – had retired. Most probably the meeting took place some time in November or December 1818, given the distance that the Thugs had travelled since the onset of the cold season in order to reach the Deccan. Wilson, op. cit. p. 64.

Bunda Ali's salary Wilson, op. cit. p. 57.

Bunda Ali's worth Each of the 100 Thugs involved in the murder of Bunda Ali's party received a minimum of two rupees as their share of the loot, those who participated in the killings themselves taking a little more. Deposition of Anundee, 2 Feb. 1824, BC F/4/1309 (52131) fos. 254–5.

Two were chuprassees . . . Smith to Prinsep, 19 Nov. 1830, *Sel.Rec.* 46–7.

. . . a full day's journey . . . Cf. Thomas Bacon, *First Impressions and Studies from Nature in Hindustan* I, 126.

On the road to Lucknadown Smith to Prinsep, 19 Nov. 1830, *Sel.Rec.* 46–7; Russell, op. cit. pp. 1–5, 169, 176–8.

The Lucknadown affair Deposition of Deena, 25 Mar. 1823, BC F/4/1404 (55517) fos. 224–5;

summary of the case of Essuree, BC F/4/1309 (52131) fos. 147–50; verdict on Bhawanee, ibid. fo. 161; verdict on Sheikh Bazeed, ibid. fo. 169; verdict on Sadee Khan, ibid. fo. 228; deposition of Sing Rae Wasilhakee, 19 Mar. 1823, ibid. fos. 251–2; deposition of Anundee, 2 Feb. 1824, ibid. fos. 253–5; deposition of Chutaree, n.d., ibid. fos. 264–70; deposition of Dulput, n.d., ibid. fo. 285; deposition of Motee, ibid. fos. 296–300; Consultation No. 27 of 25 July 1831, BPC P/126/26, OIOC; Sleeman to Smith, 19 Oct 1830, Sel.Rec. 56–61; Ramaseeana I, 169–71. For the time of the party's arrival at their camp, see BC F/4/1309 (52131) fo. 284, which puts it at 4 pm; for the time of the murders, see ibid. fo. 264.

'Bring tobacco' This appears to have been the most common of a number of signals employed by different Thug gangs to precipitate their murders. Cf. 'Deposition of Poorun Phansigar', n.d. [1829], Sel.Rec. 31; Edward Thornton, Illustrations of the History and Practices of the Thugs p. 373.

1 'Murdered in Circumstances Which Defied Detection'

Etawah's climate These unpleasant conditions have improved significantly over the last two centuries, thanks to the completion of forestry and irrigation works in the Doab.

The courtroom See Fanny Parks, Wanderings of a Pilgrim in Search of the Picturesque I, 122–3, for a description of a typical cutcherry, or magistrate's office, of the period.

A hideous discovery Perry to Dowdeswell (Secretary to Government, Calcutta), 7 Apr. 1811, Add.Mss. 5376 fos. 8–8v, CUL; for wounds see Court of Circuit Bareilly, Zillah Etawah, 2nd Sessions of 1810, in Consultation No. 46 of 18 Jan. 1811, BCJC P/130/27, OIOC.

Bodies in the wells 'It is stated,' one sceptical official observed two decades later, 'by the magistrate of Fatehpur, a district in which these offences are common, that in the course of a year in his jurisdiction not less than 120 persons fall into wells, it may therefore be suspected that in many instances persons are reported to have been murdered by thugs who have in truth died from some other accident.' See 'Court of directors on policy towards thagi', 6 Apr. 1830, in Philips (ed.), Correspondence of Lord William Cavendish Bentinck I, 425–6.

'The inhuman precaution' Perry to Dowdeswell, 1 Mar. 1812, Add.Mss. 5376 fos. 13–17.

Earlier murders 'Comparative statement of murdered bodies found on the High Roads and in the wells in the Zillah of Etawah in the years 1808, 1809 . . .', 7 Apr. 1811, ibid. fos. 8–8v.

. . . the number of murders dwarfed . . . Perry to Dowdeswell, 1 Mar. 1812, ibid. fos. 13–17.

. . . Kingdom of Oudh. . . This was the appellation the British gave it. In fact Oudh was, at this time, nominally still a part of the Mughal Empire and was ruled over by a nawab, or governor, who while in effect quite independent was not actually a king.

History of India The interested general reader should find that three recent narrative histories – Lawrence James's Raj: The Making and Unmaking of British India and John Keay's India: A History and The Honourable Company: A History of the English East India Company – sketch in the background very well. Christopher Bayly's Rulers, Townsmen and Bazaars: North Indian Society in the Age of British Expansion, 1770–1870 is the most thoughtful and detailed exploration of the social history of Hindustan in this period.

. . . nine-tenths of India . . . The Mughals' sway was exceeded only by that of the British (and then only if one assumes that the nominally independent princedoms that continued to make up half of the Subcontinent really formed part of the Raj) and is unlikely – while Pakistan and Bangladesh exist – ever to be approached again. Keay, India pp. xxii–xxiii. Nevertheless, a good deal of this magnificence was illusory. 'Outwardly, Mughal rule was a huge system of household government reinforced by an overwhelming but unwieldy military power,' writes Bayly in Rulers p. 10. '[But] one can easily overestimate its control, especially in outlying areas. The empire was . . . more like a grid of imperial towns, roads and markets which pressed heavily on [existing Indian] society and modified it, though only at certain points.'

Notes – Chapter 1   296

Etawah in ruins William Foster, *Early Travels in India, 1583–1619* p. 179.

Mughal revenues James, *Raj* p. 5.

Abandoned checkpoints Radhika Singha, *A Despotism of Law* p. 17n.

Etawah changed hands Between 1700 and 1800 Etawah was subject to the Moghul Emperor at Delhi (1700–14), to Muhammed Khan Bangash and his dynasty of Afghans (1714 49), to Nawal Rai of Oudh (1749–50), Ahmad Khan Bangash (1750–51), to the Maratha and Jat warlords of central India (1751–7), Mahmud Khan Bangash (1757), the Marathas again (1757–61), and then to the Rohillas of northern India (1762–70). Thereafter the city passed under Maratha control one final time (1770–73), before falling to Shuja-ud-Daula, the ruler of Oudh, in the last days of 1773.

The British in India Keay, *Honourable Company* pp. 73–80, 85–9, 143–68, 271–327, 362–91; idem, *India* pp. 370–72; Suresh Ghosh, *The Social Condition of the British Community in Bengal, 1757–1800* pp. 1–12, 68–9; Bernard Cohn, 'Recruitment and training of British civil servants in India, 1600–1860', in Ralph Braibanti (ed.), *Asian Bureaucratic Systems Emergent from the British Imperial Tradition* pp. 87–95.

Clive and the 200 Days Keay, *India* pp. 381–4, 392–3.

Transformation of the East India Company Ibid. pp. 392–3; Edwardes, *The Sahibs and the Lotus* pp. 13, 34–57; idem, *Glorious Sahibs* pp. 34–5; George Bearce, *British Attitudes Towards India, 1784–1858* pp. 11–39; Michael Fisher, *Indirect Rule in India* pp. 8, 11, 31, 43, 49–51.

'*had barely touched . . .*' Keay, op. cit. pp. 399–400. See also William Dalrymple, *White Mughals* pp. 57–60, and Iris Butler, *The Eldest Brother*, for more detailed appraisals of this difficult man's character.

The Marathas Stewart Gordon, *The Marathas, 1600–1818* pp. 178–93; Edwardes, *Glorious Sahibs* pp. 22–31, 39–43. The senior Maratha leaders owed allegiance of a sort to a potentate known as the Peshwa of Poona. But the Peshwa was far from the strongest of this group of princes, and lacked the authority to prevent his compatriots from making war on each other as well as fighting rival Mughal successor states. By the end of the eighteenth century he (and two other splendidly named Maratha potentates, the Gaikwad of Baroda and the Bhonsle of Nagpore) had been overshadowed by Sindhia and Holkar. Maratha titles, incidentally, worked in much the same way as those of Scottish clan chiefs. 'Sindhia' and 'Holkar' were family names used in the same way that a Highlander might speak of his chief as 'The Cameron of Locheil'. CE Luard, *Gwalior State Gazetteer* p. 15.

Famine Severe famines struck India with depressing regularity. See, e.g., Keay, *Honourable Company* pp. 115–16; WW Hunter, *The Annals of Rural Bengal* pp. 19–33; GL Corbett and RV Russell, *Central Provinces District Gazetteers: Hoshangabad District* p. 32.

Perry See *East India Register*; East India biographies, OIOC.

The beginning of British rule of Etawah DL Drake–Brockman, *District Gazetteers of the United Provinces, Etawah* pp. 95–8.

'*During the short period . . .*' Perry to Dowdeswell, 26 Nov. 1808, Add.Mss. 5375 fo. 4.

2 'An Independent Race of Men'

Etawah and surroundings Walter Hamilton, *The East-India Gazetteer* I, 544–5; Edward Thornton, *A Gazetteer of the Territories Under the Government of the East-India Company* II, 236–42; HR Nevill, *District Gazetteers of the United Provinces of Agra and Oudh: Agra* II, 241–2; Thomas Bacon, *First Impressions and Studies from Nature in Hindustan* II, 388–91; Christopher Bayly, *Empire and Information: Intelligence Gathering and Social Communication in India 1780–1870* pp. 174–5.

'*desperate and lawless*' DL Drake–Brockman, *District Gazetteers of the United Provinces, Etawah* p. 71.

'a bold, spirited and independent race . . .' Perry to Dowdeswell (Secretary, Judicial Department,
    Calcutta), 9 Dec. 1808, Perry papers Add.Mss. 5375 fos. 6–12, CUL; Bayly, *Empire and
    Information* pp. 174–5.
'very turbulent . . .' Perry to Halhed (assistant magistrate, Etawah), 27 Oct. 1812, BC F/4/389
    (9872) fos. 57–8 OIOC.
'hardly conquered' Halhed to Dowdeswell, 18 Oct. 1812, ibid. fo. 63.
Traditions of banditry See, for example, the discussion of the career of Papadu, the Hindu
    Robin Hood, in JF Richards and VN Rao, 'Banditry in Mughal India: Historical and Folk
    Perception', *IESHR* 17 (1980) pp. 99–120; also David Shulman, 'On South Indian Bandits and
    Kings', ibid. pp. 291n, 304–5.
Early travellers in India For Hsuan Tsang, see Samuel Beal, *The Life of Hiuen-Tsiang* pp. 86–7. For
    Hawkins and Withington, see William Foster, *Early Travels in India, 1583–1619* pp. 60–122,
    188–234. For the destruction of the Mughal caravan, see Bayly, *Empire and Information* p. 20.
Dacoits For the dacoits' general modus operandi, see Basudeb Chattopadhyay, *Crime and
    Control in Early Colonial Bengal, 1770–1860* pp. 21–2 and Iftikhar Ahmad, *Thugs, Dacoits and the
    Modern World-System in Nineteenth-Century India* pp. 82–3. For lathials, see Chattopadhyay pp.
    39, 79, 105–8. For the identity of dacoits and for torture, see John McLane, 'Bengali bandits,
    police and landlords after the permanent settlement' in Anand Yang (ed.), *Crime and
    Criminality in British India* pp. 31–3. On dacoity generally, see also Ranjan Chakrabarti,
    Authority and Violence in Colonial Bengal, 1800–1860 pp. 73, 79, 86, 133, 144, 186–7.
'with incredible rapidity' James Hutton, *A Popular Account of the Thugs and Dacoits* p. 101. For the
    Lucknow theft, see ibid. p. 107.
'like quicksilver . . .' William Sleeman, cited by James Sleeman, *Thug* p. 81.
'in colonies . . .' Ibid.
'we would undoubtedly . . .' This quote, from a dacoit apprehended in the Agra district around
    1855, is cited by Ahmad, op. cit. p. 103.
Unlikely to be caught Chattopadhyay, op. cit. p. 137, cites statistics for the Lower Provinces of
    Bengal for the year 1828, concerning 'all the robberies, burglaries and theft in which the
    value of the property robbed or stolen exceeded 50 rupees'.
'A crime committed . . .' Cited by Ahmad, op. cit. p. 82.
Rising crime Figures from the district court in Moorshidabad, Bengal, show that reported
    crime there rose by nearly 180% between 1790–93 and 1799; BB Misra, *The Central
    Administration of the East India Company, 1773–1834* p. 335. Chattopadhyay, op. cit. p. 127, and
    Chakrabarti, op. cit. pp. 135–6, discuss the incidence of dacoity.
Instances of dacoity in Etawah Perry to Dowdeswell, 14 June 1811, Add.Mss. 5376 fos. 11–12.
Indian roads in the Mughal period RC Majumdar (ed.), *The History and Culture of the Indian
    People* VII, 87; William Sleeman, *Ramaseeana* I, iv; Stewart Gordon, *Marathas, Marauders and
    State Formation in Eighteenth-Century India* p. 27; Asiya Siddiqi (ed.), *Trade and Finance in
    Colonial India, 1750–1860* pp. 142–3; Emily Eden, *Up the Country* p. 79; Henry Spry, *Modern
    India* I, 50–1, 110; Bayly, *Rulers, Townsmen and Bazaars* pp. 142–62.
Hucarras Bayly, *Empire and Information* pp. 64–5.
Modes of transport Thomas Bacon, *First Impressions and Studies from Nature in Hindustan* II, 65;
    Michael Edwardes, *The Sahibs and the Lotus* pp. 103, 105–6; J Dunbar (ed.), *Tigers, Durbars and
    Kings* p. 70; Pran Neville, *Rare Glimpses of the Raj* pp. 143–7. Palanquins were provided with
    mattresses and cushions, and most travellers stocked them with supplies of food and drink,
    a lantern, pistols and a book or two. There was lively disagreement concerning their merits.
    Some British officers found them surprisingly comfortable; others, including Thomas Bacon,
    finding that the jogtrot of the bearers resulted in 'abominable shaking', condemned them as
    a 'demi-barbarous method of locomotion'. The bearers were both highly skilled and militant
    (there was a general strike of palanquin bearers in Calcutta in 1828), and more than one
    high-ranking but overzealous British officer found himself abandoned by the roadside by

bearers whom he had, most unwisely, abused for the discomforts of his journey. The cost of
cross-country palanquin travel compared very unfavourably with the 20 rupees or so a
month needed to run a private palanquin within the confines of a city, and was occasioned
by the need for more bearers – generally two sets of four rather than the usual one, the
teams changing places every eight or 10 minutes on the road; the constant need to engage
fresh relays; and the necessity of hiring a foreman, a pair of torch-men to light the way at
night, and additional servants to carry such luggage as could not be fitted into the litter.

Scarred by cracks AC Newcombe, *Village, Town and Jungle Life in India* pp. 327–8.

'Such conveniences . . .' Anon., 'Ramaseeana', *Foreign Quarterly Review* 21 (1838) p. 6.

'a blanket or a quilt . . .' Ibid. pp. 6–7. For *suttoo*, see Bacon, op. cit. II, 408; for betel, see James
  Kerr, *The Domestic Life, Character and Customs of the Natives of India* p. 176.

'The traveller . . .' Bacon, op. cit. II, 65.

Fanny Eden Dunbar, op. cit. p. 121.

Emily Eden Cited by Dennis Kincaid, *British Social Life in India, 1608–1937* p. 184.

Ordered to cut the cost of his patrols Perry to Dowdeswell, 9 Dec. 1808, Add.Mss. 5375 fos. 6–12.

'Daily experience . . .' Ibid.

Incidence of murder in India Chattopadhyay, op. cit. p. 92.

Checkpoint and reward Perry to Dowdeswell, 26 Mar. 1810, Add.Mss. 5375 fos. 105–9.

First arrests 'Translation of the examination of Gholam Hossyn, inhabitant of Khurah
  Pergunnah Shekoabad', enclosed in ibid. fos. 110–14.

3 'Awful Secrets'

Etymology of the word 'thug' See John Gilchrist's *A Dictionary, English & Hindoostanee . . .* I,
486, 710, 973, where the word 'T'heg' is synonymous with 'knave', 'rascal' and 'villain', and
Robert Drummond's dictionary, *Illustrations of Grammatical Parts of the Guzerattee, Mahratta
and English Languages*, which defines the word 'thug' to mean 'a cheat, a swindler'. The Sufi
poet Bulleh Shah (1680–1757) wrote a verse in which 'thugs' feature as swindlers, while the
early nineteenth-century police officer John Shakespear reported from the Western
Provinces that 'the literal meaning is "rogue" or "knave"'. ('Observations regarding Badheks
and T'hegs, extracted from an official report dated 30 April 1816', *Asiatick Researches* 13
(1820) p. 287.) Given these discrepancies, it is worth noting that Iftikhar Ahmad, in his
Thugs, Dacoits and the Modern World-System in Nineteenth-Century India pp. 128–9, cites an April
1820 despatch from Magistrate Lycester, at Roy Barelly, which revealingly reports that in the
Western Provinces 'the word Thug is a local cant term and consequently little understood
in any uniform way'.

  Thus, while there are scattered references to 'thugs' in histories and chronicles dating as
far back as the thirteenth century, and perhaps earlier – Wilhelm Halbfass, in *Tradition and
Reflections* pp. 102–7, points to mentions of 'the sacred texts of the Thags' in Sanskrit works
composed as early as the tenth century AD – it cannot be assumed that these accounts refer
to the same murderous stranglers who used the name in later times. There are hints, here
and there, that a handful of them might; Guru Nanak (1469–1539), the founder of the Sikh
religion, once encountered 'a certain Sheikh Sajjan', who had built both a Hindu temple and
a mosque in order to 'lure travellers into his house in order that he might murder them and
so acquire their wealth', and who disposed of his victims by hurling their bodies down a
well. But a history of the Delhi sultan Firoz Shah II, dating to 1350, which contains the oldest
generally accepted use of the word, makes no mention of the crimes of which its 'thugs'
were accused, noting simply that no fewer than 1,000 of these criminals were betrayed to the
authorities by one of their own number, and that at some point between 1290 and 1296 the
entire group was rounded up and deported down the Jumna to Bengal. On Guru Nanak, see
WH MacLeod, *Guru Nanak and the Sikh Religion* pp. 38–9; Christopher Kenna, 'Resistance,

banditry and rural crime: aspects of the feudal paradigm in North India under colonial rule c.1800–1840', in E Leach and S Mukherjee (eds.), *Feudalism: Comparative Studies* p. 236. On Firoz Shah II, see HM Elliot, *History of India As Told By Its Own Historians* III, 141.

Counterfeiters Satya Sangar, *Crime and Punishment in Mughal India* pp. 85–6; Radhika Singha, *A Despotism of Law* p. 189.

Virtually all the Thugs The historian Stewart Gordon examined 2,000 fragments of oral tradition from central India, 'both in the vernacular and in translation', and found 'many stories about robbers, but none specifically about Thugs'. Gordon, 'Scarf and sword: Thugs, marauders and state-formation in 18th-century India', *IESHR* 4 (1969) pp. 408–9. For an example of a story about 'Thugs' who appear to have been common highway robbers, see V. Smith, 'The prince and the Thugs', *North Indian Notes & Queries* (March 1894) p. 212.

Identified himself as a Thug According to Hossyn's own statement, the word was actually put into his mouth by his interrogator, Amarun Zoollee Beg of Shekoabad. 'Translation of the examination of Gholam Hossyn, inhabitant of Khurah, Pergunnah Shekoabad, by trade a munerar, aged 16 or thereabouts', enclosed in Perry to Dowdeswell, 26 Mar. 1810, Perry papers Add.Mss. 5375, fos. 110–14, CUL. It took some time for the term to become established British usage. Christopher Bayly, in *Empire and Information* p. 175, notes that 'in his letters of this period Perry alternates between small and capital "t" for the word and sometimes puts it in quotation marks'.

Perry's interrogation of Gholam Hossyn Court of circuit, Bareilly, Zillah Etawah, Second Sessions of 1810, in Consultation No. 43 and Consultation No. 46 of 18 Jan. 1811, BCJC P/130/27.

. . . Gholam Hossyn's Thugs . . . 'Translation of the examination of Gholam Hossyn', Add.Mss. 5375, fos. 110–14, and 'Translation of the acknowledgement of Ghoolam Hossyn Thug made before me on the 11th April 1810' in ibid. fos. 117–22.

More than suspected Perry to Dowdeswell, 11 Apr. 1810, ibid. fos. 115–17.

Datura poisoning Thorn apple, also known as jimson weed and mad apple, is believed to be responsible for more poisonings than any other plant. The toxin it contains – hyoscyamine – is present in its leaves, roots, flowers and seeds; the Thugs seem to have used ground seeds, but herbal teas brewed from the leaves can also kill.

Dullal and others 'Deposition of Dullal, sheekh, aged 60'; 'Deposition of Kalee Khan'; 'Deposition of Acbar, son of Himmut Khan', n.d., Add.Mss. 5375 fos. 125–31, 134–5.

Cloth strips Consultation No. 46 of 1811, BCJC P/130/27.

'takes a handkerchief . . .' Ibid.

'atrocious crimes' Perry to Dowdeswell, 17 May 1810, ibid. fos. 136–8.

Size of Thug gangs relative to victims Thornton, *Illustrations* p. 181, p. 243; *Sel.Rec.* 63, 78–9. This analysis is borne out by the author's tabulation of all the cases mentioned in Thornton, *Illustrations*, Sleeman, *Ramaseeana* and *Sel.Rec.*

. . . never killed close to home . . . As well as making it harder for the police to catch the Thugs, this practice made it possible for the gangs to secure support from villagers and local landholders who could well have caused trouble had their friends or relatives been despatched. Some of the members of the Nursingpore gang described by Sleeman in *Ramaseeana* I, 30–3, do appear to have killed passing travellers in the grove outside their home village of Kundelee; they were shielded by the local landholders. On the other hand, the Murnae Thugs, tempted to strangle four merchants, who came to their village to purchase loot, for the sake of the 700 rupees they carried, were heavily fined by their protector the Rajah of Rampoora, who had to deal with the missing men's anxious relatives. He said 'that now we had begun to murder at home as well as abroad, we were no longer deserving of favour'. Ibid. I, 226.

'In this part of the country . . .' 'Deposition of Kalee Khan', Perry papers Add.Mss. 5375 fos. 125–9.

Avoid Company territories Stockwell to Perry, 11 Aug. 1815, in *Ramaseeana* II, 372.

The inhuman 'precaution . . .' Perry to Dowdeswell, 1 Mar. 1812, Add.Mss. 5376 fos. 13–17.

sipahee and cakari Nathaniel Halhed, 'Report on the state of the Pergunnahs of Sindouse from actual observation', 18 Oct. 1812, BC F/4/389 (9872) fos. 75–89; Kenna, op. cit. p. 214.

'Had this inhuman offender . . .' Perry to Dowdeswell, 17 May 1810, Add.Mss. 5375 fos. 136–8.

'There are many thieves . . .' Statement of Jheodeen, 1836, in 'Collections on Thuggee and Dacoitee', Paton papers Add.Mss, 41300 fo. 25, BL.

. . . a British traveller . . . Charles Davidson, *Diary of Travels and Adventures in Upper India* I, 186–7.

'low and dirty' Statement of Jheodeen, Paton papers, fo. 25, BL.

'men of force and violence . . .' Statement of Futteh [Futty] Khan, 1836, ibid. fo. 19v.

'The Thug is the king of all these classes!' Statements of Buhram, 1836, ibid. fos. 19v, 24.

. . . at least a hundred years . . . These traditions were first transcribed in the 1830s. The Thugs, an approver named Thukoree related, 'came to Himmutpore . . . and took up their abode under the protection of the Sengur Raja Juggummun Sa . . .' Sleeman notes that the ruler of Himmutpore in 1835 was the great-great-great-grandson of Juggummun Sa – the intervening generations giving a probable date of 1650–1720 for the arrival of the Thugs in Juggummun's dominion. Juggummun himself was said to have taxed the Thugs so heavily that they fled to the Chambel valley to escape these exactions. See 'Conversations with Thugs', in *Ramaseeana* I, 222–4.

Maratha tax on Thugs Tax was levied every three years at the rate of Rs.24–8–0 per household, and a total of 218 Thug homes were taxed. The local zamindar was supposed to send all of the proceeds – less his own fee of 100 rupees and a few expenses – to his overlord, but in practice he contrived to levy taxes from many Thugs whose names did not appear on the rent-rolls, and so made a considerable profit. Ibid. and 'List of Thug families, who paid the tax on Thugs to the Gwalior state', *Ramaseeana* II, 150–225.

Oldest Thugs Amongst those questioned by Sleeman in 1835 were Khandee, who claimed to be 83 years old, Nundun, 85, and Lalmun, who was 90. The latter might possibly have been engaged in Thuggee as early as 1760. *Ramaseeana* I, 173. Nidha, one of the Thugs questioned by Perry, had belonged to the gang of a certain Khunjah, who had been a Thug since 1785. 'Deposition of Nidha', Add.Mss. 5375 fos. 123–5.

Thug genealogies WW Hunter, in *The Annals of Rural Bengal* p. 72, refers to Thug genealogies charting as many as 20 generations, which implies a history of at least 400 years. There may well have been a significant element of embroidery and one-upmanship inherent in these purely oral accounts, however; for example, the great Thug leader Feringeea was on occasion claimed to be the product of either 10 or 17 generations of Thugs, rather than the eight he actually enumerated for Sleeman. See Sleeman to Duncan, 7 June 1832, T&D G1 fo. 12, NAI; *Ramaseeana* I, 149–50. As such claims are impossible to corroborate they cannot be accepted at face value.

Alexander the Great Consultation No. 46 of 18 Jan. 1811, BCJCP/130/27.

Expulsion of the Thugs from Delhi Paton papers, Add.Mss. 41300 fos. 125–6, BL; *Ramaseeana* I, 68.

Seven families of stranglers The original Thug clans, according to these oral traditions, were named Barsote (Bursote, Bursoth), Bhais (Bhys, Bhyns), Kachuni (Kuchunee), Hattar (Huttar), Garru (Ganoo), Tandel (Tundel) and Rathur (Bahleen or Buhleem), Robert Russell and Hira Lal report (*The Tribes and Castes of the Central Provinces of India* IV, 560), elaborating on *Ramaseeana* I, 68, 72, 222–5. The Tandels were said not to have lived in Delhi, and the Bahleens fled furthest from the capital; in Sleeman's day it was said that almost all of them lived south of the Nerbudda river. Various sons and daughters of the seven clans married into other families, the Thugs believed, and members of these other families subsequently took up the trade. At various times several groups of Thugs claimed precedence; thus the Thugs of Oudh boasted to Paton that 'up to the present day [they] were the Chief Thugs!' Paton papers fos. 126–126v. There is, however, no evidence that any of the other groups accepted these claims.

Hindus and Muslims Most Thugs had several aliases and it is difficult to be certain about their backgrounds. Reynolds, in 'Notes on the T'hags', *Journal of the Royal Asiatic Society* 4 (1837) p. 203, observes: 'No judgement of the birth or caste of a T'hag can be formed from his name, for it is not unfrequently happens that a Hindu T'hag has a Musulman name, with a Hindu alias attached to it; and vice versa with respect to T'hags who are by birth Muhammedans.'

'Here's to the spirits . . .' Account of Sheikh Inaent, *Ramaseeana* I, 162.

Camp followers Ibid. p. 144.

First use of 'thug' Kim A. Wagner, 'The Deconstructed Stranglers: A Reassessment of Thugee', *Modern Asian Studies* 38 (2004) pp. 942–3.

'stranglers and assassins' CE Bosworth, *The Mediaeval Islamic Underworld* p. 104; AS Tritton, 'Muslim Thugs', *Journal of Indian History* 8 (1929) pp. 41–4. The other categories of criminal described by Uthman al-Khayyat were housebreakers (the 'man who works by night'), con men (the 'man who works by strategems'), highwaymen ('gentlemen of the road'), and 'grave-despoilers'.

Sometimes the methods of the stranglers and the *sahib radkh* were combined. Another Arab chronicler, Al-Jahiz, writing in his *Book of Animals*, refers to a group of highway robbers called 'combiners' – 'so called because they combine strangling with "giving scent"', the contemporary criminal slang for smashing a man's face open with a rock. The striking similarity between the modus operandi of the stranglers described by Al-Jahiz and that of the Thugs in the India of the early nineteenth century does not, of course, prove any connection between the two groups. It would be more plausible to suggest that some early Indian Thug might have been inspired to adopt the methods described by Al-Jahiz after reading his book.

Thévenot Jean Thévenot (1633–67) published an account of India's stranglers in his *Travels* III, 41; it was reprinted in Russell and Lal, op. cit. IV, 559.

Fryer John Fryer travelled through much of India between the years 1672 and 1681 and described his experiences in a book made up of letters that he wrote to home: *A New Account of the East Indies and Persia . . . 1672–1681*. He writes of the stranglers he encountered in this third letter, 'A Description of Surat and Journey into Duccan'. Upon their capture, the whole group was strung up 'half a foot from the ground', after which their legs were cut off and they were left 'miserable Spectacles hanging till they dropped of their own accord'. One member of the gang, Fryer adds, was a mere boy who 'boasted, That though he were not Fourteen Years of Age, he had killed his Fifteen Men'.

Aurangzeb's farman Singha, op. cit. pp. 14–15, 189.

Varieties of Thug Sleeman, *Ramaseeana* I, 95–7, 132, 144, 161–4, 180–81, 238–9; Martine van Woerkens, *The Strangled Traveller* pp. 132–5.

Jumulud Deen Sleeman, *Ramaseeana* I, 97.

Phrases and purses Ibid. I, 67, 116; Thornton, *Illustrations* p. 332; Reynolds, 'Notes' p. 210.

'I was one day walking . . .' Sleeman, *Ramaseeana* I, 238–9.

Service with other gangs Ibid. I, 180, 182, 185, 264.

Thugs amicably share loot Cf. deposition of Feringeea on the Doolea/Malagow affair, BC F/4/1483 (55515) fos. 169–71. For an instance of cooperation between Thugs from widely distant parts of India, see Thornton, op. cit. p. 209.

4 Mr Halhed's Revenge

Early arrests and the decline in murdered bodies Perry to Dowdeswell, 17 May 1810, Perry papers, Add.Mss. 5375 fos. 136–8, CUL; 'Comparative statement of murdered bodies . . .' Add.Mss. 5376 fos. 8–8v. Whether Perry's figures proved that the Thugs had been thrown into disorder, were disposing of their victims more securely, or had simply moved on to safer territories cannot be said with any certainty; probably a combination of all three factors was at work.

Difficulty of securing a conviction Perry to Dowdeswell, 17 May 1810, Add.Mss. 5375 fos. 136–8; Perry to Dowdeswell, 6 Oct. 1812, Add.Mss. 5376 fos. 17–18v.

More bodies around Etawah Perry to Dowdeswell, 1 Mar. 1812, Add.Mss. 5376 fos. 13–17.

Flight of Thugs to Sindouse Halhed, 'Report on the state of the Pergunnahs of Sindouse from actual observation', 18 Oct. 1812, BC F/4/389 (9872) fos. 75–89.

Sindouse Ibid. Halhed to Dowdswell, 12 Oct 1812, ibid. fos. 11–15; Bengal Judicial Consultation No. 29, 31 Oct. 1812, in ibid. fos. 3–15; Edward Thornton, *Illustrations of the History and Practices of the Thugs*, pp. 472, 474–5; idem, *A Gazetteer of the Territories Under the Government of the East India Company and of the Native States of the Continent of India* II, 240–1; *Ramaseeana* I, 223; Stockwell (Assistant magistrate, Etawah) to Wauchope (Magistrate, Bundelcund), 10 June 1815, in *Ramaseeana* II, 366–8. HL Drake–Brockman, *District Gazetteers of the United Provinces, Etawah* pp. 96–8; Kim Wagner, 'The Deconstructed Stranglers', *Modern Asian Studies* 38(2004) pp. 957–60. The ravines of the northern Chambel valley remain notorious, even today, for their dacoit gangs. For an interpretive study of banditry in the region, see Paul Winther, *Chambel River Dacoity* (PhD thesis, Cornell University, 1972).

Main Thug residence Molony (Commissioner, Nerbudda territory) to Stewart (Acting Resident, Gwalior), 1 Oct. 1820, in *Ramaseeana* II, 132–3.

Numbers of Thugs 'Examination of Laljee', 11 Dec. 1812, Add.Mss. 5376 fo. 38, CUL; Halhed to Dowdeswell, 12 Oct. 1812, BC F/4/389 (9872) fos. 11–15; Halhed, 'Report on the state of the Pergunnahs of Sindouse . . .', op. cit.; deposition of Suntoke Rae, 24 Aug. 1834, in Thornton, *Illustrations* pp. 472–4.

Fort in disrepair; travellers vanish 'Report on the state of the Pergunnahs of Sindouse', op. cit.

Police Ibid.; Halhed to Hawkins (court of circuit judge, Roy Barelly), 13 Oct. 1812, BC F/4/389 (9872) fos. 52–7.

Lieutenant Maunsell See *East India Register* 1811 and 1812. Maunsell was born in Dublin on 28 July 1780 and was a Bengal Army cadet from 1802 to 1803. In 1811, he was ranked sixth in seniority among the 22 lieutenants in the regiment, having been Gazetted on 21 September 1804. The *Register* for 1812 notes his death in action against 'banditti'. The lieutenant was, incidentally, the only one of the 50 officers of the Bengal Army who died that year to be killed in action.

Military detachment Halhed to Dowdeswell, 31 Oct. 1812, BC F/4/389 (9872) fos. 3–10.

Orders to Halhed Perry to Dowdeswell, 1 Mar. + 10 Oct. + 16 Dec. 1812, Add.Mss. 5376 fos. 13–17, 19, 27–9.

Halhed See *East India Register* 1800–1812; Rosane Rocher, *Orientalism, Poetry and the Millennium* p. 81; 'Translation of the acknowledgement of Ghoolam Hossyn Thug . . .', 11 Apr. 1810, Add.Mss. 5375 fos. 117–22; for Allygurh, see Halhed to Dowdeswell, 18 Oct. 1812, BC F/4/389 (9872) fos. 63–75.

Halhed advances into Sindouse When Halhed advanced cautiously into the pargana of Sindouse that October, he had only a sketchy idea of the problems he was likely to encounter.

Even at that late date, the East India Company possessed no more than a limited understanding of the interior of India. For much of the eighteenth century, any voyage inland from Bengal or Bombay had been regarded as 'a considerable adventure'. The British road network stretched no further than Benares until the 1780s, when it was belatedly extended to Lucknow and Hyderabad; as late as 1808, even the Commander in Chief of the Bengal Army could concede that 'beyond the Jumna all is conjecture'.

The Company had, in fact, once possessed a rudimentary intelligence network in central India. It had been run by merchants based in the Mughal capital, Agra, and provided regular reports on the activities of the imperial court, supplemented by snippets of news from the further reaches of the Subcontinent picked up from travelling merchants and visiting indigo planters. But intelligence-gathering in Agra slowed dramatically as the Mughals declined, and little information of any value was received from the interior after 1740. The only regular reports available after that date came from a group of Indian clerks known as 'newswriters', who made their living by attaching themselves to native courts and circulating bulletins on local events and news likely to be of interest to other rulers. These reports were of only limited value to the Company. They contained a good deal of unreliable gossip, and the newswriters themselves, being predominantly Muslim, were far from experts concerning the nuances of Hindu society. While their bulletins did provide British administrators with the information needed to keep abreast of politics and military affairs, they contributed little to their understanding of India itself.

It was not until 1785 that the British made a concerted effort to improve their information. The old Persian Office in Calcutta – hitherto an obscure bureau charged with copying correspondence in what was then the *lingua franca* of Indian diplomacy – was turned into an intelligence-gathering department, and thereafter the Company's interest in collecting and sifting intelligence grew to such an extent that the Holkar of Indore, preparing to renew his lengthy struggle against the British in 1808, was perturbed by the invaders' 'favourite object' of receiving 'intelligence of all occurrences and transactions in every quarter'.

The activities of the Persian Office, and the increased familiarity of the Company with the Indian interior – the product of Wellesley's wars of conquest – meant that the British were by 1812 a little better-informed regarding conditions in the central provinces. They were familiar with the endemic disorder that plagued much of the land between Oudh and Hyderabad, and aware, at least in the broadest terms, of the prevalence of bandits, rebels and predatory mercenaries throughout the Native States. But even their improved intelligence had distinct limits. Most Company officers still had, at best, a crude understanding of Indian society. Knowledge of Hindu religious institutions, village life and the 'world of women' was practically non-existent. And there was a general and uneasy awareness, outside the Presidency towns, of the appalling isolation of the scattered European communities in the interior: a handful of men, and scarcely any women, adrift in a sea of tens of millions of potentially hostile 'natives' whose religion and culture – and, thus, motives and activities – seemed impossible to comprehend.

The loneliness felt by British officers stationed inland – particularly those who had failed to master the languages of the Subcontinent – was palpable. Almost all suspected they were cheated and lied to by the servants who acted as their intermediaries with the Indian world. 'Even if they served their masters loyally,' remarks one writer on this subject, 'they moved in realms of life and thought which they wished to keep hidden from their rulers. The basic fear of the colonial officer or settler was thus his lack of indigenous knowledge and ignorance of the "wiles of the native". He feared their secret letters, their drumming and "bush telegraphy", and the nightly passage of seditious agents masquerading as priests and holy men.' It was, in general, all too easy to imagine conspiracies being hatched and devilry done in the void stretching south into Gwalior. Dennis Kincaid, *British Social Life in India, 1608–1937* pp. 129, 171, 193; Christopher Bayly, *Empire and Information* pp. 6–8, 47, 58, 87, 89, 143–5, 151, 162, 174, 178; Susan Bayly, *Caste, Society and Politics in India* p. 84; George Bearce, *British Attitudes Towards India, 1784–1858* pp. 41–2; William Dalrymple, *White Mughals* pp. 50–3.

Halhed's poisoning Halhed to Dowdeswell, 31 Oct. 1812, BC F/4/389 (9872) fos. 3–11.

Chourella Halhed to Dowdeswell, 12 Oct. 1812, ibid. fos. 11–15.

Murder of Maunsell Halhed to Dowdeswell, 23 Oct. 1812, ibid. fos. 27–39.

Mutilation of Maunsell's corpse Ibid.; Hawkins to Dowdeswell, 4 Nov. 1812, ibid. fos. 47–51.

Retaliation Halhed to Dowdeswell, 30 Oct. 1812; Dowdeswell to Halhed, 7 Nov. 1812, ibid. fos. 36–9; Halhed to Dowdeswell, Consultation 81 of 30 Oct. 1812, ibid. fos. 130–5

Captain Popham Bengal Despatches Judicial, Ceded and Conquered Territories, 30 Sept. 1814, E/4/680 fos. 564–6, OIOC.

Bounty 'Deposition No. 15', enclosure in Perry to Dowdeswell, 15 Jan. 1813, Add.Mss. 5376, CUL.

Burning of Murnae Consultation No. 77, 20 Nov. 1812, BC F/4/389 (98721) fos. 112–14; Consultation No. 79, 22 Nov. 1812, ibid. fos. 127–9.

Size of the village No full account of Murnae's size or population appears in the contemporary sources, but it is described as a 'large village' in Perry to Dowdeswell, 17 Dec. 1812, Add.Mss. 5376 fos. 29–31. Maratha tax records suggest that it was larger than its neighbour, Sindouse. *Ramaseeana* II, 153.

Remains of houses ploughed under Christopher Kenna, 'Resistance, banditry and rural crime: aspects of the feudal paradigm in North India under colonial rule c.1800–1840', in E Leach and S Mukherjee (eds.), *Feudalism: Comparative Studies* p. 25. Halhed also seized the village crops, see Consultation No. 77 of 20 Nov. 1812, BCJC P/131/7. 'The burning of the village of Murnaee,' Popham wrote, 'has alarmed the evil[ly] disposed dreadfully, and will be a warning, I am persuaded, to them to wish to remain in peace and quiet.' Further reprisals, he believed, would be counter-productive: 'I am in some degree apprehensive that were more villages burnt it would drive the people in the Mahrattah frontier to desperation, particularly the sufferers who, having lost their all, might when the detachment should be withdrawn unite and make predatory incursions within our frontier.' Popham to Halhed, Nov. 1812, BC F/4/389 (9872) fos. 127–9.

Aftermath in Murnae Bengal Despatches Judicial, Ceded and Conquered Territories, 30 Sept. 1814, E/4/680 fos. 564–6, OIOC.

Thugs' flight from Murnae According to Perry to Dowdeswell, 16 Dec. 1812, Add.Mss. 5376 fos. 27–9, 'the whole of the discription of Public Offenders called Thugs have left their houses and fled into the Dekhan'. But he, of course, had a vested interest in believing this to be so. See also FC Smith, 'Report on the Sessions of 1831–32', 20 June 1832, in *Sel.Rec.* pp. 104–5; *Ramaseeana* I, 160, 226.

Capture of Laljee Halhed to Perry, 15 Oct. 1812 BC F/4/389 (9872) fos. 95–102; extract from Judicial letter from Bengal, 30 Jan. 1813, para. 144, ibid. fos. 1–2; Strachey (British Resident, Gwalior) to Halhed, 1 Nov. 1812, ibid. fos. 120–22; Consultation No. 65 of 3 Dec. 1812; Consultation No. 133 of 5 Dec. 1812, BCJC P/131/8.

Fate of Laljee and his men 'Deposition of Suntoke Rae, son of Laljoo Kuchwaha, 24 Aug. 1834', in Thornton, *Illustrations of the History and Practices of the Thugs* pp. 471–5.

Thugs settle south of the Jumna 'They now live', Perry reported in 1815, 'in a number of the Gwalior villages, stretching over an irregular tract of country from the right bank of the Kooaree to the confines of Duttea', paying taxes to the local zamindars as hitherto and enjoying their protection. Stockwell to Shakespear, 7 Aug. 1815; Stockwell to Perry, 11 Aug. 1815, printed in Thornton, op. cit. pp. 322–7.

Khyrooah 'They have always been insolent and overbearing people,' the official added, 'and their trade has been highway robbery. They hold their estate under Jhansee, and have from fifteen to twenty villages which they hold at a quit rent of 600 rupees a year.' Consultation No. 18 of 18 Mar. 1831, BPC P/126/27, OIOC. See also Smith to Prinsep, 8 Dec. 1830, BC F/4/1309 (52131) fos. 43–8.

Lack of British interest in the Thugs' arrest One Thug captured by the Marathas related that just four of Laljee's followers were sent with him for trial 'at the requisition of the Mynpooree Magistrate, who might have had the whole if he liked, but he wanted only four', and that even these men were acquitted when the only witness against them, a Thug named Aman who later became one of the Lucknadown gang, 'became so much frightened' while taking a Hindu oath 'that he let the cup of Ganges water fall out of his hands before the Magistrate, who did not in consequence believe him; and they were all four released, though they were all present at the murder of Lieutenant Maunsell'. See *Ramaseeana* I, 219–21, which also contains Thukoree's account of the visits of the great demon to the Thugs' prison.

Tranquillity returns to Sindouse Perry to Dowdeswell, 16 Dec. 1812, Add.Mss. 5376 fos. 27–9; N Halhed, 'Report on the state of the Pergunnahs of Sindouse . . . from actual observation', 18 Oct. 1812, Add.Mss. 5375 fos. 75–89.

'It is, to me, extremely doubtful . . .' Smith to Swinton, 20 June 1832, BC F/4/1406 (55521) fos. 169–70.

The movements of Thug gangs Sleeman, *Ramaseeana* I, 97, 181, 191, 222–4, 226, 245–7; II, 305, 485.

. . . largely unmolested . . . 'Deposition of Suntoke Rae, son of Laljoo Kuchwaha, 24 Aug. 1834', in Thornton, op. cit. p. 474.

5 'The Infamous System of Thuggee'

Halhed and Perry East India Register, 1814, 1823.

Stockwell Sleeman, *Ramaseeana* II, pp. 3620–75.

Forbes James Forbes, *Oriental Memoirs* II, 397. He arrived in Bombay as a writer in 1765 and remained in India until 1784, compiling an estimated 52,000 manuscript pages of notes on the natural history, archaeology and social life of the Subcontinent. The *Memoirs* that he produced from this mass of source material were composed some years later and first published in 1813–15. Thévenot, writing in about 1665, had described female stranglers who lulled victims with their beauty; see van Woerkens, *The Strangled Traveller* p. 111.

. . . seems not to have been employed . . . Sleeman, *Ramaseeana* I, 254.

Thugs at Bangalore Richard Sherwood, 'Of the Murderers Called Phansigars', *Asiatick Researches* 13 (1820) pp. 250–82.

Indians knew nothing Stewart Gordon, 'Scarf and Sword', *IEHSR* 4 (1969) pp. 408–9.

Encounters with the Phansigars in 1807 Sherwood, pp. 250–51; Thornton, p. 3.

Wright's reports Thugs and Phansigars cooperated on occasion, for example, in the Dhooma affair of 1813; Thornton, p. 207. Perry and his assistant Nathaniel Halhed were certainly familiar with Wright's descriptions of the 'Fasueegar gangs' by the time Halhed marched into Sindouse in October 1812. See Halhed, 'Report on the state of the Pergunnahs of Sindouse . . . from actual observation', 18 Oct. 1812, BC F/4/389 fos. 75–89.

On links between the Thugs and Phansigars, see *Ramaseeana* I, 163–4. For the Phansigars' activities in the Deccan, 1807–12, see Sherwood, op. cit. pp. 259n, 264; Thornton, *Illustrations* pp. 3–6; Ishwar Sahai, 'The crime of thagi and its suppression under Lord WC Bentinck', part 1, *Indian Culture* 3 (1936) p. 324; 'Extract of a letter from the Magistrate of the Zillah of Chittoor to the Register of the Foujdarry Adawlut', 6 Dec. 1809, 'Extract of a letter from the Magistrate of Chittoor to the Secretary to Government in the Judicial Department', 1 July 1812. 'Declaration given by Sheik Madar of Goottapaliam', 1 Feb. 1811, 'Declaration of Yerragaudoo', 1 Feb. 1811, 'Second declaration by Yerragaudoo', 2 Feb. 1811, all printed in *Ramaseeana* II, 304–27.

Stockwell's report of 1815 Stockwell to Acting Superintendent of Police, 7 Aug. 1815, *Ramaseeana* II, 369.

St Leger Sleeman, *Ramaseeana* I, 14–15; the Marchioness of Bute, *The Private Journals of the Marquess of Hastings*, II, 151–2. Sepoys continued to be favoured as Thug victims into the 1830s; see Smith to Swinton, 20 June 1832, BC F/4/1406 (55521) fos. 173.

Shakespear's paper J Shakespear, 'Observations Regarding Badheks and T'hegs, extracted from an official report dated 30 April 1816', *Asiatick Researches* 13 (1820) pp. 282–92.

John Malcolm Malcolm, *A Memoir of Central India* II, 187–9; see also Edwardes, *Glorious Sahibs* p. 43.

Evidence from Gwalior 'Habits and characters of the Thugs', Bengal Political dept. 86, 21 Oct. 1820, BC F/4/774 (20927) fos. 1–26. The original of this report was first copied the previous year as Consultation No. 46 of 24 July 1819. BPC P/121/59.

'*act in parties and scour . . .*' 'Captain Sheriff's Proceedings in 1823, at Jhalna', *Ramaseeana* II, 282.

Thomas Ernst 'Removal of Thomas Henry Ernst from the offices of Magistrate of the Hooghly, etc.', May 1809–June 1810, BC F/4/411 (10204) fos. 213–14, 238–41; Minto memorandum in extract BCJC, Consultation No. 25 of 24 Nov. 1810, ibid. (10205) fos.172–5.

Gorruckpore Sleeman, *Ramaseeana* II, 250–3; Thornton pp. 302–10.

Mr Gregory Madras despatches judicial, 28 Apr. 1824, E/4/929 fos. 647–66, OIOC.

Patna case Sleeman, *Ramaseeana* II, 245–7. The Thug informant seems to have been misinformed about the fate of the Nazir; he survived to be released from prison when the Thugs were rearrested in the mid-1830s, 'though [with] not long to live, from the effects of bad health produced by the cruel treatment which he experienced'. See also ibid. II, 250ff.

Encounters at Jhalna, Seonee and Mozuffurpore Jhalna, ibid. II, 271–98; Seonnee, BPC P/123/13; Mozuffurpore, *Ramaseeana* I, 185–6.

'*the infamous system of Thuggee*' Smith to Swinton, 20 June 1832, *Sel.Rec.* 102–26.

6 Scarf and Sword

Earlier destruction of Thug villages Murnae was burned down c.1800 by Blake Sahib, a European mercenary in command of a Maratha regiment seeking payment of 18,000 rupees' worth of farmed taxes owed by a well-known Thug turned revenue officer named Rae Singh (see chapter 7). *Ramaseeana* I, 175; Sleeman to Smith, Sangea 1833, T&D G1 fo. 246, NAI. At a slightly later date – probably after 1801, when the Ceded and Conquered Territories first became nominally dependent on the Company, and most likely later than 1806–7, when Sindouse was transferred to British control ('Examination of Laljee, 10 Dec. 1812, Perry papers Add.Mss. 5376 fo. 38; 'Deposition of Suntoke Rae, son of Laljoo Kuchwaha, 24 Aug. 1834', in Thornton, *Illustrations* p. 473) – 'Jacob, a commander in Sindheea's Service, sacked one or two of [the villages around Sindouse] and carried off the women as slaves.' On this occasion, 'the Inhabitants applied for and obtained redress from the Magistrate, who wrote to Jacob and in consequence most of the property taken and the women were returned.' 'Report on the state of the Pergunnahs of Sindouse . . . from actual observation', 18 Oct. 1812, BC F/4/389 (9872) fos. 75–89.

Thug geographical mobility See, for example, the evidence of the 65–year-old Thug jemadar Bheelum Burre Khan, who had lived in seven different villages and towns during his life: 'I was born in the town of Austa, pargana Wurwal, *zillah* Hyderabad, where we lived for four years, and left that place and took up our abode at Ougurga, *ellaka* [area] Ousa, and resided there for the period of 25 years, and there I married Moheroodeen Sahib Patail's daughter. We left that village and took up our residence at Lohoogoan, ellaka Droog, for 10 years and after this we came to Chincholee, ellaka Putwurdhan, where we lived for 12 years. We lived in Iowree, ellaka Beelurgee, for two years [and] nine months at Julgeera, where a party came and arrested me.' 'Deposition of Bheelum Burre Khan, Jemadar of Thugs', 1836, T&D D2/2, NAI.

Laljee funds Thugs 'Translation of the deposition of Budloo, Thug, in the Fouzdaree Court before Mr Perry, magistrate of Zillah Etawah, taken on 14 July 1812', Add.Mss. 5376 fos. 24–7.

'*Fifty times*' Sleeman, *Ramaseeana* I, 262.

Unequal relationship Ibid. I, 153, 244–5; van Woerkens, *The Strangled Traveller* pp. 52–3.

Jemadars For qualifications, see the evidence of Dorgha, in *Ramaseeana* I, 263–4; also Reynolds, 'Notes on the T'hags', *Journal of the Royal Asiatic Society* 4 (1837) p. 205, which sets out the jemadar's share of a gang's loot. On the division of spoils see also Thornton, op. cit. pp. 16, 377–8; *Ramaseeana* I, 73, 118; Fanny Parks, *Wanderings of a Pilgrim in Search of the Picturesque* p. 129; 'Deposition of Khaimraj Phansygur', 1829, *Sel.Rec.* 33. The jemadar's portion consisted of between six and 10 per cent of the loot, and he also took one equal share of what remained in common with the members of his gang.

Size of Thug gangs 'Deposition of Sheikh Dawood Newly . . .', 24 Nov. 1834; 'Deposition of Sayeed Ally . . .', 25 Nov. 1834; 'Deposition of Sheikh Burrum Thug . . .', 26 Nov. 1834, all T&D D2/1, NAI. These depositions were taken in the Deccan, but the testimony of the Thugs of Hindustan shows that the gangs of northern India were very similar in size; see *Ramaseeana* I, 82. According to Sleeman, leaders of gangs of more than 20 men received, in addition, one extra share of the loot for their troubles.

Jemadars lose authority For changes in the authority of jemadars, see 'Examination of Thug approver Rama Jemadar No. 1', July 1832, *Sel.Rec.* 127; 'Narrative of a Thuggee expedition in Oude during the cold weather, supposed to have been in 1830 . . . related by Buhram, a leader of Thugs', 20–24 Oct. 1836, in Paton papers, 41300 fo. 118.

Make-up of Thug gangs Smith to Swinton, 20 June 1832, BC F/4/1406 (55521) fo. 201; 'Translation of the examination of Shuhadule . . .', 16 May 1810, Add.Mss. 5375, fos. 138v–42, CUL.

Scouts PA Reynolds, 'Notes on the T'hags' p. 207; Smith to Swinton, 25 June 1832, BC F/4/1406 (55521) fo. 203; Thornton, *Illustrations* p. 6; see also chapter 7.

'Inquiry is also made . . .' Reynolds, 'Notes' pp. 207–8.

Inveiglers Smith to Swinton, 25 June 1832, BC F/4/1406 (55521) fos. 209–10; Sleeman, *Ramaseeana* I, 44; van Woerkens, op. cit. pp. 120–1; James Sleeman, *Thug* pp. 95–6.

Disguises 'Deposition of Rumzan, a noted Thug . . .', Paton papers fos. 122–123v.

'There was nothing to excite alarm . . .' RV Russell and Hira Lal, *Tribes and Castes of the Central Provinces of India* IV, 562.

Incautious behaviour 'At Biseynee,' the Thug Mohammed Buksh recalled, of an expedition in 1828–9, 'we fell in with some travellers, and should have secured them, but when Zolfukar came up, Bhola, who is always talking, could not help saying . . . "After all we shall not go home without something to please our wives and children." The travellers heard, suspected our designs, left our encampment on the bank of a tank, and went into the village. This was our first *bunjj* [merchandise], and to lose it thus was a bad omen: it was in fact like being seized.' *Ramaseeana* I, 234.

Transfer of a party from one inveigler to another Ibid. I, 44.

Anecdote of the Mughal officer Sleeman, *Rambles and Recollections* I, 98–101. This astonishing anecdote was picked up in the prison at Lucknow by 'a native commissioned officer of a regiment of native infantry', who recounted it to Sleeman.

'They will travel' Sleeman, *Ramaseeana* I, 53.

20 days and 200 miles Ibid. I, 169n.

Stranglers and hand-holders interchangeable Cf. BC F/4/1404 (55517) fos. 213–15, 231–62.

'I always stood at a distance . . .' Deposition of Nidha, n.d. (1810), Add.Mss. 5375 fos. 123–5.

No death penalty for strangulation Singha, *A Despotism of Law* pp. 15–16, 62.

'Do you look up to . . .' 'Dialogues with Thugs', Paton papers fo. 10.

bhurtotes The Thugs' most skilful killers, Sleeman asserts, were awarded the title *ghoor ponch*, and they killed with a weighted rumal (see below). Their less able brethren were known as bhurtotes and used an unweighted scarf. The phrase ghoor ponch does not appear in any other writings, however, and other sources refer only to the latter class of men, and assert that the bhurtotes were themselves the Thugs' most able murderers. *Ramaseeana* I, 93; van Woerkens, op. cit. p. 118; Thornton, *Illustrations* pp. 7–8.

'. . . never self-assumed . . .' 'Deposition of Poorun Phansygur', n.d. (1829), *Sel.Rec.* p. 34.

Initiation of new stranglers Reynolds, 'Notes' p. 207.

'. . . he could never acquire . . .' Henry Bevan, *Thirty Years in India* I, 257.

Hand-holders BC F/4/1309 (52131) fo. 270; Thornton, *Illustrations* p. 7.

'. . . *that part of a man* . . .' Henry Spry, 'Some account of the gang-murderers of Central India', p. 514; Thornton, op. cit. p. 8.

Strangling without assistance Russell and Lal, *Tribes and Castes* IV, 564.

Strangling a man on horseback Paton papers fo. 9.

Sleeping victims Thornton, op. cit. p. 13.

Division of spoils among the members of a gang Paton papers Add.Mss. 41300 fo. 11; Smith to Swinton, 20 June 1832, BC F/4/1406 (55521) fo. 201; Reynolds, 'Notes' p. 205.

Rumal described Reynolds, 'Notes' p. 206; for vocabulary, see van Woerkens, op. cit. p. 300; for its recent introduction see the *Calcutta Gazette*, 7 Oct. 1830, reprinted in Anil Chandra Das Gupta (ed.) *The Days of John Company* p. 584. In 1829, Poorun, an old Hindu Thug, told one Captain Borthwick: 'I have never seen the *phansy* or noose made of chord used, though I am well aware of the general supposition that it is by such an implement that people are strangled by us, but if such an implement has ever been in general use, of which I have great doubt, it has long since been laid aside for the obvious reason that, on any incidental occasion of being seized, it would inevitably lead to detection.' 'Deposition of Poorun Phansygur', n.d. (1829), *Sel.Rec.* p. 31.

. . . *difficult to master* . . . Smith to Swinton, 25 June 1832, BC F/4/1406 (55521) fo. 207.

Best technique Reynolds, op. cit. p. 206. On the importance of silence, see Paton papers, 41300, fo. 10.

'*In how short a time*' Paton papers fos. 53–6.

'*Such is the certainty* . . .' Reynolds, op. cit. p. 206.

. . . *strike in the evening* . . . 'Deposition of Poorun Phansygur', *Sel.Rec.* 31–4; Deposition of Kaimraj Phansygur', n.d. [1829], p. 23.

'*And in this state*' *Ramaseeana* I, 93.

'*Into whatever part* . . .' Deposition of Kalee Khan, 1810, Add.Mss. 5375 fos. 125–9, CUL.

Stamping and kicking Richard Sherwood, 'Of the murderers called Phansigars', *Asiatick Researches* 13 (1820) pp. 250–82; Henry Spry, op. cit. p. 514.

Stabbing Paton papers fo. 14v.

Leaded ropes This, according to Sleeman, was the weapon preferred by the Chinguree, a group of Muslim Thugs. *Ramaseeana* I, 85.

'*Kill like banditti*' Stockwell to Perry, 11 Aug. 1815, in *Ramaseeana* II, 373.

Dhotis used to strangle Ibid. II, 324; Thornton, op. cit. p. 298. 'The professed ones strangled with any part of their clothes,' added Perry's witness Ghoolam Hossyn. 'They do not make use of chords for fear of detection.' 'Translation of the acknowledgement of Ghoolam Hossyn Thug made before me on the 11th April 1810', Add.Mss. 5375 fos. 117–22.

'*Fists and elbows*' Thornton, op. cit. p. 410.

Shot Bevan, op. cit. I, 258.

Datura Ernst to Shakespear, 12 May 1810, BC F/4/411 (10204) fos. 238, 240; Extract Bengal Judicial Consultation No. 25, 24 Nov. 1810, ibid. (10205) fo. 172; 'Extract from a general letter from Hon'ble the Court of Directors', 6 Apr. 1830, *Sel.Rec.* p. 1; Robert Russell and Hira Lal, *The Tribes and Castes of the Central Provinces of India* IV, 572; Ishwar Sahai, 'The crime of thagi and its suppression under Lord WC Bentinck', part 1, *Indian Culture* 3 (1936) p. 325.

'*Mere novices*' Translation of the acknowledgement of Ghoolam Hossyn Thug made before me on the 11th April 1810', Add.Mss. 5375 fos. 117–22, CUL.

Swords used until the early nineteenth century 'Men who associated to rob travellers could travel with arms and in large numbers without arousing suspicion,' Radhika Singha observes of this period. 'They could use a greater measure of open violence and take fewer precautions over the disposal of bodies.' Singha, op. cit. pp. 185–6n, 199.

. . . *sharpened sword* . . . 'Habits and character of the Thugs', Political letter from Bengal No. 86, 21 Oct. 1820, BC F/4/774 (20927) fos. 22–6.

Examples of the use of swords 'Translation of the examination of Gholam Hossyn . . .', Mar. 1810, ibid. fos. 105–9; 'Translation of the examination of Shuhadul . . .', 16 May 1810, ibid. fos. 138v–42; 'Continuation of Trial No. 23 of 1836', BC F/4/1898 (80684) fos. 140–1; *Ramaseeana* I, 232, 243; Thornton, op. cit. p. 13.

Changing conditions for the use of swords Singha, op. cit. pp. 185, 199; Thornton, op. cit. p. 376.

Only two swords, or perhaps three 'Deposition of Poorun Phansigar', n.d. [1829], *Sel.Rec.* 32.

. . . sepoys favoured . . . Smith to Swinton, 20 June 1832, BC F/4/1406 (55521) fo. 173.

Disposing of bodies See *Ramaseeana* I, 131; van Woerkens, op. cit. pp. 122–5; Bevan, op. cit. I, 258–9. For an example of a grave prepared in advance, see Paton papers fo. 14v; Smith to Governor General, 12 Mar. 1833, T&D G1, NAI. For instances of bodies concealed and then buried later, see 'Deposition of Bheelum Burre Khan, Jemadar of Thugs', n.d., T&D D2/2, NAI; Thornton, op. cit. p. 187. For instances of bodies exhumed by animals, see 'Trial No. 12 of 1832: Nayahshahar case', BC F/4/1490 (58672) fos. 261–3; Thornton, op. cit. pp. 195–6. The care taken by some gangs to dispose of their victims, and the consequent difficulty in detecting their crimes, was noted in Madras as early as 1812; see 'Extract of a letter from the Magistrate of Chittoor to the Secretary to Government in the Judicial Department', 1 July 1812, in *Ramaseeana* II, 307.

. . . abandoned where they fell . . . During the cold season of 1829–30, the bodies of six men were found lying on the ground near a tank in Saugor & Nerbudda. They had been stripped naked and clearly bore the marks of strangulation on their necks. Nicholson to Sleeman, 10 Dec. 1829, BC F/4/1251 (50480/2) fo. 501. See also Deposition of Narooha Kumusdar, 5 Nov. 1831, cited by Thornton, op. cit. pp. 127–9.

'In these chosen spots' Thornton, op. cit. p. 9. Again, no one method was used throughout India. One gang of Deccan stranglers, noted by Bevan, op. cit. I, 72, buried their victims 'in an upright position, by doubling up the legs'.

'slightly buried' '12th or Deo Huttee Case', BC F/4/404 (55517) fo. 346; also 'Trial No. 7 of 1832: Mahsum Ali case', F/4/1490 (58671) fos. 95–6, 'Case No. 18, Jubulpoor sessions 1830', F/4/1685 (67999) fos. 52–3, and others far too numerous to list.

Thug method of burial distasteful Cf. Theon Wilkinson, *Two Monsoons* pp. 180, 215.

. . . concealed under piles of stones . . . Depositions of Heurea, 26 Apr. + 23 July 1830, BC F/4/1251 (50480/2) fos. 450–51, 481; '11th or Kundee and Juppa Case', BC F/4/1404 (55517) fo. 269.

ravines and cliffs 'Trial No. 9 of 1832: Barwaha Ghat Case', BC F/4/1490 (58671) fo. 407; Thomas Bacon, *First Impressions and Studies from Nature in Hindustan* II, 409.

'. . . where the ground is stony' Evidence of Sheeodeen, dialogue of 26 Apr. 1837, Paton papers fo. 66.

Cook and eat Evidence of Futteh Khan, ibid.

Villagers dispose of bodies Ibid. fo. 24. On blame placed on tigers see 'Deposition of Bhujda Bheel' in Smith to Prinsep, 19 Nov. 1830, *Sel.Rec.* 36; *Ramaseeana* I, 22–3.

Bodies recovered from wells 'Comparative statement of murdered bodies found on the High Roads and in the wells in the zillah of Etawah in the years 1808, 1809 and during the 12 months from the date on which the first Gang of Thugs was apprehended,' Add.Mss. 5376 fos. 8–8v.

Animal carcasses in wells Sleeman, *Ramaseeana* II, 275.

'We change the wells' Paton papers fo. 28.

7 Feringeea

Feringeea's birth Sleeman, *Ramaseeana* I, 175. On the date, see Feringeea's age (then 33) in the table 'Approvers in this case' in Sleeman to Smith, Sangea 1833, T&D G1 fo. 246, NAI. In addition to the assaults conducted by Blake Sahib and Jacob Sahib, referred to above,

Sindouse had already been burned to the ground at least once, by the Rana of Gohud, during the last quarter of the eighteenth century, according to the evidence of the Thug Thukoree in *Ramaseeana* I, 224. The Rana's motive was, as usual, the desire to impose taxes on the people of the pargana.

Feringeea's family Ibid. I, 165, 173, 223–5; Iftikhar Ahmad, *Thugs, Dacoits and the Modern World-System in Nineteenth-Century India* p. 86. Feringeea's family tree, as compiled by Sleeman, is reprinted by Martine van Woerkens, *The Strangled Traveller* pp. 140–1.

Brahmins Nicholas Dirks's recent *Castes of Mind* observes (pp. 116–17, 251–4) that caste may not originally have been the immutable, hereditary denominator it has since become, being in many cases based as much on local social politics as the exhortations of religious texts. He also suggests that the Brahmins, as the Company's main source of information on Indian society, exaggerated their own importance and role in pre-colonial India.

'every male . . .' This proud claim was not strictly true; one of Purusram's grandsons was described by the British as merely a pickpocket. Sleeman to Principal Assistant, Nursingpore, 5 Dec. 1832, T&D G1 fo. 169, NAI.

Death of Purusram See genealogical table in Sleeman, *Ramaseeana* I, facing p. 270.

Boys of eight or nine years Ibid. I, 148.

'Fathers are glad . . .' 'Dialogues with Thugs', Paton papers Add.Mss. 41300 fo. 22.

Nephew collapses in shock Sleeman, *Ramaseeana* I, 149–50.

'a father does not initiate . . .' Paton papers fo. 23.

Gurus Ibid.; 'Extract from the examination of Koshal prisoner', BC F/4/411 (10204) fo. 315; George Bruce *The Stranglers* pp. 56–7.

Initiation and the first rumal 'Deposition of Poorun Phansygur', 1829, Sel.Rec. 34.

'. . . fatal goor . . .' Sleeman, *Ramaseeana* I, 138, 216–17; HV Russell and Hira Lal, *Tribes and Castes of the Central Provinces of India* IV, 577; Stewart Gordon, 'Sword and scarf' pp. 414–15.

Elephant keeper Edward Thornton, *Illustrations of the History and Practices of the Thugs* p. 346.

Adoptive children Translation of the acknowledgement of Ghoolam Hossyn Thug made before me on the 11th April 1810' in Perry papers Add.Mss. 5375 fos. 117–22, CUL.

Thug women Thuggee was an almost exclusively male profession. There are no more than a handful of references to women serving in any capacity with Thug gangs; see JAR Stevenson, 'Some account of the P'hansigars . . .' *Journal of the Royal Asiatic Society* I, 281–2. Sleeman spoke to a Thug woman, Moosmp, who had assumed the title of jemadar alongside her husband. She was then in jail in Delhi for the murder of three families, but insisted that she had never participated directly in any murder: 'The female Thugs are only employed in taking charge of the children of the murdered people.' James Sleeman, *Thug* pp. 152–3.

'slaves' BC F/4/1251 (50480/2) fo. 579, OIOC.

'Almost one in 10 . . .' Based on an analysis of Sleeman's Thug genealogies, *Ramaseeana* I, 270–1.

Punchum Jemadar Sleeman, *Ramaseeana* I, 173–4; Thornton, *Illustrations* pp. 182–4.

Thugs and heredity For examples, see Sleeman's Thug genealogies, loc. cit; Thornton, op. cit. p. 236.

Not all children of Thugs take up Thuggee Cf. Sleeman, *Ramaseeana* I, 266.

Aseel Thugs Sleeman, *Ramaseeana* I, 158.

All gangs contained some men who were related van Woerkens, op. cit. pp. 139–42.

Gang of 1829 Sleeman to Smith, 12 Mar. 1833, T&D G/1, NAI. These men were members of the gang led by Sheikh Inaent, himself the son of a noted Thug leader. See chapters 12 and 13.

Burkas Sleeman, *Ramaseeana* I, 67–140.

Feringeea's first expeditions For 1813, see Case 40, Jubbulpore sessions of 1830, BC F/4/1689 (6799) fos. 108–9. For 1816, see deposition of Feringeea, 'Trial no. 11 of 1832: Deonagar case', BC F/4/1490 (58672) fos. 165–7.

Four Indians in every 10 Bayly, *Rulers* pp. 51–3.

'The castes to be met with . . .' van Woerkens, op. cit. pp. 129–31.

Thugs adopt high-caste disguise Ibid.

Feringeea as jemadar Sleeman, *Rambles & Recollections* I, 96–8.

Youthful appearance Sleeman to Smith, 7 Jan. 1831, Consultation No. 11 of 18 Mar. 1831, BPC P/126/27, OIOC.

Feringeea as subadar Sleeman, *Ramaseeana* I, 216.

Sujaina murders Sleeman, *Rambles & Recollections* I, 96.

Military service and Ochterlony Sleeman, *Ramaseeana* I, 235–7.

Feringeea's time in Rajpootana Ibid. I, 66, 234.

Ramzan 'Deposition of Rumzan, a noted Thug . . .', 20 Apr. 1837, Paton papers fo. 122v, BL. Suntoke Rae, son of Laljee, the zamindar of Sindhouse, noted that the Thugs of the Chambel Valley 'never returned in less than six months, and if they were unsuccessful, they sometimes remained absent two years'. Thornton, op. cit. p. 473.

Murder of the Mughulanee Sleeman, *Ramaseeana* I, 166, 206, 212–16; Thornton, op. cit. pp. 265–70.

. . . more attention . . . Based on the amount of space Sleeman devoted to the case in his works. As van Woerkens observes, he was particularly fascinated by murders involving young and pretty girls, displaying less interest in, or empathy for, older or ugly women.

'The Rule of the bones' Smith to Swinton, 20 June 1832, *Sel.Rec.* 124.

Proscriptions Sleeman, *Ramaseeana* I, 133, 181–2. Robert Russell and Hira Lal, *The Tribes and Castes of the Central Provinces of India*, pp. 580–2, provide a recapitulation and an explanatory commentary.

'These, God has afflicted . . .' Paton papers fo. 12v. See also van Woerkens, op. cit. pp. 110–11. It is interesting to note that the Thug laws and proscriptions did not apply in reverse, for there were no restrictions on maimed Thugs serving with the gangs. 'The case of Kehree,' FC Smith observed after the trial of one Thug gang in 1830, 'is in point. As a boy he had a hand cut off on conviction of belonging to a Thug association, he witnessed the appalling exhibition of his confederates being blown away from Guns, but so far from abandoning this dangerous profession, he is now, in his old age, condemned to death for the same description of crime he was punished for so severely in his youth.' Smith to Prinsep, 19 Nov. 1830, *Sel.Rec.* 54. Most remarkably of all, Bodhoo Jemadar, who had had his nose and both his hands amputated on the orders of the Rajah of Jhalone, returned to his gang even though he could hardly have hoped to resume his work as an inveigler. This was, perhaps, a special case (Bodhoo was, in Feringeea's words, 'a Thug of great repute: for sagacity we have never seen his equal: people who had been robbed used to go to him as an oracle'), but evidently even severe mutilations were not sufficient, in themselves, to prevent a longstanding member of a gang from returning to serve with his old comrades. *Ramaseeana* I, 245; Thornton, op. cit. pp. 207–8.

Temptations to break proscriptions It is evident, from the Thugs' own depositions, that at least some of these decisions were entirely pragmatic, and based on a shrewd calculation as to the likely profit to be made from a given murder. Thugs were occasionally known to decoy away potential victims whose poverty meant that they were not worth killing, even though they were not members of the proscribed groups and castes. Sleeman once related the case of a party of 25 Muslim Thugs who were travelling north from Jubbulpore: 'While they were at dinner, five travellers came up on their way to Bandah, two of them carriers of Ganges water, two tailors and a native woman. They rested a little while with the gang at the well and as soon as the Thugs were ready they all proceeded together to Shahnagar, where they all passed the night, and the next day went on together towards Beseynee, where they fell in with two other travellers on their way to Bandah. They appeared to be so poor that the Gang wished to separate them from the other five as their murder promised no advantage, and their presence might offer some obstacle to their attempts upon the others. They at first attempted to persuade them to remain when they were about to set out with the five travellers, after the third watch, but finding them obstinate they placed them with four Thugs who led them on the direct road while the main body diverged upon a byroad by which they usually took their victims. But they had not gone far before they became alarmed at being separated from the main body and insisted upon rejoining them, to which the four Thugs reluctantly agreed, and they soon overtook them on the byroad. As soon as they came up, it was determined to put them to death, and six of the gang were ordered to attend them for the purpose and move on a little ahead of the main body. They went on while the main body slackened their pace, and on reaching the nullah where the five men were to have been murdered, they strangled them and concealed their bodies till the main body came up, when the other five were strangled and the bodies of the whole seven were buried under stones . . . From the first two they got only one rupee, but from the other five they acquired property to the value of about 200 rupees.' Sleeman to Smith, 12 Mar. 1833, T&D G1, NAI.

'Horribly dangerous' See, for example, *Ramaseeana* I, 179.

Breaking of proscriptions a recent development Thornton, op. cit. p. 27.

Punchum and Himmut Sleeman, *Ramaseeana* I, 173–4; Thornton, op. cit. pp. 99, 182–4. Punchum was Feringeea's uncle on his mother's side.

Death of Himmut Ibid. I, 174.

Murder of the Kale Bebee Ibid. I, 164–5, 174–5; Thornton, op. cit. pp. 181–2.

Lack of scruple of Hindustani Thugs Sleeman, *Ramaseeana* I, 164, 166, 171, 173–4,

Refusal of Bengal and Bihar Thugs to kill women 'Do you Behar Thugs ever murder women?' Sleeman asked a group of captured stranglers in 1835. 'Never,' came the answer, 'we should not murder a woman if she had a lakh of rupees upon her.' To which a man from the Doab rejoined: 'Nor would the Dooab Thugs if she had two lakhs upon her.' Ibid. I, 171, 180.

'Some were sufficiently religious' 'We had,' Feringeea's associate Zolfukar observed, looking back on the early years of the nineteenth century after his capture in 1830, 'then some regard for religion. We have lost it since. All kinds of men have been made Thugs, and all classes of people murdered without distinction; and little attention has been paid to omens. How, after this, could we expect to escape?' Thornton, op. cit. p. 102.

'Among us, it is a rule . . .' Ibid. p. 27.

Jubber Paton papers fos. 120v–121v. For equivalent cases, see also *Ramaseeana* I, 143, 174.

'The love of money makes us kill them' Paton papers fo. 12. Bevan, in *Thirty Years in India* I, 260, tells of one Thug who, whenever he was drunk, 'would hiccough out repentance for his crimes'.

'a very handsome youth . . .' Evidence of Sheodeen, ibid. fos. 17–17v.

The Peshwa's handmaid Sleeman, *Ramaseeana* I, 166.

Arrest at Kotah Ibid. I, 177.

Murder of Newul Singh '21st or Busuynee Case', BC F/4/1406 (55520) fol. 177–333; '25th or Chuparah case', BC F/4/1406 (55521) fol. 3; 'Case no. 52 in sessions of 1830', BC F/4/1685 (67999) fos. 106–7; *Sel.Rec.* pp. 86–7; *Ramaseeana* I, 166–9.

Increase in burials Based on the author's analysis of 1,459 Thug murders dating from 1790–1839 reported in *Sel.Rec.*; Sleeman's *Ramaseeana, Rambles and Recollections* and *Depredations*; Thornton's *Illustrations*; and Spry's 'Some account of the gang murderers of Central India'.

Feringeea's precautions 'Trial no. 11 of 1832, Deonagar case', BC F/4/1490 (58672) fos. 105–252; 'Trial no. 12 of 1832, Nayahshahar case', ibid. fos. 253–346.

'Where the ground is soft . . .' Thornton, op. cit. p. 9.

Varying locations for murder See the 'Deposition of Kaimraj Phansygur', n.d. [1829], *Sel.Rec.* 19–27 for descriptions of a wide variety of murder spots.

Temple of Kamptee Sleeman to Smith, 31 January 1832, BC F/4/1406 (55520) fos. 248–55.

Mango groves and orchards Sleeman, *Rambles and Recollections* pp. 80–2; Christopher Bayly, *Rulers, Townsmen and Bazaars* p. 43; DEU Baker, *Colonialism in an Indian Hinterland* p. 28. The groves, notes Bayly, 'played an important part in the rural economy of some districts, where they accounted for as much as 5 per cent of the total cultivated acreage and provided a significant source of income for the landholders'.

Matabur beles Sleeman, *Ramaseeana* I, 243n; Paton Papers fol. 123.

High ground 'A letter explaining how Thugs selected spots for the murder of their victims', 1 Dec 1837, T&D E / 1, NAI.

'The Thugs speak of such places . . .' Thornton, op. cit. p. 9.

Kali venerated by many classes Russell and Lal, *Tribes & Castes* IV, 575.

Pickaxe consecration Ibid. IV, 574; Sleeman, *Ramaseeana* I, 155, 176; II, 304; Reynolds, *Notes* p. 204; George Bruce, *The Stranglers* pp. 60–2.

8 Sleeman

Stratton and Sleeman's youth Francis Tuker, *The Yellow Scarf: The Story of the Life of Thuggee Sleeman* pp. 3–9.

Recruitment to the East India Company and education of officers BS Cohn, 'Recruitment and training of British civil servants in India, 1600–1860', in Ralph Braibanti (ed.), *Asian Bureaucratic Systems Emergent from the British Imperial Tradition* pp. 102–24; BB Misra, *The Central Administration of the East India Company, 1773–1834* pp. 388–408; Suresh Chandra Ghosh, *The Social Condition of the British Community in Bengal, 1757–1800* pp. 16, 31–3, 43, 149; Philip Mason, *A Matter of Honour* pp. 169, 179; James, *Raj* p. 130.

Illness and mortality Wilkinson, *Two Monsoons* pp. 1–13, 45, 172–3, 180; Kincaid, *British Social Life in India* pp. xii, 37, 46; Mason, op. cit. pp. 86, 174.

Indian climate Vernede (ed.), *British Life in India . . . 1750–1947* pp. 72–5; Ghosh, op. cit. pp. 102–4; AC Newcombe, *Village, Town and Jungle Life in India* pp. 77–8, 121–2.

Calcutta in 1809 Dalrymple, *White Mughals* pp. 407–13; Kincaid, op. cit. pp. 90, 96–7, 140; Ghosh, op. cit. pp. 150–2.

Griffins Mason, op. cit. p. 175; Tuker, op. cit. p. 11.

Servants Kincaid, op. cit. p. 131; Vernede, op. cit. pp. 96–7, 104–6; Hilton Brown, *The Sahibs* pp. 210, 212; James, *Raj* p. 160, 168; Ghosh, op. cit. p. 109.

'I inquired whether the cat . . .' Cited by Brown, op. cit. p. 212.

Hookah The famous 'hubble-bubble' pipe so characteristic of eighteenth-century India. Probably because of its 'native' connotations, it fell into disuse shortly after Sleeman's arrival, and was supplanted by the cheroot.

Marriage Ghosh, op. cit. pp. 60–71; Kincaid, op. cit. pp. 164, 166–7; Mason, op. cit. p. 176; Brown, op. cit. p, 146. On the relative attractiveness of the women of the 'fishing fleet', see Fanny Eden's comments in Dunbar, *Tigers, Durbars and Kings* p. 75: 'It was a very remarkable ball owing to the extraordinary plainness – to use a light expression – of the ladies there, 20 altogether. One was pointed out with great pride as 'our only unmarried lady': that fact was not the only remarkable thing about her. She was of that hue generally denominated orange 'tawny', in a bright strawberry pink gown, one yard wide, the sort of drawn-up features which allow a view of the back of the skull, and an embroidered bag hanging over her arm while she danced.'

Daily round Kincaid, op. cit. pp. 96–7, 177–8.

Food and drink Ibid. pp. 98–9, 160; Brown, op. cit. pp. 49, 51; Ghosh, op. cit. pp. 122, 162; Wilkinson, op. cit. p. 180.

Increasing insularity of the British community Kincaid, op. cit. pp. xviii, 129, 166; Dalrymple, op. cit. p. 409; Vernede, op. cit. p. 25.

Sleeman's character, appearance and early career Tuker, op. cit. pp. 15–23, 37; PD Reeves (ed.), *Sleeman in Oudh* pp. 9–12, 14–15, 27, 30; Martine van Woerkens, *The Strangled Traveller* pp. 190–6, 201–34.

'probably the only British official . . .' Christopher Bayly, *Empire and Information* p. 75.

Civil administration Michael Edwardes, *The Sahibs and the Lotus* pp. 59–60; Meadows Taylor, *The Story of My Life* I, 265–6; Wilkinson, op. cit. p. 72; Brown, op. cit. p. 128; Amal Chatterjee, *Representation of India 1740–1840* p. 74.

'were almost invariably high-handed . . .' Edwardes, op. cit. p. 60.

'The Heaven Born' Verende, op. cit. p. 10.

Jubbulpore AE Nelson, *Central Provinces District Gazetteers: Jubbulpore District*, James Forsyth, *The Highlands of Central India* pp. 311 15.

Freebooters Philip McEldowney, *Pindari Society and the Establishment of British Paramountcy in India*; idem, 'A brief study of the Pindaris of Madhya Pradesh', *The Indian Cultures Quarterly* 27 (1971) pp. 55–70; GL Corbett and RV Russell, *Central Provinces District Gazetteers: Hoshangabad District* pp. 32–3; *Imperial Gazetteer of India, Provincial Series: Central India* pp. 23–4; Gordon, *The Marathas* pp. 114–15; Mason, op. cit. pp. 136–7; Edwardes, op. cit. pp. 60–62; Radhika Singha, *A Despotism of Law* pp. 177–8.

Insects Newcombe, op. cit. pp. 100, 103.

Thermantidotes Vernede, op. cit. p. 74.

Nursingpore RV Russell, *Central Provinces District Gazetteers: Narshingpur District* pp. 2–5, 27, 30, 70–83, 223–4; Crispin Bates, 'Class and economic change in central India: the Narmada Valley, 1820–1930', in CJ Dewey (ed.), *Arrested Development in India: The Historical Perspective* pp. 241–2.

'disastrous failure' Russell, op. cit. p. 28.

'by far the most laborious . . .' George Bruce, *The Stranglers* p. 36.

Thugs arrested in the Nerbudda valley These were the members of the Lucknadown gang, responsible for the death of Bunda Ali, and betrayed by a particularly unpleasant informant by the name of Motee. It is a complicated story, too convoluted to unravel here, and although a prompt trial of the Lucknadown gang in 1823–4 might conceivably have led the British authorities to take earlier action against the gangs, in the end the arrests led nowhere. Molony died before the case could be brought before the courts, his successor lasted no more than a few months, and in the general confusion the Lucknadown Thugs were forgotten until 1830–31. 'Disposal of several ring leaders of Thug gangs in Bundelcund', BC F/4/984 (27697) fos. 2–3; Consultation No. 27 of 25 July 1831, BPC P/126/26; 'Evidence of Motee', BC F/4/1309 (52131) fos. 296–300; Ravenshaw and Marjoribanks (Directors of the East India Company) to Bentinck (Governor General), 28 Nov. 1832, BC F/4/1483 (55514) fos. 19–26.

Thugs in Nursingpore Sleeman, *Ramaseeana* I, 32–3.

9 'A Very Good Remuneration for Murdering a Man'

Killing of stone-cutters at Baroda 'Deposition of Amanoolah Phansygur', n.d. [1829] and 'Deposition of Kaimraj Phansygur', n.d. [1829], *Sel.Rec.* 15–27.

Thugs' spend on weddings Sleeman, *Ramaseeana*, I, 173–4.

Baroda gang's loot 'Deposition of Amanoolah Phansygur', n.d. [1829], *Sel.Rec.* 15–26.

. . . a Thug who carefully listed . . . 'Deposition of Sheikh Dawood Newly', 24 Nov. 1834, T&D D2 No. 1, NAI.

Thug expenses 'Examination of Thug approver Rama Jemadar No. 1', 1832, *Sel.Rec.* 136. 'In general,' Rama concluded, 'with regard to booty acquired by myself and others, we used on our return from any excursion to dispose of it to *bunnyahs* or to give it to them in liquidation of debts.' Ibid. p. 137. From this it would appear that some Thug expeditions actually ran at a loss. It was, in any case, relatively rare for the members of the gangs to put much money aside. 'Their life,' considered FC Smith, 'is a life of pleasure; but their prosperity is evanescent. They are in a great degree during their expeditions free from the trammels of caste, and live on the fat of the land; but their wealth seldom remains with them long, being either, consumed on the spot, or expended in bribing the Jumeendars, under whose protection they reside or the authorities who connive at their atrocities or in purchasing their relief from bondage.' FC Smith, 'Report on the Sessions of 1831–32', 20 June 1832, *Sel.Rec.* p. 120. 'Thugs,' added Sleeman, 'were known to spend what they got freely, and never to have money by them.' *Rambles and Recollections* I, 108.

Loitering at customs posts See Reynolds, 'Notes on the T'hags' p. 207.

Those with no money would sometimes be spared Cf. *Ramaseeana* I, 233.

Mutilation of corpses Edward Thornton, *Illustrations of the History and Practices of the Thugs* p. 10.

'trifling' and 'paltry' 'Examination of Thug approver Mana No. 4', 1832, *Sel.Rec.* 153; Thornton, op. cit. p. 218.

. . . eight annas . . . 'two pice' Deposition of Shumsheera before the Zillah court at Benares, June–July 1833, cited by Thornton, op. cit. p. 125. 'The chance is that every man has a rupee or two about him in money or cloths,' the magistrate of Chittoor, William Wright, had noted in 1812, 'and with them the most trifling sum is a sufficient inducement to commit murder.' Wright to Secretary of Government, 1 July 1812, *Ramaseeana* II, 308–9. In 1810, Thomas Perry had interrogated a Thug named Shuhadul, who confessed to murdering one man for a share amounting to only 12 annas. This, he added, was an unusually low amount – but certainly not hugely so:

Q Did you ever receive less than 12 annas for a murder?
A Never. I have generally received 4 or 8 annas more.

[in other words, a share of Rs.1 to Rs.1–4–0]. 'Translation of the examination of Shuhadul taken before the acting magistrate on the 16th of May 1810', Perry papers, Add.Mss. 5375 fos. 138–42, CUL. A quarter of a century later, the approvers Aliyer and Dhoosoo, two of Paton's informants, were questioned along the same lines:

Q If a gang of four Thugs met a traveller at a convenient place, but knew that he had only one roopee on him, would they strangle him for that roopee?
A We never would murder for a roopee.
A If we expected eight annas each, we would murder him.

. . . the enormous sum of 200,000 rupees . . . Sleeman, *Ramaseeana* I, 189.

Jhora Naek Ibid. I, 99. The servant's name is sometimes given as Koduk Bunwaree; see James Sleeman, *Thug* p. 35.

Rae Singh's deceit Ramaseeana I, 224–6.

. . . one other group of Thugs . . . This incident occurred in the Deccan in 1816. John Malcolm, *A Memoir of Central India* II, 189.

Sixty Soul Affair Sleeman, *Ramaseeana* I, 164–5, James Sleeman, *Thug* pp. 83–5.

Murder of Forty The actual number of victims was 39, as a little girl was preserved and married to a nephew of the jemadar of Thugs. Her story was particularly wrenching, and may stand for those of all the children spared and brought up by the stranglers. The child's known relatives were all killed in the affair, and it was not until 1834 that Sleeman's men traced her, now a woman in her late 20s, still living among the Thugs. 'My mother and father resided in some town in the Deccan,' she deposed. 'Their names I do not recollect as I was only three or four years of age when my uncle and mother took me with them on a journey towards the Ganges. On the road, my mother and uncle were killed, by Thugs, with many other travellers. Kasal Singh Putuck Jemadar preserved my life and took me with him to Pahlun in Gwalior, where he brought me up; and when I became of age he married me to his son, Hunce Rao, who is now dead. As long as he lived, I lived with him; but he has been dead several years, and I have since lived with his mother, and earned my subsistence by my labour. Your sepahees found me out, and have brought me into Saugor. I had two sons by Hunce Rao; the first died when 15 months old; the other is eight or nine years of age and . . . is in Khyrawa in Jhansee with his grandmother. I was the only member of the party saved. There is now no Thug left in the family of Hunce Rao who can provide for me. If you will maintain me, I shall be glad to remain here; but I have never heard whether my parents had any surviving relations or not.' Cited by Thornton, op. cit. pp. 178–84.

Economic depression DEU Baker, *Colonialism in an Indian Hinterland* pp. 51, 55.

History of the Indian opium trade Janin, *The India–China Opium Trade in the Nineteenth Century* pp. 5–41; Farooqui, *Smuggling as Subversion* pp. 3–24, 60–3.

Opium-eating Thomas de Quincey (1785–1859), an essayist and a friend of Coleridge, became addicted to opium at Oxford University. His *Confessions of an English Opium-Eater* first appeared in 1821 and was a considerable success.

Malwa opium Farooqui, op. cit. pp. 41, 95, 115–20, 142–8, 153. Malwa opium was considered superior to the Bengali product, as it yielded smokers at least eight per cent more extract from balls of identical weight. Ibid. p. 72.

Thugs steal opium 'Deposition of Kaimraj Phansygur . . .', 1829, *Sel. Rec.* p. 23.

Indian banking LC Jain, *Indigenous Banking in India* pp. 5–45; NK Sinha, *The Economic History of Bengal*, I, 74–6, 80, 86. The quotations from Tavenier are cited by Jain, op. cit. pp. 11–14.

'this bank . . .' Anna Leonowens, *Life and Travel in India* pp. 225–6.

. . . invariably family concerns . . . Karen Leonard, 'Banking firms in nineteenth-century Hyderabad politics', *Modern Asian Studies* 15 (1981) pp. 180–1.

Hoondees Leonowens, op. cit. p. 226.

Thugs burn hoondees Cf. deposition of Amannoolah Phansygur, 1829, *Sel.Rec.* p. 17; Thornton, op. cit. p. 343.

Cash transfers and the opium trade FC Smith, 'Report on the sessions of 1831–32', 20 June 1832, *Sel.Rec.* 104–26, para 9; Farooqui, op. cit. p. 41; WH Carey, *The Good Old Days of John Company*, II, 249. There does not seem to be any evidence to support recent contentions that the anti-Thug campaign was actually motivated by the Company's desire to protect its lucrative opium trade; indeed, in so far as the Thugs' main victims were bankers and dealers operating in defiance of British attempts to impose a monopoly on the drug, it could be argued that the gangs' activities actually benefited the Bombay Presidency.

Increasing quantities Sleeman also notes the bankers' habit of sending 'remittances in precious metals and jewels' all over India 'whenever the exchange rate makes it in the smallest degree profitable'. *Ramaseeana* I, iv.

Favourable exchange rates Iftikhar Ahmad, *Thugs, Dacoits and the Modern World-System in Nineteenth-Century India* p. 96.

Dependability of treasure-bearers Sleeman, *Ramaseeana* I, 5.

'nothing but naked bodies . . .' Sleeman, *Rambles & Recollections* I, 98.

Jhansee Ghat '18th, Jhansi Ghat case', BC F/4/1405 (55519); '21st, or Basaini Case', BC F/4/1406 (55520); *Ramaseeana* II, 138.

. . . a group of Deccan Thugs . . . This crime was committed by the notorious Arcottee Thugs, and is set out by Sleeman in *Depredations* pp. xi, xii.

The case of the filthy fakir Ibid. pp. 23–4.

Gomashtas are 'invested . . .' Cited in Jain, op. cit. p. 36.

10 The Devil's Banker

Tapti river affair Statements of Dhunraj Seth, n.d.? 1831, cited by Thornton, *Illustrations of the History and Practices of the Thugs* pp. 134, 135–6; '5th or Chaupura affair', BC F/4/1685 (67999), with a summary on fos. 94–5; for Budloo Jemadar, see BC F/4/1404 (55516) fo. 71. A second treasure party fell foul of the Thugs in the same year, this time in the Deccan, where 20,000 rupees' worth of cash and gold was seized by a gang of 30 Thugs, hand-picked from among the most practised killers of several different gangs, who had pursued their quarry across 36 miles of country. 'Deposition of Amanoolah Phansygur . . .' n.d. [1829], *Sel.Rec.* 18–19.

Malagow affair The treasure in this case consisted of '13 seers of gold, with several golden necklaces, 900 golden coins, 17 gold mohurs and several bars of gold'. The cotton-cleaners had a further three rupees, and the messenger a pair of silver armlets valued at 14 rupees. Feringea's depositions, which include these details, can be found in BC F/4/1403 (55515) fos. 169–71 and BC F/4/1404 (55516) fos. 63–4. These two files give the same case different names – it is variously referred to as the '6th Dhulia Malagow' case and the '7th, Dhoree Cote' affair, but although the witnesses tell the story from different perspectives, and the total of loot taken varies by Rs.10,000, it is clear from the similarities in their evidence – notably the detail that two cotton-cleaners and a dawk carrier were among the victims – that the affairs are identical. The difference in the quantity of loot mentioned can also be accounted for; one party counted the Rs.10,000 of jewels found on the bearers, the other only the gold. Yet another account of what must be the same affair, told from a third perspective, can be found in Wellesley to Swinton, 8 Sept. 1830, *Sel.Rec.* 5–7 and statements by Dhunraj Seth, n.d.? 1831, cited by Thornton, op. cit. pp. 134, 135–6. See also Thornton, op. cit. pp. 149–53; *Ramaseeana* I, 192–4; 'Trial No. 14 of 1832: Dhulia Malagow case', BC F/4/1490 (58672) fos. 436–538 contains the evidence in two subsidiary trials of men rounded up after the first cases had been concluded. For the correct date of this affair – January 1828 – see Smith to Macnaghten, 4 Sept. 1833, BC F/4/1490 (58672) fos. 433–6. For the arrest of seven of the murderers, see 'Proceedings of Mr Fraser, Acting Agent in the Saugor and Nurbudda Territories', 4 Nov. 1829, in Sleeman correspondence, SB.

Description of Nasik and Candeish Anon., *Gazetteer of the Bombay Presidency* XII, 1–5, 207, 310–14; XVI, 345–6, 349.

Burwaha Ghat affair '8th Barwaha Gat Case', BC F/4/1404 (55516); 'Trial No. 9 of 1832,' BC F/4/1490 (58671) fos. 405ff; Thornton, op. cit. pp. 127–48; *Ramaseeana* II, 54–69.

. . . more like a highway robbery . . . See also Sleeman's comments on the Sujaina affair of 1814 in *Rambles and Recollections* I, 96–7.

'khomusna' See Sleeman's Thug vocabulary in *Ramaseeana* I, 67–140.

'by regular stages' Deposition of Moklal, n.d., cited by Thornton, op. cit. p. 145.

The Indian police system Radhika Singha, *A Despotism of Law* pp. 1–25; N Majumdar, *Justice and Police in Bengal, 1765–1793* pp. 306–13; BB Misra, *The Central Administration of the East India Company, 1773–1834* pp. 300–308, 332; Chakrabarti, *Authority and Violence* pp. 1–6. The Empire's Muslims were governed by Islamic law, its Hindus by their own code when it came to civil matters and – after the arrival of the Company in Bengal – by their conquerors' law only in criminal cases.

Thanahs The number of thanahs in a district varied widely over time. Misra, op. cit. p. 303, estimated that in the Mughal period most controlled parcels of land perhaps 4 to 10 square miles in extent – equivalent in size to an English parish. But Chakrabarti, op. cit. p. 33, shows that in two Bengal districts, in 1824, there were a mere 31 thanahs scattered among 9,500 villages controlling a total population of more than 3.2 million people – an average of one thanah to more than 300 villages.

Village watchmen Misra, op. cit. p. 304. A second class of village policeman also existed in some communities. These men, who were known as *pashans*, divided their time between collecting taxes and guarding the local fields.

Zamindars' breaches of the law Cf. Chattopadhyay, *Crime and Control* pp. 104–8.

The darogah and the Company's new system of justice Ibid. pp. xiii–xiv, 37, 52–3, 67–8, 78, 87, 89–90, 125, 128–9, 141, 165, 175; Chakrabarti, op. cit. pp. 7, 24–33, 35–46, 59, 61–2, 67, 71, 76, 79, 87–8; Misra, op. cit. pp. 332, 344–50; Basudev Chatterji, 'The darogah and the countryside: the imposition of police control in Bengal and its impact (1793–1837)', *IESHR* 18/1 (1981) pp. 19–42.

Darogah's low pay A further disincentive was the requirement that new darogahs post a security of 1,000 rupees as a guarantee of good behaviour – a sum that was forfeit in the event of dismissal. Chattopadhyay, op. cit. p. 190.

Darogahs' income, nominal and actual Ibid. pp. 165–6.

Can have no local knowledge G Thompson report, October 1806, BCJC 9 Oct. 1806; cited by Chatterji, op. cit. p. 36.

Abuses of this sort . . . Plainly, in these circumstances, the worst catastrophe that could befall any darogah was to police a district where there was little in the way of crime or violence. See Chatterji, op. cit. pp. 26, 33.

Would go to almost any lengths Few robberies ever reached the ears of the local magistrate, Bengal's Superintendent of Police conceded in 1814, because it was 'infinitely preferable to abide by the first loss than to be subjected to the inconvenience and expense attending to a prosecution'. Chatterji, op. cit. p. 35. 'The police invariably settled things with the highest bidder and remained loyal to the richest,' notes Chakrabarti, op. cit. p. 71.

Villagers conceal bodies Chakrabarti, op. cit. pp. 83, 175.

'The police is as dangerous . . .' Kedarnath Datta in *Sachitra Gulzarnagar* (1833), cited by Chattopadhyay, op. cit. p. 163.

Few cases heard Anon., *Gazetteer of the Bombay Presidency* XII pp. 310–12; Singha, op. cit. pp. 173–4, 207.

Dhunraj Seth's bank FC Smith (Agent for Saugor & Nerbudda), 'Report on the sessions of 1831–32', 20 June 1832, *Sel.Rec.* 104–26, paras 25–29; Statements of Dhunraj Seth, n.d.? 1831, cited by Thornton, op. cit. pp. 134, 135–6.

Sindhia's treasury Farooqui, *Smuggling as Subversion* p. 41.

'Some of the bodies . . .' Thornton, op. cit. p. 151.

Deposition of Oda Patel Sleeman, *Ramaseeana* II, 71.

Cubits An ancient measurement, normally said to be based on the length of a man's forearm, but varying, in practice, between 18 and 22 inches.

Recovery of the bodies at Burwaha Ghat Deposition of Narooha Kumusdar, 5 Nov. 1831, cited by Thornton, op. cit. pp. 127–9.

Beharee Lal's involvement with the Thugs This is a rather condensed account of an incident that, in reality, involved a great deal of to-ing and fro-ing between Beharee Lal, Sleeman in Jubbulpore, the Company's Resident at Indore and Agent in Bundelcund, and Holkar. The full story can be found in Sleeman to Fraser (Acting Agent, Bundulcund) 7 Jan. 1830, BC F/4/1251 (50480/2) fo. 597; Sleeman to Smith, 5 Apr. 1830, ibid. fo. 601; deposition of Sleeman's spy, n.d., ibid. fo. 603; Cartwright (Acting Resident, Indore) to Smith, 29 Apr. 1830, ibid. fos. 605–7, who expresses doubts concerning the seth's culpability; and a statement received from the authorities at Indore, n.d., ibid. fos. 607–11; Sleeman to Smith, 13 May 1830, ibid. fos. 422–43. It is not certain whether this Beharee Lal was the same man as the 'rich banker' of that name living in Lucknow in 1819 whose home was attacked by two dacoit gangs, 200 strong, which relieved the seth of treasure valued at 8,000 rupees. See James Hutton, *A Popular Account of the Thugs and Dacoits* pp. 108–9.

. . . 60 per cent . . . FC Smith, 'Report on the Sessions of 1831–32', para 27, 20 June 1832, *Sel.Rec.* 111.

Beharee Lal's Thug tribunal Ibid. See also Smith to Macnaghten, 29 May 1832, ibid. p. 82 for the Agent's views on the unreliability of Indian courts.

'King of Thugs' This was the description applied to Beharee by FC Smith in a letter to EC Revenshaw, Officiating Resident at Hyderabad, 4 Oct. 1830, Appa Sahib & Thuggee papers, SB.

'He got a good deal . . .' Testimony of Moklal, *Ramaseeana* I, 190–1. 'He moves about in state,' Sleeman charged, 'with a few of the Leaders, and whenever one of his numerous Gang is arrested he contrives to get him released under the pretence that he was employed by him

to search for his property, and wherever anyone refuses to share with him his plunder, he manages to get some native chief or public functionary to arrest him.' Sleeman to Smith, 13 May 1830, BC F/4/1251(50480/2) fo.435.

Invalid sergeant Consultation No. 15 of 9 Feb. 1831, BPC P/126/27.

British interest awakened FC Smith, 'Report on the Sessions of 1831–32', para 28, 20 June 1832, *Sel.Rec.* 111; deposition of Dhunraj Seth, n.d., cited in Thornton, p.134.

11 Approvers

Borthwick's Thugs Numerous papers related to this case are gathered in *Sel.Rec.* 10–40.

Syeed Ameer Ali See 'Deposition of Syeed Ameer Allee, jemadar of Thugs, taken before Captain Sleeman from the 14th to the 22nd April 1832 at different times', BC F/4/1406 [55521] fols. 374–464.

'The correspondence that passed' Cf. Stewart (Resident, Gwalior) to Swinton, 12 Aug. 1829, *Sel.Rec.* 11–12.

Lord William Bentinck For the Governor General's personality, see John Rosselli, *Bentinck* pp. 20, 24–5, 31–2, 57, 84, 95 and CH Philips (ed.), *The Correspondence of Lord William Cavendish Bentinck* I, xi–xxv.

Mutiny in Madras Philip Mason, *A Matter of Honour* pp. 236–42.

'A most amiable but imbecile governor' Peter Auber (Secretary to the Court of Directors) to Bentinck, cited in *Correspondence* I, xxii–xxiii.

Bentinck's motives and policies ibid. pp. xiv, xvii; Rosselli, pp. 95, 97, 185, 189–90.

Initiation of the anti Thug campaign Radhika Singha, *A Despotism of Law* pp. 203–04; Sleeman, *Ramaseeana* II, 379–84.

'We are by no means satisfied' 'General letter from the Hon'ble the Court of Directors', 6 Apr. 1830, in Philips, op. cit. I, 426.

Major Wardlow Sleeman, *Ramaseeana* I, 46n.

'The hand of these inhuman monsters' Swinton to Stewart, 23 Oct. 1829, *Sel.Rec.* 12–15.

Circular Fanny Parks, *Wanderings of a Pilgrim in Search of the Picturesque* I, 123–4.

Sleeman's marriage George Bruce, op. cit. pp. 41, 76.

Trial of 1826 Sleeman, *Ramaseeana* I, 46n.

Sleeman's Thugs Smith to Swinton, 5 Jul 1830, *Sel.Rec.* 40–4. Sleeman's attention was also drawn to the Thugs by the discovery of a number of bodies by the men of the 71st Native Infantry near Golegunge on 20 October 1829. Sleeman to Smith, 1833, T&D G/1 fos. 246–9.

Difficulties in convicting Thugs Singha, *A Despotism of Law* p.194.

'In order to make them assent to us . . .' Sleeman to Smith, T&D G/1 fos. 69–70, NAI.

'He shall make in your presence . . .' Smith to Sleeman, 20 Jan. 1831, Sleeman correspondence, SB.

'The mode of proceeding . . .' Anon., 'Ramaseeana', *Foreign Quarterly Review* 21 (1838) p. 29.

'Sent for singly . . .' Ibid.

'Curiously emotionless' Thornton, *Illustrations* pp. 198–200. The approver in this case was Sheikh Inaent; see chapter 12.

'It was on my return . . .' Ibid.

Unreliable approvers Cf. Smith to Swinton, 21 May 1832, BC F/4/1404 [55517] fo. 207; see also T&D G/1 fos. 3,5, 7.

'Thugs will strangle a King's Evidence' 'Dialogues with Thugs', Paton papers Add.Mss. 41300 fo.57v, BL.

'All I require . . .' 'Captain Sherriff's Procedings in 1823, at Jhalna', *Ramaseeana* II, 277.

Confession of Ramzan James Sleeman, *Thug* pp. 129–30.

Thugs encouraged to think they are in service Sleeman, *Ramaseeana* I, 186; Radhika Singha, *A Despotism of Law* p. 184&n.

'*All my enemies now!*' Paton papers fo. 9.

Confession of Futty Khan James Sleeman, op. cit. pp. 130–1.

General warrants Sleeman to Cavendish, 11 June 1832, T&D G/1; Philips, op. cit. II, 947.

'*setting up a dismal yell*' 'Proceedings of a Court of Enquiry . . .', 8 Oct. 1823, *Ramaseeana* II, 275; also ibid. II, 284.

Ruckbur Singh Deposition of Ruckbur Singh, ibid. II, 289–91.

The Cotwal of Sopur Ibid. I, 217–19; II, 141 3.

Case of Humeerchund and the chintz jacket Ibid. I, 64–6n.

'*Few who were in India . . .*' Cited in the introduction to Meadows Taylor, *Confessions of a Thug* pp. xv–xvi.

'*I became very busy*' Meadows Taylor, *The Story of My Life* pp. 112–13.

12 The Omen of the Owl

'*Before the establishment of tranquillity . . .*' 'Deposition of Poorun Phansygur or Thug, Caste Lodha, Age upward of 60 years . . .', n.d. [1829], *Sel.Rec.* 27–8.

'*Homes in Bundelcund*' Feringeea himself was at this time living in the town of Alumpore, in Holkar's territory. Deposition of Huraea, 21 July 1830, BC F/4/1251 (50480/2) fo. 444.

Feringeea's expedition of 1827–8 Sleeman, *Report on the Depredations Committed by the Thug Gangs* pp. 22–7. On Feringeea's short imprisonment, see deposition of Huraea, loc. cit.

Knew most Thug leaders Later British records of Thug depositions feature numerous tables showing which captured Thugs had been recognized by which approver. Feringeea regularly named twice as many suspected stranglers as any other approver, and the column headed by his name was often made twice as wide as those allotted to his fellow jemadars so as to contain the extra information he provided.

Zolfukar This jemadar's name also appears in the British records as Zoolfikar, Zoolfakar and Zoolfakir.

Origins of Sheikh Inaent Sleeman, *Ramaseeana* I, 160; Oliver (Captain, 73rd Native Infantry) to Sleeman, 10 Dec. 1829, BC F/4/1430 (55515) fo. 493. Inaent was born in 1787 or 1788 and had been active since at least 1803; see *Ramaseeana* I, 240 and II, 239–44. In 1829 he was living in the village of Gueara in Jhansee, close to Feringeea's home. Sleeman, *Depredations* p. 50.

disastrous outcome . . . The likelihood that his own finances had become strained is indicated by the fact that he returned to the roads during the hot season of 1830; see below.

Expedition of 1828–9 Depositions of Huraea, 26 Apr., 21+23 July 1830, BC F/4/1251 (50480/2) fos. 443–51; Sleeman, *Depredations* pp. 46–50 and *Ramaseeana* I, 188. The value of the loot taken at Dhoree is not certain. The first British officer on the scene put it at in excess of 100,000 rupees (9th or Dhoree affair', BC F/4/1404 (55517) fo. 3). Later estimates put it at somewhere between 70,000 and 80,000 rupees; *Ramaseeana* I, 194–6; Smith to Swinton, 20 June 1832, *Sel.Rec.* 110.

The closing net 'Proceedings of Mr Fraser . . . in the Saugor & Nerbudda Territories dated the 4th Nov. 1829', Appa Sahib & Thuggee papers, SB; Smith to Swinton, BC F/4/1251 (50480/2) fos. 408–9.

Arrest of Sheikh Inaent Sleeman, *Ramaseeana* I, 227–30; Oliver to Sleeman, 10 Dec. 1829, BC F/4/1251 (50480/2) fos. 493–4; Sleeman to Smith, 13 May 1830, ibid. fos. 422–3.

Murder of Gosains Sleeman to Smith, 13 May 1830, ibid. fos. 422–4; Nicholson (Assistant superintendent, roads) to Sleeman, 10 Dec. 1829, ibid. fo. 501; *Ramaseeana* I, 230–2; deposition of Rambuksh in Thornton, *Illustrations* pp. 399–401. On the Gosains and their wealth, see Bernard Cohn, 'The role of the Gosains in the economy of 18th and 19th century Upper India', *IESHR* 1 (1964).

Further murders by Feringeea '13th or Bhilsa affair', BC F/4/1404 (55517) fos. 393–5; *Ramaseeana* I, 231–2.

Zolfukar's foal and the chiraiya's call Sleeman, *Ramaseeana* I, 232–4. Feringeea, in ibid. I, 171, con-flates two separate incidents and says the omen was heard directly after the party buried the body of the woman, blaming their subsequent capture on disobedience of the proscription on murdering females.

Dacoit belief in omens Ranjan Chakrabarti, *Authority and Violence in Colonial Bengal, 1800–1860* p. 143. Sneezing was generally thought to be bad luck because it was taken as a sign that a *bhut* (mischief spirit) had entered or left a person. Thugs shared the same superstition. William Crooke, *Popular Religion and Folklore of Northern India* p. 223.

Thug omens and portents Sleeman to the editor of the *Government Gazette* (n.d., published 7 Oct. 1830), in AC Das Gupta (ed.), *The Days of John Company* p. 583; FC Smith, 'Report on the Sessions of 1831–32', 20 June 1832, *Sel.Rec.* 123–4; *Ramaseeana* I, 68, 87, 102, 122; Fanny Parkes, *Wanderings of a Pilgrim* I, 151. RV Russell and Hira Lal provide further examples, and a useful commentary, in *The Tribes and Castes of the Central Provinces of India* IV, 582–5. It seems worth noting that, while the Company men who set down the first accounts of these omens tended to assume that all Thugs obeyed the same portents, it is just as likely that beliefs varied from province to province, and even from gang to gang.

'. . . heard to break wind . . .' Sleeman, *Ramaseeana* I, 68.

. . . blown from the mouths of cannon Michael Edwardes, *The Sahibs and the Lotus* pp. 152–3.

Thugs more scrupulous in captivity Cited by George Bruce, *The Stranglers*, p. 67.

Feringeea's men are seized Deposition of Feringeea, BC F/4/1404 (55517) fo. 395; Sleeman to Smith, 13 May 1830, BC F/4/1251 (50480/2) fos. 422–8; deposition of Hureea, 21 July 1830, ibid. fos. 443–9; Sleeman, *Ramaseeana* I, 233–4.

Members of Feringeea's gang A list of the whole gang appears in *Ramaseeana* II, 226–7.

Sleeman becomes aware of Feringeea Sleeman to Nicholson, letter no. 133, n.d. (1830), Sleeman correspondence, SB.

13 'A Double Weight of Irons'

Capture of members of Feringeea's family Smith to Swinton, BC F/4/1404 (55517) fos. 392–3; 'Trial of Sheikh Madaree and 25 other Thugs, charged with murder at different places', BC F/4/1251 (50480/2) fos. 503–79; Sleeman, *Depredations* p. 67.

Main informer Sleeman to Smith, 13 May 1830, BC F/4/1251 (50480/2) fo. 429.

Villages of Jhansee Smith to Prinsep, 8 Dec. 1830, BC F/4/2151 (50480/1) fos. 43–8.

'by only a few seconds' Sleeman to Smith, 7 Jan. 1831, in Consultation No. 11, 18 Mar. 1831, BPC P/126/27.

The cause Sleeman to Benson, 22 Nov. 1832, in CH Philips (ed.), *The Correspondence of Lord William Cavendish Bentinck, Governor-General of India 1828–1835* II, 947.

Developing campaign against the Thugs Radhika Singha, *A Despotism of Law* pp. 186–90, 203–12; Sleeman circular 31 Aug. 1838, T&D G/8, NAI.

Sleeman commended Swinton to Smith, 3 Dec. 1830, *Sel.Rec.* 4–5.

'The extirpation of this tribe' Swinton note, dated 4 Oct. 1830 in BC F/4/1251 (50480/2) fo. 669.

'His Lordship relies . . .' Swinton to Smith, 8 Oct. 1830, *Sel.Rec.* p. 10.

Thugs, Residents and general warrants Smith to Swinton, 26 May 1832, *Sel.Rec.* 79; Macnaghton (Secretary to Governor General) to Cavendish, 25 May and 24 June 1832, ibid. pp. 87–90; Lushington (Resident, Bhurtpore) to Lockett (Agent, Ajmere), 16 July 1832, ibid. pp. 102–3; 'Report on the Sessions of 1831–32', ibid. p. 117; Singha, op. cit. pp. 204–5; 'Extract Political Letter from Fort William', 15 Dec. 1835, BC F/4/1403 (55514) fo. 16; Sleeman to Cavendish 11 June 1832, T&D G/1, NAI; Sleeman memorandum, 22 Nov. 1832, in Philips, op. cit. II, 947; Martine van Woerkens, *The Strangled Traveller* pp. 56–7; Bruce, *The Stranglers* pp. 143–4.

'To check the dreadful evil . . .' Quoted by Bruce, op. cit. pp. 145–6.

Feringeea's wife ignorant of his way of life 'Neither she nor her family knew it till you seized her and she had been brought to Jubbulpore,' the strangler insisted. *Ramaseeana* I, 237.

'I knew that Feringeea . . .' Sleeman to Smith, 7 Jan. 1831, in Consultation No. 11, 18 Mar. 1831, BPC P/126/27.

Expedition during the monsoon season of 1830 Deposition of Feringeea, '24th or Busaynee Second Trial', BC F/4/1406 (55520) fos. 544–7; Smith to Swinton 10 June 1832, ibid fos. 541–2, *Depredations* p. 66 mentions the same case without making clear the lateness of the season.

Never twice in the same bed Sleeman to Smith, 7 Jan. 1831, in Consultation No. 11, 18 Mar. 1831, BPC P/126/27.

Pursuit and final capture Ibid.; *Depredations* pp. 67–8.

In double irons Smith to Ainsley (Agent, Banda), 15 Nov. 1830, BC F/4/1251 (50480/1) fo. 34.

'Great Thugg leader' Sleeman to Smith, 7 Jan. 1831, Consultation No. 11, 18 Mar. 1831, BPC P/126/27.

'. . . though so young a man . . .' Smith to Sleeman, 20 Jan. 1831, ibid.

'. . . upon a deliberate calculation . . .' This was the opinion of the Governor General, Bentinck, himself. The fact that the matter was referred to him is another indication of the importance attached to Feringeea in the Company's eyes. BC F/4/1251 (50480/1) fos. 9–10.

'. . . given me abundant proof . . .' Sleeman to Smith, 7 Jan. 1831, Consultation No. 11, 18 Mar. 1831, BPC P/126/27.

Betrayal of Candeish gangs Sleeman, *Ramaseeana* I, 30.

Exhumation of victims' graves Ibid. I, 30–2; Sleeman to Smith, 7 Jan. 1831, Consultation No. 11, 18 Mar. 1831, BPC P/126/27.

Number of approvers James Hutton, *A Popular Account of the Thugs and Dacoits* pp. 90–2.

'I know Badaloo' Evidence of Feringeea, BC F/4/1403 (55514) fo. 91.

Golab Thug Ibid. fo. 247.

'Identified and named' Ibid. fos. 67–127.

Trial No. 6 of 1832 BC F/4/1490 (58671), fos. 22, 28.

Trial No. 7 of 1832 Ibid. fos. 95–6.

Solicited intelligence from friends and family Sleeman to Smith, 7 Jan. 1831, Consultation No. 11 of 18 Mar. 1831, BPC P/126/27.

Numbers of arrests Sleeman, *Ramaseeana* I, 38–9; *Depredations* pp. 184–5.

Feringeea's evidence questioned Sleeman to Home (Magistrate, Belsh), 31 May 1832, T&D G/1, NAI.

14 Sleeman's Machine

Anecdote of Sleeman's machine 'Dialogues with Thugs', Paton papers, Add.Mss. 41300 fo. 18v, BL.

Indian archives For Bentinck's complaint, see CH Philips (ed.), *The Correspondence of Lord William Bentinck* I, xxxviii, xlvii–xlviii.

'With regard to the mode of collecting . . .' Sleeman to Reynolds, 25 July 1832, Sleeman correspondence, T&D G/1 fo. 82, NAI.

Sleeman's register Sleeman was not the first officer to attempt to compile a register of Thugs. In the early 1820s, Lieutenant Thomas Moodie, one of the officers working with Charles Molony at Jubbulpore, had the same idea and began work on a register of his own. His work does not seem to have been taken up and continued by his fellow officers and it is impossible to say whether or not Sleeman himself was aware of it, although his position in charge of the adjoining district of Nursingpore suggests that he may well have been. He never, in any case, referred to Moodie's register, or credited it as an inspiration for his own work, in any letter or report that I have come across. See Moodie to Swinton, 3 Feb. 1824, BC F/4/984 (27697) fo. 29, OIOC, and ibid. fo. 81r.

Aliases Sleeman to Smith, 13 May 1830, Sleeman correspondence, SB; Sleeman to Smith,

10 July 1832, T&D G/1 fo. 65; Reynolds, 'Notes on the T'hags', *Journal of the Royal Asiatic Society* 4 (1837) p. 203.

Identifying marks Sleeman to Taylor (Magistrate, Cawnpore), 16 Sept. 1832, Sleeman correspondence, T&D G/1.

'. . . as soon as an accused . . .' Ishwar Sahai, 'The crime of Thagi and its suppression under Lord WC Bentinck', part 2, *Indian Culture* 3 (1936) p. 459.

Officers of the Thuggy Department Sahai, op. cit. pp. 460–61; *Ramaseeana* I, 58–9.

'exercising, as heretofore . . .' *Asiatic Journal* NS6 (1835) pp. 128–9.

Sleeman's map RH Phillimore, *Historical Records of the Survey of India, 1815–30* p. 499; George Bruce, *The Stranglers* pp. 86–7.

Paton's map BC F/4/1898 (67999) fo. 305; 'Observations upon the operations of gangs of Thug murderers in the Kingdom of Oude', 1836, Paton papers fo. 171.

Thug genealogies Sleeman, *Ramaseeana* I, after p. 270; van Woerkens, *The Strangled Traveller* pp. 140–42; Bruce, op. cit. p. 157. The information contained within the genealogies was, says Bruce, checked against the available revenue lists, which in the years before the introduction of a census provided the most reliable registry of the Company's subjects – another intensely laborious task.

Omitted mention For example, Feringeea's family tree omits mention of the jemadar's adopted sons, one of whom we know became a pickpocket rather than a Thug. Sleeman correspondence, T&D G/1 fo. 5, 169.

'they show the connection . . .' Cited by Bruce, op. cit. p. 161.

'Makun, who was hung at Indore . . .' Sleeman, *Ramaseeana* II, 128.

'There is one truth . . .' Sleeman to Taylor, 28 June 1832, T&D G/1 fos. 40–1.

Approvers grouped Sleeman to Smith, BC F/4/1404 (55517) fos. 253–5; Bruce, op. cit. p. 114. There were in any case a further 30 approvers of no fixed affiliation who could be turned to in any case where there was doubt. See also Sleeman to Wilson, 24 Dec. 1832, Sleeman correspondence T&D G/1 fos. 184–5.

Rada Kishun and Jurha Deposition of Sheikh Madaree, 22 Feb. 1830, BC F/4/1404 (55517) fos. 468, 485, 487; 'Trial of Sheikh Madaree and 25 other Thugs charged with murder at different places', ibid. fos. 513, 579; Sleeman to Smith, 7 Jan. 1831, BPC P/126/27.

Popular service, rewards 'Specific reward,' ordered Francis Curwen Smith in November 1830, 'to be offered with the sanction of the Agent to the Governor General not exceeding Rs.1,000 for each leader of Thugs proved to be of that description by trial already concluded.' Van Woerkens, op. cit. pp. 51–2. For the reward offered for Heera, alias Huree Singh, see Sleeman to Smith, 13 June 1832, T&D G/1 fo. 17. In the latter case, six sepahees and a *naik* (non-commissioned officer) from the 76th Regiment Native Infantry received 40 rupees each – several times their monthly wage – and a pair of Jubbulpore nujeebs and two approvers received the same amount, the balance of the reward being distributed to the remainder of the soldiers and militiamen involved in the arrest.

Lists of Thugs One early list of wanted Thugs, written out by FC Smith in December 1830, provided the nujeebs with details of no fewer than 98 Bundelcund men, living in 13 villages scattered throughout Jhansee. Smith to Prinsep, 8 Dec. 1830, BC F/4/1251 (50480/1) fos. 43–8; Sleeman to Smith, 12 Dec. 1830, ibid. fo. 54.

Nujeebs exceeding orders Sleeman to Smith, 20 July and 5 September 1832, T&D G/1 fos. 74–8, 113.

Lushington's complaint Lushington to Smith, 13 June 1832, and to Lockett (Agent to the Governor General, Ajmere), June 1832, *Sel.Rec.* 94–8.

'. . . are now provided with approvers' Bruce, op. cit. p. 141.

Thug loot Ibid. p. 119.

Three great results Ibid. p. 122.

'In all my experience . . . Blood for blood' Smith to Swinton, 25 June 1832, *Sel.Rec.* 125.

15 In Cutcherry

There were nearly 4,500 of them in all . . . The number of men arrested as suspected Thugs up to the end of 1840 was 3,689. A further 531 were committed in the years 1841–7 and 120 in 1848. James Hutton, *A Popular Account of the Thugs and Dacoits* pp. 92–4.

'Threatened to overwhelm' Sel.Rec. ii.

Proportion of Muslims and Hindus A breakdown of the religious affiliation of all the prisoners tried up to and including the sessions of 1832 appears in BC F/4/1685 (67999) fos. 124–8, OIOC. A slightly higher proportion of Muslim Thugs was reported in the 26 trials that made up the sessions of 1831; see BC F/4/1406 (55521) fo. 177. When Sleeman asked his approvers to tell him how many Thugs were Muslims and how many were Hindus, Feringeea replied: 'In Oude nine-tenths are Musulmans. In the Dooab, four-fifths are Hindus. South of the Nerbudda, three-fourths Musulmans. In Rajpootana one-fourth Musulmans. In Bengal, Bihar and Orissa about half and half. This is a rough guess, since we have no rule to prescribe or ascertain them.' Sleeman, *Ramaseeana* I, 178.

Hindu castes Van Woerkens, *The Strangled Traveller* pp. 129–31, summarizes lists drawn up of the prisoners tried at Indore in 1829 and in the Jubbulpore sessions of 1832–33.

Thugs in prison For Syeed Ameer Ali, see BC F/4/1406 (55521) fo. 205; for the Sindouse Thugs, *Ramaseeana* I, 219–20; for the Lucknadown gang, Ravenshaw and Marjoribanks to Governor General, 28 Nov. 1832, BC F/4/1483 (55514) fos. 19–26.

Instances of Thugs detained by British forces, 1799–1828 A provisional listing of the fate of Thugs arrested by Company officials up to the beginning of the anti-Thug campaign would include well over 20 cases and gives the lie to the commonly held assumption that the British encounter with the Thugs began only in the late 1820s.

Date	Place	Description	Outcome
1799	Seringapatem	99 Thugs captured after the fall of the city	?
1807	Chittoor, Arcot	Gang of Phansigars detained	?
	Bangalore	Trial of a gang of Phansigars	?
1809	Gorruckpore	Arrest of 16 Thugs	Acquitted
	Bihar	Apprehension of a gang of Thugs	Released
1810	Shekoabad	Arrest of 8 Thugs causes 'a sensation'	Delay in obtaining warrants leads to escape
1811	Chittoor	Gang of Phansigars detained	Some convictions
	Cuddapore	Gang of Thugs appears in court	?
1812	Calastry	Gang of Thugs arrested	Held in jail
1812–13	Mynpooree	Four Sindouse Thugs tried	Released
1813	Barelly, Benares	Execution of Thugs	49 men hanged
1813–14	Zillah Salem	500 Phansigars detained	Magistrate discharged for abuse of process
1814	Bihar	Gang detained Gorruckpore 1809 rearrested	Released on security
	?	15 members of the above gang rearrested	Acquitted
	Mynpooree	Stockwell and Perry arrest 200 Thugs	180 released on security
	Cawnpore	Wright arrests 100 Thugs	Released
c.1815	Banda	Notorious Thugs seized by Mr Wauchope	?
1816	Malwa	Gang of Thugs captured by British official	?

1820	Bhopal	Gang of Thugs arrested	Deported from Malwa by Resident at Indore
c.1820	Jubbulpore	Thugs arrested for murders in Jhansee	Held in jail
1821	Akoolah	Gang of Thugs arrested	Found guilty at Jhalna, 1823, imprisoned at Aurangabad
1822	Kotah	Gang of 46 Thugs detained by British and handed over to local ruler	Held in jail
	Seonnee	60 Thugs arrested for murders in 1820	Held until 1832, then tried
c.1823	Mynpooree	Three leading Thugs and followers held	Escaped
1823	Nerbudda valley	115 Thugs arrested for murder of 37 people	Held until 1830, then tried
1824	?	One of 1809 Gorruckpore gang rearrested	Released
c.1826	Mozuffurpore	Gang of 16 Thugs arraigned	Four hanged, 12 transported, approver released
1826	Gorruckpore	Thug trial	Two men hanged
	Nerbudda valley	26 Thugs arrested and tried at Jubbulpore	Two hanged and 24 transported
1827	Patna	Gang of Thugs detained	Prisoners released, informants lashed and jailed
1828	Candeish	6 members of Dhoolea gang tried	Two hanged and four transported

Sources: **1799**, Sherwood, *Asiatick Researches* 13; **1807** Chittoor, Thornton, p. 3; **1807** Bangalore, Sahai, *Crime of thagi* I; Gorruckpore, *Ramaseeana* II, 250–2; **1809** Bihar, *Crime of thagi* I; **1810** Shakoabad, Perry papers; **1811** Chittoor, *Ramaseeana* II, 307; **1811** Cuddapore, Thornton, p. 286; **1812**, *Ramaseeana* II, 307; **1813**, *Crime of thagi* I; **1812–13**, *Ramaseeana* I, 221; **1813–14**, E/4/929 Madras dispatches; **1814** Bihar and ?, *Ramaseeana* II, 253; **1814** Mynpooree and Cawnpore, *Ramaseeana* I, 257–60; **c.1815**, *Ramaseeana* II, 371; **1816**, Malcolm, *Memoir* II; **1820**, *Ramaseeana* II, 139–40; **c.1820**, BC F/4/1309 (52131); **1821**, *Ramaseeana* II, 273, 288; **1822** Kotah, *Ramaseeana* I, 212; II 123–31; **1822** Seonnee, BPC P/123/13; **c.1823**, *Sel.Rec.* 56–61; **1823** BC F/4/1483; **1824**, Thornton, p. 309; **c.1826**, *Ramaseeana* I, 185–6; **1826** Gorruckpore, *Ramaseeana* II, 251; **1826** Nerbudda valley, *Ramaseeana* I, 46–7; **1827**, *Ramaseeana* II, 245–7; **1828**, *Ramaseeana* I, 46.

There were undoubtedly also numerous instances in which captured Thugs appeared before Indian rulers or courts. Few if any relevant records survive from the Native States, however, and references to these cases appear only sporadically in British sources. The following instances are known:

Date	Place	Description	Outcome
c.1775	Kundul	All Thugs in area jailed for several days	Released
1785	?	Several Phansigars arrested	?
1794	Muthura	70 Thugs captured by Mahadji Sindhia	Hanged
1809	Gwalior	Gang of 21 Thugs captured by Jacob Sahib	Hanged
1812	Jetulpoor	56 Thugs captured	Imprisoned; some escaped
1813	Nodha	80 Sindouse Thugs arrested	?
1812–13	Gwalior	133 Sindouse Thugs arrested	Released after 13 months; many died in prison
1813	Ellichpore	250 Thugs arrested	Released after one month
1814/15	Jhalone	Two Thugs arrested	Trampled to death by elephants

1816	Hyderabad	Gang of Thugs arrested for murder of 10	21 men executed
c.1816	Jubbulpore	Gang of Thugs arrested	2 had nose/hands cut off; 3 released; some escaped
1818	Gwalior	Thug jemadars seized and imprisoned	Released on payment of a fine
1822	Bundelcund	Gang of Thugs arrested at Bijawar	?
1822	Kotah	Feringeea's gang of 30 men arrested	Released after one day with faces blackened
1828–9	Alumpore	Feringeea arrested	Escaped from prison

Sources: **c.1775**, *Ramaseeana* I, 157–8; **1785**, Forbes, *Oriental Memoirs* IV, 13; **1794** *Ramaseeana* I, 221; Russell and Lal, *Tribes & Castes* 573; **1809**, *Ramaseeana* I, 208; **1812**, Perry papers Add.Mss. 5376 fos. 24–7, CUL; **1812–13**, *Ramaseeana* I, 219–20; **1812**, *Ramaseeana* II, 296; **1813**, *Ramaseeana* I, 157; **1814/15**, *Ramaseeana* I, 156, 245; **1816**, *Ramaseeana* I, 34–5; **c.1816**, *Ramaseeana* II, 233–4; **1818**, *Ramaseeana* II, 133; **1822**, Bundelcund, BPC P/123/13; **1822**, Kotah, *Ramaseeana* I, 177; **1828–9**, BC F/4/1251 (50480/2) fo. 444.

A good deal more work needs to be done to make these provisional listings definitive ones.

Abortive cases Perry to Dowdeswell, 6 Oct. 1812, Perry papers, Add.Mss. 5376 fos. 17–18v, CUL; 'Deposition of Rujub, approver', 30 Nov. 1832, in *Ramaseeana* II, 245–9.

Courts and law in early nineteenth-century India Singha, *A Despotism of Law* pp. 3–6; Chakrabarti, *Authority and Violence in Colonial Bengal, 1800–1830* pp. 4–12, 33–5; van Woerkens, op. cit. p. 83; Clare Anderson, *Convicts in the Indian Ocean* p. 17; James, *Raj* p. 204. It should be added that British felons in India were tried in different courts, under English rather than Islamic law.

The inconsistent bandying about . . . Smith to Swinton, 20 June 1832, *Sel.Rec.* p. 111.

Cost of attending court Sleeman, *Rambles and Recollections* I, 97n.

Justice in the Native States . . . Smith to Swinton, 5 July 1830, BC F/4/1251 (50430/2) fo. 417; *Ramaseeana* II, 133; Singha, op. cit. pp. 31–2, 80–1, 306; *Sel.Rec.* 80–1; Bearce, *British Attitudes Towards India, 1784–1858* pp. 90–1.

'. . . carries not even the appearance . . .' Moodie to Swinton, 4 July 1822, in Consultation No. 19 of 26 July, P/123/13, OIOC; see also Smith to Swinton, 26 May 1832, *Sel.Rec.* 79; Smith to Macnaughton (Agent to the Governor General, Simla), 29 May 1832, ibid. 82.

Commencement of trials Sleeman *Ramaseeana* II, 379–84; Singha, op. cit. pp. 203–4.

Majority tried in Saugor Of the 1,803 Thugs eventually tried between 1829 and 1836, 1,514, or 84 per cent, were tried by the Agent for Saugor & Nerbudda in either Saugor or Jubbulpore. Data from *Ramaseeana* I, 38–9; for later trials see Sleeman, *Depredations* pp. 184–5.

Position of the Saugor & Nerbudda Territory The Territory thus became – the officer commanding it observed in 1836 – 'a theatre for the experiments of incipient legislation'. Singha, op. cit. pp. 173–5, 207.

Arduous trials Smith to Swinton, 20 June 1832, *Sel.Rec.* 104, 114. See also Smith to Swinton, 8 May 1832, ibid. 72; *Foreign Quarterly Review* 21 (1838) pp. 29–30.

Fanny Parks Parks, *Wanderings of a Pilgrim, in Search of the Picturesque* I, 122–3. I have translated some of Parks's Anglo-Indian phraseology.

Disinterrals See *Sel.Rec.* 35, 84; van Woerkens, op. cit. p. 77.

18 in one place T&D G/1/2 fos. 5–6.

Goldsmiths 'Trial No. 11 of 1832', BC F/4/1490 (58672) fos. 105–6. 'Even when such identifications were not possible,' added Smith, 'the credibility of the evidence of the approvers is doubtless increased by the exhumation of the bodies of the murdered at their suggestion, and by their pointing out the very graves in which they were buried.' Bruce, *The Stranglers* p. 160.

Meadows Taylor Confessions p. xviii.

Proportion of bodies recovered Sleeman, *Ramaseeana* I, 38–9; Anon., 'Ramaseeana', in *Foreign Quarterly Review* 21 (1838) p. 32.

One wife recognized . . . Bruce, op. cit. p. 91; see also Borthwick statement, n.d. [1829], *Sel.Rec.* 35

Borthwick's gang Borthwick statement, ibid. 39.

'The confession of some prisoners . . .' Sleeman to Smith, 20 Feb. 1833, T&D G/1 fos. 225–7.

'The following precautions . . .' Smith to Swinton, 20 June 1832, *Sel Rec.* 35.

Incident at Hyderabad 'Ramaseeana', *Foreign Quarterly Review* 21 (1838) p. 39.

'native defendants lie freely . . .' Moodie to Swinton, 4 July 1822, in Consultation No. 19 of 26 July, BPC P/123/13, para 17. The same was certainly true of prosecution witnesses, though the courts were less willing to accept this. The magistrate at Midnapore, early in the nineteenth century, admitted that innocent men were often punished on mere suspicion and confessions extracted by force. To make matters worse, many courts were plagued by men who earned a dubious living hiring themselves out to give false evidence. Chakrabarti, op. cit. pp. 41, 72.

Checks on Thug alibis Cf. 'Trial No. 8 of 1832', BC F/4/1490 (58671); van Woerkens, op. cit. pp. 80–1.

In a third, . . . 'Trial No. 12 of 1832', BC F/4/1490 (58672) fos. 283–5.

'These men . . .' Sleeman, *Ramaseeana* I, 38–9.

Believed old tactic of denial would still serve 'I used to think,' the Thug Sheodeen told Captain Paton, 'that, as usual, I should escape by denying guilt.' 'Dialogues with Thugs', Paton papers fo. 18v, BL.

'the change in the demeanour . . .' Smith to Swinton, 20 June 1832, *Sel Rec.* 122.

Cheinsah and Bhudalee BC F/4/1404 (55517) fos. 229–33.

Sleeman's view of Thug witnesses Sleeman, *Rambles and Recollections* I, 107.

Evidence in Thug trials Trial No. 7, BC F/4/1490 (58671) fos. 95–6; Trial No. 10, BC F/4/1490 (58672) fos. 1–2; Trial No. 13, ibid. fos. 347–8; Akola case, BC F/4/1403 (55515) fos. 384–508; Smith to Swinton, 8 May 1832, *Sel.Rec.* 77. The sepoy's name was Lalsingh Soobadar, and Smith recommended that his son, Girdharee, be allowed '3 rupees per mensem till he is sufficiently old to provide for himself, and then to make him a *Burkindaz*' (police militiaman). The child had been readily identified, not least because Dirgpal had failed even to change his name.

Khoman's identity parades BC F/4/1309 (52131) fos. 134.

. . . long association . . . Cf. Singha, op. cit. p. 184.

'never convicted upon the mere evidence of accomplices . . .' Ravenshaw and Marjoribanks (Directors, East India Company) to Governor General, 28 Nov. 1832, BC F/4/1403 (55514) fos. 19–26.

16 Demon Devotees

'Just 16 miles of Asia' George Bearce, *British Attitudes Towards India, 1784–1858* p. 42. On 'Persian poetry and Hindu metaphysics', see Dennis Kincaid, *British Social Life in India* p. 129. On Mrs Graham, see ibid.

'Oh, nothing, thank goodness' Hilton Brown, *The Sahibs* p. 225.

British officers and Indian women For a moving study of one relationship between a British officer and an Indian woman, in Hyderabad in the period 1798–1806, see Dalrymple, *White Mughals*. For the costs of running a *zenana*, see Michael Edwardes, *The Sahibs and the Lotus* p. 47.

The British and Hinduism Bernard Cohn, *An Anthropologist Among the Historians, and Other Essays* p. 146; Katherine Prior, *The British Administration of Hinduism in North India, 1780–1900*; PJ Marshall (ed.), *The British Discovery of Hinduism in the Eighteenth Century* pp. 1–43; Amal Chatterjee, *Representation of India 1740–1840* pp. 6, 8, 87, 95, 100, 103; Atis Dasgupta, *The Fakir and Sannyasi Uprisings* pp. ii, 8, 59–60.

Kali and Calcutta On important occasions, British administrators attended ceremonies at Kali's temple outside Calcutta. Michael Edwardes, *The Sahibs and the Lotus* p. 38. This led the Thugs to observe that the Company itself worshipped Kali.

'lust, injustice . . .' This quote, by the evangelical Christian William Wilberforce, is cited by John Keay, *India* p. 429.

'the horrid rite of chundee pooja' Basudeb Chattopadhyay, *Crime and Control in Early Colonial Bengal, 1770–1860* p. 8, citing BCJC, 23 May 1794.

Distrust of fakirs Amal Chatterjee, *Representation of India 1740–1840* pp. 6, 8, 87, 95, 100, 103; Atis Dasgupta, *The Fakir and Sannyasi Uprisings* pp. ii, 8, 59–60.

Female infanticide Malavika Kasturi, 'Law and Crime in India: British Policy and the Female Infanticide Act of 1870', *Indian Journal of Gender Studies* 1 (2) (1994) pp. 169–94.

Suttee In Hindu eyes this custom – which gave the widow the opportunity to perform the necessary rites of purification and select the most propitious spot to die – charged its victims with divine power. To the Mughals and their successors, the British administrators of Bengal, it seemed akin to human sacrifice, and suttees were generally discouraged on the grounds that the practice, while ancient, was not approved by any sacred text. There were about 8,200 cases in the Bengal Presidency between 1815 and 1828 – that is, 585 a year – and the custom was considerably rarer in Bombay and Madras: an average of 172 incidences a year across the latter two Presidencies combined. VN Datta, *Sati* pp. 188–92. The practice was finally outlawed by a new Governor General, Bentinck, in the late 1820s. See Chatterjee, op. cit. pp. 111–24; Singha, *A Despotism of Law* pp. 108–10.

Juggernaut The word means 'Lord of the world' and is one of the 1,000 titles accorded to the god Vishnu. The temple is in the Cuttack district, on the coast of Orissa a little over 300 miles from Calcutta, and the statues, roughly carved from sandalwood, were each about six feet high. Although they were popularly reputed to be covered in 'obscene sculptures', one sober British observer confessed that 'if there . . . it requires a very searching eye to find them out'. They were reputed to be more than 4,000 years old. The procession lasted for two or three days. Visitors who ate food prepared at Juggernaut were supposed to be absolved from the four cardinal Hindu sins, those of killing a Brahmin, drinking spirits, committing adultery and killing a cow. A second, bathing, festival was held at Juggernaut each year in addition to the more celebrated 'car festival'. In Britain, both were scarcely known before 1810, when the poet Robert Southey described Juggernaut in an epic verse 'full of the shrieks of the victims and the groans of the unfortunates who were sacrificed to bloody and superstitious rites'. After that, though, Juggernaut became part of the demonology of the Subcontinent. Walter Hamilton, *The East-India Gazetteer* II, 55–8; Thomas Bacon, *First Impressions and Studies from Nature in Hindustan* I, 174–7; Bearce, *British Attitudes* p. 104.

'hideous moral wilderness' Lawrence James, *Raj* pp. 195–6.

'universally and wholly corrupt . . .' The opinion of the Company director, Charles Grant, cited in Dalrymple, *White Mughals* p. 46.

Dacoits, Fakirs, Sanyassis, Nagas and Kallars Chattopadhyay, op. cit. pp. 8–10; David Shulman, 'On South Indian Bandits and Kings', *IESHR* 17 (1980) pp. 284–8.

Conversations with Thugs Sleeman, *Ramaseeana* I, 64–6. Sleeman offered these 'almost literal translations' on the grounds that 'these conversations were often carried on in the presence of different European gentlemen who happened to call in, and as they seemed to feel a good deal of interest in listening to them, I thought others might possibly feel the same in reading them if committed to paper'. The transcripts fill the final hundred or so pages of the first volume of *Ramaseeana* and have become the principal source – indeed in some cases the only source – for modern accounts of Thuggee. They are considerably more interesting and colourful than the dull pages of unpublished court transcripts in the Company's archives, but both, taken in isolation, can be very misleading. It is important to read them in conjunction.

Ramasee dictionary Ibid. I, 67–140; see also van Woerkens, *The Strangled Traveller* pp. 114–15, 295–315.

Sikh Thugs There seem to have been very few Sikh Thugs. But Sahib Khan, the Deccan strangler, 'knew Ram Sing Siek: he was a noted Thug leader – a very shrewd man', who also served with the Pindaris for a time and was responsible for the assassination of the notorious Pindari leader Sheikh Dulloo. Sleeman, *Ramaseeana* I, 239–40.

Common feature of folk religion Bayly, *Empire & Information* pp. 173, 176; Radhika Singha, *A Despotism of Law* pp. 189–90, 202.

Thieves and housebreakers 'Dialogues with Thugs', 29 Oct. 1836, Paton papers, Add.Mss. 41300 fo. 63v, BL.

'Having performed the usual worship . . .' 'Deposition of Bheelum Burre Khan, Jemadar of Thugs', n.d., T&D D/2/2, NAI. This is the only reference to religious affairs I have been able to find anywhere in the official papers preserved in London, Delhi and Bhopal. Nowhere else in any of the numerous files examined is any kind of worship hinted at. The reasons for the yawning discrepancy between the evidence of Sleeman's 'Conversations with Thugs' and that of the Company's legal records is hard to fathom, but a large part of the answer almost certainly lies in the manner in which the Thug trials were organized.

Mahadji Sindhia and other victims of Kali Sleeman, *Ramaseeana* I, 156–8, 220–2, Russell and Lal, *Tribes and Castes of the Central Provinces of India* IV, 572–3.

'that Bhowanee may have her blood . . .' Paton papers fo. 14v. Some Thugs explained the practice of mutilating the bodies of the Thugs' victims – which the earliest stranglers questioned by Company authorities had attributed simply to the desire to conceal their identities – in precisely these terms. 'Why do you stab the dead bodies?' Paton asked his approvers. 'That no life may remain,' answered one. But others disagreed: 'Bhowanee, whom we worship, is displeased where we do not shed the blood of our victims,' said the strangler Dhoosoo. Ibid.

'on one occasion . . .' Russell and Lal, op. cit. IV, 575.

'That Davey instituted Thuggee . . .' Sleeman, *Ramaseeana* I, 187.

'Our ancestors were never guilty of this folly' Ibid. I, 197.

'A wretched trade' 'Narrative of a Thuggee expedition in Oude . . . supposed to have been in 1830', Paton papers fo. 119.

Thugs and ghosts Sleeman, *Ramaseeana* I, 175–6. 'It is by the blessing of Davey that we escape that evil,' the approver Kuleean asserted.

'. . . irresponsible agents' Russell and Lal, op. cit. IV, 573.

Fate Feringeea deployed this argument to justify his murder of the Moghulanee: 'It was her fate to die by our hands. I had several times tried to shake [her party] off.' *Ramaseeana* I, 215.

Thugs and tigers Paton papers fo. 123.

'look forward indifferently . . .' Sleeman, *Ramaseeana* I, 150.

'How many men . . .' Ibid. I, 76.

'If a man committed . . .' Russell and Lal, op. cit. IV, 573.

'A Thug considers . . .' Sleeman, *Ramaseeana* I, 7.

Kali venerated by many classes Russell and Lal, op. cit. IV, 575.

Pickaxe worship Ibid. IV, 574.

Introduction of the pickaxe Ibid. IV, 575. This legend, Sleeman considered, originated 'in a very remote period'. *Ramaseeana* I, iii.

Beliefs similar to those of dacoits Russell and Lal, op. cit. IV, 572.

'When you have a poor traveller . . .' Sleeman, *Ramaseeana* I, 196–7.

'Do Mussellman Thugs . . .' Paton papers fo. 28.

'You paid great reverence . . .' Ibid. fo. 62v. See also *Ramaseeana* I, 186–7.

'Kali's temple at Bindachul . . .' Das Gupta, *The Days of John Company*, p. 582.

'that fiend in human form . . .' James Sleeman, *Thug* pp. 4–5.

'The histories of these men . . .' Thornton, *Illustrations* p. 407.

'However unscrupulous . . .' Sleeman, Thug p. 5.

Thugs as noble criminals See also Ramaseeana I, 235.

'noble and chivalrous instincts . . .' Charles Hervey, Some Records of Crime I, 77; Sandria Freitag, 'Crime in the social order of colonial North India', Modern Asian Studies 25 (1991) pp. 236–8.

'I know not . . .' Reynolds, 'Notes' p. 208.

'Made positive pets . . .' Extracted from the diaries of Fanny Eden. See J Dunbar (ed.), Tigers, Durbars and Kings p. 104, and the chapter 19 for further details.

'What a sad but faithful picture . . .' Cited by Bruce, The Stranglers, p. 179.

'I could not forsake them . . .' Sleeman, Ramaseeana I, 234–5.

'These common enemies of mankind . . .' Sleeman to Smith, 7 Jan. 1831, Consultation No. 11 of 18 Mar. 1831, BPC P/126/27, OIOC.

'Mr Wilson . . .' Sleeman, Ramaseeana I, 29–30n.

Hurree Singh Ibid. I, 34–5, 36–7n.

'only about two months ago . . .' Sleeman to Cavendish (resident, Gwalior), 11 June 1832, Sleeman correspondence, T&D G/1 fo. 11.

'Are you yourself . . .' Cited by James Sleeman, Thug pp. 3–4. Sleeman gives no source for this quotation and it must be regarded with a certain caution.

'consider the persons . . .' Sleeman, Ramaseeana I, 7.

'mediate his murders . . .' Ibid. I, 8.

17 The Last Days of Thuggee

'What do you think . . .?' George Bruce, The Stranglers p. 167; on the history of Sahib Khan, see William Sleeman, Ramaseeana I, 245–6

'Suppose all our operations . . .' 'Collections on Thuggee and Dacoitee', Paton papers, Add.Mss. 41300 fo. 18v, BL. The speaker in this case was the approver Futty [Futteh] Khan.

'Once a Thug . . .' Smith to Swinton, 25 June 1832, BC F/4/1406 (55521) fo. 204, OIOC.

'Suspected stranglers . . . were often disconcerted . . .' The colourful account of one of Sleeman's interrogations given by Francis Tuker, in The Yellow Scarf pp. 83–4 is, however, fictional.

Thugs move base of operations Sleeman, Ramaseeana I, 187, 246–7, 254.

'rarely seized or punished' Ibid. I, 238. These men were 'Brinjarees' – peripatetic drovers, common throughout the mofussil, some of whom supplemented their ordinary earnings by crime. Another tactic, employed by several able Thugs, was to abandon their gangs and work with only a few trusted associates. Sleeman noted that Bukshee Jemadar, 'one of the most noted Thug leaders of his day, who died in Saugor Jail in 1832, had for some 15 years ceased to accompany the large gangs, and was supposed to have left off the trade entirely'. Ibid. I, 24.

'Two seasons are still required . . .' Smith to Swinton, 25 Mar. 1832, Smith to Macnaghten, 24 Apr. 1832, Sel.Rec. pp. 73–5.

'There are many leaders . . .' Sleeman, Depredations p. xi.

Act XXX, Act XXIV and Regulation 8 Radhika Singha, A Despotism of Law pp. 214–20; van Woerkens, The Strangled Traveller pp. 100–2.

'To release on security a Thug' Smith to Swinton, 20 June 1832, in Ch Philips (ed.), The Correspondence of Lord William Cavendish Bentinck II, 844.

'affording a security net . . .' Singha, op. cit. p. 216.

Suppression in Bundelcund Sleeman, Ramaseeana I, 20.

'Completely suppressed' in Madras Bengal despatches political, 28 Nov. 1832, E/4/735 fos. 1473–91, OIOC.

Doab Smith to Macnaghton, 26 June 1832, in CH Philips (ed.), The Correspondence of Lord William Cavendish Bentinck, Governor-General of India 1828–1835 II, 1085.

Sessions from 1833–35 Sleeman, Ramaseeana I, 38–9; Depredations pp. 184–5.

Standards of proof fell Singha, op. cit. p. 212. Men could still be convicted solely on the evidence of an approver, but the maximum sentence was one of imprisonment for life, and branding on the forehead.

Sentencing after 1836 Sleeman, *Depredations* pp. 184–5; van Woerkens, op. cit. p. 101.

Agents and collaborators Sleeman, *Ramaseeana* I, 39–41.

Davey Deen Sleeman, *Ramaseeana* I, 156.

Bengal, Bihar and Orissa Ibid. pp. 40–41, 56, 181; *Depredations* p. i.

Bengal Thugs tried in Saugor The judicial independence of the Saugor & Nerbudda Territory was ended in 1835 when it became part of the newly created Presidency of Agra, local courts then falling under the supervision of Agra's *Sadar Adalat*. In practice, however, the higher court barely interfered with the by-then well-established practices of the Thug trials. See Singha, op. cit. pp. 207n, 211.

'the enormities of the Thugs . . .' Bengal despatches political, 28 Nov. 1832, E/4/735 fos. 1473–91; Singha, op. cit. pp. 205–6.

Thugs of Bengal Sleeman, *Depredations* pp. i–v.

1836 murders by Deccan thugs Ibid. pp. v, ix.

Jubbulpore sessions of 1836–1837 BC F/4/1898 (80685) fos. 66–188.

Sepoys safe Sleeman, *Ramaseeana* I, 41–2n.

Sleeman's circular The circular of 1841 likewise threw up no trace of any stranglers. James Sleeman, *Thug* pp. 189–93.

End of the anti-Thug campaign The formal end of the campaign was signalled in July 1840, when the East India Company's Court of Directors, at home in London, were informed that 'as organised associations Thug bands had been broken up'. Singha, op. cit. p. 220&n.

As many as 4,000 rank-and-file Thugs Bruce, op. cit. p. 212.

Thuggee pronounced extinct Singha, op. cit. p. 220n.

18 The Gallows and the Drop

Sleeman's register kept up to date Percival Griffiths, *To Guard My People* p. 132.

River dacoits Sukmar Sen, '"Bungoo" – River Thugs on the Hooghly', *Bengal Past & Present* 86 (1967) pp. 167–8; Chakrabarti, *Authority and Violence* pp. 140–2; Arun Mukherjee, *Crime and Public Disorder in Colonial Bengal 1861–1912* pp. 43–4; Anthony Sattin (ed.), *An Englishwoman in India* p. 26.

River Thugs Paton papers, Add.Mss. 41300 fo. 11v, BL; *Ramaseeana* I, 43, 72, 178–80, 264–8; II, 436–72; Edward Thornton, *Illustrations of the History and Practices of the Thugs* pp. 31–42, 408–20.

Seasonality of the River Thugs 'In March it becomes too hot', the Thug Shumsera explained, 'and in the rains the river becomes too rapid, and the boats cannot be pulled along the banks.' *Ramaseeana* I, 268.

Arrest of the River Thugs Arun Mukherjee, op. cit. p. 43.

Megpunnas Sleeman, *Report on the System of Megpunnaism* pp. 1–99.

Tusma-Baz Thugs Hutton, *A Popular Account of the Thugs and Dacoits* pp. 98–100; Fanny Parks, *Wanderings of a Pilgrim in Search of the Picturesque* I, 452–3. Other groups of suspected Thugs were harshly treated in this period. On one occasion, the British magistrate at Agra ordered every member of the 'tribe of Nats' – a group of acrobats – to be deported south across the Nerbudda river, an order that a second judge described as 'of the same value as would be the order from a London Magistrate to put all Italian Opera dancers and singers across the water'. Radhika Singha, 'Providential circumstances: the thuggee campaign of the 1830s and legal innovation', *Modern Asian Studies* 27 p. 115.

Dr Cheek's bearer William Tayler, *Thirty-Eight Years in India* I, 194; Russell and Lal, *The Tribes and Castes of the Central Provinces of India* IV, 570.

Sleemanabad Kevin Rushby, *Children of Kali* pp. 146, 160–1.

'*seeing that the best arrangements . . .*' Hussain Dost Khan to Captain Malcolm, 17 Aug. 1840, cited by James Hutton, op. cit. pp. 93–4.

'*Do not I pray you . . .*' Sleeman to Fraser, 22 Feb. 1838, Mss. Eur E/258/V fo. 13, OIOC.

Sentences Martine van Woerkens, *The Strangled Traveller* p. 47.

'*They should never recover their unrestricted liberty . . .*' Smith to Prinsep (Secretary to Governor General), 19 Nov. 1830, *Sel.Rec.* 54.

'*branding on the forehead . . .*' Swinton to Smith 2 Apr. 1831, 'Government of India orders confirming sentence of death . . .' T&D D/1/1, NAI.

Godna Clare Anderson, '"Godena": tattooing & branding prisoners in nineteenth-century India', in Jane Caplan (ed.), *Writing on the Body: The Tattoo in European and American History* pp. 106–9.

Plan for executions in home villages Stewart (Resident, Indore) to Swinton, 12 Aug. 1829, Appa Sahib & Thuggee papers, SB; Swinton to Stewart, 23 Oct. 1829, ibid.

Sleeman's description of the execution of Feringeea's gang This took place at Jubbulpore. Sleeman to the editor of the *Government Gazette* (n.d., published 7 Oct. 1830), in Das Gupta (ed.), *The Days of John Company* pp. 580. The letter was originally published anonymously. For Sleeman's authorship, see Smith to Prinsep, 19 Nov. 1830, *Sel.Rec.* 51.

'*met their fate . . .*' Extract Bengal Political Consultations 5 March 1830 No. 59, BC F/4/1251 fos. 379–83, OIOC. The British authorities nevertheless remained utterly convinced of the safeness of the Thugs' convictions. Indeed, the condemned men's desperate protests of innocence were – in Borthwick's view – 'clear proof of their guilt'.

. . . whether real or feigned . . . As noted, they were probably real. Cf. Andrew Ward, *Our Bones Are Scattered* pp. 441, 456–7, 668.

'*. . . coarse and disgusting levity*' Henry Spry, *Modern India* II, 165–8.

Wellington on executions Ward, op. cit. p. 441.

Number of executions Spry, op. cit. II, 168; Hutton, pp. 92–3. For the deaths of members of Feringeea's family, see Sleeman's 'Thug genealogy No. 1', printed in *Ramaseeana* I, facing p. 270.

The fate of executed Thugs For requests for cremation, see Spry, op. cit. II, 165. For bodies left on the gallows, see David Arnold, 'The colonial prison', *Subaltern Studies* 8, p. 161. For hanging in chains, see *Sel.Rec.* 92; Thornton p. 240. A photograph, dated 1859 and allegedly showing the skeletons of two Thugs, hanged in 1837, in gibbets on the road near Bangalore, was published by James Sleeman, *Thug*, facing p. 196.

Ritual mutilation of Thug corpses George Bruce, *The Stranglers* p. 162.

Number of Thug trials Sleeman *Ramaseeana* I, 38–9; *Depredations* pp. 184–5. The fate of Thugs committed up to 1840 was:

Hanged	466
Transported for life	1,504
Life imprisonment	933
Imprisonment for 7 or 14 years	81
Released on security	86
Acquitted	97
Made approver	56
Escaped	12
Died in jail before trial	208
Total	3,443

A further 246 men were held in prison awaiting trial, taking the grand total of suspected Thugs detained by the authorities to 3,689. These figures are drawn from Hutton, op. cit. pp. 92–3.

Trial of the Lucknadown Thugs The gangs of Aman Subahdar and Dhunee Khan were committed by Sleeman and examined by FC Smith at two separate Sessions. Some 75 members of this gang of 115 were tried at Saugor in the sessions of 1830–31, BC F/4/1309 (52131) fos. 124–319, 360–3; the remaining 14 surviving prisoners featured in a subsidiary trial, the 10th or Lakhnadaun Case', part of the Sessions of 1831–32. See BC F/4/1404 (55517) fos. 207–56, OIOC and Swinton to Smith, 2 Apr. 1831, *Sel.Rec.* 64–7. Swinton gives the name of the Thug who dropped Bunda Ali's baby alive into the grave as 'Sadoolah'.

The reported fates of the Lucknadown gang were as follows:

	Main trial	*Subsidiary trial*
Death	27	3
Transportation	9	2
Imprisonment for life	–	1
14 years' hard labour	5	–
7 years' hard labour	11	–
Required to provide security	18	–
Made approver	–	1
Acquitted	2	–
Died in prison after trial	–	2
Sentenced in other trials	1	5
	73	14

The remainder of the gang died in prison while awaiting trial. BC F/4/1309 (52131) fos. 128–31; BC F/4/1404 (55517) fos. 231–62; Smith to Sleeman, 31 Apr. 1831, T&D D1/1, NAI.
Execution of the Lucknadown stranglers Parks, *Wanderings of a Pilgrim* I, 201.

19   Across the Black Water

Saugor jail K. Mojumdar, 'Sleeman correspondence: 1824–1856', *The Indian Archives* 37 (1988) p. 3; Ind. BCJC, Western Provinces 1831, Consultation No. 21 of 11 Jan. 1831, Z/P/207, OIOC. Numbers continued to grow, and by 1837 two new brick jails had been built in the town. Henry Spry, *Modern India* II, 163.

Indian convict population Ibid. II, 152.

'a large proportion' Consultation No. 19 of 5 Mar. 1831, BPC P/126/27, OIOC.

Conditions in Indian jails Ranjan Chakrabarti, *Authority and Violence in Colonial Bengal, 1800–1860* pp. 100, 118–20; Radhika Singha, *A Despotism of Law* pp. 254–5, 269–72; David Arnold, 'The colonial prison: power, knowledge and penology in nineteenth-century India', *Subaltern Studies* 8 (1994) p. 167. The allowance system was superseded by the provision of set rations from 1839 and, eventually, by highly unpopular central canteens. Anand Yang, 'Disciplining "Natives": prisons and prisoners in early nineteenth-century India', *South Asia* 10 (1987) pp. 29–47; Satadru Sen, *Disciplining Punishment* pp. 10–12.

Mortality among Thugs awaiting trial James Hutton, *A Popular Account of the Thugs and Dacoits* pp. 92–4.

Wheat cakes Spry, op. cit. II, 2–3.

'Nothing is so distasteful . . .' Cited in Chakrabarti, op. cit. p. 112.

Work on the roads Spry, op. cit. II, 152–3. Charles Davidson, author of *Diary of Travels and Adventures in Upper India* I, 123–5, agreed with Spry that hard labour on the roads was far from an effective punishment, likely only to provide the prisoner with a 'superior bodily condition'.

Thugs' earlier experiences in jail Cf. *Ramaseeana* I, 261; II, 252–4; Edward Thornton, *Illustrations of the History and Practices of the Thugs*, p. 244.

Thugs confined to prison Not all magistrates took this point. Sleeman prevented one from sentencing captured Thugs to work in the fields of villages near Jubbulpore, where, he asserted, 'they would assuredly either follow their old trade . . . or teach others to follow it'. Cited by GP Edwards, *Report on the Jubbulpore School of Industry* (1854) pp. 2–3, V/23/3, OIOC.

Secured each evening . . . Sleeman correspondence, File 1832 fo. 752, SB.

'the respiration of prison-air . . .' Spry, op. cit. II, 155.

The change from extramural to intramural work Ibid. pp. 262–5; Arnold, op. cit. pp. 176–7.

Thugs at Aurangabad Neville, *Rare Glimpses of the Raj* p. 136

Cawnpore Emily Eden, *Up the Country* (London: Virago, 1983) pp. 59–60.

Agra Butler, *The Land of the Veda* p. 398.

Fanny and Emily Eden See J Dunbar (ed.), *Tigers, Durbars and Kings* p. 104; Emily Eden, *Up the Country* p. 60.

Felice Beato Vidya Dehejia (ed.), *India Through the Lens* pp. 118–47. For Beato's photograph of Thugs, see the reproduction in Tuker, *The Yellow Scarf* facing p. 144 and incorrectly dated to 1855.

Visit to the Thugs of Agra jail Butler, op. cit. p. 398.

Escape of men from Jubbulpore Jail Sleeman says there were 14 of them in all – see Sleeman correspondence 1834 fo. 842, SB – but his grandson James Sleeman, in *Thug* p. 239, puts the number of escapees at 27.

'The narratives of these pursuits . . .' Cited in GP Edwards, op. cit. p. 8, V/23/3.

Successful escapes Hutton, op. cit. p. 94.

History of transportation Anderson, *Convicts in the Indian Ocean* pp. 4–5, 12–13; for the totals of men sent to America and Australia, see Robert Hughes, *The Fatal Shore: A History of the Transportation of Convicts to Australia 1787–1868* pp. 40–2, 143.

Penal colonies in the East Indies Anderson, op. cit. pp. 4–12; McNair, *Prisoners Their Own Warders* pp. vi–vii, 1–78.

'The belief was that transportation would be polluting . . .' Anderson, op. cit. p. 16; Chakrabarti, *Authority and Violence in Colonial Bengal, 1800–1860* p. 20. The British belief that loss of caste was a mortal blow from which no Hindu could recover was similarly misplaced. James Kerr, in *The Domestic Life, Character and Customs of the Natives of India* pp. 263–5, notes: 'It is very generally supposed in Europe that loss of caste involves trials and privations indescribably awful . . . But in no case does he become an alien or outcast, shunned by everyone. The world at large transacts business with him much the same as ever . . . If he wishes to be restored to the full privileges of his caste, all he has to do is to submit to a pecuniary fine, to evince his penitence by giving a feast to some of the leading members of his caste, or to condone the offence in some equally easy way.'

'Kill and eat them . . .' CM Turnbull, 'Convicts in the Straits Settlement 1826–1867', *Journal of the Malaysian Branch of the Royal Asiatic Society* 43, 1 (1970) pp. 90, 103.

'The majority went to Penang' By way of contrast, only 11 convicted Thugs were ever sent to Mauritius. Anderson, op. cit. p. 130. There were a total of 1,250 Indian prisoners in the Straits Settlement by 1841, 1,500 by 1845 and 7,800 (one in five of them Thugs) in 1858, split between camps at Penang, Singapore and Malacca. Turnbull, op. cit. pp. 87, 96, 100.

Hunter-Weston and the Thugs James Sleeman, op. cit. p. 223.

'inconveniently low . . .' McNair, op. cit. p. 12.

Description of the prisons at Penang and Singapore Ibid. pp. 15–17, 28–9, 34, 39–42, 54, 78, 84–8, 92, 94, 143–6; Turnbull, op. cit. pp. 88–9.

'I remember being struck . . .' Cited by Anderson, op. cit. pp. 7–8.

'Harmless' According to Turnbull, op. cit. p. 100, however, Thug prisoners 'played a prominent part in the Dusserah and Muharram festivals and helped to turn them into the rowdy displays of hooliganism they became by the middle of the century'.

'It is worthy of remark . . .' McNair, op. cit. p. 13.

250 remaining Thugs Ibid. p. 146.

'utter unfamiliarity . . .' Sen, op. cit. p. 6. For a description of the Andaman colony and its prison policies in this period, see ibid. pp. 27–30, 212–14.

Approvers on the roads Edwards, op. cit. p. 8.

'There were 56 of them . . .' Hutton, op. cit. pp. 92–3.

The approvers' lock-up Edwards, op. cit. p. 4.

Description of the School of Industry See the photograph in James Sleeman, op. cit., facing p. 154.

Thuggee Lines Report on the Jails of the Central Provinces for the Year 1869, appendix 3 p. 3, and *Report on the Jails of the Central Provinces for the Year 1870*, p. 59 and appendix 3 p. 4, both V/24/2088.

'The approvers are all very fond of money . . .' Brown to Sleeman, 4 Jan. 1838, cited in Edwards, op. cit. p. 3.

Schooling This proscription lasted until the early 1840s. A few years later, the government permitted the establishment of a Night School in the Thuggee Lines where children went to study from 5pm, having already worked at their tasks from six in the morning. The boys were taught to read and write Hindi and Hindustani, and the girls to read and knit. *Report on the Jubbulpore School of Industry, 1856*, microfilm frame 670, V/23/4.

Tent- and carpet-making Ibid. pp. 9–19.

Other prisons' specialities Arnold, op. cit. p. 177.

Best carpets in India Anthony Sattin (ed.), *An Englishwoman in India* p. 25.

Great Exhibition Edward Eddrup, *The Thugs; or Secret Murderers of India* p. 7.

Carpet for Queen Victoria Kevin Rushby, *Children of Kali* p. 128. The carpet, now rather faded, is still there. It is red, with a prominent golden floral design.

'Necessary' tents *Report on the Jails of the Central Provinces for the Year 1877*, appendix B p. 3, V/24/2090, OIOC.

Employment for Thug children Edwards, op. cit. pp. 9–10, 15; *Report on the Jubbulpore School of Industry, 1856*, microfilm frame 670, V/23/4.

Commercial concerns in the annual reports Cf. *Report on the Jails of the Central Provinces for the Year 1869*, appendix 3 p. 2, V/24/2088, and *Report on the Jails of the Central Provinces for the Year 1878*, pp. 31–2, V/24/2090.

Only remained nominally profitable Report on the Jails of the Central Provinces for the Year 1888, appendix A p. 1, V/24/2092.

Sleeman on the change in Thug willingness to recreate old crimes Sleeman letter of 1848, cited by Edwards, op. cit. pp. 9–10.

Sleeman's duties East India Register, 1840–54.

'altogether too willing a horse' Tuker, op. cit. p. 143.

Size of territory under Sleeman's control The areas of the various territories of India, as they were in the 1830s, are given in Spry, op. cit. I, map facing frontispiece.

Sleeman's garden Cited in Tuker, op. cit. pp. 144–5.

The fate of Sleeman's children Ibid. pp. 110, 121, 139, 140, 146, 169–70.

Popularity of Residencies The post of Resident offered a good deal more than simply monetary rewards, of course. The opportunity to shape policy, influence native rulers and generally wield power was probably the most important lure. Michael Fisher, *Indirect Rule in India* p. 31.

'It is a noble country . . .' Tuker, op. cit. p. 123.

Sleeman strenuously opposed this policy 'His reply to Dalhousie when accepting the appointment,' notes PD Reeves (*Sleeman in Oudh* p. 16), 'had been critical of the Governor-General's propensity for annexation and he never overcame his objections to this policy.' Sleeman's position on the matter was set out in four letters published in his *Journey Through the Kingdom of Oudh*.

Sleeman in Oudh Ibid. pp. 147–59, 180; John Pemble, *The Raj, the Indian Mutiny and the Kingdom of Oudh* pp. 96–9; Reeves, op. cit. pp. 4–16.

'Mentally he was in his prime . . .' Tuker, op. cit. p. 178.

Attempted assassinations Ibid. pp. 123, 160, 175; *Rambles and Recollections* I, xxv, xxxv. James Sleeman, *Thug* pp. 125–6. Tuker's account of the 'Thug' assassin is considerably elaborated.

Sleeman's death Reeves, op. cit. p. 16; James Sleeman, op. cit. pp. 214–15.

Those too old to work Ibid. p. 19; *Report on the Jails of the Central Provinces for the Year 1871*, p. 53 and *Report on the Jails of the Central Provinces for the Year 1872*, appendix B p. 1, both V/24/2088; *Report on the Jails of the Central Provinces for the Year 1882*, V/24/2091.

Approvers' sons forced to leave See *Report on the Jails of the Central Provinces for the Year 1874* p. 17, V/24/2089.

Final closure of the School of Industry See *Report on the Jails of the Central Provinces for the Year 1892*, appendix A pp. 1, 5; *Report on the Jails of the Central Provinces for the Year 1893* pp. 23, 44, both V/24/2093; James Sleeman, op. cit. pp. 230–1. 'The only existing traces [of the Thugs],' reported RV Russell in 1916, 'are a small number of persons known as Goranda or Goyanda in Jubbulpore, the descendants of the Thugs employed at the school of industry which was established in the town. These work honestly for their living, and are believed to have no marked criminal tendencies.' Robert Russell and Hira Lal, *The Tribes and Castes of the Central Provinces of India* IV, 558–9.

Appendix: How Many Dead?

Thug murders Richard Sherwood, 'Of the Murderers Called Phansigars', *Asiatick Researches* 13 (1820) pp. 270–71; PA Reynolds, 'Notes on the T'hags', *Journal of the Royal Asiatic Society* 4 (1837) p. 213; Meadows Taylor, *Confessions of a Thug* p. vi; 'Deposition of Rumzan, a noted Thug . . . taken at Lucknow, 20 April 1837', Paton papers Add.Mss. 41300 fo. 122v.

Sumachar Durpan Cited by Iftikhar Ahmad, *Thugs, Dacoits and the Modern World-System in Nineteenth-Century India* p. 126.

James Sleeman's estimate Fearing that this total would not be believed, Sleeman reduced it to one million quite arbitrarily, by assuming the number of deaths to be 10,000 a year over no more than a century. James Sleeman, *Thug* pp. 232–6.

Futteh Khan's estimate Paton papers fos. 28, 122v.

Paton's map of Thug beles See ibid. fos. 172v, 202v–203. A copy of Paton's map of Oudh can be found at BC F/4/1898 (80685) fo. 305, and a photograph of it appears in Francis Tuker's book.

Syeed Ameer Ali's estimate Meadows Taylor, *Confessions of a Thug* p. vi.

'Not broken down' See, however, Paton papers fos. 202v–203, where Buhram's murders are broken down by location.

Quarterly Review 'A religion of murder', *Quarterly Review* Oct. 1901 pp. 506–19.

'Buhram, for one . . .' 'Narrative of a Thuggee expedition in Oude during the cold weather, supposed to have been in 1830 . . . related by Buhram, a leader of Thugs', Paton papers fo. 118.

Ramzan's estimates Ibid. fos. 122v–123, 172.

Average number of victims Median figure calculated from an analysis of all the incidents mentioned in *Ramaseeana, Depredations* and Thornton's *Illustrations*. Even this figure may be an exaggeration, since both Sleeman and Thornton naturally described the most sensational Thug murders rather than the everday.

Number of killings For the Lucknadown gang, see Smith to Swinton, 21 May 1832, BC F/4/1404 (55517) fos. 207, 209. For Feringeea's gangs and the subahdar's gang, see *Depredations* pp. 22–68. For Sayeed Ally and Dawood Newly (the latter, other depositions suggest, being actually a corruption of the name 'Duriow Nujeeb'), see 'Deposition of Sheikh Dawood Newly . . .', 24 Nov. 1834 and 'Deposition of Sayeed Ally . . .', 25 Nov. 1834, both T&D D2/1, NAI.

Sources of the opening and chapter-heading quotations

Opening quotation from the interrogation of Hurree Singh is from Sleeman, *Ramaseeana* I, 35n–36n.

The quotations at the head of each chapter are phrases drawn from Sleeman's lexicon of Thug slang, in *Ramaseeana* I, 67–140, and Martine van Woerkens, *The Strangled Traveller* pp. 295–315.

Acknowledgements

I would like to thank Fiona Jerome, drs Henk Looijesteijn, Professor Radhika Singha of Jawaharlal Nehru University, New Delhi, Sophie Watson Smyth, Dr Kim A Wagner of King's College, Cambridge, and, in particular, Osamazaid Rahman for the help they gave during many months of research. The work would not have been possible at all without access to the spectacular collections held by the Oriental and India Office Collections at the British Library and the library of the School of Oriental and African Studies in London, and I owe debts of gratitude to the excellent staff of both. Sara Holloway, my editor, the staff of Granta Books, and Patrick Walsh, my agent, offered help, encouragement and (particularly) forbearance. And Penny and Ffion, once again, endured and supported me during the protracted process of actually writing the book. I owe both much, much more than I can say.

1. Unpublished manuscripts

[a] British Library

Oriental and India Office Collections

[i] East India Company papers

E   Correspondence with India
F   Board's Collections
P   Bengal Criminal Judicial Consultations
    Bengal Political Consultations
V   Official Publications
X   Maps

[ii] Bengal Obituaries

[iii] European manuscripts

Mss. Eur E/258   Charles Fraser papers

Add.Mss.

Add.Mss. 41300   James Paton papers

[b] Manuscript department, University of Cambridge Library

Add.Mss. 5375–6   Perry letter-books

[c] National Archives of India, New Delhi

Records of the Office for the Suppression of Thuggee and Dacoitee

[d] State Archive of Madhya Pradesh, Bhopal

Satpura Bhawan
Sleeman correspondence

2. Printed private papers

Bute, Marchioness of (ed.). *The Private Journals of the Marquess of Hastings, KG.* London, 2 vols.: Saunders & Otley, 1858

Dunbar, J (ed.). *Tigers, Durbars and Kings: Fanny Eden's Indian Journals, 1837–38.* London: John Murray, 1988

Eden, Emily. *Up the Country: Letters to Her Sister from India 1837–40.* Oxford: Oxford University Press, 1937

Philips, CH (ed.). *The Correspondence of Lord William Cavendish Bentinck, Governor-General of India 1828–1835.* Oxford, 2 vols.: Oxford University Press, 1977

Sinha, AK, and AK Dasgupta (eds.). *Selections from the Ochterlony papers (1818–25) in the National Archives of India.* Calcutta: University of Calcutta Press, 1964

3. Official publications

Anon. (ed.). *East India Register,* 1800–1848

—— (ed.). *Selected Records Collected from the Central Provinces and Berar Secretariat Relating to the Suppression of Thuggee, 1829–1832.* Nagpur: Govt. Print., CP & Berar, 1939

4. Unpublished theses

Ahmad, Iftikhar. *Thugs, Dacoits and the Modern World-System in Nineteenth-Century India.* PhD thesis, SUNY at Binghamton, 1992

McEldowney, Philip. *Pindari Society and the Establishment of British Paramountcy in India.* MA thesis, University of Wisconsin, 1966

Pfirmann, Gustav. *Religiöser Charakter und Organization der Thag-Brüderschaften.* PhD thesis, Tübingen, 1970

Prior, Katherine. *The British Administration of Hinduism in North India, 1780–1900.* PhD thesis, Cambridge, 1990

Winther, Paul. *Chambal River Dacoity: A Study of Banditry in North Central India.* PhD thesis, Cornell, 1972

5. Gazetteers

Anon. *Imperial Gazetteer of India, Provincial Series: Central India.* Calcutta: Superintendent of Government Printing, 1909

Corbett, GL, and RV Russell. *Central Provinces District Gazetteers: Hoshangabad District.* Calcutta: Thacker, Spink, 1908

Drake–Brockman, DL. *District Gazetteers of the United Provinces of Agra and Oudh.* Allahabad, 48 vols., 1904–21

Hamilton, Walter. *The East-India Gazetteer.* London, 2 vols.: WH Allen, 1828

Hunter, WW. *The Imperial Gazetteer of India.* London, 14 vols.: Trübner & Co, 1885–87

Luard, CE. *Gwalior State Gazetteer.* Calcutta: Government Printing, 1908

Nelson, AE. *Central Provinces District Gazetteers: Jubbulpore District.* Bombay: Times Press, 1909

Nevill, HR. *District Gazetteers of the United Provinces of Agra and Oudh: Agra.* Allahabad: United Provinces Government Press, 1921

Russell, RV. *Central Provinces District Gazetteers: Narshingpur District.* Bombay: Times Press, 1906

—— *Central Provinces District Gazetteers: Seoni District.* Allahabad: Pioneer Press, 1907

Thornton, Edward. *A Gazetteer of the Territories Under the Government of the East-India Company and of the Native States of the Continent of India.* London, 4 vols.: WH Allen, 1854

6. Dictionaries

Crooke, William (ed.). *Hobson-Jobson: A Glossary of Colloquial Anglo-Indian Words and Phrases, and of Kindred Terms, Etymological, Historical, Geographical and Discursive.* London: John Murray, 1903
Drummond, Robert. *Illustrations of Grammatical Parts of the Guzerattee, Mahratta and English Languages.* Bombay: Courier, 1808
Gilchrist, John. *Hindoostanee Philology: A Dictionary, English & Hindoostanee . . .* Edinburgh: A. Constable, 1810

7. Secondary sources

Anderson, Clare. *Convicts in the Indian Ocean: Transportation from South Asia to Mauritius, 1815–1853.* Basingstoke: Palgrave & Macmillan, 2000
—— '"Godena": tattooing & branding prisoners in nineteenth-century India'. In Jane Caplan (ed.), *Writing on the Body: The Tattoo in European and American History.* London: Reaktion Books, 2000
Anon. 'Ramaseeana'. *Foreign Quarterly Review* 21 (1838)
—— 'A religion of murder'. *Quarterly Review*, October 1901
Arnold, David. 'The colonial prison: power, knowledge and penology in nineteenth-century India'. *Subaltern Studies* 8 (1994)
Bacon, Thomas. *First Impressions and Studies from Nature in Hindustan, Embracing an Outline of the Voyage to Calcutta and Five Years' Residence in Bengal and the Doab, from 1831 to 1836.* London, 2 vols.: WH Allen, 1837
Baker, DEU. *Colonialism in an Indian Hinterland: The Central Provinces, 1820–1920.* Delhi: Oxford University Press, 1993
Bates, Crispin. 'Class and economic change in central India: the Narmada Valley, 1820–1930'. In CJ Dewey (ed.), *Arrested Development in India: The Historical Perspective.* New Delhi: Manshar Publications, 1988
Bayly, CA. *Rulers, Townsmen and Bazaars: North Indian Society in the Age of British Expansion, 1770–1870.* New Delhi: Oxford University Press, 1992
—— *Empire and Information: Intelligence Gathering and Social Communication in India, 1780–1870.* Cambridge: Cambridge University Press, 1996
Bayly, Susan. *Caste, Society and Politics in India from the Eighteenth Century to the Modern Age.* Cambridge: Cambridge University Press, 1999
Beal, Samuel. *The Life of Hiuen-Tsiang by the Shamen Hwui Li.* London: Kegan Paul, Trench, Trübner & Co., 1911
Bearce, George. *British Attitudes Towards India, 1784–1858.* Oxford: Oxford University Press, 1961
Bevan, H. *Thirty Years in India, or, A Soldier's Reminiscences of Native and European Life in the Presidencies, from 1808 to 1836.* London, 2 vols.: Pelham Richardson, 1839
Bosworth, CE. *The Mediaeval Islamic Underworld: The Banu Sasan in Arabic Society and Literature.* Leiden, 2 vols.: EJ Brill, 1976
Brown, Hilton. *The Sahibs: The Life and Ways of the British in India as Recorded by Themselves.* London: William Hodge, 1948
Bruce, George. *The Stranglers: The Cult of Thuggee and its Overthrow in British India.* New York: Harcourt, Brace & World, 1968
Butler, Iris. *The Eldest Brother: The Marquess Wellesley, 1760–1842.* London: Hodder & Stoughton, 1973

Butler, William. *The Land of the Veda, Being Personal Reminiscences of India, Its People, Castes, Thugs & Fakirs* . . . New York: Carlton & Lanahan, 1872

Carey, WH. *The Good Old Days of Honorable John Company, Being Curious Reminiscences Illustrating Manners & Customs of the British in India During the Rule of the East India Company, from 1600 to 1858* . . . Calcutta, 2 vols.: R. Cambray, 1907

Chakrabarti, Ranjan. *Authority and Violence in Colonial Bengal, 1800–1860.* Calcutta: Bookland Private, 1997

Chatterjee, Amal. *Representation of India 1740–1840: The Creation of India in the Colonial Imagination.* Basingstoke: Macmillan, 1998

Chatterji, Basudev. 'The darogah and the countryside: the imposition of police control in Bengal and its impact (1793–1837)'. *Indian Economic and Social History Review* 18 (1981)

Chattopadhyay, Basudeb. *Crime and Control in Early Colonial Bengal, 1770–1860.* Calcutta: KP Bagchi & Co., 2000

Chitnis, Krishnaji. *Glimpses of Maratha Socio-Economic History.* Delhi: Atlantic Publishers & Distributors, 1994

Cohn, BS. 'The role of the Gosains in the economy of 18th and 19th century Upper India'. *Indian Economic and Social History Review* 1 (1964)

—— 'Recruitment and training of British civil servants in India, 1600–1860'. In Ralph Braibanti (ed.). *Asian Bureaucratic Systems Emergent from the British Imperial Tradition.* Durham, NC: Duke University Press, 1966

Crooke, William. *An Introduction to the Popular Religion and Folklore of Northern India.* London: Humphrey Milford, 1926

Dalhousie Login, E (ed.). *Lady Login's Recollections of Court and Camp Life 1820–1904.* London: Smith, Elder, 1916

Dalrymple, William. *White Mughals: Love and Betrayal in Eighteenth-Century India.* London: HarperCollins, 2002

Das Gupta, Anil Chandra (ed.). *The Days of John Company: Selections from the Calcutta Gazette, 1824–1832.* Calcutta: West Bengal Government Press, 1959

Dasgupta, Atis. *The Fakir and Sannyasi Uprisings.* Calcutta: KP Bagchi & Company, 1992

Datta, VN. *Sati: A Historical, Social and Philosophical Enquiry into the Hindu Rite of Widow Burning.* London: Sangam Books, 1988

Davidson, Charles. *Diary of Travels and Adventures in Upper India, from Bareilly, in Rohilcund, to Hurdwar and Nahun, in the Himalaya Mountains, With a Tour in Bundelcund, a Sporting Excursion in the Kingdom of Oude, and a Voyage Down the Ganges.* London, 2 vols.: Henry Coburn, 1843

Dehejia, Vidya (ed.). *India Through the Lens: Photography 1840–1911.* Washington: Smithsonian Institution, 2000

Dirks, Nicholas. *Castes of Mind: Colonialism and the Making of Modern India.* Princeton: Princeton University Press, 2001

Eddrup, Edward. *The Thugs; or Secret Murderers of India.* London: Society for Promoting Christian Knowledge, 1853

Edwardes, Michael. *Glorious Sahibs: The Romantic as Empire-Builder 1799–1838.* London: Eyre & Spottiswoode, 1968

—— *The Sahibs and the Lotus: The British in India.* London: Constable, 1988

Elliot, HM. *History of India. As Told by its Own Historians.* London, 8 vols.: Trubner, 1867–77

Farooqui, Amar. *Smuggling as Subversion: Colonialism, Indian Merchants, and the Politics of Opium.* New Delhi: New Age International, 1998

Fhlathúin, Máire ní. 'The travels of M. de Thévenot through the Thug archive'. *Journal of the Royal Asiatic Society*, series 3, 11 (2001)

Fisher, Michael. *Indirect Rule in India: Residents and the Residency System, 1764–1857*. Delhi: Oxford University Press, 1991

Forbes, James. *Oriental Memoirs: Selected and Abridged from a Series of Familiar Letters Written during Seventeen Years' Residence in India*. London, 2 vols.: R Bentley, 1834

Forsyth, James. *The Highlands of Central India: Notes on Their Forests and Wild Tribes, Natural History, and Sports*. London: Chapman and Hall, 1871

Foster, William. *Early Travels in India, 1583–1619*. London: Humphrey Milford, 1921

Freitag, Sandria. 'Crime in the social order of colonial North India'. *Modern Asian Studies* 25 (1991)

Fryer, John. *A New Account of the East Indies and Persia . . . 1672–1681*. London, 3 vols.: Hakluyt Society, 1909–15

Ghosh, Suresh Chandra. *The Social Condition of the British Community in Bengal, 1757–1800*. Leiden: EJ Brill, 1970

Gordon, Stewart. 'Scarf and sword: Thugs, marauders and state-formation in 18th-century India'. *Indian Economic and Social History Review* 4 (1969)

—— *The Marathas, 1600–1818*. Cambridge: Cambridge University Press, 1993

—— *Marathas, Marauders and State Formation in Eighteenth-Century India*. Delhi: Oxford University Press, 1994

Griffiths, Percival. *To Guard My People: The History of the Indian Police*. London: Ernest Benn, 1971

Gupta, Hiralal. 'A critical study of the Thugs and their activities'. *Journal of Indian History* 37 (1959)

Halbfass, Wilhelm. *Tradition and Reflection: Explorations in Indian Thought*. Delhi: Sri Satguru Publications, 1992

Hervey, Albert. *A Soldier of the Company: Life of an Indian Ensign 1833–43*. London: Michael Joseph, 1988

Hervey, Charles. *Some Records of Crime (Being the Diary of a Year, Official and Particular, of an Officer of the Thuggee and Dacoitie Police)*. London, 2 vols.: Sampson Low, Marston & Co., 1892

Hunter, WW. *The Annals of Rural Bengal*. London: Smith, Elder & Co., 1868

Hutton, James. *A Popular Account of the Thugs and Dacoits, the Hereditary Garrotters and Gang-Robbers of India*. London: WH Allen, 1857

Jain, LC. *Indigenous Banking in India*. London: Macmillan, 1929

James, Lawrence. *Raj: The Making and Unmaking of British India*. London: Abacus, 1998

Janin, Hunt. *The India–China Opium Trade in the Nineteenth-Century*. Jefferson, North Carolina: McFarland, 1999

Kasturi, Malavika. 'Law and Crime in India: British Policy and the Female Infanticide Act of 1870'. In *Indian Journal of Gender Studies* 1 (1994)

Keay, John. *The Honourable Company: A History of the English East India Company*. London: HarperCollins, 1993

—— *India: A History*. London: HarperCollins, 2000

Kenna, Christopher. 'Resistance, banditry and rural crime: aspects of the feudal paradigm in North India under colonial rule c.1800–1840'. In E Leach and S Mukherjee (eds.). *Feudalism: Comparative Studies*. Sydney, 1985

Kerr, James. *The Domestic Life, Character and Customs of the Natives of India*. London: WH Allen, 1865

Kincaid, Dennis. *British Social Life in India, 1608–1937*. London: RKP, 1973

Kinsley, D. *Hindu Goddesses: Visions of the Divine Feminine in Hindu Religious Tradition*. Berkeley: University of California Press, 1986

Kolff, DHA. *Naukar, Rajput and Sepoy: the Ethno-History of the Military Labour Market in Hindustan, 1450–1850*. Cambridge: Cambridge University Press, 1990

Leonard, Karen. 'Banking firms in nineteenth-century Hyderabad politics'. *Modern Asian Studies* 15 (1981)

Leonowens, Anna. *Life and Travel in India, Being Recollections of a Journey Before the Days of Railroads*. Philadelphia: Porter & Coates, 1884

McEldowney, Philip. 'A brief study of the Pindaris of Madhya Pradesh'. In *The Indian Cultures Quarterly* 27 (1971)

MacLeod, WH. *Guru Nanak and the Sikh Religion*. Oxford: Clarendon Press, 1968

McNair, JFA. *Prisoners Their Own Warders; A Record of the Convict Prison at Singapore in the Straits Settlement Established in 1825, Discontinued 1873, Together With a Cursory History of the Convict Establishments at Bencoolen, Penang and Malacca from the Year 1797*. London: Archibald Constable, 1899

Majeed, Javed. 'Meadows Taylor's *Confessions of a Thug*: the Anglo-Indian novel as a genre in the making'. In Bart Moore-Gilbert (ed.), *Writing India 1757–1990*. Manchester: Manchester University Press, 1996

Majumdar, N. *Justice and Police in Bengal, 1765–1793: A Study of the Nizamat in Decline*. Calcutta: Firma KL Mukhopadhyay, 1960

Majumdar, RC (ed.). *The History and Culture of the Indian People*. Mumbai, 12 vols.: Bharatiya Vidya Bhavan, 1996

Malcolm, John. *A Memoir of Central India, including Malwa, and Adjoining Provinces . . .* London, 2 vols.: Kingsbury, Parbury & Allen, 1823

Marshall, PJ (ed.). *The British Discovery of Hinduism in the Eighteenth-Century*. Cambridge: Cambridge University Press, 1970

Mason, Philip. *A Matter of Honour: An Account of the Indian Army, Its Officers and Men*. London: Papermac, 1986

Misra, BB. *The Central Administration of the East India Company, 1773–1834*. Manchester: Manchester University Press, 1959

Mojumdar, K. 'Sleeman correspondence: 1824–1856'. *The Indian Archives* 37 (1988)

Mookerjee, Ajit. *Kali: The Feminine Force*. London: Thames and Hudson, 1988

Mukherjee, Arun. *Crime and Public Disorder in Colonial Bengal 1861–1912*. Calcutta: KP Bagchi & Co., 1995

Nair, Thankappan (ed.). *British Social Life in Ancient Calcutta (1750 to 1850)*. Calcutta: Sanskrit Pustak Bhandar, 1983

Neville, Pran. *Rare Glimpses of the Raj*. Mumbai: Somaiya Publications, 1998

Newcombe, AC. *Village, Town and Jungle Life in India*. Edinburgh: William Blackwood, 1905

Parks, Fanny. *Wanderings of a Pilgrim in Search of the Picturesque, During Four-and-Twenty Years in the East*. London: Pelham Richardson, 2 vols, 1850

Pemble, John. *The Raj, the Indian Mutiny and the Kingdom of Oudh*. Hassocks: Harvester Press, 1977

Phillimore, RH. *Historical Records of the Survey of India, 1815–30*. Dehra Dun: Office of the Geodetic Branch, Survey of India, 1954

Reeves, PD (ed.). *Sleeman in Oudh: An Abridgement of WH Sleeman's 'A Journey Through the Kingdom of Oudh'*. Cambridge: Cambridge University Press, 1971

Reynolds, PA. 'Notes on the T'hags'. *Journal of the Royal Asiatic Society* 4 (1837)

Richards, JF, and VN Rao. 'Banditry in Mughal India: Historical and Folk Perception'. *Indian Economic and Social History Review* 17, 1980

Rocher, Rosane. *Orientalism, Poetry and the Millennium: The Checkered Life of Nathaniel Brassey Halhed (1751–1830)*. Delhi: Motilal Banarsidass, 1983

Rosselli, John. *Lord William Bentinck: The Making of a Liberal Imperialist, 1774–1839*. Delhi: Thomson Press, 1974

Roy, Parama. 'Discovering India, imagining Thuggee'. *The Yale Journal of Criticism* 9 (1996)

Rushby, Kevin. *Children of Kali: Through India in Search of Bandits, the Thug Cult and the British Raj*. London: Constable, 2002

Russell, Robert, and Hira Lal. *The Tribes and Castes of the Central Provinces of India*. London, 4 vols.: Macmillan, 1916

Sahai, Ishwar. 'The crime of thagi and its suppression under Lord WC Bentinck', parts 1 and 2. *Indian Culture* 3 (1936)

Sangar, Satya. *Crime and Punishment in Mughal India*. Delhi: Sterling Publishers, 1967

Sattin, Anthony (ed.). *An Englishwoman in India: The Memoirs of Harriet Tytler 1828–1858*. Oxford: Oxford University Press, 1986

Sen, Satadru. *Disciplining Punishment: Colonialism and Convict Society in the Andaman Islands*. Delhi: Oxford University Press, 2000

Sen, Sukumar. '"Bungoo" – River Thugs on the Hooghly'. *Bengal Past & Present* 86 (1967)

Shakespear, John. 'Observations regarding Badheks and T'hegs, extracted from an official report dated 30 April 1816'. *Asiatick Researches* 13 (1820)

Sherwood, RC. 'Of the murderers called Phansigars'. *Asiatick Researches* 13 (1820)

Shulman, D. 'On South Indian Bandits and Kings'. *Indian Economic and Social History Review* 17 (1980)

Siddiqi, Asiya (ed.). *Trade and Finance in Colonial India, 1750–1860*. Delhi: Oxford University Press, 1995

Singha, Radhika. *A Despotism of Law: Crime and Justice in Early Colonial India*. Delhi: Oxford University Press, 1998

Sinha, DP. *British Relations with Oudh 1801–1856*. New Delhi: KP Bagchi & Company, 1988

Sinha, NK. *The Economic History of Bengal: From Plassey to the Permanent Settlement* vol. I. Calcutta: the Author, 1956

Sleeman, James. *Thug, or A Million Murders*. London: Sampson Low, Marston & Co., 1920

Sleeman, William. *Ramaseeana, or a Vocabulary of the Peculiar Language Used by the Thugs*. Calcutta, 2 vols.: JC Sheriff, Bengal Military Orphan Press, 1836

—— *A Report on the System of Megpunnaism, or the Murder of Indigent Parents for their Young Children (Who Are Sold as Slaves) as it Prevails in the Delhie Territories, and the Native States of Rajpootana, Ulwar and Bhurtpore*. Serampore: Serampore Press, 1839

—— *Report on the Depredations Committed by the Thug Gangs of Upper and Central India, from the Cold Season of 1836–37, down to their Gradual Suppression, Under the Operations of the Measures Adopted Against Them by the Supreme Government, in the Year 1839*. Calcutta: GH Huttmann, 1840

—— *Rambles and Recollections of an Indian Official*. London, 2 vols.: London, Archibald Constable, 1893

Smith, VA. 'Thuggee'. *North Indian Notes and Queries* 3 (1894)

Spry, Henry. 'Some account of the gang murderers of Central India, commonly called the Thugs; accompanying the skulls of seven of them'. *The Phrenological Journal and Miscellany* 8 (1832–34)
—— *Modern India: With Illustrations of the Resources and Capabilities of Hindustan*. London, 2 vols.: Whittaker & Co., 1837

Stevenson, JAR. 'Some account of the P'Hansigars, or gang-robbers, and of the Shudgarshids, or tribe of jugglers'. *Journal of the Royal Asiatic Society* I (1836)

Sue, Eugene. *The Wandering Jew*. London: Chapman & Hall, 1844

Talyer, William. *Thirty-Eight Years in India, From Juganath to the Himalaya Mountains*. London: WH Allen, 2 vols, 1881

Taylor, Meadows. *Confessions of a Thug*. London, 3 vols.: Richard Bentley, 1839
—— *The Story of My Life*. London, 2 vols.: William Blackwood, 1877

Thornton, Edward. *Illustrations of the History and Practices of the Thugs. And Notices of Some of the Proceedings of the Government of India, for the Suppression of the Crime of Thuggee*. London: Nattali and Bond, 1851

Tritton, AS. 'Muslim Thugs'. *Journal of Indian History* 8 (1929)

Tuker, Francis. *The Yellow Scarf: The Story of the Life of Thuggee Sleeman*. London: JM Dent, 1961

Turnbull, CM. 'Convicts in the Straits Settlements 1826–1867'. *Journal of the Malaysian Branch of the Royal Asiatic Society* 43 (1970)

Vernede, RV (ed.). *British Life in India . . . 1750–1947*. Delhi: Oxford University Press, 1995

Wagner, Kim. 'The Deconstructed Stranglers: A Reassessment of Thugee'. *Modern Asian Studies* 38 (2004)

Ward, Andrew. *Our Bones Are Scattered: The Cawnpore Massacres and the Indian Mutiny of 1857*. London: John Murray, 2004

Wilkinson, Theon. *Two Monsoons: The Life and Death of Europeans in India*. London: Duckworth, 1987

Wilson, William. *Historical Record of the Fourth 'Prince of Wales's Own' Regiment Madras Light Cavalry*. Madras: C Foster & Co., 1877

Woerkens, Martine van. *The Strangled Traveller: Colonial Imaginings and the Thugs of India*. Chicago: University of Chicago Press, 2002

Yang, Anand. 'Disciplining Natives: Prisons and prisoners in early nineteenth-century India'. *South Asia* 10 (1987)
—— (ed.). *Crime and Criminality in British India*. Tuscon: University of Arizona Press, 1985

INDEX

The endnotes are not indexed

escapes from jail, 266–7

execution of, 83, 151, 153, 244, 255, 256–60

exhumation of victims of, xii, 161–2, 186–8, 210–11, 217

feelings of remorse and pity among, 85, 96–7

flight from homes: (before 1800), 36, 64; (1800), 64; (1810), 42; (1812), 48–52, 64; (1830s), 238–9

forcible adoption of children by, 86–7

geographical and social mobility of, 65

gravediggers employed by, 79–81

gurus of, 84–5

handholders employed by, 72, 74

hereditary, 83, 87–8, 89, 195–6, 235, 238, 246–7, 251

Hindu, 36, 89, 95, 172, 204, 258, 268

historians' views of, x–xii

income of, 51, 75, 122–3, 124, 133, 134, 167

increase in numbers during later 1820s, 166

indifference of to capital punishment, 258&n, 259–60

induction of children into gangs of, 83–4

initial disbelief in efficacy of approvers, 166

inveigling of victims by, 32, 68–72, 77, 93–4, 247

irons worn by, 158, 264, 270

jailed 49&n, 57, 94, 98, 143, 151, 161, 164, 169, 182, 204, 244, 255, 264–7, 272–6, 281–2

jemadars of, 66–7, 87, 102, 122

latrine tents and, 274

in literature, x

loss of caste and, 268–9

love for families, 181–2, 227, 232–3

make up of gangs of, 66–81

modus operandi of, xii, 56–7, 247–8, 286–7

murder of Europeans by, 46–8

murder by individuals acting alone, 75, 271

murder by strangulation, xii, 5–6, 8, 72–8

murder of women by, 91–5

Muslim, 36–7, 89, 95, 204, 229, 269

mutilation of victims by, 32, 249

non-hereditary, 86, 87–8, 196

number of murders committed by, 31–2, 283–9

number of victims killed at one time, 79,

numbers of, 31, 288–9

old, retained as camp followers, 68, 84

origins of, 35–8

peculiarities of evidence supplied by, 156

Phansiagars and, 54–6

plunder seized by, 164, 202

proscribed victims of, 91–5, 98–9, 227

quality of evidence against, 153, 155–6, 158–9, 192–203, 208, 210–18

recovery of, after 1812 campaign, 50–1

reform of, 275–6

relations and cooperation between gangs, 40, 95, 168–9

relations with zamindars, 44, 65–6, 67

religious beliefs of, ix, xi–xii, 224–31

rituals of, 85, 101–3

scouts employed by, 67–9, 121, 123, 130, 133–4

shedding of blood by, 73, 135

size of gangs of, 66–7, 122,

soothsayers employed by, 174, 176

status of in village communities, 35

subadars of, 66–7, 122

supersititons of, 49n, 92, 172, 173–6, 227–30

swords used by, 32, 79

tattooed and branded, 255–6

technique for murdering a man on horseback, 75&n

techniques of, 27–8, 31, 32, 33, 67–81

training of novices by, 74

transfer of loyalties from gang to gang, 66

transportation of, 244, 253, 267–72

trials of, 41, 49, 151, 189, 193, 203, 204–18, 242, 244, 254–9

uniqueness of, 35, 40